Also in the Variorum Collected Studies Series:

E. J. ASHWORTH
Studies in Post-Medieval Semantics

JAN PINBORG
Medieval Semantics
Selected Studies on Medieval Logic and Grammar

WILLIAM J. COURTENAY
Covenant and Causality in Medieval Thought
Studies in Philosophy, Theology and Economic Practice

JEAN CHÂTILLON
D'Isidore de Séville à saint Thomas d'Aquin
Etudes et théologie et d'histoire

YVES CONGAR
Thomas d'Aquin. Sa vision de théologie et de l'Eglise

KARL F. MORRISON
Holiness and Politics in Early Medieval Thought

FRANCIS OAKLEY
Natural Law, Conciliarism and Consent in the Late Middle Ages

DONALD R. KELLEY
History, Law and the Human Sciences
Medieval and Renaissance Perspectives

JOHN W. O'MALLEY
Rome and the Renaissance: Studies in Culture and Religion

CHARLES B. SCHMITT
Studies in Renaissance Philosophy and Science

CHARLES B. SCHMITT
The Aristotelian Tradition and Renaissance Universities

JOHN WHITTAKER
Studies in Platonism and Patristic Thought

JOHN M. RIST
Platonism and its Christian Heritage

A. H. ARMSTRONG
Plotinian and Christian Studies

Lies, Language and Logic in the Late Middle Ages

Professor Paul Vincent Spade

Paul Vincent Spade

Lies, Language and Logic in the Late Middle Ages

Routledge
Taylor & Francis Group
LONDON AND NEW YORK

First published 1988 by Ashgate Publishing

Published 2016 by Routledge
2 Park Square, Milton Park, Abingdon, Oxon OX14 4RN
711 Third Avenue, New York, NY 10017, USA

Routledge is an imprint of the Taylor & Francis Group, an informa business

British Library CIP data

Spade, Paul Vincent
Lies, language and logic in the late Middle Ages
— (Collected studies series; CS272).
1. Scholasticism
I. Title
189'.4 B734

ISBN 9780860782209 (hbk)

Transferred to Digital Printing 2014

VARIORUM REPRINT CS272

CONTENTS

OCKHAM'S SEMANTICS

This volume contains a total of x + 302 pages.

PUBLISHER'S NOTE

The articles in this volume, as in all others in the Collected Studies Series, have not been given a new, continuous pagination. In order to avoid confusion, and to facilitate their use where these same studies have been referred to elsewhere, the original pagination has been maintained wherever possible.

Each article has been given a Roman number in order of appearance, as listed in the Contents. This number is repeated on each page and quoted in the index entries.

PREFACE

The seventeen papers reproduced in this collection were all originally published between 1973 and 1983. They are devoted to topics in mediaeval logic and semantic theory. Within that general area, my work has been concentrated in three main subfields, represented here by the three main divisions of this volume: (1) The mediaeval treatments of antinomies such as the "Liar" paradox (papers II–VIII); (2) mediaeval semantic theory, particularly the logical doctrine of "supposition" and the theory of the relation between language and thought (papers IX–XV); and (3) the peculiar genre of disputation known as "*obligationes*" (papers XVI–XVII). Paper I is a general overview of research in the field, and may serve as an introduction to the volume as a whole.

The three main parts of this collection correspond to the three chapters I contributed to *The Cambridge History of Later Medieval Philosophy*, Norman Kretzmann, ed., (Cambridge: Cambridge University Press, 1982): Chs. 9 (pp. 188–96), 12 (pp. 246–53), and 13B (pp. 335–41). I refer the reader to those chapters for further information on the topics covered in the present volume.

With the exception of the first two, all the papers collected here deal exclusively with the first half of the fourteenth century. Except for papers I–II and VI, they are all focussed on Oxford University. If there is one name that dominates these pages, it is that of William of Ockham. All the papers in the second part of the collection (IX–XV) are studies of Ockham, as is paper III. The results of these studies are often negative; they find fault with this or that aspect of Ockham's theory. Nevertheless, I hasten to add that I have never thought of my task as one of "debunking" Ockham. On the contrary, I find Ockham an extraordinarily appealing thinker, one with whom I am in considerable philosophical sympathy. I hope that, through the papers reproduced here, the reader will perhaps come to appreciate the depth and richness of this part of Ockham's thought, and of mediaeval logic and semantic theory more generally.

For this volume, simple misprints have been corrected in the texts themselves. Other mistakes, together with further information supplementing and updating what is said in the papers, have been incorporated into the section of *Addenda et corrigenda* at the end of this volume. References to the *Addenda et corrigenda* are indicated by daggers (†) in the margin by the relevant passages.

I am happy to acknowledge the following editors and publishers for their kind permission to reproduce the articles in this collection: The editors of *Synthese* and D. Reidel Publishers for paper I; the editor of *Franciscan Studies* for II, X and XII; the editors of *Medioevo: Rivista di storia della filosofia medievale* and Studio Bibliografico Antenore for IV; the editors of *Vivarium* and E. J. Brill Publishers for V, IX, XI, and XIV; the editor of *Notre Dame Journal of Formal Logic* for III and VI; Librairie philosophique J. Vrin, publishers of *Archives d'histoire doctrinale et littéraire du moyen âge*, for VII and XVI; John Benjamins Publishers for VIII; the Editor of *Journal of the History of Philosophy* for XIII; the editors of *Histoire, Epistémologie, Langage* for XV, and the editor of *History and Philosophy of Logic* and Taylor & Francis, Ltd., XVII.

Finally, I should like to acknowledge and thank the many colleagues who, through their conversation, correspondence, advice and criticism, have made much of my work easier and have saved me from many an error.

PAUL VINCENT SPADE

Bloomington, Indiana
August 1987

I

RECENT RESEARCH ON MEDIEVAL LOGIC

In this paper I shall survey some of the main areas of recent research on the logic of the Middle Ages. A large and flourishing body of scholars is now actively at work in this field; interest in the topic is no longer by any means confined to a relatively small group of specialists. Perhaps the most characteristic feature of this recent research is the symbiotic relationship between pure historical and textual scholarship of the highest quality – the edition of texts, the identification of authors and their sources, the establishment of their interrelations – and the critically exegetical work of scholars familiar with the results and techniques of modern logic and analytic philosophy. This fruitful relationship has begun to make the immense field of medieval logic accessible not only to specialized medievalists but also to the philosophical profession at large.

Although it is impossible to date the beginning of this collaboration with any precision, it had taken hold firmly by about 1960. At that time, thanks to the work of Bocheński, Boehner and Moody, among others, medieval logic had been established as a rich and sophisticated field worthy of serious study. But this claim was not established without resistance. For many years, students of medieval philosophy had concentrated mainly on issues in metaphysics and epistemology. There were perhaps several reasons for this – the sociology of the revival of medieval studies in Europe and America, the preeminence of Thomas Aquinas until recently in the intellectual life of the Catholic Church, and so on. Whatever the reasons, historians of medieval philosophy tended to focus on the great metaphysical and epistemological questions, and largely overlooked medieval work in other areas of philosophy.

Of course there had been some scattered interest in medieval logic all along. See, for example, the extended – but by no means sympathetic – treatment in Prantl (1855–1867), the editions of some of Peter Abelard's [1079–1142] logical works in Cousin (1836) and Geyer (1919–1933), and the texts and studies in Grabmann (1937a, 1937b, 1938, 1940, 1943). But this work was sporadic and did not reflect any widespread scholarly interest in medieval logic. It was not until Moody (1935, 1953) and the work of

Boehner (1945, 1951–1954, 1952, 1955, 1957, 1958) and Bocheński (1937, 1938, 1940, 1955, 1956, 1961) that it began to be realized that medieval logic had its own characteristic form, that it was not at all just a series of tinkerings with the syllogistic and warmed over Aristotle, and that it was of real historical and philosophical interest. Moody and Boehner, of course, were not trained logicians, so that they did not adequately treat many of the foundational questions that are now being asked. In this respect recent work is superior to theirs. It goes without saying, however, that we still owe them an incalculable debt.

I cannot of course do justice to all the facets of recent research in the field. I shall mention only a few points, and hope thereby to convey some idea of its extent. For the most part, although not exclusively, I shall confine myself to work done since 1960. My discussion will be organized in two parts. The first part will be a general review of some of the major trends and results in the area. Space does not permit extended critical and evaluative comments, although I will insert remarks on particular points here and there, and suggest areas where future research might profitably be directed. The second part will be a selective bibliographical essay designed to inform the interested layman of a few central studies and translations, and of where he may go to find out more.

I

One of the most significant aspects of recent work in the field is the appearance of reliable editions of many of the important original texts. For centuries, historians of medieval philosophy generally, and of medieval logic especially, suffered from a lack of readily available sources. Even major known works were extant only in medieval manuscripts or incunabula editions, scattered throughout the libraries of Europe. They were accessible only to the relatively few scholars who had mastered the arcane art of Latin palaeography. Since these texts are the raw material for all other work in the field, it was impossible to form a clear picture of medieval logic until they were edited and published. Although much work remains to be done, the situation has improved dramatically in recent years. Many of the major logical texts have appeared, together with a large number of relatively minor ones that serve to fill out the picture.

For the early period, we now possess a new edition of Augustine's [354–430] *De dialectica* by Jan Pinborg together with a translation, in Jackson (1975).[1] Boethius' [ca. 480–524] *De syllogismis hypotheticis* has been recently edited in Obertello (1969), and Anselm's [1033–1109] important *De grammatico* edited and translated in Henry (1964, 1974). For the twelfth and thirteenth centuries there are several important new editions. De Rijk (1962–1967) is invaluable here. For Peter Abelard, the texts in Minio-Paluello (1958b), Dal Pra (1969) and De Rijk (1970) supplement the earlier editions in Cousin (1836) and Geyer (1919–1933), and provide us now with essentially all of Abelard's logical writings. As for the thirteenth century, we now at last possess a critical edition of Peter of Spain's immensely important *Summulae logicales* in De Rijk (1972), and a working edition of Lambert of Auxerre's *Logica* in Alessio (1971), together with the older but still usable edition of William of Sherwood's *Introductiones in logicam* in Grabmann (1937b).[2] These three *summae* have often been regarded as the most influential works of thirteenth-century logic, although that is perhaps questionable in the light of further research. Several other works of Sherwood have also been edited in O'Donnell (1941), Roure (1970) – of doubtful authenticity, see De Rijk (1966, pp. 90–93) – and Green (forthcoming).

For the fourteenth century, the most important work is the project now † being conducted at the Franciscan Institute by Gedeon Gál and his colleagues, to edit critically the theological and philosophical works of William of Ockham. Building on the earlier work of Boehner (1951–1954), Gál and Brown (1974) have published the first complete critical edition of Ockham's *Summa logicae*, his main work on logic. This is an event of major importance in the field. In the next few years, we may expect similarly excellent editions of Ockham's *Commentary on Aristotle's Sophistic Refutations*, which has never before been edited in any form; his *Expositio aurea*, including a revised edition of Moody (1965); and revised editions of Buytaert (1964), Buytaert (1965–1966), and Boehner (1945). These last three items are now regarded as of somewhat doubtful authenticity – especially the first two of them. Also † for the fourteenth century, several of the logical writings of Walter Burleigh are now available, in Boehner (1955), Roure (1970), Brown (1972, 1973, 1974) and Green (forthcoming). The situation with John Buridan is also rapidly improving. See Reina (1957), Hubien (1976) and Scott (forth- † coming). For the later part of the century, Ralph Strode's *Logica* [ca.

1350–1370] is being edited by Alfonso Maierù. Except for the sections on *consequentiae* and *obligationes* which were published in early printed editions, this text had been thought to be lost. In fact, however, there is a copy in Oxford, Bodl., Canon. Misc. 219, fols. 13ra-52vb, and individual tracts are extant also in other manuscripts. For the fifteenth century, the *Logica* of Paul of Pergula has been edited in Brown (1961), and parts of Paul of Venice's huge *Logica magna* have been edited and translated in Perreiah † (1971) and in Adams and del Punta (1976).

On the basis of such editions, we are now in a position to draw some tentative conclusions. Thus, to cite just one example, the position of William of Ockham in the main stream of medieval logic must now be rethought. Ockham has long been regarded as the founding father of the 'new way' of philosophy in the fourteenth century, the way of the '*nominalistae*' characterized in part by their enthusiastic application of so called 'terminist' logical techniques and distinctions to the solution of a broad range of philosophical problems. Understandably, Ockham's own considerable work on logic has been given great emphasis.

Without denying Ockham's importance or his influence on subsequent logicians, we are now beginning to see that, on the one hand, his was by no means 'standard doctrine' in later years and that, on the other hand, he not only inherited the terminist logical tradition of his thirteenth-century predecessors, he also in some cases simply took over his logical views ready-made from his contemporaries. A striking instance of the latter is the fact, shown by Brown (1972), that Ockham's discussion of the 'supposition' or reference of relative pronouns was taken over almost verbatim from Walter Burleigh, Ockham's realist opponent. Again, Gál and Brown (1974, p. 744 n. 1) have argued that Ockham's treatment of the Liar and related paradoxes (the so called '*insolubilia*') was also taken from Burleigh.

In other respects, Ockham's logic had certain peculiarities not universally adopted by his successors. His division of the kinds of consequences, for instance (see Adams 1973), did not become standard. In his treatment of tensed and modal sentences, Ockham curiously avoided the word 'ampliation', the standard term, both before and after him, for the effect tensed and modally modified copulae have on the supposition or reference of terms. Ockham in effect has a doctrine of ampliation, but for some reason he avoids the term. Again, Ockham treats these sentences as ambiguous, and so as having more than one truth condition, whereas most later authors regarded them in effect as disjunctions, and so as having a single disjunctive truth condition.[3]

We are now beginning to sort out distinct traditions in medieval logic. There is some speculation about the existence of separate 'schools' of logic at Oxford and Paris as early as the thirteenth century. See, for example, De Rijk (1972, Introduction) and Kretzmann *et al.* (1975). Again, the work of Maierù (1969) and De Rijk (1975a, 1975b, 1976) has indicated an important stream, associated with but not originated by Richard Billingham [mid-fourteenth century], concerning – in a very rough modern approximation – the doctrines of canonical logical form and opaque contexts. Ockham's influence is minimal here.

Important recent studies have also been done on Boethius, in Minio-Paluello (1958a), Shiel (1958), Engels (1963), De Rijk (1964) and Stump (1974). Anselm is treated in Henry (1964, 1967, 1974). For the twelfth and thirteenth centuries, De Rijk (1962–1967) is again invaluable. Several recent studies of Abelard's logical and semantical doctrine are available in Beonio-Brocchieri Fumagalli (1964), Jolivet (1969), Nuchelmans (1973, Ch. 9), and Tweedale (1976). At the other chronological extreme, the work of Hickman (1971) and Ashworth (1974) have shown that the tradition of scholastic logic was strong well into the seventeenth century. The still largely unexplored field of Arabic logic is also now beginning to get the attention it deserves, for instance in Rescher (1963a, 1963b, 1964, 1967), Lohr (1965), Zabeeh (1971) and Shehaby (1973). So too, the connections are being investigated between medieval logic and grammatical theory, e.g., in Pinborg (1967), and between medieval logic and science, e.g., in Murdoch (1974, 1975) and Kretzmann (1976, 1977).

There are of course many other important studies. Although each of them warrants a separate and full discussion of its own, I shall confine myself to a few evaluative and critical remarks on those aspects of the literature with which I am most familiar.

The medieval literature on *obligationes* and *insolubilia* remained largely unknown until recently. The *obligationes* – highly structured and rigorous forms of debate or disputation – were discussed to some extent in Brown (1966) and Angelelli (1970), although on the basis of only a few late texts, and by Hamblin (1970, pp. 125–134 & 260–263) on the basis of a few

† others. De Rijk (1974–1976), Green (forthcoming) and Spade (1977, forthcoming a, forthcoming b) have recently begun to investigate the genre more thoroughly, and several new texts are now, or soon will be, available. It is already possible to distinguish at least two broad streams in the tradition. See Spade (forthcoming b). As this research continues, I suspect we shall find the influence of the *obligationes* to be more pervasive than one might have anticipated. Such seemingly innocuous locutions as '*concedendum est*' (It is to be granted) and '*admisso casu*' (When the situation has been admitted), found in virtually all medieval logical texts, turn out to be highly rule-governed technical phrases in the *obligationes*-literature. Once the *obligationes* are thoroughly understood, I suspect we shall be able to unravel many previously puzzling arguments throughout the logical literature.

The *insolubilia* or semantic antinomies have been the topic of much of my own research, e.g., Spade (1973, 1975). I shall not review that work here, but only call attention to a curious point for further speculation. Much research on the antinomies in modern logic and set-theory has been done in a kind of 'crisis' atmosphere. Quine (1966, p. 11), for instance, says:

> A veridical paradox packs a surprise, but the surprise quickly dissipates itself as we ponder the proof. A falsidical paradox packs a surprise, but it is seen as a false alarm when we solve the underlying fallacy. An antinomy, however, packs a surprise that can be accommodated by nothing less than a repudiation of part of our conceptual heritage.

No medieval author ever talked like that about the *insolubilia*. Despite the remark in Bottin (1976, p. 10) that in the face of the *insolubilia*, "many generally accepted logical rules are left seriously invalidated, thus putting the whole medieval logical 'system' in crisis",[4] no medieval author, to my knowledge, recognized any such 'crisis'. Even as sophisticated an author as the fourteenth-century William Heytesbury, who at least in certain passages[5] recognized that there can be no entirely satisfactory solution to these paradoxes, did not seem to think that was a fact of any great theoretical significance. In general, the *insolubilia* seem to have been regarded more as nuisances than as crucial theoretical test-cases. Bottin, it seems to me, has projected a modern attitude into the medieval discussions. It is interesting to speculate what might account for this difference of attitudes.

Boehner (1952) and Moody (1953), among others, surveyed the medieval literature on 'consequences' some twenty-five years ago. They showed, for instance, that many of the now accepted rules of the assertoric and modal propositional calculus were recognized and used by medieval logicians. Their work was valuable for establishing that this medieval doctrine is of some interest for modern philosophers, and for showing such things as that disjunction was taken in the inclusive sense. But they did not probe deeply into the foundations of the theory. Recent work has gone beyond them in this respect. See, e.g., McDermott (1972) and Adams (1973).

Boehner (1951; 1952, pp. 53–70) and Moody (1953, pp. 64–80; 1967) wrote a great deal, for instance, on the question whether Ockham had the notion of material implication in the modern, truth-functional sense. For the most part, it must be said, they did not understand the problem. The issue has now been settled, in my view, in Adams (1973). There she shows that "Ockham's basic notion of inference does, as Boehner suggests, coincide with material implication", but that no one of Ockham's subdivisions of valid consequences – and in particular not his notion of '*ut nunc*' or 'as of now' consequence – exactly captures that notion. She also shows that Ockham's notion of 'simple consequence' captures the modern notion of strict implication.

Two things, however, should be observed. First, Ockham's division of consequences, as said above, was not standard in the Middle Ages, so that much work remains to be done on other authors. Second, with respect to strict implication, it should be observed that medieval logicians in general rarely discussed iterated modalities. In the absence of such discussions, it is often assumed that their notion of modality was *S*-5 modality. This should perhaps be investigated more closely, especially in contexts where the medievals linked tense and modal notions. On this, see Adams and Kretzmann (1969), Normore (1975), Karger (1976) and Knuuttila (1976). These investigations are shedding light on some important issues in medieval metaphysics as well – the extent, for instance, to which Ockham is ontologically committed to *possibilia*. On this question, contrast the approaches in Normore (1975) and Karger (1976).

With respect to quantification theory, it has been recognised for some time that medieval logicians used a restricted form of quantification, over terms – thus 'Every man is an animal' rather than 'For all x, if x is a man then x is an animal'. The interrelations between the medieval and the modern styles of quantification are now being investigated, e.g., in Matthews (1964, 1973), Priest and Read (1977), and especially Karger (1976).

Much valuable research has recently been done on medieval semantic theory. Nuchelmans (1973) has given us an excellent study of the semantics of propositions, one that should be read by every serious student of medieval logic. Most work, however, has been devoted to the semantics of terms, the characteristically medieval theory of 'supposition'. As a result, we now have a fairly clear picture of that doctrine. See especially Scott (1966, pp. 29–42) and Swiniarski (1970). It needs to be pointed out how much progress has been made here. As recently as Moody (1953, pp. 11 & 22), it was unclear whether supposition was a semantic relation (which it is) or a syntactic one.

One curious facet of this investigation should be mentioned. Ockham and many others claimed that the predicates of particular negative sentences (*O*-form categoricals, e.g., 'Some man is not a philosopher') had what they called 'confused and distributive supposition'. But if the doctrine of the 'modes of supposition' is meant to give an account of truth-conditions, that claim is false. As far as I know, Swiniarski (1970) and Matthews (1973) were the first to realize this. The fact seems to have been entirely overlooked in the Middle Ages. This is so suspicious that I think it requires a rethinking of just † what purpose the theory of 'modes of supposition' was meant to serve. The texts with which I am mainly familiar are exasperatingly silent on this point.

In addition to the incidental remarks above, I should like here to suggest some areas for future research. We need, for instance, much more work on the theory of consequence in a variety of authors; we are not yet in a position to form general conclusions about the doctrine. Again, the connections between the theory of supposition and medieval theology are only just beginning to be explored. (One place to look for such a connection is in the various commentaries on Peter Lombard's *Sentences*, Book I, distinction 4.) Again – and very important – the links between medieval Latin and Byzantine logic have scarcely been touched.[6]

We are still badly in need of texts and studies of individual authors who have not yet been given the attention they deserve. A critical edition of Albert of Saxony's *Perutilis logica*, for instance, would be most welcome. The early edition with which I am most familiar (Venice, 1518) is not entirely reliable. Perhaps a critical edition of the Pseudo-Scotus' commentaries on the *Prior Analytics* would be in order, or at least a careful study of the state of the Luke Wadding text. Certainly, despite the valuable work of McDermott (1972), we need more exegetical studies of this exciting author. The list is very long; students who wish to enter the fertile field of medieval logic may be assured that there will be much work for them to do for many years to come.

This brief survey has omitted many important topics and the work of many valuable researchers, and has touched on others only fleetingly. I hope it will nevertheless convey some idea of the extent and nature of recent work in the field.

II

The following bibliographical information is intended for the interested layman. I have selected only a few major items he should know about, and included references he may go to to find out more. Although such a selection is inevitably arbitrary to some extent, I think the result is more useful to the general reader than a fuller bibliography would be.

There are several general surveys of medieval logic. Boehner (1952) and Moody (1953) are classics and, although dated, should be read by anyone interested in the field. Bocheński (1956, 1961) includes a large number of quotations, although not as much exegesis as do Moody and Boehner. Perhaps the best single survey for modern readers is Kneale and Kneale (1962). The authors are, in my opinion, rather too quick in some of their evaluations, and the historical information in the book has in some cases been superseded, but it is very good nonetheless. Pinborg (1972), which is more selective, is also very helpful. Prantl (1855–1867) is still useful for the wealth of texts in his footnotes. (But see n. 6 above.) Under no circumstances should one rely on Styazhkin (1969, Ch. 1), although the rest of the book is good for the post-medieval period from Leibniz on.

There are extensive bibliographies in Bocheński (1956, 1961) and Pinborg (1972), up to the date of publication. Ashworth (forthcoming) † is extremely useful, and should be consulted wherever possible. Surveys of the original medieval manuscripts may be found in Mohan (1952), Thorndike and Kibre (1963), Lohr (1967–1974), Lohr (1972), Spade (1975) and Mohan † (forthcoming).

Several English translations will help the non-reader of Latin. I should mention especially Mullally (1945), including Peter of Spain's tract on supposition; Mullally (1964), a difficult translation; Henry (1964, 1974); Boh (1965); Scott (1966), quite good; Kretzmann (1966) and Kretzmann

(1968), both excellent; Adams and Kretzmann (1969), also excellent; Perreiah (1971); Seaton (1973); Shehaby (1973); Kluge (1973–1974); Loux (1974), to be used with caution; and Adams and del Punta (1976).

Finally, I should mention Maierù (1972), an important aid to understanding medieval logical terminology. For other recommended studies and critical exegeses, see Part I of this essay.

Indiana University

NOTES

[1] The authenticity of this text has long been disputed. Jackson reviews the question carefully, and concludes that the preponderence of evidence is on the side of authenticity. I find his argument convincing.

[2] On this text, see Malcolm (1971).

[3] In this respect I think Loux (1974, pp. 23–46) wrongly imposes the later doctrine on Ockham.

[4] "Molte regole logiche communemente accettate restano gravemente infirmate, mettendo cosí in crisi l'intero 'sistema' logico medievale."

[5] E.g., Heytesbury (1494, fol. 7rb): "*insolubilia*, as their name implies, cannot be solved without evident objection" ("insolubilia, juxta significationem nominis, absque evidenti objectione solvi non possunt").

[6] Prantl (1855–1867) held that medieval logic was a product of three sources: (a) the recovery of Aristotle, (b) Byzantine influence, and (c) Arabic influence. His particular thesis about the influence of Byzantine logic – that Peter of Spain's *Summulae logicales* was simply a translation of a Greek *Synopsis* Prantl attributed to the eleventh century Byzantine author Michael Psellus – has been decisively refuted. On this issue, see De Rijk (1962–1967, Vol. 1, p. 18, and 1972, pp. lxi–lxvii). Perhaps because of this, the question of other possible Byzantine influences has not been given the attention it deserves.

REFERENCES

Adams, M. M.: 1973, 'Did Ockham Know of Material and Strict Implication? A Reconsideration', *Franciscan Studies* 33, 5–37.

Adams, M. M., and N. Kretzmann (trs.): 1969, *William Ockham: Predestination, God's Foreknowledge, and Future Contingents* (Century Philosophy Sourcebooks), Appleton-Century-Crofts, New York. Translation of the edition in Boehner (1945), with study.

Adams, M. M. (tr.), and F. del Punta (ed.): 1976, *Logica magna of Paul of Venice, Fasc. 6.2: De veritate et falsitate propositionis et De significato propositionis* (Classical and Medieval Logic texts), University Press, Oxford.

Alessio, F. (ed.): 1971, *Lamberto d'Auxerre: Logica (Summa Lamberti)* (Pubblicazioni della facoltà di lettere e filosofia dell'Università di Milano, Vol. 59), La Nuova Italia Editrice, Firenze.

Angelelli, I.: 1970, 'The Techniques of Disputation in the History of Logic', *The Journal of Philosophy* 67, 800–815.

Ashworth, E.J.: 1974, *Language and Logic in the Post-Medieval Period* (Synthese Historical Library, Vol. 12), D. Reidel Publishing Company, Dordrecht.

Ashworth, E. J.: forthcoming, *The Tradition of Medieval Logic and Speculative Grammar from Anselm to the End of the Seventeenth Century: A Bibliography from 1836 Onwards* (Subsidia Mediaevalia), Pontifical Institute of Mediaeval Studies, Toronto. †

Beonio-Brocchieri Fumagalli, M. T.: 1964, *La logica di Abelardo* (Pubblicazioni dell'istituto di storia della filosofia dell'Università di Milano, Vol. 6), La Nuova Italia Editrice, Firenze.

Bocheński, I. M.: 1937, 'Notes historiques sur les propositions modales', *Revue des sciences philosophiques et théologiques* 26, 673–692.

Bocheński, I. M.: 1938, 'De consequentiis scholasticarum earumque origine', *Angelicum* 15, 92–109.

Bocheński, I. M.: 1940, 'Sancti Thomae Aquinatis de modalibus opusculum et doctrina', *Angelicum* 17, 180–218.

Bocheński, I. M.: 1955, 'Communications sur la logique médiévale', *The Journal of Symbolic Logic* 20, 90–91.

Bocheński I. M.: 1956, *Formale Logik* (Orbis Academicus, Bd. III, 2), Verlag Karl Alber, Freiburg. Translated in Bocheński (1961).

Bocheński, I. M.: 1961, *A History of Formal Logic*, University of Notre Dame Press, Notre Dame, Ind. Translation of Bocheński (1956).

Boehner, P. (ed): 1945, *The Tractatus de praedestinatione et de praescientia dei et de futuris contingentibus of William Ockham* (Franciscan Institute Publications, Vol. 2), The Franciscan Institute, St. Bonaventure, N.Y. Translated in Adams and Kretzmann (1969).

Boehner, P.: 1951, 'Does Ockham Know of Material Implication?', *Franciscan Studies* 11, 203–230. Reprinted in Boehner (1958, pp. 319–351).

Boehner, P. (ed.): 1951–1954, *William Ockham: Summa logicae, Pars prima et Pars secunda et tertiae prima*, Vols. 1–2 (Franciscan Institute Publications Text Series, Vol. 2), The Franciscan Institue, St. Bonaventure, N.Y. *Pars prima* translated in Loux (1974).

Boehner, P.: 1952, *Medieval Logic: An Outline of Its Development from 1250 to c. 1400*, Manchester University Press, Manchester.

Boehner, P. (ed.): 1955, *Walter Burleigh: De puritate artis logicae tractatus longior, with a Revised Edition of the Tractatus brevior* (Franciscan Institute Publications Text Series, Vol. 9), The Franciscan Institute, St. Bonaventure, N.Y.

Boehner, P. (ed. & tr.): 1957, *Ockham: Philosophical Writings*, Thomas Nelson and Sons, London.

Boehner, P.: 1958, *Collected Articles on Ockham* (Franciscan Institute Publications Philosophy Series, Vol. 12), The Franciscan Institute, St. Bonaventure, N.Y.

Boh, I. (tr): 1965, 'Paul of Pergula on Supposition and Consequences', *Franciscan Studies* 25, 30–89. Translation of part of Brown (1961).

Bottin, F.: 1976, *Le antinomie semantiche nella logica medievale* (Pubblicazioni dell'istituto di storia della filosofia e del centro per ricerche di filosofia medievale, nuova serie, Vol. 25), Editrice Antenore, Padua.

Brown, M. A. (ed.): 1961, *Paul of Pergula: Logica and Tractatus de sensu composito et diviso* (Franciscan Institute Text Series, Vol. 13), The Franciscan Institute, St. Bonaventure, N.Y.

Brown, M. A.: 1966, 'The Role of the *Tractatus de obligationibus* in Mediaeval Logic', *Franciscan Studies* **26**, 26–35.

Brown, S. F. (ed.): 1972, 'Walter Burleigh's Treatise *De suppositionibus* and Its Influence on William of Ockham', *Franciscan Studies* **32**, 15–64.

Brown, S. F. (ed.): 1973, 'Walter Burleigh's Middle Commentary on Aristotle's *Perihermeneias*', *Franciscan Studies* **33**, 42–134.

Brown, S. F. (ed.): 1974, 'Walter Burley's *Quaestiones in librum Perihermeneias*', *Franciscan Studies* **34**, 200–295.

Buytaert, E. M. (ed.): 1964, 'The *Tractatus logicae minor* of Ockham', *Franciscan Studies* **24**, 34–100.

Buytaert, E. M. (ed.): 1965–1966, 'The *Elementarium logicae* of Ockham', *Franciscan Studies* **25**, 151–276, and **26**, 66–173.

Cousin, V. (ed.): 1836, *Ouvrages inédits d'Abélard*, Imprimerie royale, Paris.

Dal Pra, M. (ed.): 1969, *Pietro Abelardo: Scritti di logica*, 2nd ed. (Pubblicazioni dell'istituto di storia della filosofia dell'Università di Milano, Vol. 3), La Nuova Italia Editrice, Firenze.

De Rijk, L. M.: 1962–1967, *Logica Modernorum: A Contribution to the History of Early Terminist Logic*, Vols. 1–2 bound in 3 (Wijsgerige Teksten en Studies), Van Gorcum, Assen.

De Rijk, L. M.: 1964, 'On the Chronology of Boethius' Works on Logic', *Vivarium* **2**, 1–49 and 125–162.

De Rijk, L. M.: 1966, 'Some Notes on the Mediaeval Tract *De insolubilibus*, with the Edition of a Tract Dating from the End of the Twelfth Century', *Vivarium* **4**, 83–115.

De Rijk, L. M. (ed.): 1970, *Petrus Abaelardus: Dialectica, First Complete Edition of the Parisian Manuscript*, 2nd ed. (Wijsgerige Teksten en Studies), Van Gorcum, Assen.

De Rijk, L. M. (ed.): 1972, *Peter of Spain: Tractatus, Called afterwards Summule logicales* (Wijsgerige Teksten en Studies), Van Gorcum, Assen.

De Rijk, L. M.: 1974–1976, 'Some Thirteenth Century Tracts on the Game of Obligation', *Vivarium* **12**, 94–123; **13**, 22–54; and **14**, 26–49.

De Rijk, L. M.: 1975a, 'Another "*Speculum puerorum*" Attributed to Richard Billingham: Introduction and Text', *Medioevo* **1**, 203–235.

De Rijk, L. M.: 1975b, 'The Place of Billingham's *Speculum puerorum* in 14th and 15th Century Logical Tradition, with the Edition of Some Alternative Tracts', *Studi Mediewistyczne* **16**, 99–153.

De Rijk, L. M.: 1976, 'Richard Billingham's Works on Logic', *Vivarium* **14**, 121–138.

Engels, J.: 1963, 'Origine, sens et survie du terme boécien "secundum placitum"', *Vivarium* **1**, 87–114.

Gál, G., and S. F. Brown (eds.): 1974, *Venerabilis Inceptoris Guillelmi de Ockham Summa logicae* (Opera philosophica, Vol. 1), The Franciscan Institute, St. Bonaventure, N.Y.

Geyer, B. (ed.): 1919–1933, *Peter Abaelards philosophische Schriften* (Beiträge zur Geschichte der Philosophie des Mittelalters, Bd. 21), Hefte 1–4, Aschendorffsche Verlagsbuchhandlung, Münster i. W.

Grabmann, M.: 1937a, *Bearbeitungen und Auslegungen der aristotelischen Logik aus der Zeit von Peter Abaelard bis Petrus Hispanus* (Abhandlungen der Preussischen

Akademie der Wissenschaften, Jg. 1937, Phil.-hist. Klasse nr. 5), Walter de Gruyter u. Co., Berlin.

Grabmann, M. (ed.): 1937b, *Die Introductiones in logicam des Wilhelm von Shyreswood († nach 1267)* (Sitzungsberichte der Bayerischen Akademie der Wissenschaften, Phil.-hist. Abt., Jg. 1937, Heft 10), Verlag der Bayerischen Akademie der Wissenschaften, München.

Grabmann, M.: 1938, *Kommentare zur aristotelischen Logik aus dem 12. und 13. Jahrhundert in MS Lat. Fol. 624 der Preussischen Staatsbibliothek in Berlin* (Sitzungsberichte der Preussischen Akademie der Wissenschaften, Jg. 1938, Phil.-hist. Klasse nr. 18), Walter de Gruyter u. Co., Berlin.

Grabmann, M.: 1940, *Die Sophismatenliteratur des 12. und 13. Jahrhunderts mit Textausgabe eines Sophisma des Boetius von Dacien* (Beiträge zur Geschichte der Philosophie und Theologie des Mittelalters, Bd. 36, Heft 1), Aschendorffsche Verlagsbuchhandlung, Münster i. W.

Grabmann, M.: 1943, *Thomas von Erfurt und die Sprachlogik des mittelalterlichen Aristotelismus* (Sitzungsberichte der Bayerischen Akademie der Wissenschaften, Phil.-hist. Abt., Jg. 1943, Heft 2), Verlag der Bayerischen Akademie der Wissenschaften, Berlin.

Green, R.: forthcoming, *The Logical Treatise 'De obligationibus': An Introduction with Critical Texts of William of Sherwood and Walter Burley*, The Franciscan Institute, St. Bonaventure, N.Y. †

Hamblin, C. L.: 1970, *Fallacies*, Methuen & Co., London.

Henry, D. P.: 1964, *The De grammatico of St. Anselm: The Theory of Paronymy* (Publications in Mediaeval Studies, Vol. 18), University of Notre Dame Press, Notre Dame, Indiana. Contains text, translation, and study.

Henry, D. P.: 1967, *The Logic of Saint Anselm*, Clarendon Press, Oxford.

Henry, D. P.: 1974, *Commentary on De grammatico: The Historical–Logical Dimension of a Dialogue of St. Anselm's* (Synthese Historical Library, Vol. 8), D. Reidel Publishing Company, Dordrecht. Also contains text and translation.

Heytesbury, W.: 1494, *Tractatus gulielmi Hentisberi de sensu composito et diviso, Regulae ejusdem cum sophismatibus, Declaratio gaetani supra easdem. . .* , Bonetus Locatellus for Octavianus Scotus, Venice.

Hickman, L. A.: 1971, *Logical Second Intentions: Late Scholastic Theories of Higher Level Predicates* (Ph.D. dissertation), University of Texas, Austin.

Hubien, H. (ed.): 1976, *Iohannis Buridani Tractatus de consequentiis*, Publications universitaires, Louvain.

Jackson, B. D. (tr.): 1975, *Augustine: De dialectica* (Synthese Historical Library, Vol. 16), D. Reidel Publishing Company, Dordrecht.

Jolivet, J.: 1969, *Arts du langage et théologie chez Abélard* (Études de philosophie médiévale, Vol. 57), Librairie philosophique J. Vrin, Paris.

Karger, E.: 1976, *A Study in Ockham's Modal Logic* (Ph.D. dissertation), University of California, Berkeley.

Kluge, E.-H. W. (tr.): 1973–1974, 'William of Ockham's Commentary on Porphyry: Introduction and English Translation', *Franciscan Studies* **33**, 171–254; **34**, 306–382.

Kneale, W., and M. Kneale: 1962, *The Development of Logic*, Clarendon Press, Oxford.

Knuuttila, S.: 1976, 'Time and Possibility in Scholasticism: A Summary', *Reports from the Institute of Philosophy, University of Helsinki*, No. 4, 1976. (Summary of a dissertation to be published in English.)

Kretzmann, N. (tr.): 1966, *William of Sherwood's Introduction to Logic*, University of Minnesota Press, Minneapolis.

Kretzmann, N. (tr.): 1968, *William of Sherwood's Treatise on Syncategorematic Words*, University of Minnesota Press, Minneapolis.

Kretzmann, N.: 1976, 'Incipit/Desinit' in P. K. Machamer and R. G. Turnbull (eds.), *Motion and Time, Space and Matter: Interrelations in the History of Philosophy and Science*, Ohio State University Press, Columbus, Ohio, pp. 101–136.

Kretzmann, N.: 1977, 'Socrates Is Whiter than Plato Begins to Be White', *Noûs* **11**, 3–15.

Kretzmann, N., J. Longeway, E. Stump, and J. van Dyk: 1975, Review of De Rijk (1972), *The Philosophical Review* **84**, 560–566.

Lohr, C. H. (ed.): 1965, '*Logica Algazelis*: Introduction and Text', *Traditio* **21**, 223–290.

Lohr, C. H.: 1967–1974, 'Medieval Latin Aristotle Commentaries', *Traditio* **23**, 313–413; **24**, 149–245; **26**, 135–216; **27**, 251–351; **28**, 281 – 396; **29**, 93–197; **30**, 119–144.

Lohr, C. H.: 1972, 'Medieval Latin Aristotle Commentaries: Addenda et Corrigenda', *Bulletin de philosophie médiévale* **14**, 116–126.

Loux, M. J. (tr.): 1974, *Ockham's Theory of Terms: Part I of the Summa logicae*, University of Notre Dame Press, Notre Dame, Ind. Translation of Boehner (1951–1954, *pars prima*).

Maierù, A. (ed.): 1969, 'Lo *Speculum puerorum sive Terminus est in quem* di Riccardo Billingham', *Studi Medievali*, ser. III, Vol. 10.3, 297–397.

Maierù, A: 1972, *Terminologia logica della tarda scolastica* (Lessico intellettuale Europeo, Vol. 8), Edizioni dell'Ateneo, Roma.

Malcolm, J.: 1971, 'On Grabmann's Text of William of Sherwood', *Vivarium* **9**, 108–118.

Matthews, G. B.: 1964, 'Ockham's Supposition Theory and Modern Logic', *The Philosophical Review* **73**, 91–99.

Matthews, G. B.: 1973, '*Suppositio* and Quantification in Ockham', *Noûs* **7**, 13–24.

McDermott, A. C. S.: 1972, 'Notes on the Assertoric and Modal Propositional Logic of the Pseudo-Scotus', *Journal of the History of Philosophy* **10**, 273–306.

Minio-Paluello, L.: 1958a, 'Les traductions et les commentaires aristotéliciens de Boèce', Studia Patristica II, series 5, Vol. 9, pp. 358–365.

Minio-Paluello, L.: 1958b, *Twelfth Century Logic, Texts and Studies. II: Abaelardiana inedita*, Edizioni di storia e letteratura, Roma.

Mohan, G. E.: 1952, 'Incipits of Logical Writings of the XIIIth–XVth Centuries', *Franciscan Studies* **12**, 349–489.

† Mohan, G. E.: forthcoming, 'Incipits of Philosophical Writings in Latin of the XIIIth–XVth Centuries' (Franciscan Institute Text Series), The Franciscan Institute, St. Bonaventure, N. Y. See the announcement in *Franciscan Studies* **35** (1975), p. 279.

Moody, E. A.: 1935, *The Logic of William of Ockham*, Sheed & Ward, New York.

Moody, E. A.: 1953, *Truth and Consequence in Mediaeval Logic* (Studies in Logic and the Foundations of Mathematics), North-Holland Publishing Company, Amsterdam.

Moody, E. A. (ed.): 1965, *Gulielmi Ockham. Expositionis in libros artis logicae prooemium et expositio in librum Porphyrii de praedicabilibus* (Franciscan Institute Text Series, Vol. 14), The Franciscan Institute, St. Bonaventure, N.Y.

Moody, E. A.: 1967, 'Medieval Logic', in P. Edwards (ed.), *The Encyclopedia of Philosophy*, Macmillan Company and The Free Press, New York, Vol. 4, pp. 528–534.

Mullally, J. P. (ed. & tr.): 1945, *The Summulae logicales of Peter of Spain* (Publications in Mediaeval Studies, Vol. 8), University of Notre Dame Press, Notre Dame, Ind.

Mullally, J. P. (tr.): 1964, *Peter of Spain: Tractatus Syncategorematum and Selected Anonymous Treatises* (Mediaeval Philosophical Texts in Translation, Vol. 13), Marquette University Press, Milwaukee, Wis.

Murdoch, J. E.: 1974, 'Philosophy and the Enterprise of Science in the Later Middle Ages', in Y. Elkana (ed.), *The Interaction between Science and Philosophy*, Humanities Press, Atlantic Highlands, N.J., pp. 51–113.

Murdoch, J. E.: 1975, 'From Social into Intellectual Factors: An Aspect of the Unitary Character of Late Medieval Learning', in J. E. Murdoch and E. D. Sylla (eds.), *The Cultural Context of Medieval Learning*, D. Reidel Publishing Company, Dordrecht, pp. 271–348.

Normore, C. G.: 1975, *The Logic of Time and Modality in the Later Middle Ages: The Contribution of William of Ockham* (Ph.D. dissertation), University of Toronto, Toronto.

Nuchelmans, G.: 1973, *Theories of the Proposition: Ancient and Medieval Conceptions of the Bearers of Truth and Falsity* (North-Holland Linguistic Series, Vol. 8), North-Holland Publishing Company, Amsterdam.

Obertello, L. (ed. & tr.): 1969, *A.M. Severino Boezio: De syllogismis hypotheticis* (Istituto di filosofia dell'Università di Parma, Logicalia: Testi classici di logica), Paideia Editrice, Brescia.

O'Donnell, J. R. (ed.): 1941, 'The *Syncategoremata* of William of Sherwood', *Mediaeval Studies* **3**, 46–93.

Perreiah, A. R. (ed. & tr.): 1971, *Paul of Venice: Logica magna (Tractatus de suppositionibus)* (Franciscan Institute Text Series, Vol. 15), The Franciscan Institute, St. Bonaventure, N.Y.

Pinborg, J.: 1967, *Die Entwicklung der Sprachtheorie im Mittelalter* (Beiträge zur Geschichte der Philosophie und Theologie des Mittelalters, Bd. 42, Heft 2), Aschendorffsche Verlagsbuchhandlung, Münster i.W.

Pinborg, J.: 1972, *Logik und Semantik im Mittelalter: Ein Überlick* (Grammatica Speculativa), Frommann-Holzboog, Stuttgart-Bad Canstatt.

Prantl, C.: 1855–1867, *Geschichte der Logik im Abendlande*, Vols. 1–4, S. Hirzel, Leipzig.

Priest, G., and S. Read: 1977, 'The Formalization of Ockham's Theory of Supposition', *Mind* **86**, 109–113.

Quine, W. V.: 1966, *The Ways of Paradox and Other Essays*, Random House, New York.

Reina, M. E. (ed.): 1957, 'Giovanni Buridano: "*Tractatus de suppositionibus*" ', *Rivista critica di storia della filosofia* **12**, 175–208 & 323–352.

Rescher, N. (tr.): 1963a, *Al-Fārābi's Short Commentary on Aristotle's Prior Analytics*, University of Pittsburgh Press, Pittsburgh.

Rescher, N.: 1963b, *Studies in the History of Arabic Logic*, University of Pittsburgh Press, Pittsburgh.

Rescher, N.: 1964, *The Development of Arabic Logic*, University of Pittsburgh Press, Pittsburgh.

Rescher, N.: 1967, *Temporal Modalities in Arabic Logic* (Foundations of Logic, Suppl. Series, Vol. 2), D. Reidel Publishing Company, Dordrecht.

Roure, M. L.: 1970, 'Le problématique des propositions insolubles au XIIIe siècle et au début du XIVe, suivie de l'édition des traités de W. Shyreswood, W. Burleigh et Th. Bradwardine', *Archives d'histoire doctrinale et littéraire du moyen âge* 37, 205–326.

Scott, T. K. (tr.): 1966, *John Buridan: Sophisms on Meaning and Truth* (Century Philosophy Sourcebooks), Appleton-Century-Crofts, New York. Translation of Scott (forthcoming).

† Scott, T. K. (ed.): forthcoming, *Johannes Buridanus: Sophismata* (Grammatica Speculativa), Frommann-Holzboog, Stuttgart-Bad Canstatt.

Seaton, W. K. (ed. & tr.): 1973, *An Edition and Translation of the Tractatus de consequentiis by Ralph Strode, Fourteenth-Century Logician and Friend of Geoffrey Chaucer* (Ph.D. dissertation), University of California, Berkeley.

Shehaby, N. (tr.): 1973, *The Propositional Logic of Avicenna: A Translation from al-Shifā': al Qiyās with Introduction, Commentary and Glossary* (Synthese Historical Library, Vol. 7), D. Reidel Publishing Company, Dordrecht.

Shiel, J.: 1958, 'Boethius' Commentaries on Aristotle', *Mediaeval and Renaissance Studies* 4, 217–244.

Spade, P. V.: 1973, 'The Origins of the Mediaeval *Insolubilia*-Literature', *Franciscan Studies* 33, 292–309.

Spade, P. V.: 1975, *The Mediaeval Liar: A Catalogue of the Insolubilia-Literature* (Subsidia Mediaevalia, Vol. 5), Pontifical Institute of Mediaeval Studies, Toronto.

Spade, P. V.: 1977, 'Roger Swyneshed's *Obligationes*: Edition and Comments', *Archives d'histoire doctrinale et littéraire du moyen âge* 44, 243–285.

† Spade, P. V.: forthcoming a, 'Richard Lavenham's *Obligationes*: Edition and Comments', *Rivista critica di storia della filosofia*.

† Spade, P. V.: forthcoming b, 'Robert Fland's *Obligationes*: An Edition', *Mediaeval Studies*.

Stump, E.: 1974, 'Boethius' Works on the Topics', *Vivarium* 12, 77–93.

Styazhkin, N. I.: 1969, *History of Mathematical Logic from Leibniz to Peano*, M.I.T. Press, Cambridge, Mass.

Swiniarski, J. J.: 1970, 'A New Presentation of Ockham's Theory of Supposition with an Evaluation of Some Contemporary Criticisms', *Franciscan Studies* 30, 181–217.

Thorndike, L., and P. Kibre: 1963, *A Catalogue of Incipits of Mediaeval Scientific Writings in Latin*, rev. ed., The Mediaeval Academy of America, Cambridge, Mass.

Tweedale, M. M.: 1976, *Abailard on Universals*, North-Holland Publishing Company, Amsterdam.

Zabeeh, F. (tr.): 1971, *Avicenna's Treatise on Logic: Part One of Danesh-Name Alai (A Concise Philosophical Encyclopedia) and Autobiography*, Martinus Nijhoff, The Hague.

II

THE ORIGINS OF THE MEDIAEVAL *INSOLUBILIA* LITERATURE

One of the problems discussed at great length by the logicians of the later Middle Ages was that of the so-called *insolubilia*. In brief, an *insolubile* is a paradox or sophism of the sort that are today sometimes called "semantic antinomies." They are typified by the Liar paradox, in which a speaker utters the following sentence and it alone : 'I am lying.' Again, the problem may be illustrated by the following sentence : 'This sentence is false,' referring to itself. Such paradoxes constitute a point of interest common to modern logicians and to mediaeval. The modern literature on the paradoxes is immense. [1] The mediaeval literature too is quite considerable, but has only begun to be tapped. [2]

What were the origins of the discussion of the *insolubilia* in the Middle Ages ? We shall treat this question under two rubrics : first, *when* did the mediaevals begin to discuss such paradoxes, and second, *where* did they learn about them ? Did they inherit the Liar, or did they discover it for themselves ?

With respect to the first question, one sometimes finds the view expressed that, although there were antecedents as early as the middle of the thirteenth century, the real nature of the problem was not realized until the very end of that century and the beginning of the fourteenth. T. K. Scott expresses this view. He writes : [3]

---

[1] For a bibliography of this literature, see Robert L. Martin, ed., *The Paradox of the Liar* (New Haven, Conn. : Yale Univ. Press, 1970), pp. 135–149.

[2] For a catalogue of this mediaeval literature, with a list of MSS and editions, and quotations of some key passages, see my *The Mediaeval Liar: A Catalogue of the Insolubilia–Literature*, forthcoming in the series "Subsidia Mediaevalia", (Toronto : Pontifical Institute of Mediaeval Studies). †

[3] Theodore Kermit Scott, tr., *John Buridan : Sophisms on Meaning and Truth* ("Century Philosophy Sourcebooks" ; New York : Appleton–Century–Crofts, 1966), p. 50, n. 89.

Even in the middle of the thirteenth century, a thinker as eminent as Albert the Great... merely repeats Aristotle's remarks.[4] But by the end of that century, interest in the paradox was growing, and Buridan's own discussion indicates the importance assigned to it by fourteenth-century logicians.

I. M. Bocheński too seems to support this position. He indicates that it was not until the end of the thirteenth century that authors began to go beyond the very sketchy remarks made by Aristotle. He writes:[5]

Concerning also the search for solutions of antinomies in the Middle Ages insufficient knowledge is available for us to be able to survey the whole development here, though J. Salamucha devoted a serious paper to it.[6] The connected problems seem to have been well known in the middle of the 13th century, but without their importance being realized. Albert the Great merely repeats the Aristotelian solution of the Liar, and again Giles of Rome (in the second half of the 13th century) only treats this antinomy briefly and quite in the Aristotelian way. Peter of Spain, whose *Summulae* treat of all the problems then considered important, considers the fallacy of what is 'simply and in a certain respect' (under which heading Aristotle deals with the Liar), but says nothing about antinomies.

This view, however, is now demonstrably mistaken. L. M. De Rijk has published an edition of a tract from the early thirteenth century — or possibly even from the late twelfth — that treats the paradoxes in a fully conscious way.[7] This is the earliest text known to date.[8] In addition, at least five other texts show that the problem †
was understood by the middle thirteenth century.[9]

---

[4] The remarks in question occur in Aristotle, *Sophistici elenchi* 25, 180a27–b4. As we shall see, these remarks do not seem really to bear on the logical-semantical paradoxes of the Liar type.

[5] I. M. Bocheński, *A History of Formal Logic*, Ivo Thomas, tr., (Notre Dame, Ind.: Univ. of Notre Dame Press, 1961), p. 237. I have deleted Bocheński's reference numbers from the passage.

[6] Jan Salamucha, " Pojawienie się zagadnień antynomialnych na gruncie logiki średniowiecznej, " *Przglad filozoficzny* 40 (1937), pp. 68–89, 320–343.

[7] L. M. De Rijk, " Some Notes on the Mediaeval Tract *De insolubilibus* with the Edition of a Tract Dating from the End of the Twelfth Century, " *Vivarium* 4 (1966), pp. 83–115.

[8] *Ibid.*, p. 86.

[9] The five are 1) Anonymous, Paris, B.N. lat. 16617, ff. 46v–50v, edited by M. L. Roure, " La problématique des propositions insolubles au xiiie siècle

On the other hand, we sometimes find the other extreme view expressed. J. A. Weisheipl, OP, says, " Variants of the Liar paradox were discussed in the twelfth century. " [10] And William Kneale writes, " Adam of Balsham mentions as something well known the puzzle of the man *qui se mentiri dicit.* " [11] De Rijk says that Adam mentions it as a " current complicated question. " [12] The texts that form the basis for all of these remarks occur in Adam's *Ars disserendi,* written in 1132. [13] The first text runs : [14]

Of the fifth, [15] as " Whether *pronoes* (which in Latin is called 'providence') rules the world, " as the Stoics said, " or not, " as the Epicureans said. (But for us it is from the first useless to inquire into this as if it were doubtful, since we have put our faith in its truth. Indeed, the question is not allowed, since the law forbids it and rightly coerces those who set themselves up in opposition with respect to the matter in question.

---

et au début du xive, suivie de l'édition des traités de W. Shyreswood, W. Burleigh et Th. Bradwardine, " *Archives d'histoire doctrinale et littéraire du moyen age,* 1970, pp. 205–326 at 248–261. Roure, following Grabmann, tentatively attributes this tract to William of Sherwood, but De Rijk has argued, I think conclusively, that the attribution is not well-founded (De Rijk, *op. cit.*, p. 93). 2) Anonymous, Paris, B.N. lat. 16617, ff. 50v–54v, edited by H. A. G. Braakhuis, " The second Tract on *Insolubilia* Found in Paris, B.N. Lat. 16.617 : An Edition of the Text with an Analysis of its Contents, " *Vivarium* 5 (1967), pp. 111–145. 3) Anonymous, Paris, B.N. lat. 11412, ff. 88ra–91va. 4) Lambert of Auxerre, *Summulae logicales,* † at least thirteen known MSS. 5) Robert Grosseteste, *Commentarium in Sophisticos elenchos Aristotelis,* Oxford, Merton, MS 280, ff. 1ra–37va at 33va. In addition, Richard of Sherwood's tract, Cambridge, St. John's, MS 100, ff. 135ra–138va, may possibly be that early. (These texts are numbers VI, XX, XXI, XLV, LIX and LVII in my *The Mediaeval Liar.* See above, n. 2.)

[10] James A. Weisheipl, OP, " Developments in the Arts Curriculum at Oxford in the Early Fourteenth Century, " *Mediaeval Studies* 28 (1966), pp. 151–175 at 165.

[11] William and Martha Kneale, *The Development of Logic* (Oxford : Clarendon Press, 1962), p. 227.

[12] De Rijk, *op. cit.*, p. 83.

[13] *Adam Balsamiensis Parvipontani Ars Disserendi* (*Dialectica Alexandri*), L. Minio-Paluello, ed., (" Twelfth Century Logic : Texts and Studies, " v. 1 ; Rome : Edizioni di storia e letteratura, 1956), p. xxi.

[14] *Ibid.*, p. 86 : " Quinti ut 'utrum pronoes (que latine providentia vocatur) mundum regat' ut Stoici dixerunt 'an non' ut Epicurei (at et hoc apud nostros ut ambiguum disquiri iam est ociosum, fide facta veri ; immo et illicitum lege prohibente et ipsa de qua queritur sibi adversantes digne cohercente ; sit ergo quinti generis exemplum 'an mentiatur qui nichil nisi se mentiri dicit'). "

[15] I.e., an example of the fifth type of " elective " proposition, the type which asks about the category of act.

Therefore, let the example of the fifth kind be " Whether he lies who says nothing but that he lies ").

The second is : [16]

Such also is that question " Whether he speaks truly who says that he lies ; " but also that question " Whether he says the truth who says nothing but that he lies. "

These passages are problematic. They certainly contain the earliest mediaeval formulaton of the Liar paradox known to date. But it must be observed that Adam's remarks show only that the formula, which was later recognized to be a paradox, was known to him. Adam does not try to solve the paradox, does not say that it was well-known, does not say that it was being discussed in his time, and for that matter does not even indicate that he realized that the sentence is a paradoxical one. We can hardly conclude from these passages that the problems posed by the Liar were recognized and discussed at such an early date.

De Rijk claims that the term 'insolubile' was used as early as John of Salisbury's *Metalogicon* (1159) [17] as the technical name for paradoxes of the Liar type. [18] The passage in question is : [19]

In the school of philosophers at that time, the insoluble question was discussed whether a pig led to market is held by a man or by a rope. Again, whether he who bought the whole cape gets the hood.

---

[16] *Ibid.*, p. 107 : " Tale est et illud 'an vere enuntiet qui se mentiri dicit' ; sed et illud 'an verum dicat qui nichil nisi se mentiri dicit'. " The 'tale' refers to " elective interrogables " (choice questions) which are multiple questions in virtue of some determination added to simple questions (" determinationes simplicibus adiecta, " *ibid.*). Thus, " Whether the sun is moved against the firmament or not " is a multiple elective interrogable in virtue of the determination " against the firmament " added to the simple elective interrogable " Whether ⟨the sun⟩ is moved or not. " (" An sol moveatur contra firmamentum an non, " " An moveatur an non. " *Ibid.*)

[17] On the date, see *The Metalogicon of John of Salisbury : A Twelfth–Century Defense of the Verbal and Logical Arts of the Trivium*, Daniel D. McGarry, tr., (Berkeley, Cal. : Univ. of Cal. Press, 1962), p. xix.

[18] De Rijk, *op. cit.*, p. 85 text and n. 4. Also p. 86, n. 1.

[19] I have used my own translation. McGarry's loses the word 'insoluble'. The Latin is : " Insolubilis in illa philosophantium scola tunc temporis quaestio habebatur, an porcus, qui ad uenalicium agitur, ab homine an a funiculo teneatur. Item, an capucium emerit qui cappam integram comparauit. " (*Ioannis Saresberiensis episcopi carnotensis Metalogicon libri IIII*, C. Webb, ed., (Oxford: Clarendon Press, 1929), p. 10, lines 20–23.)

But it seems obvious that the "insoluble questions" mentioned in this text were not at all of the Liar type, and that the term 'insoluble' there means simply "unsolvable" — that is, futile. [20]

In short, there seems to be no conclusive reason to push the mediaeval discussion of the Liar back earlier than the first part of the thirteenth century. This is not to say that there was no discussion before then ; indeed, the passages from Adam of Balsham are suggestive. But to the best of present-day knowledge, no treatment from the earlier period has survived.

Let us turn now to the second question before us, namely, where did the mediaevals learn about the paradoxes? It might as well be said at the outset that no one knows the answer to this question. For that matter, we cannot rule out the possibility that the mediaevals thought it up themselves, although that seems unlikely, as we shall see. Nevertheless, there are some bits of evidence, which will be reviewed here. [21]

Some classical references to the paradox can be pretty well discarded as possible sources for the mediaeval discussions. [22] One might have expected, for instance, something to have been made of St. Paul's famous remark on Epimenides (*Titus* 1 : 12–13). [23] But to the best of my knowledge, there is not a single reference to this text in the corpus of mediaeval *insolubilia*-literature. Moreover, commentators on the passage seem to have ignored or overlooked the paradox it suggests. [24]

---

[20] It is not clear in fact just when the term 'insolubile' acquired its later, technical meaning. In the earliest known tract we already read : "An insoluble is a circular and necessary deduction to both parts of a contradiction." (De Rijk, *op. cit.*, p. 105 : "Insolubile est ad utramque partem contradictionis circularis et necessaria deductio.")

[21] See also *ibid.*, pp. 83–85.

[22] On the history of the question in the pre-mediaeval period, see Bocheński, *op. cit.*, pp. 130–133 ; Benson Mates, *Stoic Logic* (Berkeley, Cal. : Univ. of Cal. Press, 1961), p. 84 ; Alexander Rüstow, *Der Lügner : Theorie/Geschichte und Auflösung* (Leipzig : B. G. Teubner, 1910), pp. 15–107.

[23] "One of themselves, a prophet of their own, said 'Cretans, always liars, evil beasts, lazy gluttons'. This statement is true." (Vulgate text : "Dixit quidam ex illis, prorsus ipsorum propheta : Cretenses semper mendaces, malae bestiae, ventres pigri. Testimonium hoc verum est.")

[24] Augustine refers to the passage in *Contra adversarium legis et prophetarum* III, 4, 13, PL 42, 646 f., but only to ask why Sacred Scripture should quote pagan sources. Jerome does not seem to think that the passage presents any special difficulties (*Commentariorum in epistolam ad Titum liber unus*, PL 26,

There is perhaps a reference to the paradox in Augustine's *Contra academicos.* [25] But as De Rijk points out, [26] the *Contra academicos* was not part of the mediaeval curriculum, and in any case, the passage is cryptic enough that it could hardly suggest the paradox to anyone who did not already know about it. There are no known references to the passage in the *insolubilia*-literature.

Seneca too refers obliquely to the paradox, calling it by its Greek name 'pseudomenon,' but only hints at its nature. [27] Aulus Gellius, in the second century A. D., provides a relatively explicit formulation : [28] " When I lie and say that I lie, do I lie or speak the truth ? " It is just possible that this was the source for Adam of Balsham's examples, quoted earlier. Adam certainly knew and used Gellius, [29] and indeed, seems to have used him in the proximate context of the first passage quoted above. On the other hand, Adam's version of the paradox differs from Gellius' in a significant detail. Adam's passages both contain the important words " who says *nothing but* that he lies." In Gellius' version, on the other hand, it seems that I not only say that I lie, but *in addition* lie. In short, Gellius' formulation seems to be more an example of the Aristotelian fallacy *secundum quid et simpliciter* than a real antinomy. We shall

605c–609c). See also the following texts : PL 30, 897b–c ; PL 68, 681b–c; PL 100, 1016d–1017c ; PL 103, 244a–d ; PL 112, 669d–672a ; PL 134, 708a–b ; PL 175, 606c–d ; PL 181, 1486c–1487d ; PL 192, 387c–388b, for other references. Most of these are based on either Jerome or Augustine. Aquinas too sees no problem (*Expositio in epistolam ad Titum*, in *Opera omnia* (Parma text), v. 13, (New York : Musurgia Publishers, 1949), c. 1, lect. 3, pp. 648 f).

[25] *Contra academicos* III, 13, 29, in *Aurelii Augustini Contra academicos, De beata vita, necnon De ordine libri*, W. M. Green, ed., (" Stromata Patristica et Mediaevalia, " fasciculus II ; Utrecht : Spectrum, 1956), p. 62, lines 33–37 : " Verum ille sapiens aut haec neglegit aut, si perfecta dialectica ipsa scientia ueritatis est, sic illam nouit, ut istorum mendacissimam calumniam : si uerum est, falsum, si falsum est, uerum est, contemnendo et non miserando fame necet. "

[26] De Rijk, *op. cit.*, p. 84, n. 3.

[27] Ep. 45, 10, in *L. Annaei Senecae ad Lucilium epistulae morales*, L. D. Reynolds, ed., (Oxford : Clarendon Press, 1965), v. 1, p. 118, lines 10–13 : " Quid me detines in eo quem tu ipse pseudomenon appellas, de quo tantum librorum conpositum est ? Ecce tota mihi vita mentitur : hanc coargue, hanc ad verum, si acutus es, redige. "

[28] *Noctes Atticae*, XVIII, ii, 10, in *A. Gellii Noctes Atticae*, P. K. Marshall, ed., (Oxford : Clarendon Press, 1968), v. 1, p. 540, lines 20 f. : " cum mentior et mentiri me dico, mentior an uerum dico ? "

[29] See the references in the index to Minio–Paluello's edition of Adam of Balsham, p. 121 (see n. 13, above).

discuss this difference later. At any rate, no later mediaeval author, to my knowledge, cites Gellius in this context.

Somewhat more promising is a passage from Cicero's *Academica*, in which the Liar is formulated this way: [30]

Certainly it is the foundation of dialectic that whatever is uttered — and they call it an ἀξίωμα, which is as it were a proposition — is true or false. What then? Are such things as these true or false: "If you lie, and speak that truth, do you lie or speak the truth?" These of course you say are "inexplicable," which is more unpleasant than what we say are incomprehensible or imperceptible.

But I overlook this, and ask: If they cannot be explained, and there is no verdict found about them, so that you might answer the question whether they are true or false, where does that definition go: "A proposition is that which is either true or false?" Having taken up these matters, I shall add that among things which are classed as opposites, some are to be accepted, some rejected. How then do you decide that this is well-argued: 'If you say that it is now light, and you speak the

[30] The translation is mine. See Cicero *Acad. Pr.* II, xxix, 95–xxx, 97, in *Academica: The Text Revised and Explained,* James S. Reid, ed., (Hildesheim: Georg Olms Verlagsbuchhandlung, 1966 – "Reprographischer Nachdruck der Ausgabe London 1885"), p. 290 line 10 – p. 293 line 14: "Nempe fundamentum dialecticae est, quidquid enuntietur — id autem appellant ἀξίωμα, quod est quasi effatum — aut uerum esse aut falsum. Quid igitur? Haec uera an falsa sunt? Si te mentiri dicis idque uerum dicis, mentiris an uerum dicis? Haec scilicet inexplicabilia esse dicitis, quod est odiosius quam illa, quae nos non comprehensa et non percepta dicimus.

"Sed hoc omitto, illud quaero; si ista explicari non possunt, nec eorum ullum iudicium inuenitur, ut respondere possitis uerane an falsa sint, ubi est illa definitio, 'effatum esse id, quod aut uerum aut falsum sit'? Rebus sumptis adiungam ex his sequandas esse alias, alias improbandas, quae sint in genere contrario. Quo modo igitur hoc conclusum esse iudicas? 'Si dicis nunc lucere et uerum dicis, lucet; dicis autem nunc lucere et uerum dicis: lucet igitur'. Probatis certe genus et rectissime conclusum dicitis; itaque in docendo eum primum concludendi modum traditis. Aut quidquid igitur eodem modo concluditur probabitis aut ars ista nulla est. Vide ergo hanc conclusionem probaturusne sis: 'si dicis te mentiri uerumque dicis, mentiris; dicis autem te mentiri uerumque dicis, mentiris igitur'. Qui potes hanc non probare, cum probaueris eiusdem generis superiorem? Haec Chrysippia sunt, ne ab ipso quidem dissoluta. Quid enim faceret huic conclusioni? 'Si lucet, lucet; lucet autem: lucet igitur'. Cederet scilicet. Ipsa enim ratio conexi, cum concesseris superius, cogit inferius concedere. Quid ergo haec ab illa conclusione differt? 'Si mentiris, mentiris: mentiris autem: mentiris igitur'. Hoc negas te posse nec approbare nec improbare. Qui igitur magis illud? Si ars, si ratio, si uia, si uis denique conclusionis ualet, eadem est in utroque. Sed hoc extremum eorum est: postulant ut excipiantur haec inexplicabilia."

truth, it is light; but you say that it is now light and you speak the truth; therefore, it is light'? You rigorously test the generic form, and you say quite correctly that it is well-argued. Accordingly, when you teach, you propound it as the first mood of argumentation. So either you will approve whatever is inferred in the same way, or this dialectical art is worthless. See then whether you will confirm this argument: 'If you say you lie, and you speak the truth, you lie; but you say you lie, and you speak the truth; therefore, you lie'. How can you not approve this, since you approved the former one of the same kind? These things are Chrysippian, although indeed they have not been solved by him. For what would he do to this argument: 'If it is light, it is light; but it is light; therefore, it is light'? He would grant it, of course. For the very structure of the conditional, since you granted the antecedent, compels you to grant the consequent. How then does this differ from the other one: 'If you lie, you lie; but you lie; therefore, you lie'? You deny that you can neither confirm nor reject the former. Then how in the other case any the more? If art, if structure, if the way — if the force of the argument, in short, carries any weight, it is the same for both. But this is how far they go: they ask that an exception be made for these "inexplicables."

There are at least two extant MSS of the *Academica* from before the twelfth century, and at least one from the twelfth century itself. [31] Moreover, the gist of this passage was excerpted and included in a ninth-century compilation of Cicero's philosophical writings. [32] So it was available to the Middle Ages. Nevertheless, like the other passages we have cited so far, no mention is ever made of it in the literature. Furthermore, as De Rijk observes: [33]

---

[31] See Reid's introduction, *ibid.*, p. 66.

[32] De Rijk, *op. cit.*, p. 84, quotes the relevant passage. The compilation is Hadoard's *Excerpta*. See Paul Schwenke, ed., "Des Presbyter Hadoardus Cicero-Excerpte," *Philologus*, Suppl. Band 5 (1911), pp. 397–588.

[33] De Rijk, *op. cit.*, p. 85. Joseph Owens, CSsR, (*The Doctrine of Being in the Aristotelian Metaphysics*, 2nd ed., (Toronto: Pontifical Institute of Mediaeval Studies, 1963, p. 211) says: "In an aporia the intellect has no passage. It can make no headway. Something is holding it back. The meaning of the Greek, however, may be toned down merely to embarrassment or difficulty in one's progress." This seems to be just what happened with the term 'insolubile'. In the earliest known tract (De Rijk, *op. cit.*, p. 105, lines 5–9) we read: "And because of this it must be known that there are insolubles absolutely speaking and insolubles in a certain respect. An insoluble absolutely speaking I call that which can in no way be solved, as what was said before. [He had given the example: 'God is one in essence and three in persons'.] An insoluble in a certain respect is that which can in one way be solved, in another not, as 'I speak falsely', 'I lie', and the like." ("Et propter hoc notandum quod sunt insolubilia simpliciter

If the insolubilia-literature had found its starting-point in the Ciceronian tradition, one would rather have expected the Roman's term *inexplicabile* instead of *insolubile*. The latter might have been a translation for the Greek ἀπορία.

None of these possible sources, as we have seen, is referred to in literature. By contrast, very frequently, and from almost the earliest treatises we know, the paradox is discussed explicitly within the framework of the Aristotelian fallacy *secundum quid et simpliciter*. [34] In the first quarter of the fourteenth century, Thomas Bradwardine could say that this was the usual way of viewing the Liar. [35]

The Aristotelian passage in question is *Sophistici elenchi* 25, 180a27–b7 : [36]

All arguments of the following kind have this feature : 'Is it possible for what is-not to be' ? 'No'. 'But, you see, it *is* something, despite its not *being*'. Likewise also, Being will not be; for it will *not be* some particular form of being. 'Is it possible for the same man at the same time to be a keeper and a breaker of his oath' ? 'Can the same man at the

---

et insolubilia secundum quid. Insolubile simpliciter dico quod nullo modo potest solvi, ut id quod predictum est. Insolubile secundum quid est id quod uno modo potest solvi, alio modo non, sicut '*me dicere falsum*', '*me mentiri*', et similia. ") In fact, it was the standard practice to point out that the " insolubles " were not really insoluble, but only *very difficult* to solve. See my " An Anonymous Fourteenth-Century Treatise on 'Insolubles' : Text and Study, " (M.S.L. diss. : Pontifical Institute of Mediaeval Studies, Toronto, 1969), pp. *9f.

[34] See all the texts, except the second, mentioned in n. 9, above.

[35] Thomas Bradwardine, *Insolubilia*, ca. 2, edited in Roure, *op. cit.*, par. 2.04, p. 287.

† [36] Oxford translation. The Vulgate text, in PL 64, 1034b–c, is : " Sunt autem hujusmodi orationes omnes id habentes, putasne contingit quod non est esse ? attamen non est aliquid id quod non est. Similiter autem et quod est non erit, nam non erit aliquid cum sunt. Nunquid contingit eumdem simul bene jurare et pejerare ? Nunquid possibile est simul eidem suadere et dissuadere ? An neque esse quid, et esse, idem ? quod autem non est, non si est quid, etiam est simpliciter. Neque si bene jurat id quidem, et qua, necesse est et bene jurare, nam qui jurat se pejeraturum, bene jurat perjurans hoc solum, at non bene jurat. Neque qui dissuadet, suadet, sed secundum quid suadet. Similis autem ratio est et de eo quod est mentiri eundem simul et verum dicere, sed propter id quod non est facile inspicere utrum quis assignet simpliciter veracem esse, vel mendacem difficile apparet. Prohibet autem eundem nihil simpliciter quidem esse mendacem, qua autem veracem, vel alicujus esse veracem aliquem, veracem autem non. " On this vulgate text, see L. Minio-Paluello, " Note sull'Aristotele latino-medievale, " V, *Rivista di filosofia neo-scolastica* 44 (1952), pp. 389–411 at 398.

same time both obey and disobey the same man' ? Or isn't it the case that being something in particular and Being are not the same ? On the other hand, Not-being, even if it be something, need not also have absolute 'being' as well. Nor if a man keeps his oath in this particular instance or in this particular respect, is he bound also to be a keeper of oaths absolutely, but he who swears that he will break his oath, and then breaks it, keeps this particular oath only ; he is not a keeper of his oath ; nor is the disobedient man 'obedient', though he obeys one particular command. The argument is similar, also, as regards the problem whether the same man can at the same time say what is both false and true : but it appears to be a troublesome question because it is not easy to see in which of the two connexions the word 'absolutely' is to be rendered — with 'true' or with 'false' There is, however, nothing to prevent it from being false absolutely, though true in some particular respect or relation, i.e., being true in some things, though not 'true' absolutely.

The *Sophistici elenchi* first appeared in the Latin West around 1130. [37] At first sight, this might seem to solve several problems. Adam of Balsham, so it would go, got the paradox from Aristotle, [38] and the discussion of the Liar — whenever it began in earnest — took its origin in the passage just quoted.

But the matter is not quite so simple. In order to see one of the reasons why not, let us look again at Aristotle's text, and then follow for a while the tradition of commentary on, and use made of, the *Elenchi*.

Two parts of Aristotle's text concern us, and must be distinguished. The first may be called the " Perjurer " (" Is it possible for the same man at the same time to be a keeper and a breaker of his oath ? ") ; the second is the " Liar " (" The argument is similar, also, as regards the problem whether the same man can at the same time say what is both false and true. "). [39]

---

[37] See L. M. De Rijk, *Logica Modernorum : A Contribution to the History of Early Terminist Logic*, vol. 1 : *On the Twelfth Century Theories of Fallacy*, (" Wijsgerige Teksten en Studies, " VI ; Assen : Van Gorcum & Comp. B.V., 1962), p. 24, and W. D. Wingate, *The Mediaeval Latin Versions of the Aristotelian Scientific Corpus, with Special Reference to the Biological Works*, (London : The Courier Press, 1931), pp. 5 f. See also De Rijk, " Some Notes..., " p. 85, n. 1.

[38] In fact, Adam did know the *Sophistici elenchi*. See L. Minio-Paluello, " The Ars Disserendi of Adam of Balsham 'Parvipontanus', " *Mediaeval and Renaissance Studies* 3 (1954), pp. 136–140.

[39] We henceforth use the capitalized term 'Liar' to refer not just to actual antinomies of the kind exemplified in the first paragraph of this paper, but also

The common fourteenth century formulation of the Liar was as follows: 'Socrates speaks falsely', where Socrates, who utters no other sentence, is the speaker. Two features must be noted here. First, the liar (Socrates) speaks in the *present* tense ("Socrates *speaks* falsely"). Second, the liar says *only* this one sentence.

Aristotle's text is relatively clear on the matter of the Perjurer. He says: "For he who swears that he will break his oath keeps his oath in breaking that oath only, but he does not keep his oath." [40] The meaning seems to be roughly as follows: Suppose, for instance, that a man swears that he will break his oath. Suppose, further, that some time later he swears an oath that he will go to Athens, but then in fact breaks that oath and refuses to go. Then, it might be argued, that man has both kept and broken his oath, which is a contradiction. Not so, says Aristotle, for this is a fallacy *secundum quid et simpliciter*. Absolutely speaking, that man is a perjurer. He keeps his oath only with respect to the particular oath 'I shall break my oath.'

Aristotle goes on to say that the Liar is a case of the same sort of problem ("The argument is similar"). But this is all he says, other than to observe that it is a difficult problem. The reader was left to reconstruct the Liar example along lines similar to the Perjurer.

Many mediaeval writers overlooked the Perjurer and the Liar altogether. Presumably they did not think these two examples deserved to be singled out for special consideration. Their works include the twelfth-century *Glose in Aristotelis Sophisticos elenchos*,[41] and *Fallacie Parvipontane*, [42] and the thirteenth century *Introductiones in logicam* of William of Sherwood, [43] the *Summulae dialectices*

---

to *any* attempt to formulate the sophism that Aristotle hints at here. Analogously for the capitalized term 'Perjurer' The liar and the perjurer (not capitalized), on the other hand, are the speakers in the Liar and the Perjurer.

[40] I have translated directly from the vulgate Latin text (see above, n. 36) where, as here, it differs significantly from the Oxford translation.

[41] Anonymous, *Glose in Aristotelis Sophisticos elenchos*, v. 2, c. 25, in De Rijk, *Logica Modernorum*, v. 1, Appendix A, p. 250.

[42] Anonymous, *Fallacie Parvipontane*, lib. 2, c. 7, in De Rijk, *op. cit.*, Appendix E, pp. 596–598.

[43] William of Sherwood, *Introduction to Logic*, Norman Kretzmann, tr., (Minneapolis: Univ. of Minn., 1966), pp. 153–155; and *Die Introductiones in logicam des Wilhelm von Shyreswood* († *nach 1267*), Martin Grabmann, ed., ("Sitzungsberichte der Bayerischen Akademie der Wissenschaften," Philosophisch-historisch Abteilung, Jahrgang 1937, Heft 10; Munich: Verlag der Bayerischen Akademie der Wissenschaften, 1937), pp. 96 f.

formerly attributed to Roger Bacon,[44] and the immensely important *Summulae logicales* of Peter of Spain.[45]

Some twelfth century authors, however, considered one or both of Aristotle's examples more or less explicitly in the Aristotelian fashion. The *Fallacie Vindobonenses*, for instance, presents the following version of the Perjurer as an example of the fallacy *secundum quid et simpliciter*:[46] " This man swears that he will break his oath in all cases, and afterwards swears that God does not exist. He swears well with respect to his first oath; therefore, he swears well. " Nothing is said of the Liar, however.

On the other hand, the twelfth century *Summa Sophisticorum elenchorum* presents a full reconstruction of the Liar as, formally at least, an exact parallel to the Perjurer:[47]

> Supposing that Socrates promises that he will say only falsehoods to me, afterwards when he comes to me, he says that I am a stone. Then he speaks the truth with respect to discharging his promise; therefore, he speaks the truth. Likewise he lies, because he speaks falsely. Therefore the same man lies and speaks the truth.

But note that this formulation presents a situation of quite a different kind than does the Perjurer. The Perjurer could be solved only by observing that it was a fallacy *secundum quid et simpliciter*. The form of the Liar presented above can, on the other hand, be solved without an appeal to that fallacy, by simply observing that

---

[44] In *Opera hactenus inedita Rogeri Baconi*, fasc. xv, Robert Steele, ed., (Oxford: Clarendon Press, 1940), pp. 351 f. This text has more recently been attributed to Robert Bacon. See De Rijk, *Logica Modernorum*, vol. 2, part 1: *The Origin and Early Development of the Theory of Supposition* (Assen: Van Gorcum & Comp. B.V., 1967), p. 445.

[45] L. M. De Rijk, ed. *Peter of Spain* (*Petrus Hispanus Portugalensis*): *Tractatus: called afterwands Summule logicales*, (Assen: Van Gorcum & Comp. B.V., 1972), tract. VII, pars. 120–130, pp. 157–161.

[46] Anonymous, *Fallacie Vindobonenses*, v. 1, c. 8, in De Rijk, *op. cit.*, Appendix D, p. 531: " iste iurat se deieratum in omnibus et postea iurat Deum non esse / iste bene iurat quantum ad primum iuramentum, / ergo bene iurat. " The form " deieratum' does not seem to make sense here. Perhaps read 'deieraturum'. "

[47] Anonymous, *Summa Sophisticorum elenchorum*, dist. I, vol. 1, lib. 2, c. 2, in De Rijk, *op. cit.*, Appendix B, p. 375: " Posito quod Socrates promittit se michi dicturum tantum falsa. Postea cum venit ad me, dicit me esse lapidem. Tunc verum dicit quantum ad promissum persolvendum; ergo, verum dicit. Similiter mentitur quia falsum dicit. Ergo idem mentitur et dicit verum. "

the Liar does indeed both lie and speak the truth, but at different times and in different utterances. The perjurer by a single act — e.g., by his refusing to go to Athens — both fulfilled his oath and broke it, although with respect to different oaths. The liar, on the other hand, in the version formulated above, by a single act both fulfills a promise and speaks falsely, which, of course, is no paradox at all. It is only by two distinct acts, two utterances, the one after the other, that the liar speaks both truth and falsehood. The solution of the Perjurer consists of pointing out the confusion between breaking (or keeping) one's oath *simpliciter* and doing so *secundum quid*. The solution to the Liar in this formulation consists of simply observing that the liar speaks truly and falsely at different times.

Thus the Liar cannot be made fully parallel to the Perjurer, contrary to what Aristotle seems to imply in his text. For, even when the two are set up in exactly the same way, their solutions will be different.

In the thirteenth century, Thomas Aquinas formulated the problem with a significant new feature.[48] In his *De fallaciis* (1244–1245),[49] Thomas says : " Likewise here, 'The Liar speaks the truth in saying that he speaks falsely. Therefore, he speaks the truth.' It does not follow. For to speak the truth is opposed to what it is to speak falsely, and conversely. "[50]

Thomas' version has the liar say that he *is* speaking falsely — *present* tense. Aristotle is ambiguous on this point. The perjurer swears that he *will* break his oath. The Liar is said to be " similar, " but the details are not given. Accordingly, as we have seen, the author of the *Summa Sophisticorum elenchorum* has the liar also speak in the future tense (" promises that he *will* say only falsehoods to me ").

To put the liar's words into the *present* tense is a significant de-

[48] This is not to say he originated the formulation. Indeed, it occurs as early as Adam of Balsham, *outside* the tradition of commentary on the *Elenchi* and tracts *De fallaciis* which follow the *Elenchi*.

[49] On the date, see I. T. Eschmann, " A Catalogue of St. Thomas Aquinas's Works, " in Etienne Gilson, *The Christian Philosophy of St. Thomas Aquinas*, L. K. Shook, tr., (New York : Random House, 1956), p. 410 (item no. 49), and the references there. The authenticity of this work has been questioned. See *ibid.*

[50] Thomas Aquinas, *De fallaciis ad quosdam nobiles artistas*, in *Opera omnia* (Parma text), v. 16, (New York : Musurgia Publishers, 1950), p. 384 : " Similiter hic, Mendax dicit verum dicendo se dicere falsum. Ergo dicit verum. Non sequitur : nam dicere verum opponitur ei quod est dicere falsum, et e converso. "

velopment. For, once the liar is thought to say "I speak falsely," rather than "I shall speak falsely," it is but a small step to suppose that he says "I speak falsely," and *nothing else.* This would be a sophism which could not be solved in simply the Aristotelian manner. It would demand a new approach. Aquinas himself does not take this step, but continues to regard the Liar in the Aristotelian manner.

Albert the Great, writing between 1248 and 1264, [51] not only has the liar speaking in the present tense, but the perjurer as well, although he is not consistent about the latter. The relevant texts are these : "...and let it be set down that someone swears that he *breaks* his oath... " [52] ; " ...he who swears that he *will break* his oath swears that well, that is, in this respect ; absolutely, however, he does not swear well " [53] ; " ...for let it be set down that someone says 'I *speak* falsely,' and that he speak falsely " [54] ; and [55]

> If he swears that he breaks his oath, and he swears the truth, namely, that he breaks his oath, no one by swearing the truth breaks his oath ; therefore, he would not break his oath. And it was given that he does break his oath. But if he does not break his oath, and he swears that he breaks his oath, he does not swear the truth ; therefore, he breaks his oath. For otherwise he would not swear the truth when he swears that he breaks his oath. Therefore, he breaks his oath. For otherwise it would not be true that he breaks his oath.

Albert, however, like Thomas, continues to regard the sophism in the Aristotelian way, as a fallacy *secundum quid et simpliciter.* [56]

Giles of Rome, writing between 1286 and 1291, [57] has the liar

---

[51] See James A. Weisheipl, OP, " Albert the Great, " in *New Catholic Encyclopedia,* v. 1, p. 257.

[52] Albert the Great, *Libri duo elenchorum,* in *Opera omnia,* (Paris : Vivès, 1890–1899), v. 2, p. 694 : " ...et ponatur, quod aliquis juret se perjurare... "

[53] *Ibid. :* " ...qui jurat se perjuraturum, bene jurat hoc, hoc est, secundum hoc : simpliciter autem non bene jurat. "

[54] *Ibid. :* " ...ponatur enim, quod aliquis dicat, ėgo dico falsum : et dicat falsum. "

[55] *Ibid.*, p. 696 : " Si jurat se perjurare et jurat verum, scilicet se perjurare, nemo jurando verum perjurat ; ergo iste non perjuraret ; et datum fuit quod perjurat ; sed si non perjurat et jurat se perjurare, non jurat verum : ergo perjurat : quia aliter non juraret verum, quando jurat se perjurare : ergo perjurat : quia aliter non esset verum quod perjurat. "

[56] *Ibid.* f.

[57] See P. Glorieux, *Répertoire des maîtres en theologie de Paris au xiiie siècle,* (Paris : Librairie philosophique J. Vrin, 1933), v. 2, p. 301 (no. 400).

speak in the present tense and in the future tense interchangeably. He presumably did not think it made much difference. He writes, for instance :[58] " Therefore let this situation be posited, that someone says that he *will speak* falsely, and afterwards speaks falsely, as for example, if someone should say 'I *speak* falsely. An ass flies.' " He too solves the sophism in quite the Aristotelian way. In fact, Giles is so far from being concerned with any logical problems that he is worried instead about the moral implications of the sophism. If one swears that he will break his oath, ought he to do what he has thus sworn to do or not ? Giles concludes that he ought not, for while it is wrong to swear that one will break one's oath, it is even worse to fulfill that oath.[59]

Thus, even in the last quarter of the thirteenth century, there were men who commented on and wrote about Aristotle's Perjurer and Liar examples, and who gave no indication whatever that they were aware of the antinomical problems that might be suggested by Aristotle's text. These men continued to construe the paradox in the Aristotelian way, as an example of the fallacy *secundum quid et simpliciter*. Their solutions involve the liar in *two* utterances: 'I speak falsely' (or 'I shall speak falsely'), and a second, false sentence such as 'An ass flies.' Before the antinomical problems could be seen, someone would have to take the step to suppose that the liar said 'I speak falsely' and *that alone*.

But of course that step had already been taken long before. Adam of Balsham formulates the sentence this way, as we have seen. And already by the beginning of the thirteenth century, we find the Liar discussed in this form in special treatises devoted exclusively to the topic.[60]

This points out a curious problem. If the Aristotelian passage in the *Sophistici elenchi* is the source for the mediaeval discussions,

---

[58] Giles of Rome, *In Aristotelis De sophisticis elenchis commentum* (Venice : Bonetus Locatellus, for Octavianus Scotus, 1496/97 (Hain 140)), f. 58va : " Ponatur ergo talis casus quod aliquis dicat se dicturum falsum, et postea dicat falsum, utputa, si quis diceret 'Ego dico falsum. Asinus volat'. "

[59] *Ibid.*, f. 58rb–va.

[60] See the third text mentioned in n. 9, above, and the text edited by De Rijk, " Some Notes... " This fact also eliminates the initially plausible suggestion that it was the mediaevals' tampering with Aristotle's recalcitrant Liar example, which would not fit the Perjurer pattern despite the Philosopher's own words, that led them to a discovery of the fully antinomical formulation common in the fourteenth century.

how do we explain the fact that the earliest treatments we know appear *outside* the tradition of commentary on the *Elenchi?* Such commentaries, and the tracts *De fallaciis* which follow the outline of Aristotle's book, show a marked tendency to ignore the problem or to treat it as more or less a parallel to the Perjurer. This is so even after a separate tradition, one which treated the Liar in explicit and fully antinomical form, had developed and long been flourishing. We might have expected otherwise.

There is also another reason to question — or at least to qualify — the thesis that the mediaeval discussion took its origin in Aristotle's text. For the earliest known tract makes no use of the Aristotelian distinction between *simpliciter* and *secundum quid* in setting out its solution. [61] In fact, its approach is quite a different one. The anonymous author maintains the position known as *cassatio*: to someone who says that he is lying, we ought to reply " You say nothing. " [62] Indeed, the anonymous author of another treatise, around 1225, says that this opinion is "according to the common judgment." [63] He himself maintains a version of the *cassatio* doctrine, trying to fit it at the same time into the frame of the fallacy *secundum quid et simpliciter*.[64]

---

[61] De Rijk, *op. cit.* The anonymous author does, however, appeal to the distinction when he discusses two senses of the term 'insolubile'. See above, n. 33.

[62] " nil dicis. " De Rijk, *op. cit.*, p. 106, line 1.

[63] " secundum communem judicium. " See the third text mentioned in n. 9, above, and my *The Mediaeval Liar*, item XXI.

[64] *Ibid.* At least two other approaches to the paradox were taken very early in the history of the discussion. Both are exemplified in the second text mentioned in n. 9, above. One was the way of the so-called " restringentes " — those who impose restrictions (on the reference of terms) — who denied self-reference. This must have been a common opinion quite early, for the thirteenth century tracts mentioned as items one and three in n. 9, above, explicitly argue against it — and also against the *cassatio* doctrine. (Nevertheless, the third text in n. 9 in the end accepts a version of *cassatio*.)

The other way was to argue that although the verb in an insoluble is in the present tense, it refers to some *prior* time. Thus, if I say 'I speak falsely', and have not uttered any falsehoods before making that statement, my utterance is false. This view might just possibly have arisen from considerations of the question of tense in trying to make Aristotle's Perjurer and his Liar parallel. See the discussion above.

Thomas Bradwardine's *Insolubilia*, ca. 2–5 (Roure, *op. cit.*, pp. 286–296), provides a useful survey of these and other opinions held before his time. Ralph Strode credits Bradwardine with being the first to break away from these approaches and to come up with something that really worked. See the passages quoted in my *The Mediaeval Liar*, item LIII.

Cassatio seems to have fallen rapidly into disrepute. We do not find it maintained in any form after about 1225. By the time of Bradwardine's tract, 1321–1324,[65] it seems to be regarded as a rather preposterous opinion, and refuted by taking it with excruciating literalness. Bradwardine argues that he who says that he speaks falsely utters letters — we would say phonemes — syllables and words, and thus not nothing.[66]

The doctrine of *cassatio* bears a striking and suggestive resemblance to what seems at least to have been the view of the Stoic Chrysippus, preserved in a very fragmentary text:[67]

> The (fallacy) about the truth-speaker and similar ones are to be... (solved in a similar way). One should not say that they are true and (also) false; nor should one conjecture in another way, that the same (statement) is expressive of true and false simultaneously, but that they have no meaning at all. And he rejects the afore-mentioned proposition and also the proposition that one can say true and false simultaneously and that in all such (matters) the sentence is sometimes simple, sometimes expressive of more.

Finally, let us note that "during the first half of the twelfth century the Parisian masters came into acquaintance with James of Venice's (translation and) commentary on the *Soph. El.*"[68]

From all this we can perhaps draw two tentative conclusions. First, the mediaevals probably did not think up the paradox on their own. This is not to say that they did not exercise their ingenuity on the problem, but only that it was first presented to them through some intermediary. The almost universal testimony of the early texts leaves little doubt that Aristotle's fallacy *secundum quid et simpliciter* had something to do with it.

Second, there seems to be little doubt that there were other forces at play too. The peculiar formulation of Aristotle's text, and the tendency of the commentary tradition to ignore problems with the Liar that go beyond that text, indicate that it was probably

---

[65] On the date, see James A. Weisheipl, OP, "Ockham and Some Mertonians," *Mediaeval Studies* 30 (1968), p. 190.

[66] Roure, *op. cit.*, p. 295, par. 5.06.

[67] Bocheński, *op. cit.*, p. 133. (The omission is in Bocheński.) The text is edited in Rüstow, *op. cit.*, p. 73 line 22 – p. 74 line 25. See Bocheński, *loc. cit.*, for a discussion.

[68] De Rijk, "Some Notes...," p. 85. See Minio-Paluello, "Note sull'Aristotele...," pp. 401–405.

not Aristotle's words themselves that stimulated the discussion. Moreover, the early appearance of quite non-Aristotelian views points to other, perhaps Stoic, influences.

This Aristotelian and yet not-so-Aristotelian situation suggests a commentary on the *Sophistici elenchi*, one which drew on other sources. Perhaps James of Venice's commentary was responsible. The text is lost, however, and the hypothesis cannot be verified. [69] If it was indeed James of Venice who precipitated the mediaeval discussion, we still have to explain the fifty years or so between the appearance of his commentary and the first extant treatments of the paradox. [70]

Indiana University

---

[69] See *ibid.* on this commentary.

[70] This paper is based on a chapter of my Ph.D. dissertation for the University of Toronto. I should like to thank Profs. Hans G. Herzberger and E. A. Synan for their patient direction and advice. My indebtedness to De Rijk's " Some Notes... " should be obvious.

III

OCKHAM ON SELF-REFERENCE

It seems now to be the accepted view that Ockham's reply to the Liar paradox consisted of a rejection of self-reference across the board.[1] I think that accepted view is wrong. On the contrary, Ockham allowed self-reference in all but exceptional cases.

The accepted view is based on two passages. The first is from † Ockham's *Summa logicae* III, 3, 45,[2] the second from his commentary on † Aristotle's *Sophistici elenchi*.[3] In both texts, we have a situation in which Socrates says only 'Socrates utters a falsehood' (*Sortes dicit falsum*). Ockham disarms the paradox by holding that the term 'falsehood' in Socrates' utterance cannot refer to (*supponit pro*) that very utterance itself. In the first text he goes on to observe that what Socrates' proposition then amounts to is 'Socrates utters a falsehood *other than this proposition*.' Since by hypothesis that is not so, the proposition is false. Earlier in the same text Ockham gives an analogous account of the situation in which Socrates says only 'Socrates does not speak a truth' (*Sortes non dicit verum*). The term 'truth' in that proposition cannot refer to (*supponit pro*) that very proposition, and so the whole utterance amounts to 'Socrates does not utter a truth *other than this proposition*.' Since that is so by hypothesis, the proposition is true. It is clear from this that Ockham's reply is indeed a denial of self-reference. The question is whether that denial extends across the board to innocuous cases as well as to vicious ones. Ockham never says that a part cannot refer to (*supponit pro*) the whole of which it is a part—the usual mediaeval way of formulating a general rejection of self-reference. What he does say is this:[4]

> In the proposition *Sortes non dicit verum*, the predicate cannot supposit for this entire proposition of which it is a part, yet not precisely because it is a part.

In fact, *whenever* Ockham denies the possibility of self-reference, it is always qualified, as here, by a phrase such as "in this proposition." This is negative evidence. More positive is the clause "yet not precisely because it is a part." This certainly suggests that some parts of at least some propositions can refer to their wholes.

The suggestion is confirmed by a passage from Ockham's treatise on *obligationes*.[5] There he distinguishes six species of obligation. The first † is "institution," which he defines thus: "Institution is a new convention for some word throughout the time of disputation, and is not meant to last any longer."[6] What he has in mind is, for example, the geometrician's use of letters to signify certain points or lines for the duration of a proof. Ockham goes on:[7]

> About this species some rules are given. One is that a part can never signify the whole of which it is a part. But this rule takes an exception. For in this proposition 'Every proposition is true', the subject signifies the whole proposition. Likewise, the same thing can signify itself; therefore, a part by the same reason can signify the whole. The antecedent is clear. For this noun 'utterance' signifies every utterance, and as a consequent itself. Likewise, this noun 'noun' signifies every noun, because the definition of a noun agrees with every noun. Therefore it is to be said that, although a part can signify the whole of which it is a part, nevertheless such an institution is not always to be admitted. For when through the institution of a part having the same institution, the signified whole would be changed from truth to falsehood and conversely, then such an institution is not to be admitted.

The last sentence is rather obscure; it is not clear what exceptions Ockham intends to make. Nevertheless, he certainly does want to say that, in all but exceptional cases, there is nothing wrong with a part signifying its whole. But signification is not reference (supposition). In order to pass from self-signification to self-reference, we need only observe that in personal supposition—the only kind of supposition at stake here—a term refers to just what it signifies.[8] In short, Ockham allows self-reference in all but exceptional cases. The Liar and related paradoxes are such exceptional cases.

In fact, Ockham was not at all alone in adopting this attenuated denial of self-reference. Others in the same period were Roger Roseth, Walter Burley and Walter Sexgrave.[9] Indeed, Burley adopts essentially the same position as Ockham, and explicitly rejects the view that self-reference is never licit.[10] I know of only two mediaeval authors who adopted this latter view, both of them on the basis of shockingly bad arguments.[11]

Ockham's view then seems to be that self-reference is to be allowed except where it would lead to paradox—in short, it is licit except where it is illicit. In the absence of any independent account of what makes certain cases illicit, such a position is not very revealing. And Ockham provides no independent account.

NOTES

1. *Cf.*, e.g., Philotheus Boehner, "Ockham's theory of supposition and the notion of truth," in his *Collected Articles on Ockham*, Eligius M. Buytaert, ed., (St.

Bonaventure, N.Y.: The Franciscan Institute, 1958), pp. 257ff.; James A. Weisheipl, "Developments in the arts curriculum at Oxford in the early fourteenth century," *Mediaeval Studies*, vol. 28 (1966), p. 166; E. J. Ashworth, "The treatment of semantic paradoxes from 1400 to 1700," *Notre Dame Journal of Formal Logic*, vol. XIII (1972), p. 38.

† 2. The chapter is edited on the basis of one incunabula and two MSS as an appendix to my "An Anonymous Fourteenth-Century Treatise on 'Insolubles': Text and Study," (M.S.L. dissertation: The Pontifical Institute of Mediaeval Studies, 1969). Part of it is translated in Boehner, *op. cit.*, pp. 258f.

† 3. The relevant passage is printed *ibid.*, p. 259, n. 34.

4. *Ibid.*, p. 258.

5. On *obligationes* in this sense, *cf.* Ignacio Angelelli, "The techniques of disputation in the history of logic," *The Journal of Philosophy*, vol. 67 (1970), pp. 800-815.

† 6. *Summa logicae* III, 3, 38. The passage is edited in Spade, *loc. cit.*

7. *Ibid.*

8. This statement needs qualification in view of the fact that Ockham gives no fewer than four senses of 'to signify' (*Summa logicae* I, 33), and in view of the complications raised by tense and modal contexts. These qualifications do not affect my point.

† 9. *Cf.* my *The Mediaeval Liar: A Catalogue of the Insolubilia-Literature* (forthcoming as a volume in the series "Subsidia Mediaevalia," Toronto: Pontifical Institute of Mediaeval Studies), items LXII, LXVII and LXVIII, respectively.

10. *Cf.* M. L. Roure, "La problématique des propositions insolubles au XIIIe siècle et au début du XIVe, suivie de l'édition des traités de W. Shyreswood, W. Burleigh et Th. Bradwardine," *Archives d'histoire doctrinale et littéraire du moyen âge*, 1970, pp. 269f.

† 11. The first is the anonymous author of the text edited in my "An Anonymous Fourteenth-Century . . . ". The second is also anonymous, and is edited by H. A. G. Braakhuis, "The Second Tract on *Insolubilia* Found in Paris, B. N. Lat. 16.617: An Edition of the Text with an Analysis of its Contents," *Vivarium*, vol. 5 (1967), pp. 111-145. Robert Holcot may also have held such a view. *Cf.* my *The Mediaeval Liar*, item LX.

Indiana University
Bloomington, Indiana

IV

INSOLUBILIA AND BRADWARDINE'S THEORY OF SIGNIFICATION

In the Middle ages the term for an antinomy or paradox of the Liar type ('This sentence is false' or 'This sentence is not true') was '*insolubile*' – an «insoluble». There was a great deal of literature on the topic of such insolubles in the Middle Ages, and that literature has recently begun to be investigated in detail.[1] As a result of this research, it has become clear that the views of Thomas Bradwardine on this topic were especially influential. They are the topic of this paper.

Bradwardine was born around 1295 and died as Archbishop of Canterbury in 1349, presumably of plague. He is not widely known among historians of logic, but he is quite well known in the history of science and the history of theology – of science because of his important *Tractatus de proportionibus* on the physics of motion,[2] and of theology because of his famous *De causa dei.*[3] Nevertheless, sometime between 1321 and 1324,[4] Bradwardine also wrote an *Insolubilia* that I regard as a turning point in the history of the mediaeval discussion of this topic.[5]

1. For general surveys of the mediaeval literature, see F. Bottin, *Le antinomie semantiche nella logica medievale*, Editrice Antenore, Padova 1976 and P.V. Spade, *The Mediaeval Liar: A Catalogue of the Insolubilia-Literature*, Pontifical Institute of Mediaeval Studies, Toronto 1975.

2. H. Lamar Crosby, Jr., ed. and tr., *Thomas of Bradwardine: His Tractatus de Proportionibus; Its Significance for the Development of Mathematical Physics*, University of Wisconsin Press, Madison Wis. 1955.

3. Thomas Bradwardine, *De causa dei contra Pelagium et de virtute causarum*, Joannes Billius, Londini 1618 (photoreprint Minerva, Frankfurt am Main 1964).

4. On the date, see J.A. Weisheipl, *Ockham and Some Mertonians*, «Med. Stud.», 30 (1968), 163-213 at 190.

5. Edited in M.L. Roure, *La problématique des propositions insolubles au xiiie siècle et au début du xive, suive de l'édition des traités de W. Shyreswood, W. Burleigh et Th. Bradwardine*, «Arch. Hist. doctr. litt. M.A.», 37 (1970), 205-326 at 285-326. Roure's edition is based on Erfurt, *CA 8°* ms. 76, ff. 6-21. In the present paper, I have sometimes corrected the edition on the basis of Bruges, Bibl. publ. de la ville, ms. 500, ff. 134r-143v, and *Vat. lat.* 2154, ff. 13ra-22rb. For other manuscripts, see J.A. Weisheipl, *Repertorium Mertonense*, «Med. Stud.», 31 (1969), 174-224 at 178, and the note in Spade, *The Mediaeval Liar*, 106 n. 195. Discussions of

Before Bradwardine, several authors had proposed various theories to solve the paradoxes.[6] With Bradwardine, however, the discussion entered a new and, in my view, much more sophisticated stage. Indeed, in the third quarter of the fourteenth century Ralph Strode, who was writing on insolubles in the sixth and last treatise of his own *Logica*,[7] surveyed the literature before Bradwardine[8] and then observed[9]:

> For the above opinions were those of the old writers, who correctly understood little or nothing about insolubles. After them there arose the first among the modern philosophers of nature, namely, master Thomas Bradwardine, who was the first to come upon something worthwhile concerning insolubles.

Despite Strode's high praise, it must be said that neither Bradwardine nor for that matter anyone else has succeded in «solving» the paradoxes in any completely satisfactory way. Indeed, I think there are sound theoretical reasons for saying that cannot be done. We shall have to evaluate Bradwardine's views therefore in the light of their own intrinsic interest and in the light of their implications for semantic theory more generally, quite apart from their success or failure as an ultimate solution to the Liar paradox.

Bradwardine reasoned like this. A true sentence, he said, is by definition one that signifies *only* as is the case (*tantum sicut est*); a false sentence is one that signifies otherwise than is the case

Bradwardine's text may be found in Roure, *La problématique*, 234-243; Bottin, *Le antinomie*, 79-86; Spade, *The Mediaeval Liar*, 105-110; and P.V. Spade, *Peter of Ailly: Concepts and Insolubles. An Annotated Translation*, D. Reidel, Dordrecht 1980, 5-6.

6. See the discussion in Bottin, *Le antinomie*; Spade, *The Mediaeval Liar*; P.V. Spade, *The Origins of the Mediaeval 'Insolubilia' Literature*, « Francisc. Stud. », 33 (1973), 292-309; † and P.V. Spade, *Early Theories in the Medieval 'Insolubilia' Literature* (forthcoming).

7. On Strode's *Logica* and his logical views, see A. Maierù, *Terminologia logica della tarda scolastica*, Edizioni dell'Ateneo, Roma 1972, index. Maierù is preparing a partial edition of the *Logica*. For his discussion of insolubles, see Spade, *The Mediaeval Liar*, 87-91; and P.V. Spade, *Robert Fland's 'Insolubilia': An Edition, with Comments on the Dating of Fland's Works*, « Med. Stud. », 40 (1978), 56-80.

8. Strode's survey is taken almost verbatim from Bradwardine's own discussion of previous opinions.

9. Erfurt, *CA 4°*, ms. 255, f. 3vb: « Praedictae namque opiniones fuerunt antiquorum [antiquorum], qui parum vel nihil de insolubilibus recte sapuerunt. Post quos surrexit princeps modernorum physicorum, videlicet magister Thomas Bradwardine, qui aliquid quod valuerit de insolubilibus primitus adinvenit » (all translations in this paper are my own).

(*aliter quam est*).[10] These definitions encapsulate a rudimentary correspondence theory of truth. In addition, Bradwardine adds an explicit acceptance of the Principle of Bivalence, that every sentence is true or false.[11]

Given just this much, it follows already that any sentence that signifies itself to be not true, as at least the simplest kinds of insolubles do, is automatically false and not true. For suppose it is true. Then, since it signifies itself to be not true, it does not signify only as is the case. Something it signifies is not so. Hence it fails to satisfy the definition of a true sentence. In short, such a sentence cannot be true on pain of violating the very definition of a true sentence. And, since it is not true, the Principle of Bivalence tells us that the sentence must be false. Hence by definition, the sentence must signify somehow otherwise than is the case; it must signify something that is not so. But of course, it signifies that it is not true, and that is indeed so. Hence – and here is the crucial move – any sentence that signifies itself to be not true does not signify *only* that, but must also signify something else as well, something else that is not the case.

Sentences are true if they signify only as is the case. They are

10. Roure, *La problématique*, 297, § 6.03 (here and below I have felt free to revise Roure's orthography and punctuation): « Definitiones etiam sunt duae. Quarum prima est ista: Propositio vera est oratio significans tantum sicut est. Secunda est ista: Propositio falsa est oratio significans aliter quam est ». Notice that sentences are here not said to signify « things » in the ten Aristotelian categories, although Bradwardine does not deny that they might signify in that way too. Rather signification is here a propositional notion. Sentences signify *that* such and such is so, and that such and such is so either is the case or is not the case.

11. Roure, *La problématique*, 297, § 6.04: « Suppositiones sunt sex (*following Bruges, Bibl. publ. ms. 500, f. 137r*). Prima est ista: Quaelibet propositio est vera vel falsa ». [« The assumptions are six. The first is this: Every sentence is true of false »]. Throughout this paper I translate 'propositio' by 'sentence', where this is to be understood as a *declarative* sentence, with a truth-value. Commands, prayers, questions, and in general sentences without truth-value were not regarded as « propositiones ». The translation 'proposition' risks confusion with the modern notion of a proposition as that which is *expressed* by a sentence. 'Statement' likewise suffers inappropriate connotations from modern philosophical literature. I know of no way to translate 'propositio' that does not require some explanation). The Principle of Bivalence is a semantic principle, and should be carefully distinguished from the Law of Excluded Middle '*p* or not-*p*'. The two are independent of one another. There are logics (for instance, supervaluational logics) for which bivalence fails but excluded middle holds, and there are logics (for instance, logics without negation) for which bivalence holds but in which excluded middle cannot even be formulated.

false if they signify otherwise than is the case. But Bradwardine does not say that false sentences must signify *only* otherwise than is the case. The idea then is that a sentence may signify many things to be so. In order for the sentence to be true, all those things must be indeed so. If any one of them fails, that spoils the whole thing; the sentence is in that case false. In particular, insolubles are false not because they signify themselves to be not true, because that much of what they signify is so, but rather because of something else they signify too, something that is *not* so.

But what else is it that insolubles signify? What could it be that would not seem contrived and *ad hoc*? Bradwardine's answer was: such a sentence not only signifies that it is not true, it also signifies that it *is* true.[12] And it is the latter that fails to be the case. Let us look first at how this suggestion breaks the paradox. Then we will look at the reasoning behind the move, and at some of the problems and consequences of the theory.

Let *k* be a sentence that signifies itself to be not true. For example, let *k* = '*k* is not true'. Now according to Bradwardine's definition of truth, *k* is true if and only if it signifies only as is the case. And, as we have just seen, according to Bradwardine's theory *k* signifies two things, not just one. It not only signifies itself to be *not* true, it also signifies itself to *be* true. Hence, we have

k is true if and only if both *k* is not true and *k* is true.

The right side of this biconditional is just a straightforward contradiction, and so we have no special problem with it; it is just false. So too, therefore, the left side of the biconditional is false, since the two sides are equivalent. That is, *k* is not true, on pain of contradiction.

On the other hand, there is no corresponding contradiction if we say that *k* is false – as we now must, given the Principle of

12. Roure, *La problématique*, 298, § 6.05 (here corrected on the basis of Bruges, ms. 500, f. 137r): « Si aliqua propositio significat se non esse veram vel se esse falsam, ipsa significat se esse veram, et est falsa » [« If some sentence signifies itself not to be true, or ‹signifies› itself to be false, it signifies itself to be true, and it is false »].

Bivalence and the fact that, as we have just seen, *k* is not true. For according to the definition of falsehood, *k* is false if and only if it signifies otherwise than is the case. And it certainly does signify otherwise than is the case, since it signifies a contradiction, as we have just seen. Furthermore, we know which half of the contradiction fails. It is the right half of the conjunction on the right of the biconditional above, the half that says that *k* is true.

The sentence *k* is false, therefore, not insofar as it signifies itself to be *not* true, because that much of what it signifies is so, but because it also signifies itself to *be* true, and that is not so. To say that *k* is true leads to contradiction, as we have just seen. To say that *k* is false, however, does not lead to contradiction. Hence the paradox is broken.

This, in summary fashion, is how Bradwardine's view works. But what is the rationale behind it? Why does Bradwardine say that insolubles not only signify themselves to be *not* true, but also signify themselves to *be* true? The fundamental principles here are two. First[13]:

> Any sentence signifies or denotes as of now or simply whatever follows from it as of now or simply.

The terminology of «simple» and «as of now» consequence is part of the vocabulary of the mediaeval theory of consequence in general. And, although Bradwardine does not explicitly say so,[14] it is probably safe to suppose that for him the division of consequences into «simple» and «as of now» ones is meant to be exhaustive, as it was for Ockham.[15] In that case, the principle just quoted reduces to what I will call the «Bradwardine Principle»:

13. Roure, *La problématique*, 297, § 6.04: «Quaelibet propositio significat sive denotat ut nunc vel simpliciter omne quod sequitur ad illam ut nunc vel simpliciter». This is the second of Bradwardine's «assumptions», following the text in n. 11 above.

14. Bradwardine left no special treatise *De consequentiis* and, at least as far as I know, no other systematic presentation of his theory of consequence.

15. See M. McCord Adams, *Did Ockham Know of Material and Strict Implication? A Reconsideration*, «Francisc. Stud.», 33 (1973), 5-37.

(*BP*) Any sentence signifies or denotes whatever follows from it.
If *p* only if *q*, then *P* signifies that *q*,

where the name replacing '*P*' names the sentence replacing '*p*'.[16]

The second basic principle of Bradwardine's reasoning is the converse of this, what I will call the «Converse Bradwardine Principle»:

(*CBP*) Whatever a sentence signifies follows from it.
If *P* signifies that *q*, then *p* only if *q*.

Although Bradwardine does not explicitly state *CBP* as one of the bases of his theory, it is presupposed by some of his reasoning.[17]

Given *BP* and *CBP*, here is how Bradwardine argues that insolubles signify that they are true[18]:

16. I take Bradwardine's 'or denotes' to be an equivalent for sentential signification (signifying that such and such is so). See n. 10 above.

17. Several writers earlier than Bradwardine had maintained that whatever is « understood » in something « follows » from it. See, e.g., Iohannes Duns Scotus, *Quaestiones super libros Elenchorum Aristotelis*, q. 51, obj. 1(*Opera omnia*, ed. L. Wadding, L. Durand, Lugduni 1639, vol. 1 [photoreprint Georg Olms, Hildesheim 1968], 267); Simon of Faversham, *Quaestiones novae super Sophisticos elenchos*, q. 22 (or q. 23 according to a different numbering): « Utrum sequatur 'homo mortuus, ergo homo' ». Both texts are cited in S. Ebbesen, *The Dead Man Is Alive*, « Synth. », 40 (1979), 43-70 at 65 n. 6. See also the anonymous but probably English text from roughly the 1280s, *Quaestiones super Sophisticos elenchos*, in Cambridge, Gonville & Caius, ms. 611/341, ff. 1-24v at f. 12va, quoted in Ebbesen, *The Dead Man*, 63. Given the traditional psychological notion of signification (see P.V. Spade, *Some Epistemological Implications of the Burley-Ockham Dispute*, « Francisc. Stud. », 35 [1975], 212-222), it was but a short step from these claims to *CBP*. On the other hand, I know of no author before Bradwardine who maintained *BP* or anything that commits one to *BP*. Some authors before Bradwardine had maintained that all sentences (not just insoluble ones) « assert » that they are true. (See, e.g., Bonaventurae, *Quaestiones disputatae de mysterio trinitatis*, q. 1, a. 1, ad 5, in *Opera omnia*, Coll. S. Bonaventurae Quaracchi 1882-1902, V, 50; Iohannes Duns Scotus, *Opus secundum in Perihermenias*, q. 8, obj. 1, in *Opera omnia*, 1, 221; Walter Burleigh, *De puritate artis logicae tractatus longior*, tract. 1, i, Ch. 4, Ph. Boehner ed., The Franciscan Institute, St. Bonaventure, N.Y. 1955, 25, lines 36-38; Burley, *Insolubilia*, in Roure, *La problématique*, 272, § 3.02). But Bradwardine is the first I know to maintain *BP* in its full generality, or to use this principle systematically as the basis for a solution to the paradoxes.

18. Roure, *La problématique*, 299, § 6.054: « Secunda conclusio quantum ad primam sui partem totaliter demonstratur. Sit *A* propositio significans se non esse veram. Vel ergo significat aliquid aliud vel non. Si non, et sequitur: '*A* non est verum; ergo, non est ita totaliter sicut significatur per *A*, per primam definitionem; et per *A* tantum significatur *A* non esse veram, ut ponitur; ergo, per secundam partem primae conclusionis, non est ita quod *A* ‹non› est verum'. Ergo, per secundam suppositionem, *A* significat se esse verum. Si enim significat aliquid aliud quam se non esse verum, sit illud '*B* est *C*'. Tunc sequitur: '*A* non est verum; ergo, non est ita totaliter sicut significatur per *A*; et per *A* tantum significatur *A* non esse verum et *B* est *C*; ergo, non est ita quod *A* non est verum et quod *B* est *C*; ergo, per quartam suppositionem, *A* est verum vel nullum *B* est *C*'. Ergo, per

The second conclusion [19] is completely demonstrated with respect to its first part. Let *A* be a sentence signifying itself not to be true. Therefore, either it signifies something else or it does not. If (i) it does not, then it follows: '*A* is not true; therefore, it is not entirely the case as is signified by *A*, by the first definition [20]; and by *A* it is signified only that *A* is not true, as is assumed; therefore, by the second part of the first conclusion,[21] it is not the case that *A* is not true'. Therefore, by the second assumption,[22] *A* signifies itself to be true. If (ii) it does signify something other than that it is not true, let that be: *B* is *C*.[23] Then it follows: '*A* is not true; therefore, it is not entirely the case as is signified by *A*; and by *A* it is signified only that *A* is not true and *B* is *C*; therefore, it is not the case that *A* is not true and that *B* is *C*; threfore, by the fourth assumption,[24] *A* is true or no *B* is *C*'. Therefore, by the second assumption, *A* signifies that *A* is true or that no *B* is *C*. And it signifies the opposite of the second part of this disjunction, as is assumed, namely that *B* is *C*. And by the fifth assumption,[25] from this disjunction together with the opposite of the second part, the first one follows, namely that *A* is true. Therefore, by the second assumption, *A* signifies *A* to be true. The argument is entirely the same if it is assumed that *A* signifies itself not to be true and *many* other things.

The argument may be paraphrased as follows. As before, let *k* =

suppositionem secundam, *A* significat quod *A* est verum vel quod nullum *B* est *C*. Et significat oppositum secundae partis hujus disjunctivae, ut ponitur, scilicet quod *B* est *C*. Et per quintam suppositionem, ex ista disjunctiva cum opposito secundae partis sequitur prima, scilicet quod *A* est verum. Ergo, per secundam suppositionem, *A* significat *A* esse verum. Consimiliter omnino est arguendum si ponatur *A* significare se non esse verum et multa alia » (The editorial insertion is Roure's). Roure discusses the argument in this passage at 238 ff.

19. The « second conclusion » is quoted in n. 12 above.

20. The definition of truth, quoted in n. 10 above.

21. For the « first conclusion », see Roure, *La problématique*, 298, § 6.05 (here corrected according to *Vat. lat.* 2154, f. 15vb): « Quaelibet propositio cujus extremum multa habet supposita significat sive denotat affirmationem vel negationem pro aliquo illorum, et si unicum habet, denotat pro illo » [« Any sentence the extreme [*i.e., the subject or predicate*] of which has many supposita signifies or denotes an affirmation or negation for one of them, and if it has a single suppositum, it denotes [*understand*: an affirmation or negation] for that »]. The second part of this conclusion concerns sentences, like *A* in Bradwardine's example, that contain singular terms. But the conclusion seems irrelevant to the argument at this point.

22. The « Bradwardine Principle ». See n. 13 above.

23. This is merely an example. Any arbitrary sentence may be substituted.

24. De Morgan's Law. See Roure, *La problématique*, 297, § 6.04 (with word-order here revised according to Bruges, ms. 500, f. 137rb): « Quarta est ista: copulativa et disjunctiva ex partibus contradicentibus sibi invicem contradicunt » [« The fourth assumption is this: a conjunction and the disjunction made up of contradictory parts contradict one another] ». That is, '*p* and *q*' and 'not-*p* or not-*q*' are contradictories, as are 'not-*p* and not-*q*' and '*p* or *q*'.

25. Disjunctive syllogism. See Roure, *La problématique*: « Quinta: ex qualibet disjunctiva cum opposito unius suarum partium infertur reliqua pars » [« The fifth assumption: From any disjunction together with the opposite of one of its parts the other part is inferred »].

'*k* is not true', and let *k signify* that *k* is not true, just as one would expect from looking at it.[26] Now either *k* signifies nothing else in addition, or else it does. Hence we have two cases:

Case 1: *k* signifies that *k* is not true, and nothing else. Then

1. Assume for conditional proof that *k* is not true.
2. Hence (from step 1 and the definition of truth), *k* does not signify only as is the case.
3. Therefore (from step 2 and the assumption of Case 1), it is not the case that *k* is not true.
4. Hence (by double negation), *k* is true after all.
5. In short (from steps 1 through 4 by conditional proof), *k* is not true only if *k* is true.
6. Therefore (by *BP*), *k* signifies that *k* is true, which is what we wanted to prove.

Case 2: *k* not only signifies that *k* is not true, but something else as well - say, that *p*. (Notice how this is put: *k* signifies two things, *that-k-is-not-true* and *that-p*. It does not signify only the conjunction of those two things, *that-k-is-not-true-and-p*, although it will also signify that conjunction in virtue of *BP* and *CBP*).[27] Then

1. As before, assume for conditional proof that *k* is not true.
2. Hence (from step 1 and the definition of truth), *k* does not signify only as is the case.
3. Therefore (from step 2 and the assumption of Case 2), it is not the case both that *k* is not true and that *p*.
4. That is (by De Morgan's Law[28]), either *k* is true or else it is not the case that *p*.
5. In short (from steps 1 through 4 by conditional proof), *k* is not true only if either *k* is true or else it is not the case that *p*.[29]
6. But (by the assumption of Case 2), *k* signifies that *p*.[30]
7. Hence (from step 6 and *CBP*), *k* is not true only if *p*.

26. This second stipulation, as we shall see, is unnecessary in virtue of *BP*. The importance of this fact will be discussed below.

27. Let '*P*' name the sentence replacing '*p*'. Then in general if *P* signifies that *q* and *P* also signifies that *r*, then *p* only if *q* and *p* only if *r*, by *CBP*. Hence *p* only if both *q* and *r*. And therefore, by *BP*, *P* signifies (conjunctively) that *q-and-r*. The converse reasoning also holds.

28. See n. 24 above.

29. Bradwardine here adds the step (see n. 18 above): *k* signifies that either *k* is true or else it is not the case that *p*. (This follows from step 5 by *BP*). But the step is never used later in the proof and so is completely idle.

30. It was to justify this step that I pointed out above that *k* signifies two things and not just their conjunction.

8. Therefore (from steps 5 and 7 and a little propositional logic), *k* is not true only if *k* is true.
9. Thus (from step 8 and *BP*), *k* signifies that *k* is true, which is what we wanted to prove.

So on either of the two alternatives, Case 1 or Case 2, *k* signifies that *k* is true. And, as Bradwardine remarks,[31] Case 2 can obviously be generalized to allow still further significations, so that in any event *k* will signify that *k* is true. *Q.E.D.*

This is the core of Bradwardine's theory of insolubles. His view was immensely influential. Versions of it were maintained, or at least discussed, down to the end of the Middle Ages.[32] Indeed, Bradwardine's theory was perhaps the most broadly influential theory of insolubles during the entire subsequent mediaeval discussion of the topic.[33]

The structure of Bradwardine's two-case argument as examined above may at first appear strange. After all, one might object, if insolubles signify that they are true, then Case 1 cannot in fact arise, so that the argument there amounts to a *reductio*. Likewise, unless '*p*' is replaced by '*k* is true' itself, the argument under Case 2 is in effect a *reductio* of the claim that *k* signifies *only* that *k* is not true and that *p*. And similarly for the generalized forms of Case 2. Could Bradwardine not have found a more straightforward way to prove his point?

Yes, he could have. Note first that, although many later authors generalized Bradwardine's view and maintained that *every* sentence signifies itself to be true,[34] Bradwardine himself

31. See the end of the text quoted in n. 18 above.

32. See Spade, *The Mediaeval Liar*, anonymous items IV, VIII and XII (Pseudo-Heytesbury), and items XXIV (Albert of Saxony), XXXI (anonymous, but attributed there to Henry Hopton; on the attribution see L.M. de Rijk, *Logica Oxoniensis: An Attempt to Reconstruct a Fifteenth Century Oxford Manual of Logic*, « Medioevo », 3 [1977], 121-164 at 140), XXXIII-XXXIV (John Buridan), XXXVIII (John of Holland), XXXIX (John Huntman (Venator), there called John Hunter), XLIX (Paul of Pergula), LIII (Ralph Strode), LVI (Richard Lavenham), and LVIII (Robert Fland).

33. His only major competitor in this respect seems to have been William Heytesbury. See William Heytesbury, *On « Insoluble » Sentences: Chapter One of His Rules for Solving Sophisms*, transl. with an introd. and study by P.V. Spade, Pontifical Institute of Mediaeval Studies, Toronto 1979. These judgments of influence are tentative and of course do not imply that Bradwardine's and Heytesbury's were the only two theories in circulation. Neither do they imply anything about the adequacy of those views.

34. For instance, Albert of Saxony. See Spade, *The Mediaeval Liar*, 48; and Albertus de

does not explicitly say that. Nevertheless, the generalized claim follows from *BP* and *CBP* by a quite direct argument. Let '*P*' name the sentence replacing '*p*'.[35] Then in general:

1. Assume for conditional proof that *p*.
2. For arbitrary *q*, assume also that *P* signifies that *q*.
3. Then (from step 2 and *CBP*), *p* only if *q*.
4. Therefore (from step 1 and *modus ponens*), *q*.
5. Hence (since steps 2 through 4 are general with respect to *q*), for every *q*, if *P* signifies that *q*, then *q*.
6. Therefore (from step 5 and Bradwardine's definition of truth), *P* is true.
7. In short (from steps 1 through 6 by conditional proof), *p* only if *P* is true.
8. Thus (from step 7 by *BP*), *P* signifies that *P* is true.

Hence, Bradwardine could have made his point generally and much more straightforwardly. Nevertheless, some light can be shed on the structure of the argument he actually gave if we ignore step 8 of the above argument and continue:

9. Assume for conditional proof that if for all *q*, if *P* signifies that *q* then *q*, then *r*.
10. Now (by Bradwardine's definition of truth), *P* is true if and only if, for all *q*, if *P* signifies that *q*, then *q*.
11. Hence (from steps 9 and 10 and substitution of equivalents), *P* is true only if *r*.
12. Therefore (from steps 7 and 11), *p* only if *r*.
13. Hence (from step 12 by *BP*), *P* signifies that *r*.
14. In short (by conditional proof, since steps 9-13 are general with respect to *r*), *the signification of P is closed under the consequence relation.*[36]

Saxonia, *Perutilis logica*, Venetiis 1522 (photoreprint Olms, Hildesheim - N.Y. 1974), f. 43rb, the third conclusion: « Omnis propositio mundi significat se esse veram » [« Every sentence in the world signifies itself to be true »]. See also n. 17 above, on the pre-Bradwardinian authors Bonaventure and Walter Burley.

35. We assume nothing about the signification of *P*. But see below.

36. A weaker version of this result may be obtained from *BP* and *CBP* much more quickly by simply observing that if *P* signifies that *q*, then (by *CBP*) *p* only if *q*, so that if in addition *q* only if *r*, then it follows that *p* only if *r*, so that (by *BP*), *P* signifies that *r*. This result is weaker insofar as there may arise infinitary cases in which all that *P* signifies *jointly* implies that *r* even though (barring conjunctions of infinite length), for no single *q* such that *P* signifies that *q* is it the case that *q* only if *r*. This nicety no doubt escaped Bradwardine, so that it is not at all implausible to suppose that Bradwardine actually intended the signification of sentences to be, as we say, closed under the consequence relation, even though he very likely never went through the fourteen-step argument above.

This result perhaps explains the structure of Bradwardine's two-case argument examined above. In each of the two cases we are to understand that the signification of *k* is closed under the consequence relation. Thus, in Case 1 we assume that *k* signifies that *k* is not true *and the consequences of that*, and nothing else, and in Case 2 we assume that *k* signifies that *k* is not true and that *p*, *and the consequences of those things*, and nothing else. Under neither case then does the argument amount to a *reductio*; in both cases, that *k* is true is one of the consequences of *k*'s stipulated signification.

We have seen how Bradwardine's theory resolves the paradoxes, and we have seen the rationale behind the theory. Let us explore some of its implications further.

Alfred Tarski, as is well known, set up what he called a «criterion of adequacy» for any acceptable theory of truth. Any such theory, he said, must verify all biconditionals of the form '*P* is true if and only if *p*', where '*p*' is replaced by a sentence and '*P*' by a name of that sentence.[37] I shall call such biconditionals «Tarski biconditionals» and, corresponding to them, I shall speak of «Tarski inferences», of the form '*P* is true, therefore *p*' and conversely. The one direction of these biconditionals or inferences, the direction ending with the claim that *P* is true, I shall call «semantic ascent»; the other direction is «semantic descent».

Bradwardine is clearly committed to accepting semantic descent in virtue of *BP*. For since (tautologically) *p* only if *p*, it follows by *BP* that *P* signifies that *p*,[38] and so by Bradwardine's definition of truth *P* is true only if *p*.

But semantic descent is by no means an innocuous feature of Bradwardine's theory. It violates the almost universally held mediaeval view that signification is through and through conventional, that expressions play whatever semantic role we

37. See A. Tarski, *The Concept of Truth in Formalized Languages*, in A. Tarski, *Logic, Semantics, Metamathematics: Papers from 1923 to 1938*, J.H. Woodger, tr., Clarendon Press, Oxford 1956, 152-278 at 155-156.

38. See notes 26 and 35 above.

care to assign to them.[39] As a result of this radical conventionality, one can quite consistently suppose that the sentence 'God exists' signifies, for instance, that you are an ass. Some authors in fact explicitly discussed how one should argue from such a supposition. Thus Roger Swyneshed, writing some ten to fifteen years after Bradwardine's *Insolubilia*,[40] argued that if one assumes that 'God exists' signifies that you are an ass, one does not thereby have to deny the sentence 'God exists'. On the contrary, one still has to grant it; what one has to deny is that the sentence 'God exists' is true. Swyneshed's point is simply that in actual reasoning one must grant or deny sentences according to the significations they actually have, not according to whatever significations they are counterfactually assumed to have. Reasoning *about* circumstances in which sentences signify in some other way does not alter the fact that in the *actual* circumstances they signify the way they do. And since the reasoning takes place under actual circumstances, not under the counterfactual circumstances the reasoning is about, one must grant or deny sentences according to their actual significations. If we think of a language abstractly as a an ordered pair consisting of a set of sentences and a semantics, then Swyneshed here is in effect distinguishing a metalanguage, in which the reasoning takes place, from an object-language that the reasoning is about and that differs from the metalanguage only with respect to its semantics, not with respect to its set of sentences.

It is clear that Swyneshed, who thus accepts the thoroughgoing conventionality of signification, has to reject both semantic ascent and semantic descent as formulated above. From 'God

39. At least this is true for spoken and written language. Many mediaeval authors recognized a « mental language », in which signification was fixed by nature, not by convention. See, e.g., J. Trentman, *Ockham on Mental*, « Mind », 79 (1970), 586-590.

40. P.V. Spade, *Roger Swyneshed's Obligationes: Edition and Comments*, « Arch. hist. doctr. litt. M.A. », 44, (1977), 243-285 at 254, § 21 and 264-265, §§ 58-61. On the date, see 246, and the references there. Swyneshed's claim in these passages was by no means universally accepted. See P.V. Spade, *Obligations: Developments in the Fourteenth Century*, in *Cambridge History of Later Medieval Philosophy*, N. Kretzmann *et al.*, eds., Cambridge University Press, Cambridge 1982, Ch. 16B, 335-341 at 339-340. The issue turned on whether one considered *impositio*, as a species of *obligatio*, to be an actual assignment of signification to terms or sentences, or only an assumption (usually counterfactual) of such an assignment.

exists', which must always be granted, one cannot semantically ascend to the claim that 'God exists' is true, since that must sometimes be denied as in the example. Similarly, semantic descent will fail if one assumes that 'You are an ass' signifies that God exists. On the other hand, the following modified versions of semantic ascent and descent will hold:

> If *p* and *P* signifies only that *p*,[41] then *P* is true.[42]
> If *P* is true and *P* signifies that *p*,[43] then *p*.

Bradwardine, as we have seen, accepts a stronger version of semantic descent because for him *BP* guarantees that *P* signifies that *p*. This amounts to an important restriction on the conventionality of signification. It is inconsistent to suppose, as Swyneshed did with the sentence 'God exists', that where '*P*' names the sentence replacing '*p*', *P* does not signify that *p*. Such a restriction, to be sure, does not fix the signification of *P* entirely. For while *P* signifies that *p* (and the consequences of that), it may signify other things as well. Nevertheless *BP* does commit Bradwardine to compromising the radical conventionality of signification, and thus to rejecting an important traditional feature of mediaeval semantics.

With respect to semantic ascent, the situation is more complex. On the one hand, Bradwardine's theory seems to accept semantic ascent explicitly in the case of insolubles. It is the availability of such an ascent that allows him, in his argument examined above, to infer by *BP* that insolubles signify that they

41. And perhaps the consequences of that, although it is not clear that for Swyneshed signification is closed under the consequence relation.

42. See also Guillelmi Hentisberi *De veritate et falsitate propositionis*, in *Tractatus* [...] *de sensu composito et diviso, Regulae ejusdem cum sophismatibus* [...], Venetiis 1494, ff. 183va-188rb at f. 185rb: « cum respectu cujuscumque propositionis verae sint aliquae praemissae inferentes sicut aliquam talem conclusionem 'Haec est vera', sicut illae duae praemissae ‹'Tu sedes' et› 'Haec propositio 'Tu sedes' praecise significat quod tu sedes'‹inferunt› 'Ergo, haec est vera 'Tu sedes'' » [« Nevertheless, with respect to any true sentence whatever, there are some premises implying such a conclusion as 'This is true'. For instance, these two premises 'You sit' and 'The sentence 'You sit' precisely signifies that you sit' imply 'Therefore, this is true 'You sit'' »]. The emendations are required for the sense, and also to conform to an example earlier in the passage. Maierù's suggested emendation, 'sicut illae duae praemissae: haec propositio 'tu sedes' ‹est vera, quae› praecise significat' etc., would have the result that the 'quae' -clause would be unnecessary to the inference. See Maierù, *Terminologia logica*, 457. †

43. Whether or not it signifies other things as well.

are true.[44] Indeed, although Bradwardine does not explicitly recognize the fact, *CBP* commits him to allowing semantic ascent in all cases.[45] This is just as one would expect. If *BP* commits Bradwardine to semantic descent, *CBP* commits him to semantic ascent.

On the other hand, it also seems as if Bradwardine's theory goes on to *suspend* semantic ascent in the case of insolubles. Once again, let *k* = '*k* is not true'. As we have seen, it follows that *k* signifies that *k* is not true, so that *k*'s not being true is a necessary condition for *k*'s being true. But while this is a necessary condition, it is not sufficient. On the assumption that *k* signifies *only* that *k* is not true (and the consequences of that),[46] the necessary and sufficient conditions for the truth of *k* are given by

> *k* is true if and only if both *k* is not true and *k* is true,

again as we have seen. And since the right half of the biconditional is a contradiction, *k* is not true but false. It was because Bradwardine wanted the necessary and sufficient truth-conditions for insolubles to be expressed in this manner that he needed to argue that insolubles signify that they are true.

But if semantic ascent held for insolubles, we would have

> if *k* is not true then *k* is true,

so that the second conjunct on the right of the above biconditional would be redundant; it would be implied by the first conjunct and so could be deleted. But if it could be deleted, then *k*'s not being true would be after all a sufficient condition for *k*'s being true, so that we would have

> *k* is true if and only if *k* is not true,

which is just the Tarski biconditional for *k* and gives us exactly the paradox we are trying to avoid. In short, Bradwardine needs to suspend semantic ascent in order to make the extra clause necessary in the truth-conditions for insolubles. Yet his justifi-

44. See the penultimate step of the argument under each of the two cases considered.
45. See step 7 of the above proof that signification is closed under consequence.
46. If *k* signifies yet further things, then *a fortiori* semantic ascent will fail.

cation for adding that extra clause is based on an acceptance of semantic ascent.[47] What is going on?

Bradwardine does not make the situation very clear, but we can perhaps explain it like this: Bradwardine accepts semantic ascent object-linguistically, but rejects it at least for insolubles metalinguistically. The above discussion of Swyneshed shows that, while the terminology of «object-language» and «metalanguage» is of course not mediaeval, nevertheless the distinction is not altogether anachronistic. In the present context, it applies as follows.

Let *k* be the Latin insoluble sentence '*k non est verum*' (translation: *k* is not true). Then if I am speaking in English about that Latin sentence *k*, Bradwardine's truth-conditions for *k* can be expressed as: *k* is true if and only if both *k* is not true and *k* is true. And that amounts, by a little propositional logic, to saying only: *k* is true only if *k* is not true. The converse implication, semantic ascent, is indeed suspended, and *k* is not true but false. Hence «metalinguistically», Bradwardine rejects semantic ascent at least for insolubles. On the other hand, if *k* is the English insoluble sentence '*k* is not true' and I am speaking in English about *k*, then once again I can state Bradwardine's truth-conditions for *k* by: *k* is true if and only if *k* is not true and *k* is true. But in this case the second conjunct on the right is redundant; it is already implicit in the first conjunct insofar as every sentence signifies, and so implies, that it is true. Contrast this with the former case, in which the second conjunct did not say that the first conjunct is true in English, but rather that a certain sentence is true in Latin. In short, when we are speaking in English about English, the second conjunct on the right of the biconditional can be simply deleted. All its work is done by the first conjunct. But if we do delete it, we have the full Tarski biconditional, in both directions, including semantic ascent. Ob-

47. It is not clear whether this problem is general and applies to all sentences whatever. For while Bradwardine is at least implicitly committed to saying that every sentence signifies that it is true he is not committed to saying that this requires an additional clause in the truth-conditions for all sentences.

ject-linguistically, then, semantic ascent holds. The situation is the same if the distinction between object-language and metalanguage is drawn not in terms of the set of sentences of the language but only in terms of the semantics of those sentences.

On Bradwardine's theory, as we have seen, insolubles are false not because of what they signify on the face of it, because what they signify in that way holds. Rather they are false because they also signify that they are true, and that does not hold. On the other hand, the contradictory or denial of an insoluble, Bradwardine says, is *true* because it signifies disjunctively the contradictories of what the insoluble signified conjunctively.[48] For instance, where *k* is once again the insoluble sentence '*k* is not true', it signifies *that-k-is-not-true-and-k-is-true*, and so is false. But its contradictory or denial, '*k* is true', signifies the denial of this, which by De Morgan's Law[49] is *that-k-is-true-or-k-is-not-true*, which holds tautologically. Hence '*k* is true', the contradictory of the insoluble *k*, is indeed true.

48. Roure, *La problématique*, 303, § 7.06 (the situation assumed here is that Socrates says only the sentence *A*, namely 'A falsehood is said by Socrates'): « Retento casu priori, si *A* sit falsum, suum oppositum erit verum, scilicet 'Nullum falsum dicitur a Sorte', quae sit *B*. Consequens falsum, quia per suppositionem secundam subjectum *B* supponit pro *A*. Ergo, *B* est una universalis habens unam singularem falsam, scilicet '*A* falsum non dicitur a Sorte'. Ergo, *B* est falsum. Ergo, contradictoria sunt falsa. Dicendum quod paenultima consequentia non valet. Et si regula 'Inconvenientem' allegatur, dicendum quod intelligitur de universalibus significantibus inhaerentiam extremorum pro omnibus suis suppositis singularibus copulative. Sed in proposito non est sic. Nam sic *A* significat sua significata copulative, scilicet: falsum dicitur a Sorte et *A* est verum, ita *B* significat sua significata disjunctive, scilicet: nullum falsum dicitur a Sorte vel *A* non est verum » [« Keeping the same situation, if *A* is false its opposite will be true, namely 'Nothing false is said by Socrates'. Let that be *B*. The consequent is false, because by the second assumption (*see n. 12 above - the reference seems to be incorrect*) the subject of *B* supposits for *A*. Therefore, *B* is a universal that has a false singular, namely, 'This false *A* is not said by Socrates'. Therefore, *B* is false. Therefore, contradictories are false. It must be said ‹in reply› that the penultimate consequence is not valid. (*I.e., despite appearances, B is not really universal*). And if the rule 'The inconsistent...' (*I do not know exactly what this rule is*) is appealed to, it is to be said that ‹that rule› is understood with respect to universal sentences signifyng the inherence of the extremes for all their singular supposita copulatively. But in the case at hand this is not so. For just as *A* signifies its significates copulatively, namely: a falsehood is said by Socrates and *A* is true, so *B* signifies its significates disjunctively, namely: nothing false is said by Socrates or *A* is not true »]. Recall that because an insoluble signifies at least two things, it also signifies the conjunction of those two. See n. 27 above.

49. See n. 24 above.

Bradwardine's motivation here is obvious. He wants to be sure that contradictories always have opposite truth values, even in the case of the paradoxes. Nevertheless this seems to be a hopelessly wrong approach. First of all, Bradwardine is implicitly committed to holding that all sentences, not just insolubles, signify conjunctively insofar as all sentences, in addition to whatever else they signify, also signify that they are true. Hence, every sentence will signify both conjunctively (since all sentences do that) and disjunctively (since every sentence is the contradictory of some other sentence that signifies conjunctively). There may be some way to work all this out, but Bradwardine certainly has not done it.

But further, Bradwardine's treatment of contradictories conflicts with the fact that he accepts the full Tarski biconditionals, including semantic ascent, when speaking in the «object-language» tone of voice. Where *k* = '*k* is not true', Bradwardine accepts '*k* is true if and only if *k* is not true' object-linguistically. He could not do that if one half of that biconditional were false because it is the insoluble, while the other half is true because it is the contradictory of the insoluble. That would falsify, not verify, the biconditional.

What Bradwardine ought to have done, and what some others – for instance, Buridan[50] – in the tradition stemming from Bradwardine did in fact do, is to say that the *syntactical* con-

50. See Johannes Buridanus, *Sophismata*, T.K. Scott, ed., Frommann-Holzboog, Stuttgart-Bad Cannstatt 1977, Ch. 8, sophisma 8, 140 (the situation is that Socrates says only 'Plato speaks falsely', and Plato says only 'Socrates speaks falsely', both of which Buridan regards as insoluble and false. Robert tries to contradict Socrates by saying only 'Plato does not speak falsely'. Of course Robert's sentence is the *syntactic* contradictory of Socrates' sentence - i.e., its negation. What Buridan wants to know is whether it is in addition the *semantic* contradictory of Socrates' sentence - i.e., of opposite truth-value): « Et consimili modo puto esse dicendum de quarta ratione. Nam propositio Sortis et propositio Roberti sunt ambae falsae et non contradicunt, quia possibile est esse reflectionem supra unam ex qua sequitur ipsam esse falsam, quod tamen non sit sic reflectio supra aliam, sicut est in casu posito. Et ideo ad contradicendum propositioni Sortis oportet contradicere copulativae ex ista et consequente in ipsa implicato, scilicet illa quae ponebatur illi aequipollere, ut quod Robertus dicat 'Plato non dicit falsum vel *a* non est verum'. Sic enim nullo modo poterant illae duae simul esse verae nec falsae » [« And I think the same thing has to be said for the fourth argument. For Socrates' sentence and Robert's sentence are both false and do not ‹semantically› contradict ‹one another›. For it is possible for there to be reflection (*i.e., self-reference*) on the one, from which it follows that it

tradictory – i.e., the denial or negation – of an insoluble sentence is just as false as the insoluble itself. In the above example, *k* is false not because on the face of it it signifies itself to be not true, since that is so, but because it also signifies itself to be indeed true, and that is not so. The syntactical contradictory of *k*, on the other hand, namely '*k* is true', is false as well because, whatever else it signifies, it signifies that *k* is true, and that is simply *not* so.

Hence the «correct» way to develop Bradwardine's view, it seems to me, is to say that in the case of insolubles, syntactically contradictory sentences are both false. I hasten to add that this odd result is in no way a violation of the Principle of Non-Contradiction, either in the syntactic form 'not both *p* and not-*p*' (indeed not both – not even one!), or in the semantic form, since no sentence is assigned both truth and falsehood.

This odd situation, which Bradwardine himself resists, is nevertheless the only reason Bradwardine would be able to accept the full Tarski biconditionals, including semantic ascent, object-linguistically. Where *k* is as above, both sides of the biconditional are false. And that is why the biconditional can be upheld as true object-linguistically.

Of course in classical or standard propositional logic, any sentence of the form '*p* if and only if not-*p*' deductively implies the straightforward contradiction '*p* and not-*p*'. How then do we prevent Bradwardine's view – in what I regard as the «corrected» and preferred form in which one finds it in Buridan and others – from yielding out and out contradiction? The answer is obvious. If the contradiction follows on standard or classical deductive theory, then a suitable Bradwardinian deductive theory is going to have to be non-standard or non-classical. In fact, as it turns out, *reductio* fails. For, once again, let *k* = '*k* is not true'. If we assume that *k* is true, then *k* must signify only as is the case. But we know that for Bradwardine *k* signifies in a con-

is false, and yet there is no such reflection on the other, as happens in the present case. And therefore, in order ‹semantically› to contradict Socrates' sentence, one has to contradict the copulative composed of it and the consequent implicit in it, namely what was claimed to be equipollent to it, so that Robert says 'Plato does not speak falsely or *a* is not true'. For these two could in no way be true or false together »].

tradictory way. Hence if *k* is true a contradiction is so. Now if *reductio* held, we could conclude categorically from this that *k* is *not* true. But of course we cannot validly conclude that, since that is just the insoluble sentence *k* itself and so is false. Unfortunately, we also cannot conclude that *k is* true, since that is false too. In the end, we cannot truly say anything about the truth value of *k* either way – at least not object-linguistically. But that is the price we pay.

Reductio therefore fails. On the other hand, all the other primitive rules of introduction and elimination in standard systems of natural deduction for a classical propositional logic appear to hold. In short, it seems to me that the propositional logic that underlies a correctly developed theory in the Bradwardine-tradition – i.e., a theory like Buridan's that knows how to handle the contradictories of insolubles[51] – is very much like the non-classical propositional logic developed by Frederick Fitch in his *Symbolic Logic: An Introduction*, which likewise suspends *reductio* but retains all the other usual primitive rules of introduction and elimination.[52] This suggestion is very tentative, of course, since it is hard to know finally what Bradwardine would say about certain introduction and elimination rules. But if it is true it is very interesting, since one of Fitch's explicit motivations for his non-standard logic was to find a way to handle the paradoxes.[53]

All of this of course is in the «object-linguistic» tone of voice. When speaking metalinguistically, the theory will not accept the full Tarski biconditionals; it will suspend semantic

51. In P.V. Spade, *John Buridan on the Liar: A study and Reconstruction*, « Notre Dame J. form. Log. », 19 (1978), 579-590, I give a reconstruction of Buridan's theory that differs in some respects from the way I am interpreting Buridan here. The difference centers on the rules of double negation, which are there suspended in the case of insolubles. The interpretation there may be brought into line with the present paper by adjusting the valuation rules for negation. Since both interpretations extrapolate to some extent (I think not irresponsibly) from Buridan's text, there is room for each of them.

52. F.B. Fitch, *Symbolic Logic: An Introduction*, The Ronald Press, New York 1952.

53. Fitch, *Symbolic Logic*, 8, §§ 2.12-2.14. Nevertheless, the formal semantics that have been developed for Fitch's logic do not capture this motivation in any very obvious way. See, e.g., R. Routley, *Semantical Analyses of Propositional Systems of Fitch and Nelson*, « Stud. log. », 33 (1974), 283-298.

ascent. But it will use *all* the classical propositional inferences, including *reductio.*

Even in its «developed» and «corrected» form, however, there is something not quite satisfactory about this theory. Metalinguistically, as we have seen, the theory suspends one half of the Tarski biconditionals. This means that, in the absence of any fuller explanation, we simply do not have any account of the necessary and sufficient condition for the truth of an insoluble sentence, but only of the necessary conditions. In short, it appears that this tradition has bought a «solution» to the paradoxes at the price of a full theory of their truth-conditions. It does not have a full theory of their truth-conditions; it has only half a theory.

But, it may be objected, that is so only metalinguistically. Object-linguistically, we have full Tarski biconditionals, and so truth-conditions that are both necessary and sufficient. That is so, but object-linguistically we also have situations, as we saw in the discussion of *reductio*, where we cannot truthfully say just what the truth-values of certain sentences are. Either way we pay a price.

Bradwardine's theory, therefore, even in its revised and «corrected» form, does not provide a completely satisfactory solution to the paradoxes. But then neither does any other theory. The paradoxes are here to stay.[54]

54. Earlier versions of this paper were read to the 1980 Summer Institute on Medieval Philosophy at Cornell University, and to the Society for Medieval and Renaissance Philosophy at the 1981 American Philosophical Association Western Division meetings in Milwaukee, Wisconsin. I am grateful to the participants for their helpful comments.

V

William Heytesbury's Position on "Insolubles": One Possible Source

I

In the first chapter of his *Regulae solvendi sophismata,*[1] William Heytesbury sets out his view on the so-called "insolubles"—paradoxes or antinomial sentences such as the famous Liar paradox.[2] Heytesbury's position was very influential in the subsequent *insolubilia*-literature.[3] In the Prologue to his *Regulae*, however, Heytesbury denies that the position he maintains in that first chapter is original with him; it was already known when he wrote the *Regulae* in 1335.[4]

> Primum igitur capitulum notam sed non novam de insolubilibus summam declarabit.[5]

This disclaimer presents a puzzle. For in fact there is no known treatment of the insolubles that both antedates Heytesbury's chapter, at least so far as we can tell, and also maintains, or even mentions,

[1] See William Heytesbury, *Tractatus gulielmi Hentisberi de sensu composito et diviso, Regulae eiusdem cum sophismatibus, Declaratio Gaetani supra easdem ...*, (Venice: Bonetus Locatellus for Octavianus Scotus, 1494 [Hain 8437]). Copy at University of Chicago Library. I am preparing a translation and study of the † first chapter of the *Regulae*.

[2] On the early history of the mediaeval discussions of these "insolubles", see my *The Origins of the Mediaeval* Insolubilia-*Literature*, in: Franciscan Studies 33 (1973), pp. 292-309. The mediaeval literature is surveyed and studied in my *The Mediaeval Liar: A Catalogue of the Insolubilia-Literature*, ("Subsidia Mediaevalia", vol. 5; Toronto: Pontifical Institute of Mediaeval Studies, 1975).

[3] In addition to several anonymous authors, the following logicians adopted or at least used Heytesbury's position in their own writings: Angelo of Fossambrone, Cajetan of Thiene, John of Constance, John Dumbleton, John of Holland, John Hunter, John of Wesel, John Wyclif, Paul of Pergula, Paul of Venice, Ralph Strode and Robert Fland. See the discussion in *The Mediaeval Liar, ad loc.*

[4] The date is given by James A. Weisheipl, *Ockham and Some Mertonians*, in: Mediaeval Studies 30 (1968), pp. 163-213 at p. 196, where Weisheipl quotes the colophon of one MS. of the *Regulae*: "Datus Oxonie a mag. Wilhelmo de Hyttisbyri a.D. M°CCC°XXXV°."

[5] *Regulae, ed. cit.*, f. 4va.

exactly the position he adopts there. There are several treatises that hold the same view, but none that can be dated with any confidence before Heytesbury's. Moreover, the later authors who explicitly attribute this view to someone by name always mention Heytesbury, or a subsequent writer influenced by Heytesbury (such as John of Holland [6]), and no one earlier.[7]

I believe that, as a result of a recent publication by L. M. de Rijk, we are now in a position to resolve this puzzle and to offer one possible source for Heytesbury's view. In order to understand what is going on, let us look first at Heytesbury's procedure in his first chapter. He begins by considering four attempts to "solve" the insolubles. The first such attempt is Roger Swyneshed's.[8] The second and third views are attributed to John Dumbleton and Richard Kilmington in Cajetan † of Thiene's commentary on this chapter, although these attributions appear to be spurious [9]:

> Prima harum positionum est Suisset. Secunda ponitur a Dulmentone. Tertia est Richardi Clientonis in *Sophismatibus* suis.[10]

The fourth view Heytesbury describes as follows [11]:

> Quarta opinio et ultima recitanda statuit sibi tamquam principium quod nullus est casus [12] possibilis qui aliquid simpliciter insolubile qualitercumque includat. Unde non est iste casus possibilis, scilicet, quod haec propositio 'Falsum est' vel aliqua talis sit omnis propositio [13] et quod illa praecise significet quod falsum est, quia ex hoc sequitur falsum esse verum et ambo contradictoria simul esse falsa. Sequuntur etiam multa talia inconvenientia quae pro nunc non expedit recitare. Et ideo sufficiunt haec pro nunc.

This fourth view, Heytesbury says, will be his own. He raises objections to each of the four opinions in turn, and observes that the

[6] See *The Mediaeval Liar*, item XXXVIII.

[7] See *The Mediaeval Liar*, *passim*.

[8] See my *Roger Swyneshed's* Insolubilia: *Edition and Comments*, forthcoming. †

[9] See *The Mediaeval Liar*, items XXXVI and LV.

[10] Cajetan of Thiene, *In Regulas Gulielmi Hentisberi recollectae*, published with the edition of the *Regulae* cited above, f. 7va.

[11] *Ed. cit.*, f. 4vb.

[12] A "casus" is a hypothetical situation, the "case" The term is also used for a set of sentences describing a hypothetical situation or "case".

[13] For mediaeval nominalists such as Heytesbury, a sentence is a particular utterance or inscription (a sentence-token, not the type). Since utterances fade away and inscriptions can be erased, the existence of sentences is for Heytesbury a contingent affair. Hence it is perfectly possible that the single sentence (utterance or inscription) 'A falsehood exists' should have been the only sentence.

objections to the fourth view are difficult if not impossible to answer with complete satisfaction [14]:

> Multae possent fieri hujusmodi objectiones contra istam responsionem quibus esset difficile vel impossibile in toto satisfacere.

Heytesbury claims indeed that this is so for any attempt to solve the paradoxes; he recognizes that "something has to give somewhere".[15] Nevertheless, he thinks that the fourth view is the best of the lot, and ought, despite the objections, to be upheld [16]:

> Contra tres primas opiniones arguitur primo conjunctim per unum medium, deinde contra singulas singulatim. Postea contra quartam quam inter alias reputo sustinendam. Eam vero non in totum satisfacere assero sicut nec aliquam quia hoc non video esse possibile. Aestimo tamen ipsam inter omnes magis esse propinquam veritati.

After considering the objections against the first four opinions, Heytesbury sets out his definitions of an insoluble casus and of an insoluble sentence, and gives his five famous rules for responding to insolubles in disputation.[17] The details of these definitions and rules need not detain us now.[18] Suffice it here to say (a) that they do not appear in any earlier writer, to the best of my knowledge, and (b) that in view of Heytesbury's statement that the fourth opinion is the one that ought to be maintained, it would seem to follow that the definitions and rules later in the chapter give simply a more detailed account

[14] *Ed. cit.*, f. 6rb.

[15] This is a significant admission. Most mediaeval authors, like the early writers in the modern history of the paradoxes, thought the insolubles rested on a simple, although perhaps subtle, "mistake". Once the mistake was found and corrected, that would be all there was to it. In the passage quoted at n. 16, however, Heytesbury at least implicitly recognizes that the lesson of the paradoxes goes deeper than that, that no solution can be had without sacrificing part of our tried and trusted convictions about truth and logic. To the best of my knowledge, Heytesbury is the first mediaeval writer to have reached this realization—if not the only one. Nevertheless, Heytesbury himself is not altogether consistent in this point of view. For at the very beginning of the first chapter, immediately after the general prologue to the *Regulae*, Heytesbury expresses the earlier, more confident view: there is a "correct" solution to the paradoxes, but we simply have not found it yet: "Ad propositum igitur rediens de insolubilibus dicam quid aestimo affirmandum. Dicit Philosophus in *Praedicamentis* quarto capitulo [*Categories* 7, 7b 31-33], 'Quadratura circuli etsi sit scibilis, nondum tamen scita est'. Cum quo consimiliter dicendum esse sentio quod licet insolubilia solvi possunt nondum tamen soluta sunt." (*Ed. cit.*, f. 4va.)

[16] *Ed. cit.*, f. 5ra.

[17] *Ed. cit.*, ff. 6rb-7ra.

[18] See *The Mediaeval Liar*, item LXIX, and my forthcoming translation and study of the text.

of the fourth opinion described more briefly earlier in the chapter, in the passage quoted above. The conjunction of (a) and (b) makes Heytesbury's disclaimer of originality, in his Prologue, puzzling.[19] My proposed resolution focusses on (b).

II

In a recent study of the early mediaeval *obligationes*-literature, published in this journal, L. M. De Rijk has presented a text that might just possibly be Heytesbury's source.[20] This text De Rijk calls *Obligationes Parisienses*. It is not about insolubles at all, at least not directly; instead it concerns that still little-known type of disputation called "obligatio". Nevertheless, the anonymous author of this text, writing at the beginning of the thirteenth century,[21] says some things in passing that bear on our question. Consider, for example, the following passages.

> Si vero non fiat convertibile cum '*falsum poni*' in tempore positionis, considerandum est an ex ea fit insolubile et si sic, casus tibi terminatur. Solet tamen nullum tale a quibusdam in positione recipi quod non potest cadere, quia fit insolubile ex casu.[22]

> Ad aliud dicendum quod bene sequitur: '*tu concedis falsum*', non tamen concedenda est conclusio—ea enim concessa fit insolubile—nec est exigenda eius probatio nec est neganda.[23]

> Que autem habent unum contradictorie oppositorum necessarium, alterum impossibile, pro impossibili tantum recipiatur in depositione, nisi impediat insolubile. Et propter hoc hec disiuncta: '*falsum deponi vel non deponi*', non est deponibilis, nec pro toto nec pro partibus, quia hec per se est necessaria: *falsum non deponi*, hec autem est impossibilis: *falsum deponi*; et cum hoc est insolubile si deponatur.[24]

> Alie circumstantie que causant insolubile in falsa positione, cassande sunt etiam in depositione.[25]

The exact force of these passages can, of course, only be seen in context. Nevertheless, it is clear from the passages that the anonymous

[19] Note that Cajetan of Thiene, in his commentary on this chapter, attributes the first three opinions by name, but is strangely silent about the prior authorship of the fourth, despite Heytesbury's explicit denial of originality. See the text quoted above at n. 10.

[20] L. M. de Rijk, *Some Thirteenth Century Tracts on the Game of Obligation, II*, in: Vivarium 13 (1975), pp. 22-54.

[21] On the date, see *ibid.*, p. 26.

[22] *Ibid.*, p. 36 lines 29-32.

[23] *Ibid.*, p. 38 lines 24-26.

[24] *Ibid.*, p. 48 lines 26-32.

[25] *Ibid.*, p. 49 lines 11-12.

author will not allow the respondent in a "disputatio de obligationibus" to admit any casus, or to concede any proposed sentence, that leads to what he calls an "insoluble". This is just the way Heytesbury described the fourth previous opinion when he first introduced it early in his chapter: "no casus is possible which in any way includes anything that is simply insoluble." [26]

Moreover, there is additional reason to think that perhaps this text, or one in the same tradition, lies behind Heytesbury's position on insolubles. Heytesbury's view has it that no insoluble sentence, in the circumstances that make it paradoxical, signifies exactly as it seems to. For instance, suppose that Socrates utters only the sentence 'Socrates is speaking falsely'. Heytesbury holds that if that sentence signifies exactly as it seems to, that is, if it is taken at face value, a contradiction results: the sentence is true if and only if what Socrates is saying, namely, that very same sentence, is false. Hence the sentence in those circumstances does not signify exactly as it seems to; it is not to be taken at face value. How then is it to be taken? Heytesbury's answer is that, if it is not stipulated by the opponent when he sets up the hypothetical case, the respondent is under no duty to say exactly how the sentence signifies. He should simply decline to answer that question.

This is the import of Heytesbury's famous third rule,[27] and was taken by later authors to be one of the most characteristic aspects of Heytesbury's position. Some later authors objected to this feature, thinking it was nothing more than an evasion of the most important issue. A respondent in disputation might well avoid an embarrassing contradiction by adopting Heytesbury's position, but he has hardly advanced our understanding of insolubles very much. In short, the objection goes, Heytesbury's position is "sophistry" in the worst sense.[28]

Compare this characteristic feature of Heytesbury's view with the following passage from the *Obligationes Parisienses*:[29]

> Solutio. Positio est recipienda. Et negato Sortem esse asinum concedenda est hec; *'tu respondes: falsum'*. Et non sequitur: *'ergo tu negas, Sortem esse asinum'*. Possum enim respondere *'falsum est'*, non negando Sortem esse asinum. Hec autem neganda *'tu respondes: falsum est aliud falsum* <*a*>

[26] See the text above, at n. 11.
[27] *Ed. cit.*, f. 6va.
[28] See, for example, the anonymous *Commentarium in insolubilia Hollandrini* in *The Mediaeval Liar*, item V, at pp. 24-25.
[29] De Rijk, *op. cit.*, p. 38 lines 3-11.

> *Sortem esse asinum'* Ex cuius opposito et hac: *'tu respondes: falsum'* sequitur te negare <aliud> a *Sortem esse asinum*. Quo concesso si queratur quid aliud, huic questioni non debet satisfieri in falsa positione, quia quidquid redderetur, hoc esset falsum non sequens.

The exact logic of this passage is obscure, even in context. The situation is this. The opponent in the disputation observes that it is possible for you (the respondent) to concede that Socrates is an ass. Whether such a concession is right or wrong, it is still possible. And since it is possible, the opponent assumes that it is the case. (This is the "positing" of a hypothetical "casus".) Then he proposes to you the sentence 'Socrates is an ass'. If you concede it, then you have conceded something impossible on the basis of a hypothetical casus that is quite possible. Such a response on your part would be incorrect. On the other hand, if you deny 'Socrates is an ass', then the opponent proposes to you the sentence 'You reply "It is false" '. That is true in fact, since that is what you replied, and it is moreover consistent with the hypothetical casus. Therefore, you should concede it. If you do, however, then it seems to follow from what you have conceded that you have denied that Socrates is an ass. But this is inconsistent with the hypothetical casus, which was that you concede that Socrates is an ass. Hence there is a dilemma which the anonymous author tries to resolve in the passage just quoted.

The author's solution consists in observing that from the sentence 'You reply "It is false" ', which you have conceded, it does not follow that you have denied that Socrates is an ass. On the contrary, you denied something other than that Socrates is an ass. (It is here that the logic of the passage is obscure.) But if you are asked just what else it is that you have denied, you do not have to answer that question.

The parallel between this and the characteristic feature of Heytesbury's third rule should be obvious. This supports the hypothesis that it was this text, or another one in the same tradition, that stood behind Heytesbury's chapter on insolubles. But whether this hypothesis is true or not, whether there is any real influence on Heytesbury by this text, or by another one in the same tradition, it certainly is true that Heytesbury's position was already, in certain essential respects, a "known but not a new" position, as he puts it, at the time he wrote the first chapter of his *Regulae*.

The exact sense in which this is so must, however, be carefully delineated. It remains true that no known author prior to Heytesbury maintained the definitions and rules in the later parts of his chapter.

Nevertheless, it is also true that the anonymous author of the *Obligationes Parisienses* already maintained the kernel of Heytesbury's view: that no casus is to be admitted as possible if it in any way "includes" anything that is "simply insoluble". The anonymous author does not tell us what he means by an "insoluble". Heytesbury's definition, it seems, is his own original contribution.[30] Again, it is true that the anonymous author of the *Obligationes Parisienses* already maintained something remarkably like the characteristic feature of Heytesbury's third rule. It was left to Heytesbury, however, to generalize and formulate this rule precisely, and to apply it to insolubles.

Thus it appears that point (b) at the end of section I, above, must be properly understood. Heytesbury does think that his definitions and rules are part of the fourth opinion he had earlier described. But they are part of that opinion not, at least so far as we know, in the sense that anyone before Heytesbury had actually formulated those definitions and rules as carefully and systematically as Heytesbury did. Rather they are part of that opinion only in the sense that they conform to it and are suggested by it. Heytesbury's apparent originality in his definitions and rules may therefore be reconciled with the explicit disclaimer in his Prologue.

Bloomington, Indiana
Indiana University

[30] Note that, for Heytesbury, to say that a casus is a "casus of an insoluble" is not to say that it "includes something simply insoluble" in the sense in which that is ruled out by the fourth opinion. In effect, a casus "includes something simply insoluble" if and only if it is a "casus of an insoluble" in the sense specified by Heytesbury's definition, and also provided that the insoluble sentence in that casus signifies exactly as it appears to—that is, that it is to be taken at face value. See Heytesbury's two definitions and the second of his five rules, *ed. cit.*, f. 6rb-6va.

VI

JOHN BURIDAN ON THE LIAR: A STUDY AND RECONSTRUCTION

This paper is a partial study of the position taken by the 14th century † logician and philosopher John Buridan (see [4]) on the Liar and related paradoxes—the "insolubles" (*insolubilia*) as they were called then. Buridan's position is most extensively set out in the eighth chapter of his Sophismata ([2], translated in [3]. There is also a discussion in [1].). Although at least three brief treatments have appeared in English ([3], introduction; [7], [9]), and although the *Sophismata* has recently been translated into English (in [3]), no study has yet examined Buridan's view in depth. This paper attempts a partial rectification of that situation.

We shall begin by setting out some preliminary notions and notation. Then we shall cite some passages from Buridan that set out his position. On the basis of these passages, we shall extract several theses which may be regarded as "principles" of his approach. Our reconstruction of Buridan's position will have to conform as much as possible to these theses. I said that this paper is a "partial" study of Buridan's position. Our overall policy will be to reconstruct that position within a very simple framework, allowing only the most straightforward kinds of paradox. Accordingly, we shall set out a very limited syntax **SYN**—containing only singular terms, two predicates, and a negation operator—and a very restricted set of models, which allow only the simplest and most direct kind of vicious self-reference. Insolubility will then be defined for this context. Such a narrow approach permits us to abstract from certain kinds of cases that Buridan simply does not discuss, and to put off to another occasion a treatment of some of the more complicated cases he does discuss. An initial obstacle is the fact that the Buridanian theses to be extracted from his text will turn out to be inconsistent even within this simple framework. Some compromise must be made if our study is to get off the ground. We shall discuss some possible ways of making this compromise, and choose from among them. Our choice will involve giving up the rules of double negation in certain cases. It will also involve adopting the principle that the correspondence theory of truth fails exactly in the cases of the insolubles. Once all this has been done, we shall set up a language $\mathcal{L}_1$ within the simple context provided by **SYN** and $\mathcal{L}_1$-models. $\mathcal{L}_1$ will satisfy all the Buridanian theses extracted from his text, except for the rules of double negation, which we resolved to sacrifice. We shall look at $\mathcal{L}_1$ in some detail.

1 For simplicity, we shall not consider languages with polyadic predicates. If ϕ is a primitive monadic predicate of some language $\mathcal{L}$, and if $V_{\mathfrak{M}}$ is a valuation function assigning a truth value 0, . . ., 1 to the sentences of $\mathcal{L}$ with respect to a model $\mathfrak{M}$, and if $f_{\mathfrak{M}}$ is the denotation function for $\mathfrak{M}$, assigning denotations to the singular terms x of $\mathcal{L}$, then we shall say by definition that $\mathrm{EXT}_{\mathfrak{M}}(\phi) = \{f_{\mathfrak{M}}(x): V_{\mathfrak{M}}(\phi x) = 1\}$, and we shall call $\mathrm{EXT}_{\mathfrak{M}}(\phi)$ the "extension of ϕ with respect to $\mathfrak{M}$". This definition will be extended later to cover predicates formed by prefixing a string of negations to a primitive predicate ϕ. The definition demands that everything contained in the extension of any predicate of $\mathcal{L}$ have a name. We accept this condition for the purposes of our discussion. (A further consequence of the definition is that, where T is a truth-predicate, $\mathrm{EXT}_{\mathfrak{M}}(T)$ is defined *not* as the class of true sentences, but rather as the class of sentences with true truth-sentences. In virtue of Theorem 3 below, however, these two classes are identical.)

2 Buridan's suppositional truth-rules ([3], pp. 90-93), with which the reader is assumed to be familiar, provide a reasonably good account of the correspondence theory of truth according to which a sentence is true iff it corresponds to reality, to the facts (see [13], §3). We shall say that a sentence *corresponds* (to reality, to the facts) iff the world is as the sentence "signifies according to formal significations" ([3], p. 195). That is, a sentence corresponds iff the *normal* suppositional truth-conditions for such a sentence are met ([3], pp. 90-93). If the sentence is an insoluble one, then that condition is not in fact its actual truth-condition, as we shall see. But that is of no account here.

We shall be discussing only atomic sentences and sentences formed from atomic sentences by negation. Within this context we can say that an atomic sentence corresponds in a model $\mathfrak{M}$ iff its subject and predicate "stand for the same" ([3], pp. 90-93, conclusions 9 and 10)—that is, iff the denotation of its subject term is contained in the extension of its predicate term in $\mathfrak{M}$. The negation $n(s)$ of a sentence s corresponds in $\mathfrak{M}$ iff s itself does not correspond in $\mathfrak{M}$. Thus, if ϕ is a primitive predicate, then by definition $\phi_x \in \mathrm{CORR}_{\mathfrak{M}}$ iff $f_{\mathfrak{M}}(x) \in \mathrm{EXT}_{\mathfrak{M}}(\phi)$, and $n(s) \in \mathrm{CORR}_{\mathfrak{M}}$ iff $s \notin \mathrm{CORR}_{\mathfrak{M}}$. The correspondence theory of truth may now be expressed as follows: A sentence is true in $\mathfrak{M}$ iff it corresponds in $\mathfrak{M}$: $V_{\mathfrak{M}}(s) = 1$ iff $s \in \mathrm{CORR}_{\mathfrak{M}}$.

3 In order to provide a framework for the discussion to follow, I want here to set out eight "theses", which, I shall argue, are in one way or another theses of Buridan's position. I say "in one way or another", because they do not all have the same status. Some of them Buridan explicitly holds; some can be inferred from things he explicitly holds. Some, finally, seem to be only tacitly accepted. The status of each will be discussed briefly in turn. For a fuller discussion, see [11]. The eight are these:

(1) *"From every proposition, together with the condition that it exists, there follows the conclusion that it is true."* ([3], p. 196). This is explicitly held by Buridan. The context is this ([3], pp. 195f.):

> Thus, it is otherwise said, nearer the truth, that every proposition virtually implies another proposition, so that of the subject standing for it, there is affirmed this predicate "true" I say it implies virtually just as an antecedent implies that which follows from it. Thus, any proposition is not true, if in this consequent affirmation, the subject and predicate do not stand for the same.

Buridan agrees with this view, but adds the proviso that the "proposition" must exist. For him, a sentence (what he calls a "propositio") is a sentence-*token*, an individual utterance or inscription. As such, its existence is a contingent affair. Utterances die away, and inscriptions can be erased. For Buridan, it is only *existing* sentences (tokens) that can be said to have a truth-value. (See [3], p. 17.) For simplicity, we shall confine ourselves in this paper by *fiat* to contexts in which the existential condition is satisfied for all sentences. (Compare [3], p. 57.)

Let us call (1) the "virtual implication principle" (VIP). It, or a version of it, was a characteristic of a long line of mediaeval views on the paradoxes. (See [10], items [IV], [VIII], [XII], [XXIV], [XXVII], [XXXI], [XXXVIII], [XXXIX], [XLIX], [LIII], [LVI], [LVIII], [LXIV].) In the form above, the principle says in effect that if $f_{\mathfrak{M}}(x) = s$, then if s has in $\mathfrak{M}$ whatever properties are preserved under the consequence relation, so too does Tx. (See thesis (7) for one choice of such a property.)

(2) *Insolubles are false.* This too is explicitly held by Buridan, in his explanation of the suppositional rules of truth ([3], p. 92). We call this thesis (IF).

(3) *The normal suppositional rules of truth fail exactly in the cases of the insolubles.* This too is more or less explicitly held by Buridan. He does explicitly say that the usual rules hold for all non-insoluble cases ([3], p. 93). He also says that the rules fail in the case of affirmative insolubles ([3], p. 198; compare [3], pp. 90-93). It does not seem illegitimate to add to this that they also fail for insoluble negatives, although Buridan does not stipulate this explicitly. Since the normal suppositional rules give us an account of correspondence, as observed above, thesis (3) amounts to saying that *the correspondence theory of truth fails exactly in the cases of the insolubles:* $s \in \text{INS}_{\mathfrak{M}}$ *iff it is not the case, that* $s \in \text{CORR}_{\mathfrak{M}}$ *iff* $V_{\mathfrak{M}}(s) = 1$. Hence we call it (CT-INS).

(4) *Bivalence: Every (existing) sentence is either true or false.* Buridan does not explicitly hold this. Nevertheless, he mentions only two values, and we ought to follow him as closely as possible. I know of only two mediaeval authors ([10], items [LXIII] and [X], 4th previous opinion) who allowed for failure of bivalence in the case of insolubles. We call this thesis (BIV).

(5) *If it is true that a sentence s is true, then s is true.* Buridan does not explicitly hold this either. But he says nothing that indicates that he would

reject it, and indeed maintains some things that lead directly up to it. (See [11], pp. 41-42.) I know of no mediaeval who questioned it. Call this thesis (TT).

(6) *If x does not stand for a sentence, then* ⌜*x is true*⌝ *is false*. This principle is the basis for Buridan's solution of a sophism in [3], p. 189f. Call this thesis (NS).

(7) *Between sentences that exist, the valid consequences are just the truth-preserving transformations*. Buridan explicitly holds one half of this: "It is true that of every valid consequence, it is impossible for the antecedent to be true without the truth of the consequent formed at the same time as it." ([3], p. 183) On the other hand, in the same place he holds that

> it is not sufficient for a consequence to be valid that it is impossible for the antecedent to be true without the consequent formed at the same time as it. . . So more is required, namely, that it could not be as the antecedent signifies unless it were as is signified by the consequent.

The point of this revision is to accomodate certain problems raised by his view that only existing sentence-tokens have truth-values. If valid consequences were just the truth-preserving transformations, then consequences such as 'Every proposition is affirmative, so none is negative' ([3], p. 183) would not be valid. Whenever the antecedent is true, the consequent cannot exist, and so cannot be true.

Buridan resolves this problem by observing that the world may be as a certain sentence-token would signify it to be, even though that sentence-token might not in fact exist. Thus, if Socrates is running, then the world is as would be signified by a sentence-token of the type 'Socrates is running', even if that sentence-token did not in fact exist. We shall say that the sentence-token is "secure" in this case. If in addition, the sentence-token happens to exist, then it is true. A sentence-token is true iff it is secure and exists (see [6] and [9]. The term 'secure' is taken from [6]). Buridan's revised notion of consequence, then, amounts to saying that the valid consequences are just the transformations that always preserve security. As long as we confine ourselves to contexts in which all sentence-tokens exist, truth and security collapse, and principle (7) holds. We call the principle (TC).

(8) *The valid consequences are just the traditional ones*. Buridan nowhere explicitly say this. But if we look closely at his text ([3], pp. 180-185), it appears that the problem which led him to base consequence on security rather than on truth was just that certain traditionally valid argument-forms would have to be given up, and certain traditionally invalid forms would have to be admitted—once the bearer of a truth-value was made the existing sentence-token—if the usual notion of consequence as truth-preserving were retained. Thus, Buridan's goal seems to have been to revise the notion of consequence in such a way that just the traditionally valid argument-forms could be retained. Since the traditional consequences which will concern us will be the double-negation rules, we call this thesis (DN).

4 The eight theses above must be kept in mind as we attempt to reconstruct Buridan's position. As we shall see, they are mutually incompatible. Let us begin with the simple syntax **SYN** of [12], with a primitive vocabulary consisting of denumerable singular terms, two primitive predicates P and T, and a negation operator. If a sentence s has an atomic constituent of the form Tx, then we shall call s a *semantic sentence*. Let $n(s)$ be the negation of s. This allows us to write '$n^i(s)$' for the i-fold negation of s. If i is odd and s is of the form Tx, we call $n^i(s)$ an *odd semantic sentence*. A *model* for **SYN** will be a triple $\mathfrak{M} = \langle X_{\mathfrak{M}}, f_{\mathfrak{M}}, g_{\mathfrak{M}} \rangle$, where $X_{\mathfrak{M}}$ includes the set of all sentences of **SYN**, $f_{\mathfrak{M}}$ is a one-one function whose domain is the set of singular terms of **SYN** and whose range is $X_{\mathfrak{M}}$, and $g_{\mathfrak{M}}$ assigns a subset of $X_{\mathfrak{M}}$ to P. These restrictions allow us to define for each model $\mathfrak{M}$ a function $t_{\mathfrak{M}}$ assigning to each sentence s its unique *truth sentence*, the sentence Tx such that $f_{\mathfrak{M}}(x) = s$. (Compare [12].) Finally, for any set Y of sentences of **SYN**, form the smallest set Y^* including Y and such that if $n(s)$ is in Y^*, so is s. (Y^* is thus the smallest set containing every constituent sentence of every member of Y.) Then a *naive valuation* over a set Y of sentences with respect to a model $\mathfrak{M}$ for **SYN** is a function $V_{\mathfrak{M}}$ with domain Y^* and range $\{0, 1\}$, such that: (a) $V_{\mathfrak{M}}(Px) = 1$ iff $f_{\mathfrak{M}}(x) \in g_{\mathfrak{M}}(P)$; (b) $V_{\mathfrak{M}}(n(s)) = 1 \quad V_{\mathfrak{M}}(s)$; (c) $V_{\mathfrak{M}}(t_{\mathfrak{M}}(s)) = V_{\mathfrak{M}}(s)$. Observe that (a) and (b) follow from the Buridanian thesis of bivalence (BIV) and the correspondence theory of truth. On the other hand, (c) follows from the theses (VIP), (BIV), (TT), and (TC).

5 We introduce the auxiliary notion of the syntactic relation G which a semantic sentence bears to its grammatical subject. Then, with respect to a model $\mathfrak{M}$, we define the relation $R_{\mathfrak{M}}$ of "semantic descent" to be the proper ancestral of the relative product of G into $f_{\mathfrak{M}}$. Now an $\mathcal{L}_1$*-model* will be a model $\mathfrak{M}$ for **SYN** such that: (1) if s is $R_{\mathfrak{M}}$-ungrounded (see [5]), then for some s' (possibly $s = s'$), $R_{\mathfrak{M}}(s, s')$ and $R_{\mathfrak{M}}(s', s')$. That is, there are no non-cyclic infinite chains of semantic descent in $\mathfrak{M}$. (2) $R_{\mathfrak{M}}$ is antisymmetric. There are no $R_{\mathfrak{M}}$-cycles of length greater than one. If a sentence is a semantic descendant of itself, it is an *immediate* semantic descendant of itself. (3) Only odd semantic sentences are semantic descendants of themselves. Cases such as $s = t_{\mathfrak{M}}(s)$ are ruled out. Thus in $\mathcal{L}_1$-models a sentence is $R_{\mathfrak{M}}$-ungrounded iff it either is or leads by an $R_{\mathfrak{M}}$-path to a directly self-referential odd semantic sentence. Self-reference of this kind is paradoxical. The paradigm is: $s = n(t_{\mathfrak{M}}(s))$, but we also have in general $s = n^i(t_{\mathfrak{M}}(s))$ for odd i. Condition (2) above is imposed in order to allow us to study this simple kind of paradox in isolation, without worrying about more complicated cases in which reference is passed from hand to hand, as it were, around a cycle with several members. They are a topic for another paper. Conditions (1) and (3), on the other hand, are imposed in order to rule out cases that Buridan simply does not treat.

6 For a language whose syntax is **SYN** and whose admissible models are $\mathcal{L}_1$-models, we define: *A sentence* s *is an insoluble in an admissible model* $\mathfrak{M}$ (*i.e.*, $s \in \mathsf{INS}_{\mathfrak{M}}$) iff $R_{\mathfrak{M}}(s, s)$. This definition appears to capture just the sentences that Buridan would want to call insoluble within our restricted framework. He several times mentions an insoluble's "reflection on itself'' ([3], p. 180 and *passim*). Yet, he makes it clear that not all such ''reflection'' or self-reference generates paradox ([3], pp. 192f.). The ''reflection'' in question appears to be the kind in which a sentence is its own semantic descendant. That Buridan would want to call *all* such cases within our context insoluble follows from Lemma 2, below. Where $R_{\mathfrak{M}}(s, s)$, there is no naive valuation over $\{s\}$. Hence s requires an exception to (VIP), (BIV), (TT), (TC) or the correspondence theory of truth. But since Buridan holds the first four theses, it is the correspondence theory that is violated. Hence, by (CT-INS), s is insoluble. Within the context provided by **SYN** and $\mathcal{L}_1$-models, we can prove the following preliminary results.

Lemma 1 *The insolubles are just the odd semantic sentences that refer directly to themselves*: $s \in \mathrm{INS}_{\mathfrak{M}}$ *iff for some odd* i, $s = n^i(t_{\mathfrak{M}}(s))$.

The proof follows by the definition of $\mathrm{INS}_{\mathfrak{M}}$ and conditions (2) and (3) on $\mathcal{L}_1$-models.

Lemma 2 *Is* s *is insoluble in a model* $\mathfrak{M}$, *then there is no naive valuation* $V_{\mathfrak{M}}$ *over* $\{s\}$.

For suppose $s \in \mathrm{INS}_{\mathfrak{M}}$. Then for some odd i, $s = n^i(t_{\mathfrak{M}}(s))$, by Lemma 1. Suppose further that there is a naive valuation $V_{\mathfrak{M}}$ over $\{s\}$. Then $V_{\mathfrak{M}}(s) = V_{\mathfrak{M}}(n^i(t_{\mathfrak{M}}(s)))$. Hence, by condition (b) on naive valuations, $V_{\mathfrak{M}}(s) \neq V_{\mathfrak{M}}(t_{\mathfrak{M}}(s))$, since i is odd by hypothesis. Thus by condition (c) on naive valuations, $V_{\mathfrak{M}}(s) \neq V_{\mathfrak{M}}(s)$. The Lemma follows by *reductio*.

Notice that for models (not $\mathcal{L}_1$-models) in which $s = n^i(t_{\mathfrak{M}}(s))$ for i *not* odd, there are naive valuations over $\{s\}$. $\mathcal{L}_1$-models thus rule out all but ''vicious'' kinds of direct self-reference, in which cases the naive rules of valuation break down.

Where s is atomic, let us call the sequence: $\langle s, n(s), n^2(s), n^3(s), \ldots \rangle$ a *negation sequence*. Then:

Lemma 3 *A negation sequence contains at most one insoluble in a given model: if* $n^i(s)$ *and* $n^j(s)$ *are both insoluble in* $\mathfrak{M}$, *then* $i = j$.

The proof is straightforward, from Lemma 1.

7 It turns out that even within the simple context of **SYN** and $\mathcal{L}_1$-models, the Buridanian theses extracted above are mutually inconsistent. In fact, we need only three of the theses to derive a contradiction:

Theorem 1 *The theses* (CT-INS), (TC), *and* (DN) *are mutually inconsistent*.

For (1), suppose that $s \in \mathrm{INS}_{\mathfrak{M}}$. Then (2), $n^2(s) \notin \mathrm{INS}_{\mathfrak{M}}$ by Lemma 3. Now (3), suppose further that $s \in \mathrm{CORR}_{\mathfrak{M}}$. Then (4), $n^2(s) \in \mathrm{CORR}_{\mathfrak{M}}$. Moreover (5), $V_{\mathfrak{M}}(s) \neq 1$, by (1), (3) and (CT-INS). Thus (6), $V_{\mathfrak{M}}(n^2(s)) \neq 1$, by (5), (TC) and (DN). But nevertheless (7), $V_{\mathfrak{M}}(n^2(s)) = 1$, by (2), (4) and (CT-INS). Hence (8), $s \notin \mathrm{CORR}_{\mathfrak{M}}$, from (3)-(7) by *reductio*. Therefore (9), $n^2(s) \notin \mathrm{CORR}_{\mathfrak{M}}$. Now (10), $V_{\mathfrak{M}}(s) = 1$, by (1), (8) and (CT-INS). And so (11), $V_{\mathfrak{M}}(n^2(s)) = 1$, from (10), (TC) and (DN). But (12), $V_{\mathfrak{M}}(n^2(s)) \neq 1$, by (2), (9) and (CT-INS). Steps (11) and (12) are of course contradictory.

What Theorem 1 shows is that Buridan's position is incoherent. The tension can be resolved only by departing from one or more of the three theses involved in Theorem 1. Several modern approaches make the compromise at (CT-INS). For instance, any solution in which the Liar sentence fails of bivalence and in which negation is choice-negation (see [6], p. 27) is of this kind. Such an approach departs from the correspondence theory not only in the case of insolubles, but also in the case of their double negations, which are *not* insoluble, by Lemma 3. However much such approaches have to offer, we shall not follow them in sacrificing (CT-INS). For it seems that Buridan himself would have chosen to make the compromise elsewhere, as I shall argue presently. Accordingly, we can give up either (TC) or (DN). If we give up (TC), we must ask whether any interesting property will replace truth as being preserved under valid consequence. The most plausible candidate is perhaps correspondence. Thesis (TC) would then be replaced by (CC): *Between sentences that exist, the valid consequences are just the correspondence-preserving transformations*. But it is easy to show that this maneuver forces us to give up at least one more of our Buridanian theses. For suppose that $s \in \mathsf{INS}_{\mathfrak{M}}$. Then $V_{\mathfrak{M}}(s) = 0$ by (IF). Hence $s \in \mathsf{CORR}_{\mathfrak{M}}$ by (CT-INS). From this two things follow. First, $t_{\mathfrak{M}}(s) \in \mathsf{CORR}_{\mathfrak{M}}$, using (VIP) and (CC). But also $t_{\mathfrak{M}}(s) \notin \mathsf{CORR}_{\mathfrak{M}}$, using Lemma 1 and the fact that $s \in \mathsf{INS}_{\mathfrak{M}}$, together with the definition of $\mathsf{CORR}_{\mathfrak{M}}$. Hence we would have to give up either (IF) or (VIP). For the sake of keeping as close as possible to Buridan, we shall not adopt this policy. Instead, we shall make our compromise at (DN)—negation is going to behave in a peculiar way.

There is some indication that Buridan himself would make the compromise here. For despite his wanting to retain the traditionally valid argument-forms, he appears also to have recognized that his negation did peculiar things. In [3], ch. 8, sophism 8, Buridan has Socrates say only 'Plato speaks falsely' and Plato say only 'Socrates speaks falsely'. This is not a situation that can be represented in the limited context of **SYN** and $\mathcal{L}_1$-models, and indeed we should not normally think of the case as generating a paradox. But Buridan does; he holds that both Socrates and Plato utter insolubles. For our purposes, the interesting point in this discussion is that Buridan allows that an insoluble and its negation are both false ([3], p. 199).

8 In the remaining sections of this paper, we shall study the language $\mathcal{L}_1$ whose syntax is **SYN** and whose admissible models are just the $\mathcal{L}_1$-models. The rules of valuation for $\mathcal{L}_1$ are these: (A) $V_{\mathfrak{M}}(Px) = 1$ iff $f_{\mathfrak{M}}(x) \in g_{\mathfrak{M}}(P)$, and $V_{\mathfrak{M}}(Px) = 0$ otherwise. (B) $V_{\mathfrak{M}}(t_{\mathfrak{M}}(s)) = V_{\mathfrak{M}}(s)$. (C) If $f_{\mathfrak{M}}(x)$ is not a sentence of **SYN**, then $V_{\mathfrak{M}}(Tx) = 0$. (D) If $s \in \mathsf{INS}_{\mathfrak{M}}$ or $n(s) \in \mathsf{INS}_{\mathfrak{M}}$, then $V_{\mathfrak{M}}(n(s)) = 0$. (E) If $s \notin \mathsf{INS}_{\mathfrak{M}}$ and $n(s) \notin \mathsf{INS}_{\mathfrak{M}}$, then $V_{\mathfrak{M}}(n(s)) = 1 - V_{\mathfrak{M}}(s)$. It can be shown that for each admissible model $\mathfrak{M}$ for $\mathcal{L}_1$, these rules assign exactly one of 0, 1 to each sentence of **SYN**. For the proof, which is straightforward but rather lengthy, see [11]. (The definition of insolubility is slightly different there, but equivalent.)

Theorem 1 showed that Buridan's position cannot be consistently represented as a whole. But making the necessary sacrifices, $\mathcal{L}_1$ is a good reconstruction within the limits of its own syntax and models. The Buridanian theses (IF), (BIV) and (NS) are satisfied directly by the rules (A)-(E) above. Thesis (TT) follows at once from (B). (CT-INS) will be proven below as Theorem 4. Since we agreed that valid consequences were to be truth-preserving, thus satisfying (TC), we also thereby satisfy (VIP), in view of (B). But the double negation rules (DN) fail whenever they lead to or from an insoluble, in virtue of Theorem 8 below. Conversely, given a language with the syntax and models of $\mathcal{L}_1$, and given the definition of $\mathsf{INS}_{\mathfrak{M}}$, rule (A) follows from (CT-INS) and (BIV). One half of (B), namely, $V_{\mathfrak{M}}(s) \leq V_{\mathfrak{M}}(t(s))$, follows from (VIP), (TC) and (BIV). The other half follows from (TT) and (BIV). Rule (C) is just (NS). Rule (D) follows from (IF), (CT-INS) and (BIV). Rule (E) follows from (CT-INS) and (BIV). Thus, given the syntax and models of $\mathcal{L}_1$, and given the definition of an insoluble, Buridan's own principles entail (A)-(E). (DN) is of course suspended.

Buridan does not discuss infinite non-cyclic chains, nor cycles of length one that are not vicious (e.g., $s = t_{\mathfrak{M}}(s)$). His silence on these matters is honored by the fact that $\mathcal{L}_1$-models do not admit such cases. He does discuss cycles of length greater than one, and sentences formed with binary connectives, but these are beyond the resources of $\mathcal{L}_1$, which takes no stand on them. They are matters for another study.

9 Theorem 2 *The extension of P is given by* $g_{\mathfrak{M}}$: $\mathsf{EXT}_{\mathfrak{M}}(P) = g_{\mathfrak{M}}(P)$.

For $\mathsf{EXT}_{\mathfrak{M}}(P) = \{f_{\mathfrak{M}}(x): f_{\mathfrak{M}}(x) \in g_{\mathfrak{M}}(P)\}$, by rule (A) and the definition of $\mathsf{EXT}_{\mathfrak{M}}$. The theorem follows by the conditions on models.

Theorem 3 *The extension of T in a model is the class of sentences true in that model*: $\mathsf{EXT}_{\mathfrak{M}}(T) = \{s: V_{\mathfrak{M}}(s) = 1\}$.

This follows from rules (B) and (C) and the definition of $\mathsf{EXT}_{\mathfrak{M}}$.

We shall say that ϕ is a *predicate* of $\mathcal{L}_1$ iff ϕ is either a primitive predicate of $\mathcal{L}_1$, i.e., either P or T, or else formed from a primitive predicate of $\mathcal{L}_1$ by prefixing a string of i negations ($i \geq 0$). We let $N^i(\phi)$ be the result of prefixing i negation operators to ϕ. We now extend the definition of $\mathsf{EXT}_{\mathfrak{M}}$ to all predicates of $\mathcal{L}_1$. If ϕ is a primitive predicate of $\mathcal{L}_1$, then $\mathsf{EXT}_{\mathfrak{M}}(N^i(\phi)) = \mathsf{EXT}_{\mathfrak{M}}(\phi)$ for i not odd, and $\mathsf{EXT}_{\mathfrak{M}}(N^i(\phi)) = X_{\mathfrak{M}} \quad \mathsf{EXT}_{\mathfrak{M}}(\phi)$ for odd i. (It might have seemed more natural to allow $\mathsf{EXT}_{\mathfrak{M}}(\phi)$ to be defined at the outset as $\{f_{\mathfrak{M}}(x): V_{\mathfrak{M}}(\phi x) = 1\}$ for *all* predicates ϕ, primitive or not. But this would have had the effect of excluding insolubles from the extension of the non-truth predicate $N(T)$, even though they are non-truths. In terms of personal supposition theory—where a predicate stands for (*supponit pro*) the members of its extension—this would mean that in the insoluble $s = n(t_{\mathfrak{M}}(s))$, $N(T)$ would not stand for the whole sentence of which it is a part. Buridan unequivocally rejects that approach. (See [3], pp. 192f.)

Lemma 4 *The correspondence theory of truth holds for non-insolubles*: *if* $s \notin \mathsf{INS}_{\mathfrak{M}}$, *then* $s \in \mathsf{CORR}_{\mathfrak{M}}$ *iff* $V_{\mathfrak{M}}(s) = 1$.

For suppose $s \notin \text{INS}_{\mathfrak{M}}$. Then if s is a non-semantic sentence $n^i(Px)$, $Px \in \text{CORR}_{\mathfrak{M}}$ iff $f_{\mathfrak{M}}(x) \in \text{EXT}_{\mathfrak{M}}(P)$. Hence, by Theorem 2 and rule (A), $Px \in \text{CORR}_{\mathfrak{M}}$ iff $V_{\mathfrak{M}}(Px) = 1$. Thus the Lemma follows by i applications of rule (E) and the definition of $\text{CORR}_{\mathfrak{M}}$. If, on the other hand, s is a semantic sentence $n^i(Tx)$, then

Case 1: $f_{\mathfrak{M}}(x)$ is not a semantic sentence. Then $f_{\mathfrak{M}}(x) \notin \text{EXT}_{\mathfrak{M}}(T)$ by Theorem 3. Hence $Tx \in \text{CORR}_{\mathfrak{M}}$ iff $V_{\mathfrak{M}}(Tx) = 1$ by rule (C) and the definition of $\text{CORR}_{\mathfrak{M}}$. Thus again, the Lemma follows by i applications of rule (E) and the definition of $\text{CORR}_{\mathfrak{M}}$.

Case 2: $f_{\mathfrak{M}}(x)$ is a sentence s', and s is $R_{\mathfrak{M}}$-grounded. Then $s = n^i(t_{\mathfrak{M}}(s'))$. Now $t_{\mathfrak{M}}(s') \in \text{CORR}_{\mathfrak{M}}$ iff $s' \in \text{EXT}_{\mathfrak{M}}(T)$, by the definition of $\text{CORR}_{\mathfrak{M}}$. By Theorem 3 and rule (B), it follows that $t_{\mathfrak{M}}(s') \in \text{CORR}_{\mathfrak{M}}$ iff $V_{\mathfrak{M}}(t_{\mathfrak{M}}(s')) = 1$. Hence the Lemma follows by i applications of rule (E) and the definition of $\text{CORR}_{\mathfrak{M}}$.

Case 3: s is $R_{\mathfrak{M}}$-ungrounded. Again, for some s', $s = n^i(t_{\mathfrak{M}}(s'))$. If for no $0 \leq j \leq i$ is $n^j(t_{\mathfrak{M}}(s')) \in \text{INS}_{\mathfrak{M}}$, the argument is just as for Case 2. If the contrary, j is odd by Lemma 1. Thus $n^{j+1}(t_{\mathfrak{M}}(s')) \in \text{CORR}_{\mathfrak{M}}$ iff $V_{\mathfrak{M}}(s') = 1$, by the definition of $\text{CORR}_{\mathfrak{M}}$ and rule (B). Now since $n^j(t_{\mathfrak{M}}(s')) \in \text{INS}_{\mathfrak{M}}$, Lemma 1 yields $n^j(t_{\mathfrak{M}}(s')) = s'$. Thus $V_{\mathfrak{M}}(s') = 0$ and $V_{\mathfrak{M}}(n^{j+1}(t_{\mathfrak{M}}(s'))) = 0$ by rule (D). From (BIV) and the above, we have $n^{j+1}(t_{\mathfrak{M}}(s')) \in \text{CORR}_{\mathfrak{M}}$ iff $V_{\mathfrak{M}}(n^{j+1}(t_{\mathfrak{M}}(s'))) = 1$. Now $j \neq i$, since by the hypothesis of the Lemma $s \notin \text{INS}_{\mathfrak{M}}$. Hence by Lemma 3, there will be no insolubles from $n^{j+1}(t_{\mathfrak{M}}(s'))$ to $n^i(t_{\mathfrak{M}}(s'))$. So from the above, by $i - (j + 1)$ applications of rule (E) and the definition of $\text{CORR}_{\mathfrak{M}}$, the Lemma follows. This completes the proof.

Lemma 5 *Every insoluble corresponds*: $s \in \text{INS}_{\mathfrak{M}}$ *only if* $s \in \text{CORR}_{\mathfrak{M}}$.

For suppose $s \in \text{INS}_{\mathfrak{M}}$. Then for some odd i, $s = n^i(t_{\mathfrak{M}}(s))$, by Lemma 1. Now the definition of $\text{CORR}_{\mathfrak{M}}$ and Theorem 3 yield $t_{\mathfrak{M}}(s) \in \text{CORR}_{\mathfrak{M}}$ iff $V_{\mathfrak{M}}(s) = 1$. Hence by rule (D), $t_{\mathfrak{M}}(s) \notin \text{CORR}_{\mathfrak{M}}$. So $s \in \text{CORR}_{\mathfrak{M}}$ by the definition of $\text{CORR}_{\mathfrak{M}}$, since i is odd.

Theorem 4 *The correspondence theory of truth fails exactly for insolubles*: (CT-INS).

This follows from Lemmata 4 and 5 and rule (D).

If ϕ is a primitive predicate of $\mathcal{L}_1$, we shall say that $N^i(\phi)$ is *safe* just in case for all admissible models $\mathfrak{M}$, $\text{EXT}_{\mathfrak{M}}(N^i(\phi)) = \{f_{\mathfrak{M}}(x)\colon V_{\mathfrak{M}}(n^i(\phi x)) = 1\}$. Then:

Lemma 6 *If ϕ is a primitive predicate and i is not odd, then $N^i(\phi)$ is safe.*

For in that case $n^i(\phi x) \notin \text{INS}_{\mathfrak{M}}$, by Lemma 1, and so $V_{\mathfrak{M}}(n^i(\phi x)) = 1$ iff $f_{\mathfrak{M}}(x) \in \text{EXT}_{\mathfrak{M}}(\phi)$ by Theorem 4. Now $\text{EXT}_{\mathfrak{M}}(N^i(\phi)) = \text{EXT}_{\mathfrak{M}}(\phi) = \{f_{\mathfrak{M}}(x)\colon f_{\mathfrak{M}}(x) \in \text{EXT}_{\mathfrak{M}}(\phi)\}$, from the (extended) definition of $\text{EXT}_{\mathfrak{M}}$. The Lemma follows by substitution.

Lemma 7 *If i is odd, then $N^i(P)$ is safe.*

For in that case $n^i(Px) \notin \text{INS}_{\mathfrak{M}}$ by Lemma 1, and so $V_{\mathfrak{M}}(n^i(Px)) = 1$ iff $f_{\mathfrak{M}}(x) \notin \text{EXT}_{\mathfrak{M}}(P)$ by Theorem 4 and the definition of $\text{CORR}_{\mathfrak{M}}$, since i is odd. Now $\text{EXT}_{\mathfrak{M}}(N^i(P)) = X_{\mathfrak{M}} - \text{EXT}_{\mathfrak{M}}(P) = \{f_{\mathfrak{M}}(x)\colon f_{\mathfrak{M}}(x) \notin \text{EXT}_{\mathfrak{M}}(P)\}$, by the (extended) definition of $\mathsf{EXT}_{\mathfrak{M}}$, since the range of $f_{\mathfrak{M}}$ is $X_{\mathfrak{M}}$. The Lemma follows by substitution.

Theorem 5 *The unsafe predicates of $\mathcal{L}_1$ are just the predicates $N^i(T)$ for odd i.*

That the other predicates are safe follows from Lemmata 6 and 7. Let $s = n^i(t_{\mathfrak{M}}(s))$ for odd i. Then $s \in \mathsf{INS}_{\mathfrak{M}}$ by Lemma 1, and so $s \in X_{\mathfrak{M}} - \mathsf{EXT}_{\mathfrak{M}}(T)$ by rule (D) and Theorem 3. Thus $s \in \mathsf{EXT}_{\mathfrak{M}}(N^i(T))$, by the (extended) definition of $\mathsf{EXT}_{\mathfrak{M}}$. Now $V_{\mathfrak{M}}(n^i(t_{\mathfrak{M}}(s))) = 0$, by rule (D), and so $s \notin \{f_{\mathfrak{M}}(x): V_{\mathfrak{M}}(n^i(Tx)) = 1\}$. Thus by extensionality, the model $\mathfrak{M}$ shows that $N^i(T)$ is unsafe.

An unsafe predicate $N^i(T)$ will be said to *fail in* those models $\mathfrak{M}$ and *for* those sentences s such that $s \in \mathsf{EXT}_{\mathfrak{M}}(N^i(T)) - \{f_{\mathfrak{M}}(x): V_{\mathfrak{M}}(n^i(Tx)) = 1\}$. Then:

Theorem 6 *No two unsafe predicates of $\mathcal{L}_1$ fail in exactly the same models for exactly the same sentences: If i and j are odd, and $i \neq j$, then there is and s and $\mathfrak{M}$ such that $N^i(T)$ fails in $\mathfrak{M}$ for s and $N^j(T)$ does not.*

For, given the conditions, suppose that $s = n^i(t_{\mathfrak{M}}(s))$ and $s' = n^j(t_{\mathfrak{M}}(s))$. Then $s \in \mathsf{EXT}_{\mathfrak{M}}(N^i(T))$ and $s \notin \{f_{\mathfrak{M}}(x): V_{\mathfrak{M}}(n^i(Tx)) = 1\}$, as in the proof of Theorem 5. Thus $N^i(T)$ fails in $\mathfrak{M}$ for s. Now $s' \notin \mathsf{INS}_{\mathfrak{M}}$ by Lemmata 1 and 3. Thus $V_{\mathfrak{M}}(s') = 1$ iff $s' \in \mathsf{CORR}_{\mathfrak{M}}$ by Theorem 4. Hence $V_{\mathfrak{M}}(s') = 1$ iff $V_{\mathfrak{M}}(s) = 0$ by the definition of $\mathsf{CORR}_{\mathfrak{M}}$, Theorem 3 and (BIV), since j is odd. Then since $V_{\mathfrak{M}}(s) = 0$ by Lemma 1 and rule (D), $V_{\mathfrak{M}}(s') = 1$. Hence $s \in \{f_{\mathfrak{M}}(x): V_{\mathfrak{M}}(n^j(Tx)) = 1\}$, and so $N^j(T)$ does not fail in $\mathfrak{M}$ for s.

On the other hand, there are admissible models in which every unsafe predicate fails for some sentence. Let $s_1 = n(t_{\mathfrak{M}}(s_1))$, $s_2 = n^3(t_{\mathfrak{M}}(s_2))$, and in general $s_i = n^{2i-1}(t_{\mathfrak{M}}(s_i))$. Nevertheless, in a given model and for a given sentence, at most one predicate fails:

Theorem 7 *If i and j are odd and $i \neq j$, then if $s \notin \mathsf{EXT}_{\mathfrak{M}}(T)$ and $s \notin \{f_{\mathfrak{M}}(x): V_{\mathfrak{M}}(n^i(Tx)) = 1\}$, then $s \in \{f_{\mathfrak{M}}(x): V_{\mathfrak{M}}(n^j(Tx)) = 1\}$.*

For given the conditions, $V_{\mathfrak{M}}(t_{\mathfrak{M}}(s)) = 0$ by Theorem 3, and also $V_{\mathfrak{M}}(n^i(t_{\mathfrak{M}}(s))) = 0$. Suppose $n^i(t_{\mathfrak{M}}(s)) \notin \mathsf{INS}_{\mathfrak{M}}$. Then $n^i(t_{\mathfrak{M}}(s)) \notin \mathsf{CORR}_{\mathfrak{M}}$ by Theorem 4, and $t_{\mathfrak{M}}(s) \in \mathsf{CORR}_{\mathfrak{M}}$, since i is odd. But since $V_{\mathfrak{M}}(t_{\mathfrak{M}}(s)) = 0$, Theorem 4 requires by *reductio* that $n^i(t_{\mathfrak{M}}(s)) \in \mathsf{INS}_{\mathfrak{M}}$ after all. Hence $n^j(t_{\mathfrak{M}}(s)) \notin \mathsf{INS}_{\mathfrak{M}}$ by Lemma 3, and so $V_{\mathfrak{M}}(n^j(t_{\mathfrak{M}}(s))) = 1$ iff $s \notin \mathsf{EXT}_{\mathfrak{M}}(T)$, by Theorem 4 and the definition of $\mathsf{CORR}_{\mathfrak{M}}$, since j is odd. This and the given conditions yield $V_{\mathfrak{M}}(n^j(t_{\mathfrak{M}}(s))) = 1$, and so the Theorem holds.

Theorems 5-7 indicate some of the peculiar behavior of negation in $\mathcal{L}_1$. The following Theorem shows the basis of this peculiarity. Let s be an atomic sentence. If for some $i \geq 0$, $V_{\mathfrak{M}}(n^i(s)) = V_{\mathfrak{M}}(s)$ iff i is not odd, then we say that negation *behaves classically in $\mathfrak{M}$ for $n^i(s)$*. Then:

Theorem 8 *Negation behaves classically in $\mathfrak{M}$ except just for the insolubles in $\mathfrak{M}$.*

First, if s is atomic and for no $i \geqslant 0$ is $n^i(s) \in \text{INS}_{\mathfrak{M}}$, then negation behaves classically for $i = 0$, trivially. For $i > 0$, $V_{\mathfrak{M}}(n^i(s))$ is calculated on the basis of $V_{\mathfrak{M}}(s)$ by i applications of rule (E), and so behaves classically. On the other hand, if s is atomic and for some $j \geqslant 0$, $n^j(s) \in \text{INS}_{\mathfrak{M}}$, then $V_{\mathfrak{M}}(s) = 0$ and for all $i \geqslant 0$, negation behaves classically in $\mathfrak{M}$ for $n^i(s)$, *except* where $i = j$, as we shall now show. $V_{\mathfrak{M}}(n^j(s)) = 0$ by rule (D). Also, $n^j(s) = n^j(t_{\mathfrak{M}}(n^j(s)))$ and j is odd by Lemma 1. Thus $V_{\mathfrak{M}}(s) = V_{\mathfrak{M}}(t_{\mathfrak{M}}(n^j(s))) = 0$, by rule (B). So $V_{\mathfrak{M}}(s) = V_{\mathfrak{M}}(n^j(s))$. But since j is odd, this means that negation does not behave classically in $\mathfrak{M}$ for the insoluble $n^j(s)$. On the other hand, it does behave classically for the atomic s, trivially. By Lemma 3, there are no insolubles between s and $n^j(s)$. So for $0 < i < j$, $n^i(s)$ is evaluated by rule (E), guaranteeing that negation behave classically in these cases. By rule (D), $V_{\mathfrak{M}}(n^{j+1}(s)) = 0$, and since $j + 1$ is even, negation behaves classically for $n^{j+1}(s)$. By Lemma 3 again, for no $i > j$ is $n^i(s) \in \text{INS}_{\mathfrak{M}}$. Thus $n^i(s)$ for $i > j + 1$ is evaluated on the basis of $V_{\mathfrak{M}}(n^{j+1}(s))$ by rule (E), and so negation behaves classically in these cases too.

From Theorem 8, we see that in the "normal" case, negation marches through the sequence $\langle s, n(s), n^2(s), \ldots \rangle$ by *alternating* between the values 0 and 1 or 1 and 0. But in the case of such a sequence that contains an insoluble, the insoluble forces negation out of step, as it were, so that a 0 is followed by a 0. Recovery occurs at once, and the next step is a 0, as it should be. From here on, the march is back "in step", and proceeds as if nothing had happened.

In future papers, I shall examine some of the complications that arise when Buridan considers situations in which two or more sentences are arranged in an $R_{\mathfrak{M}}$-cycle, and in which sentences with binary connectives are taken into account.

REFERENCES

[1] Buridan, J., *In Metaphysicen Aristotelis quaestiones argutissimae magistri Joannis Buridani*, Paris, Jodocus Badius Ascensus, 1518.

[2] Buridan, J., *Sophismata Buridani*, Paris: Antoine Denidel and Nicole de la Barre, [c. 1495-1500] (*Incunabula in American Libraries*, 3rd census, B-1295). Copy at Harvard University Library, incunabula 8325.5.

[3] Buridan, J., *Sophisms on Meaning and Truth*, Theodore Kermit Scott, tr., "Century Philosophy Sourcebooks"; New York: Appleton-Century-Crofts (1966).

[4] Faral, E., "Jean Buridan: Maître ès arts de l'Université de Paris" in *Histoire littéraire de la France*, vol. 38, Paris, Imprimerie nationale (1949), pp. 462-605.

[5] Herzberger, H. G., "Paradoxes of grounding in semantics," *The Journal of Philosophy*, vol. 67 (1970), pp. 145-167.

[6] Herzberger, H. G., "Truth and modality in semantically closed languages," in Robert L. Martin, ed., *The Paradox of the Liar*, New Haven, Connecticut: Yale University Press (1970), pp. 25-46.

[7] Moody, Ernest A., *Truth and Consequence in Mediaeval Logic*, "Studies in Logic and the Foundations of Mathematics"; Amsterdam, North-Holland Publishing Company (1953).

[8] Prior, A. N., "The possibly-true and the possible", *Mind*, vol. 78 (1969), pp. 481-492.

[9] Prior, A. N., "Some problems of self-reference in John Buridan," *Proceedings of the British Academy*, vol. 48 (1962), pp. 281-296.

[10] Spade, P. V., *The Mediaeval Liar: A Catalogue of the Insolubilia-Literature*, Subsidia Mediavalia, vol. 5, Toronto, Pontifical Institute of Mediaeval Studies (1975).

[11] Spade, P. V., *The Mediaeval Liar: A Study of John Buridan's Position on the Paradox with a Catalogue of the Insolubilia-Literature of the Middle Ages*, Ph.D. dissertation, University of Toronto (1972).

[12] Spade, P. V., "On a conservative attitude toward some naive semantic principles," *Notre Dame Journal of Formal Logic*, vol. XVI (1975), pp. 597-602.

[13] Tarski, A., "The semantic conception of truth," in Herbert Feigl and Wilfrid Sellars, eds., *Readings in Philosophical Analysis*, New York, Appleton-Century-Crofts (1949), pp. 52-84.

Indiana University
Bloomington, Indiana

VII

ROGER SWYNESHED'S *INSOLUBILIA* : EDITION AND COMMENTS

The text edited below is the second of two influential tracts by Roger Swyneshed[1] which frequently appear together in the MSS. The first of these tracts, Swyneshed's *Obligationes*, was edited in an earlier paper.[2] The present tract, his *Insolubilia*, concerns sophisms of the kind illustrated by the so-called "Liar paradox", in which someone utters the sentence 'What I am now saying is false' and that alone. Modern interest in the mediaeval literature on such paradoxes has grown markedly in recent years.[3] Swyneshed's text is of considerable importance in this literature. His position was criticized at length in William Heytesbury's famous *Regulae solvendi sophismata*, ch. 1,[4] and so shared in the latter's wide circulation. Despite Heytesbury's criticisms, however, Swyneshed's view was adopted in a revised and amplified form by the

(1) On Roger Swyneshed, who is not to be confused with the Merton "Calculator", Richard Swyneshed, see James A. WEISHEIPL, "Roger Swyneshed, O.S.B., Logician, Natural Philosopher, and Theologian," in *Oxford Studies Presented to Daniel Callus* ("Oxford Historical Society", new series, vol. 16; Oxford: Clarendon Press for the Oxford Historical Society, 1964 for 1959-60), pp. 231-252. Weisheipl's paper is the most complete source for Swyneshed's life and works. The confusion of Roger with Richard Swyneshed occurs in some of the MSS. See, e.g., the colophon to MS. V^*, n. 91 to par. 112, below.

(2) Paul Vincent SPADE, "Roger Swyneshed's *Obligationes*: Edition and Comments," *Archives d'histoire doctrinale et littéraire du moyen âge*, 44 (1977), p. 243-285.

(3) On the origins of this literature in the Middle Ages, see my "The Origins of the Mediaeval *Insolubilia*-Literature," *Franciscan Studies* 33 (1973), pp. 292-309. For a catalogue of the mediaeval texts, see my *The Mediaeval Liar: A Catalogue of the Insolubilia-Literature*. Toronto, Pontifical Institute of Mediaeval Studies, 1975 ("Subsidia Mediaevalia", vol. 5).

(4) Printed in *Tractatus gulielmi Hentisberi de sensu composito et diviso, Regulae ejusdem cum sophismatibus, Declaratio Gaetani supra easdem...*, Venice: Bonetus Locatellus for Octavianus Scotus, 1494 [Hain 8437], ff. 4va-7rb. Copy at University of Chicago Library.

late mediaeval encyclopedist of logic, Paul of Venice.[5] Moreover, Swyneshed's three "conclusions" (below, pars. 25-27) became famous in their own right, and were the subjects of some dispute.[6]

Swyneshed's text was written after roughly 1330 and certainly before 1335, the date of Heytesbury's *Regulae.*[7] Weisheipl lists MSS. containing one or both of Swyneshed's tracts. Of these, I have examined three[8]:

Bruges, Bibl. publ. MS. 500, ff. 150va-157va (mid-14c).[9]
Vatican, Vat. lat. 2130, ff. 154vb-159va (15c).
Vatican, Vat. lat. 2154, ff. 6va-12va (15c).[10]

In addition, I have examined two other MSS. of Swyneshed's text, not cited by Weisheipl[11]:

Cambridge, Corpus Christi College 244 (245), ff. 59r-76v (15c).[12]
Cambridge, Corpus Christi College 378, ff. 77r-80r (incomplete) (15c).[13]

In my *The Mediaeval Liar* (item XVII), I listed these two MSS. as anonymous but bearing a close relation to Swyneshed's text. On closer examination, however, they prove to be copies of Swyneshed's tract itself.

(5) See my *The Mediaeval Liar*, item L. John of Celaya's text also appears to have been influenced by Swyneshed. See Marie-Louise Roure, "Le traité 'Des propositions insolubles' de Jean de Celaya", *Archives d'histoire doctrinale et littéraire du moyen âge*, 29 (1962), pp. 235-338.

(6) See *The Mediaeval Liar*, item XLI (John of Wesel's *Quaestiones super insolubilibus*), q. 1; and item LXII (Roger Roseth). See also item XXVI (Anthony de Monte), conclusion 2. Swyneshed's position is also discussed by the anonymous authors of items III, VII, XIII, by Cajetan of Thiene (item XXVIII), John Dumbleton (item XXXVI), Marsilius of Inghen (item XLVII) and Ralph Strode (item LIII).

(7) See Weisheipl, *op. cit.*, p. 247, and supporting arguments, pp. 244-247.

(8) *Ibid.*, p. 243. See also *The Mediaeval Liar*, item LXIII. I have not examined Prague, Metropol. 1645 [O. LXI], ff. 138-153v (14c), with Swyneshed's *Obligationes*.

(9) See A. de Poorter, *Catalogue des manuscrits de la Bibliothèque publique de la ville de Bruges* ("Catalogue général des manuscrits des bibliothèques de Belgique" II. Gembloux, J. Duculot, 1934).

(10) On these last two MSS., see *Codices vaticani latini : codices 2118-2192*, Anneliese Maier, ed., Vatican, 1961. Weisheipl, *op. cit.*, p. 243, says that Vat. lat. 2154 is 14c.

(11) Weisheipl, *op. cit.*, p. 234, cites Bale's attribution to Swyneshed of a text "De divisionibus", with the *incipit* "Quattuor sunt divisiones proposi[tionum]". Bale's *Index* refers to Magdalen College, Oxford, but gives no MS. number. The *incipit* agrees with the *incipit* of Swyneshed's *Insolubilia* in the two Cambridge MSS., below. Edith Sylla informs me that there is an additional copy, with this same *incipit*, in Bodleian, Bodley 676 (S.C. 2593), ff. 126r-131r; the *explicit* is "Et tunc arguitur sic: hoc est verum. Ergo ita est sicut hoc principaliter significat. Consequentia patet per definitionem tertiam" (see perhaps the middle of par. 40, following *VV**, in the edition below). (Letters of February 9 and March 24, 1976.)

(12) Folio 68v of the MS. is inscribed '69' and f. 69r is inscribed '70'. I have followed these inscriptions in the edition below.

(13) This copy breaks off at the bottom of f. 80r, in the middle of par. 52 of the edition. Folios 80v-81r are blank. On these two Cambridge MSS., see Montague Rhodes James, *A Descriptive Catalogue of the Manuscripts in the Library of Corpus Christi College Cambridge*, 2 vols. Cambridge: University Press, 1912.

Unlike the *Obligationes*, which appeared even in the early MSS. in two redactions,[14] the text of the *Insolubilia* is relatively constant in the MSS. For the following edition, I have used Vat. lat. 2154 (with the sign "*V**") as the basis, departing from it only where required by the syntax or by the sense of the argument. I have collated this copy with Vat. lat. 2130 (with the sign "*V*"), Cambridge 244 (245) (with the sign "*C*"), and Cambridge 378 (with the sign "*C**"). Although the Bruges MS. is the earliest of those I have examined, I have not used it in the edition. It agrees very closely with *V*, and where the two disagree, *V* is usually to be preferred. Of the MSS. I have used, *V** is in general the most reliable, followed in order by *V*, *C** and *C*.

Since the edition below is a working edition, and not a critical one, I have recorded only major variants, those that may affect the doctrine and those that involve significant changes in wording. Where subordinate MSS. differ significantly from the text in *V**, but differ only insignificantly among themselves, I have quoted the variant according to the most preferred MS. in which it occurs (*V* preferred to *C**, and *C** to *C*), but have referred to all the MSS. in which it occurs. I have not recorded marginalia unless they affect the text; for the most part, they serve only to mark articulations of the argument. I have, however, recorded all departures from *V**, and all interlinear and marginal corrections in *V**. The phrases 'significare principaliter', 'significare primarie', 'significare praecise', and the like, while they do not appear to play an important role in Swyneshed's doctrine, do play an important role in the doctrine of other authors and in later revisions and amplifications of Swyneshed's position. I have accordingly thought it best to record all variants of these phrases.

I have normalized the orthography according to *Thesaurus linguae latinae*. Editorial additions are enclosed in pointed brackets. The division into paragraphs is mine. I have also numbered the main parts of the text according to the division given in the prologue to the *Obligationes*, immediately preceding the *Insolubilia*, in *V**.[15] I have inserted the folio and column references in the text. Where the reading in a subordinate MS. spans two columns in a variant recorded in the apparatus, I have marked the division precisely in the notes, and as accurately as possible in the main text.

As in my edition of the *Obligationes*, I have added some comments in the notes. These are for the most part meant to clarify points or arguments in the text. They do not constitute a full commentary.

(14) See my introduction to "Roger Swyneshed's *Obligationes*".
(15) See "Roger Swyneshed's *Obligationes*", par. 1.

<Rogerii Swyneshed Insolubilia>[16]

(1) (*V*154vb, *V**6va) Dicto de obligationibus restat de insolubilibus secundum processum prohemii determinare[17].

I

(2) (*C*59r, *C**77r) Divisiones autem ad hoc pertinentes sunt quattuor[18]. Prima est haec : Propositionum alia significat principaliter sicut est vel principaliter[19] aliter quam est, alia nec principaliter sicut est nec aliter quam est. Propositio significans principaliter sicut est est sicut propositio significans principaliter[20] quod deus est vel quod tu sedes, si ita sit[21], et sic de consimilibus. Propositio significans principaliter[22] aliter quam est est sicut propositio[23] significans quod[24] homo est asinus vel quod tu sedeas, si tu non[25] sedes[26]. Propositio nec principaliter significans sicut est nec aliter quam est, id est, quae nec est vera nec falsa[27], est propositio[28] significans aliqualiter esse et illa sic significando est pertinens ad inferendum se ipsam non significare principaliter sicut est[29], sicut

(16) Expliciunt obligationes reverendi doctoris Suiset. Incipiunt insolubilia ejusdem *V*. Richardi Suiset Angli insolubilia *V** (second hand, at top of f. 6v). On the confusion of Roger with Richard Swyneshed, see Weisheipl, *op. cit.*

(17) restat...determinare/jam restat in processum prohemialiter tactum de insolubilibus determinare *V*. For the prologue referred to here, see Swyneshed's *Obligationes*, par. 1. Par. 1 of the *Insolubilia* is lacking in *CC**.

(18) duae *V*. Nevertheless, *V* subsequently gives all four divisions. Divisiones... quattuor/ Quattuor sunt divisiones propositionum quarum *CC**.

(19) principaliter *om.* *C** *V*

(20) principaliter *om.* *C**.

(21) significans... sit/ per quam primarie et adaequate significatur, et illa sic significando non est pertinens ad inferendum se ipsam significare aliter quam est vel non principaliter sicut est, ut ista propositio ' Deus est ' vel ' Vos sedetis ', si ita sit quod vos sedeatis *C*.

(22) principaliter *om.* *V*.

(23) principaliter *add.* *V*.

(24) sicut non est, ut illa *C**.

(25) *Interl.* non *V**.

(26) sicut... sedes/ quando per illam sicut adaequate et primarie significatur non est, ut ' Homo est asinus ' vel ' Vos sedetis ' si ita sit quod vos non sedetis *C*. vel...sedes *om.* *C**. vel... sedes/ vel quod tu non sedes, si tu sedes *V*.

(27) id... falsa *om.* *CC** *V*. Although the passage is omitted by all MSS. except *V**, it conforms to Swyneshed's doctrine. See, e.g., par. 28.

(28) principaliter *add.* *V*.

(29) nec principaliter (principaliter *om.* *C**) aliter quam est *add.* *CC**.

haec propositio ' Haec propositio non significat[30] sicut est ', demonstrata illa eadem, quae principaliter significet quod ipsa non significat sicut est[31]. Et haec similiter ' Omnis propositio significat aliter quam est ' quae principaliter[32] significet quod omnis propositio significat aliter quam est[33]. Et sic de similibus.

(3) Pro quo est notandum quod propositio pertinens ad inferendum se ipsam non significare principaliter sicut est est talis ex qua[34] cum totaliter sic esse sicut est[35] sequitur vel natum[36] est sequi illam non significare principaliter sicut est[37]. Exemplum : Significet haec propositio ' Haec significat aliter quam est ' principaliter quod[38] haec significat aliter quam est[39], ipsamet demonstrata. Tunc sequitur « Haec propositio significat aliter quam est[40] ; et principaliter[41] sic significat ; igitur, haec (*C*59v) non significat principaliter sicut est ». Et ita ex illa cum totaliter sic esse sicut est sequitur quod ipsa non significat[42] sicut est[43]. Et ideo nec significat aliter quam est nec sicut est[44]. Et sicut est de illa, ita est de similibus[45].

(30) principaliter *add.* *C**
(31) non... est/ significat *C**.
(32) principaliter *om.* *C**.
(33) quae... est *om.* *C*.
(34) sic significando *add.* *C*. per se posita *add.* *C**. per se vel *add.* *V*.
(35) ex parte rei *add.* *C*. sic... est/ sicut est *C**, sic esse est *V**. The sense seems to be : with some additional premiss (« sic esse ») expressing the supposed situation (« sicut est »). The phrase ' sic esse sicut est ', in this sense, is common throughout the tract.
(36) nata *CV**.
(37) In general, throughout Swyneshed's *Insolubilia*, a sentence ' *p* ' is « pertinens ad inferendum » that *q* if and only if, from the premiss ' *p* ', and perhaps some needed additional premisses, it follows that *q*. Sometimes Swyneshed adds the stipulation that the conclusion not follow from the additional premisses alone. I.e., if ' *p* ' is « pertinens », its presence must make a difference. (See par. 6. Also, pars. 89, 92, and replies 95, 98, and also especially par. 97.) Note that this notion is quite different from the notion used in Swyneshed's *Obligationes*, that a sentence is « pertinens » to an « obligatum » if and only if it either follows from or is inconsistent with the « obligatum ». See his *Obligationes*, par. 4.
(38) significet... quod *om.* *C**. principaliter quod/ quae principaliter significet quod *V**.
(39) principaliter... est *om.* *C*.
(40) aliter... est *om.* *V**.
(41) principaliter *om.* *C**.
(42) principaliter *add.* *CC***V*.
(43) nec aliter quam est *add.* *C**.
(44) aliter... est/ principaliter sicut est nec (principaliter *add.* *C*) aliter quam est *CV*. Et... est *om.* *C**.
(45) It is clear why such a sentence would not signify principally as is the case. But it is not clear why in general the sentence would not signify principally otherwise than is the case. In the example, of course, it is obvious enough. For if it is not the case as the sentence principally signifies, and the sentence principally signifies just that, then it is after all the case as the sentence principally signifies. But the argument in

(4) Secunda divisio est haec : Propositionum alia falsificat se ipsam, alia non. Propositio falsificans se ipsam est duplex. Quaedam falsificat se mediate, quaedam immediate. Propositio falsificans se mediate est propositio significans principaliter[46] sicut est vel[47] aliter quam est et ipsa sic significando[48] falsificat propositionem aliam a se falsificantem se. Exemplum : Sit *a* una propositio significans principaliter quod *b* est falsum, et *b* una propositio significans principaliter[49] quod *a* est falsum. Et sit tantum[50] unum *a* et tantum unum *b*. Tunc hoc posito, non potest poni quod utrumque sit verum, sed oportet ponere quod alterum sit falsum. Nec potest ratio assignari quare magis *a*[51] est falsum quam *b* est falsum nec e converso. Igitur, illo casu posito, oportet ponere utrumque[52] fore falsum[53]. Et sic ex *a* sequitur *b* fore falsum[54], et ex *b* sequitur *a* fore falsum[55]. Et ita ex *a* sequitur *a* fore falsum (V^*6vb) mediante *b*. Et ex *b* sequitur *b* fore falsum mediante *a*[56]. Et ita *a* falsificat *b* immediate et se ipsam mediate[57].

(5) Propositio falsificans se immediate est propositio significans principaliter sicut est vel[58] aliter quam est pertinens ad inferendum se ipsam fore falsam. Et illa est duplex. Quaedam est pertinens sufficiens, quaedam est pertinens insufficiens. Pertinens sufficiens est propositio significans principaliter[59] sicut est vel[60] aliter quam est ex qua sic significando immediate sequitur vel est natum sequi ipsam fore falsam. Exemplum :

the paragraph shows that to be impossible. What Swyneshed needs is some guarantee that a similar consequence holds for every sentence which is « pertinens ad inferendum se ipsam non significare principaliter sicut est ». But there would seem to be no such guarantee. For the sentence ' Omnis propositio significat aliter quam est ', which Swyneshed himself mentions in par. 2, provides a counterexample : if it is not the case as the sentence principally signifies, and if the sentence principally signifies that every sentence signifies otherwise than is the case, then some sentence principally signifies as is the case. But it does not follow that the original sentence signifies as is the case.

(46) principaliter *om.* C^*.

(47) principaliter *add.* *C*.

(48) sic significando *om.* CC^*. *In marg.* sic significando *V*.

(49) principaliter *om.* *CV*.

(50) sit tantum/ sint scilicet *V*.

(51) *Interl.* *a* V^*.

(52) *a* *V*.

(53) On this kind of argumentation, see my « On A Conservative Attitude toward Some Naive Semantic Principles », *Notre Dame Journal of Formal Logic* 16 (1975), pp. 597-602.

(54) et e contra *add.* *C*.

(55) et... falsum *om.* *C*. *Add.* mediante *b* V^*.

(56) Et ita... *a* *om.* CC^*.

(57) Et *b* falsificat *a* immediate et se ipsam mediate *add.* CC^*. Et sic... mediate/ et se ipsam falsificantem *V*.

(58) principaliter *add.* *C*.

(59) principaliter *om.* C^*.

(60) principaliter *add* *C*.

Significet[61] illa propositio ' Hoc est falsum ' principaliter[62] quod hoc est falsum, (*V*155ra) ipsamet demonstrata. Tunc sequitur immediate « Hoc est falsum ; igitur, hoc est falsum »[63]. Et sic illa est pertinens sufficiens ad inferendum se ipsam[64] fore (*C*60r) falsam[65].

(6) Pertinens insufficiens est duplex. Quaedam est pertinens insufficiens[66] ad inferendum solum se ipsam fore falsam, et quaedam est pertinens insufficiens[67] ad inferendum se ipsam fore falsam et aliam[68] similiter. Propositio pertinens insufficiens primo modo est propositio[69] significans sicut est[70] ex qua sic significando cum totaliter sic esse sicut est ex parte rei sequitur vel natum[71] est sequi[72] ipsam fore falsam et ex ita esse[73] sine illa non sequitur illud[74]. Exemplum : Ponatur quod tantum sit unus Sortes et quod solum dicat illam (*C**77v) ' Sortes dicit falsum ' et quod illa ex impositione[75] principaliter significet quod Sortes dicit falsum. Tunc sequitur « Sortes dicit falsum[76] ; et solum dicit illam ' Sortes dicit falsum ' ; igitur, illa est falsa »[77]. Et illa est pertinens ad inferendum cum casu posito quod illa ' Sortes dicit falsum ' significat principaliter sicut est[78].

(7) Propositio pertinens insufficiens[79] secundo modo est propositio pertinens ad inferendum se ipsam fore falsum[80] et similiter aliam. Exemplum : Ponatur quod illa propositio ' Omnis propositio est falsa ' praecise[81] significet quod omnis propositio est falsa. Et sint multae falsae propositiones aliae ab illa[82]. Tunc ex illa significante totaliter esse sicut

(61) Significetur *V**.
(62) quae principaliter significat *V**.
(63) igitur... falsum *om. V**.
(64) *Add. interl.* solam *C*.
(65) Et quaedam est pertinens ad inferendum se ipsam et aliam fore falsam *add. C*.
(66) insufficiens *om. CC* V*
(67) insufficiens *om. CC* V*.
(68) a se sibi similem *add. V*.
(69) principaliter *add. CC* V*.
(70) vel aliter quam est *add. C*. (This reading should perhaps be preferred.)
(71) nata *CV**.
(72) solum *add C**.
(73) ita esse/ illa sic esse sicut est *C*.
(74) et... illud *om. C**
(75) positione *C**.
(76) Tunc... falsum *V in marg.*
(77) demonstrando eandem propositionem *add. C*.
(78) Et... est/ Et hoc arguitur ex illa et ex eadem cum hoc quod solum dicit illam (vel *add. C**) quod verum (ita *CC**) est per casum. Et non (non *om. C*) potest poni isto casu posito quin illa significet principaliter sicut est *CC* V*.
(79) insufficiens *om. C**.
(80) fore falsum *om. C**.
(81) primarie *CC**, principaliter *V*.
(82) Et... illa/ Et sint multae aliae propositiones ab illa *V in marg.*

est[83] sequitur vel est natum[84] sequi[85] illam eandem fore falsam et aliam similiter ab illa. Et ideo illa est pertinens insufficiens ad inferendum se et aliam ab illa fore falsam. Antecedens probatur sic[86] : Omnis propositio est falsa ; ipsamet est propositio ; igitur, ipsamet est falsa. Et sic infert se ipsam fore falsam. Sequitur etiam « Omnis propositio est falsa ; propositio alia ab illa est propositio ; igitur, propositio alia ab illa est falsa ». Et sic sequitur propositionem aliam ab illa fore falsam.

(8) Propositio non falsificans se est propositio habens conditiones propositionum falsificantium se[87] conditionibus contrarias[88], sicut sunt universaliter omnes propositiones in se falsae[89], sicut de tali ' Homo est asinus ' principaliter significante[90] quod homo est asinus. Et universaliter de omni propositione tali[91].

(9) Contra illas divisiones dicetur[92]. Ideo hic (*V**7ra) transeo.

(10) Tertia divisio est haec : Omne insolubile provenit ex proprietate vocis vel ex actu nostro vel ex mixtione actus nostri cum proprietate (*C*60v) vocis[93]. Proprietates vocum sunt illae : esse verum, esse falsum[94], esse necessarium, esse impossibile, et sic similia. Actus nostri sunt duplices, scilicet, interiores et exteriores. Primi sunt sicut scire, intellegere, cogitare, credere, dubitare[95], et similia. Secundi sicut ambulare, scribere, et hujusmodi[96].

(11) Ultima divisio est haec : Propositionum alia significat complexe naturaliter[97], alia complexe actualiter[98]. Primo modo sunt propositiones

(83) significante... est/ (cum *add. C*) totaliter sic esse *CC**.
(84) nata *V**.
(85) vel... sequi *om. CC**.
(86) Tunc... sic/ Tunc sic *V*.
(87) sub *add. C*.
(88) contrariis *CC*V**.
(89) omnes... falsae/ omnes (multae *C**) propositiones verae et multae (verae... multae *om. C*) falsae *CC*V*.
(90) significat *V**.
(91) impossibili *CC*V*.
(92) See pars. 28-29, and reply, pars. 30-32 (against the first division), and pars. 89-93, and reply, pars 95-99 (against the second division).
(93) proprietate vocis/ voce *V*.
(94) esse falsum *om. V*.
(95) intellegere... dubitare/ cognoscere vel intellegere *CC**, cognoscere, credere *V*.
(96) ambulare... hujusmodi/ audire, scribere, percutere, et similia. Insolubile proveniens ex mixtione actus nostri cum proprietate vocis est ut posito quod Sortes dicat quod Sortes dicit falsum esse *C*, scribere, audire, et similia *C**. Secundi... hujusmodi *V. in marg.*
(97) complexe naturaliter/ materialiter complexive *C**.
(98) complexe actualiter/ complexive artificialiter *C**, complexe accidentaliter *V*.

in anima, si quae sint[99]. Secundo modo est dupliciter : Quaedam significat actualiter[1] ex impositione vel impositionibus, quaedam non actualiter[2] ex impositione vel ex impositionibus. Propositio significans actualiter[3] ex impositione est[4] ut ' Deus est '[5] imposita ad significandum principaliter[6] quod deus est, et sic de aliis. Propositio significans[7] ex impositionibus est ut haec propositio ' Deus est ', si imponebatur ab uno ad significandum quod deus est et ab alio imponebatur ad significandum quod hono est asinus[8]. Tunc utroque modo sic significat.

(12) Propositio significans actualiter[9] non ex impositione[10] ut sic : Talis propositio ' Deus est ' imponatur ad significandum principaliter quod deus est et aliquis[11] concipiat per illam aliter quam fuerit imposita ad significandum, sicut quod homo est asinus. Tunc illa actualiter[12] et non ex impositione sic significat.

(13) Post illa sequuntur quattuor definitiones[13] seu descriptiones. Prima est haec : Propositio est oratio indicativa congrua[14] naturaliter (*V*155rb), ex impositione, vel impositionibus qua vel quibus ultimo fuit imposita complexe ad significandum significativa[15]. Haec patet discurrendo per singulas propositiones.

(14) Secunda est haec : Propositio (*C**78r) vera est propositio non falsificans se principaliter sicut est significans naturaliter aut ex impositione vel impositionibus qua vel quibus ultimo fuit imposita ad significandum.

(15) Tertia definitio : Propositio falsa est oratio falsificans se vel oratio non falsificans se[16] principaliter aliter[17] quam est[18] significans (*C*61r)

(99) Swyneshed thus hesitates over the existence of a mental language. Contrast William of Ockham, *Summa logicae* I, 3, Gedeon Gál and Stephen F. Brown, eds., (St. Bonaventure, N.Y., The Franciscan Institute, 1974), and William Ockham, *Quodlibeta septem* (Strasbourg, 1491), quod. 5, q.8.

(1) artificialiter *C**, accidentaliter *V*.
(2) actualiter *om. CC**. non actualiter/ accidentaliter non *V*.
(3) artificialiter *C**, accidentaliter *V*. actualiter *om. C*.
(4) ex... est *om. V*.
(5) est *om. V**.
(6) actualiter *C*. principaliter *om. V*.
(7) artificialiter *add. C**. propositio significans *add. V**.
(8) principaliter *add CC**.
(9) artificialiter *C**. accidentaliter *V*.
(10) nec ex impositionibus *add. C**.
(11) continue *add. V*.
(12) artificialiter *C**. accidentaliter *V*.
(13) divisiones *C**.
(14) et perfecta *add. C*.
(15) Note that it is not required that the « oratio » signify principally as is the case or otherwise than is the case. See par. 2.
(16) vel... se *om. C*.
(17) sicut est vel principaliter (principaliter *om. C*) aliter *CC**.
(18) quam est *om. V**.

naturaliter, ex impositione, vel impositionibus qua vel quibus ultimo fuit imposita ad significandum.

(16) Quarta est haec : Insolubile ad propositum est propositio significans principaliter sicut est vel[19] aliter quam est[20] pertinens ad inferendum se ipsam fore falsam vel nescitam vel creditam, et sic de singulis[21].

(17) Postea sequuntur octo suppositiones quarum prima est haec : Omnis propositio pertinens ad inferen- (*V**7rb) dum se ipsam fore falsam est falsificans se. Haec patet ex intentione Philosophi quarto *Metaphysicae*[22] ubi ponit quasdam orationes se ipsas destruere[23]. Et planum est quod ibi nihil aliud intellegitur per orationem destruentem[24] se nisi orationem pertinentem ad inferendum se ipsam fore falsam, quod significatur per illum terminum ' falsificans se '. Et melius sonat in lingua latina nominare talem propositionem falsificare se quam destruere eo quod nec oratio est destructiva sui ipsius nec alterius a se. Melius tamen sonat in lingua graeca nominare talem propositionem destruere quam falsificare se. Et ideo translator utitur hoc verbo ' destruere se ' ubi nos utimur ' falsificare se '[25] eo quod verius tali propositioni competit.

(18) Secunda est haec : Omnis propositio falsificans se est propositio falsa. Haec probatur : Omnis propositio[26] falsificans se significat sicut est vel aliter quam est[27]. Si aliter quam est[28], igitur[29] falsa per definitionem tertiam. Si significat sicut est, tunc ex illa cum[30] totaliter sic esse sicut est sequitur quod illa est falsa[31].

(19) principaliter *add. CC**.

(20) Hence the sentences described in par. 2 as « neither true nor false » are not insolubles.

(21) nescitam... singulis/ veram *CC**, non necessariam *V*.

(22) Aristotle, *Metaphysics* 4, 8, 1012 b 13-14.

(23) describere *V**

(24) describentem *V**.

(25) se *V**. *interl.*

(26) Omnis propositio/ Quaecumque propositio falsa *C*.

(27) See pars. 4-5.

(28) Si... est *om. CV**.

(29) Si... igitur/ et omnis talis est *V*.

(30) significatione *V*. cum *om. C*.

(31) pertinens ad inferendum se ipsam fore falsam est falsa in se, ut patet per primam suppositionem *add. C.* Sequitur quod ita est quod illa est falsa *add. V.* The argument here is obscure. The third definition (par. 15) may be construed in two ways : (1) a false sentence is one that either (a) falsifies itself or else (b) does not falsify itself but signifies principally otherwise than is the case ; (2) a false sentence is one that signifies principally otherwise than is the case, whether it falsifies itself or not. On interpretation (1), the entire argument in par. 18 is unnecessary. For a sentence that falsifies itself is automatically false by part (a) of the definition. On interpretation (2), the second part of the argument amounts to a *reductio* : If the sentence signifies as is the case, then from it and the fact that it signifies as is the case, it follows that it is false (since it falsifies itself — see par. 17, which must in this case be construed as

(19) Tertia est haec : Propositio verificans se est propositio (*C*61v) pertinens ad inferendum se ipsam fore veram. Haec patet per probationem prioris[32] suppositionis. Nam sicut propositio pertinens ad inferendum se fore falsam dicitur falsificans se, sic propositio pertinens ad inferendum se fore veram dicitur verificans se.

(20) Quarta : Non omnis propositio verificans se est vera. Haec probatur sic : Ponatur quod sunt multae propositiones verae et multae falsae. Tunc illa propositio ' Omnis propositio est vera ' principaliter significans quod omnis propositio est vera, ut notum, est falsa. Patet per definitionem tertiam eo quod principaliter significat aliter quam est. Et quod illa verificat se patet. Nam ipsa est pertinens ad inferendum se ipsam fore veram, quia sequitur « Omnis propositio est vera ; ipsamet est propositio ; igitur, ipsamet est vera ».

(21) Quinta est haec : Nulla propositio est suae partes. Haec patet per Philosophum septimo *Metaphysicae*, circa finem[33], ubi declarat quod haec syllaba ' ba ' non est haec illae litterae ' b ' et ' a ' et quod illae litterae possunt esse quando non est illa syllaba. Ideo illae litterae non sunt illa syllaba vel communiter dicendo[34] nulla propositio est suae partes[35].

(22) Sexta : Nulla propositio vera est falsa et e converso. Haec patet de se[36].

(23) (*C**78v) Septima : Qualitercumque concipiens propositionem concipit per propositionem, illa sic sibi significat. Haec patet ex descriptione illius termini ' significare '. Nam significare non est aliud quam conceptui aliquid (*V*155va) repraesentare ; sed qualitercumque concipiens propositionem concipit per propositionem taliter propositio conceptui (*C*62r) repraesentat ; igitur, et cetera.

(24) Octava et ultima : Propositio in voce vel in scripto solum[37] propter taliter esse qualiter ex impositione (*V**7va) vel impositionibus

giving a *definition* of self-falsification and as being simply convertible. For justification see pars. 19, 26), and so, by the definition in par. 15 on interpretation (2), that it signifies otherwise than is the case. Hence, by *reductio*, it does not signify as is the case, after all. It would perhaps seem that interpretation (2) is the more likely. For on that interpretation, the definitions in pars. 14-15 do not suffice by themselves to ensure that every sentence principally signifying as is the case or otherwise than is the case is true or false. Hence the need for suppositions 1 and 2.

(32) primae *CC* V*.

(33) Aristotle, *Metaphysics* 7, 17, 1041 b 12-20.

(34) dicenda *V**.

(35) vel... partes/ Consimili ratione omnino probatur quod haec (omnis *C**. haec *om.* *C*) propositio non est suae partes *CC*V*.

(36) Intellegendum est quod nulla propositio vera est falsa pro eodem significato, quia pro diversis significatis potest bene esse vera pro uno et *add* *C**.

(37) non *C**. solum *om.* *C*.

significat[38] est vera vel falsa[39]. Haec patet. Nam si propositio in voce vel in scripto foret vera vel falsa propter hoc quod aliquis[40] concipit per eam sic esse, vel taliter vel aliter, tunc purus latinus sciret plures propositiones graecas[41] quam perfectissimus graecus. Quod probatur sic : Capitur purus latinus[42] qui per omne scriptum quod videat et per omne[43] prolatum quod audiat[44] concipiat solum quod deus est. Capiatur alius perfectissimus graecus qui concipit[45] taliter esse per propositiones qualiter ex impositione vel impositionibus significant[46]. Et pono quod ille latinus audiat et videat omnes propositiones graecas quas videt et audit ille graecus. Tunc ille latinus scit omnes propositiones illas[47] esse veras eo quod per[48] omnes propositiones[49] concipit sicut est. Sed iste graecus non[50], eo quod per aliquas concipit sicut est et per aliquas aliter quam est[51].

(25) Ultimo ex istis sequuntur tres conclusiones quarum prima est haec : Aliqua propositio falsa significat principaliter[52] sicut est[53]. Haec probatur sic : Aliqua est propositio significans principaliter[54] sicut est quae falsificat se ; et omnis propositio falsificans se est falsa ; igitur, aliqua propositio falsa significat principaliter[55] sicut est. Major patet per praedicta in secunda[56] divisione hujus particulae[57]. Et minor patet per secundam suppositionem. Ex quibus sequitur conclusio probata.

(38) non *add.* *C.*

(39) This rules out truth or falsehood based on signification of the type discussed in par. 12.

(40) est... aliquis/ non dicitur esse vera vel falsa propter hoc quod aliquis *C* in marg.*

(41) veras *add.* *C*.*

(42) sciret... latinus *om.* *C.*

(43) scriptum *add.* *C*.*

(44) studeat *V*.* ' Audiat ' is preferred ; see later in the paragraph.

(45) quod... concipit *om.* *V.* qui concipit *om.* *V*.* Capiatur... concipit/ Causatur etiam graecus qui concipit *C.*

(46) primarie *add.* *C.* taliter... significant/ aliter esse propositiones vel ex impositione vel impositionibus *V*.*

(47) scit... illas/ omnes istas propositiones *C*.*

(48) per *om.* *C.*

(49) solum *CC*.*

(50) non *om.* *C.*

(51) Sed... est/ Sed graecus concipit per alias sicut est et per alias aliter quam est. Et sic sit pauciores fore veras *C*,* per aliquas non sed aliter quam est ; igitur, et cetera *V*.*

(52) principaliter *om.* *C.*

(53) et praecise hoc *add.* *V.*

(54) principaliter *om.* *C**

(55) principaliter *om.* *CC*.*

(56) quarta *V*.*

(57) Swyneshed never explicitly says this in the discussion of the second division. See pars. 4-8.

(26) Secunda conclusio : In[58] aliqua consequentia bona formali ex vero sequitur falsum. Haec probatur sic[59] : In aliqua consequentia bona et formali ex vero sequitur propositio falsificans se ; et quaelibet talis (*C*62v) est falsa, ut patet per secundam[60] suppositionem ; igitur, et cetera. Antecedens probatur : Haec consequentia est bona et[61] formalis « Consequens illius consequentiae est falsum ; igitur, consequens est falsum »[62]. Et illius consequentiae antecedens est verum et consequens falsum. Quod probatur sic : Et ponatur quod tantum illa consequentia sit et nulla alia et quod antecedens[63] illius principaliter[64] significet quod consequens illius consequentiae sit falsum, ipsa eadem demonstrata per ly ' illius ', et quod[65] consequens principaliter[66] significet quod consequens sit falsum. Hoc posito, illud consequens falsificat se, quod patet. Nam consequens est pertinens ad inferendum se ipsam fore falsam ; igitur, falsificat se. Consequentia patet per primam suppositionem. Et antecendens probatur sic : Ex consequente[67] cum totaliter sic esse sicut est[68] sequitur illud consequens fore falsum ; igitur, consequens est pertinens[69]. Et consequentia patet per dicta in divisione secunda. Antecedens probatur. Nam sequitur « Consequens est falsum ; et tantum[70] illud consequens est[71] ; igitur, illud consequens est falsum ». Et quod antecedens[72] sit verum probatur. Nam antecedens principaliter[73] significat sicut est ; et non falsificat se ; igitur, antecedens[74] est verum. Consequentia illa est bona[75]. Et major et minor patent intuenti.

(27) Ultima conclusio, quod duo contradictoria sibi mutuo contradicentia sunt simul falsa. Haec probatur sic : Aliqua sunt contradictoria

(58) Ex *V**.
(59) In... sic *om. V*.
(60) tertiam *C**, istam *V*.
(61) bona et *om. C**.
(62) Antecedens... falsum *om. V*.
(63) consequens *C*.
(64) principaliter *om. C**.
(65) per consequens *C*.
(66) principaliter *om. C**.
(67) antecedente *CC**.
(68) et ex isto sic esse sine (sive ?) ex consequente omnino *add. C*. et ex sic esse sine illo consequente non *add. V*.
(69) impertinens *C**.
(70) totum *C**.
(71) This is the « totaliter sic esse sicut est ». It follows from the assumption « quod tantum illa consequentia sit et nulla alia » earlier in the paragraph. See above, n. 35 to par. 3.
(72) I.e., the antecedent of the consequence « Consequens illius consequentiae est falsum ; igitur, consequens est falsum ».
(73) principaliter *om. C*.
(74) principaliter significat sicut est et non *add. sed vacat V**.
(75) bona *om. V**.

quorum unum principaliter significat aliter quam est et (*V**7vb) aliud falsificat se ; igitur, aliqua duo contradictoria sibi invicem contradicentia sunt simul falsa. Consequentia patet per suppositionem secundam et definitionam tertiam[76]. (*C**79r) Assumptum probatur sic : Et capio illa duo contradictoria ' Hoc est falsum ' et ' Hoc non est falsum ', et volo quod per utrumque pronomen demonstretur illa ' Hoc est falsum ' , videlicet, primam[77], et quod illa ' Hoc est falsum ' principaliter significet quod hoc est falsum, et quod illa ' Hoc non est falsum '[78] principaliter significet quod hoc non est falsum. Tunc primum illorum est falsum quia (*C*63r) falsificat se. Nam sequitur « Hoc est falsum ; igitur, hoc est falsum ». Et secundum illorum est falsum eo quod significat aliter quam est, quia significat quod prima propositio non est[79] falsum ; et hoc est falsum ; igitur, secunda est falsa[80].

(28) (*V*155vb) Contra illas propositiones arguitur multipliciter. Primo sic[81] : Una illarum propositionum ponit aliquam propositionem fore nec veram nec falsam[82], quod est contra Aristotelem in *Praedicamentis*[83] ubi dicit in uno loco[84] sic : « Videtur autem omnis affirmatio[85] vera vel falsa ». Ex qua sequitur quod omnis affirmativa est vera vel falsa. Et si hoc est verum de istis affirmativis, eadem ratione erit verum de negativis.

(29) Item, in eodem libro alibi dicit sic[86] : « In eo quod res est vel non est oratio dicitur vera vel falsa ». Sed quaecumque propositio detur, ita est ex parte rei sicut illa[87] significat vel non est ita. Igitur, quaecumque propositio detur, ista erit vera vel falsa[88].

(30) Solutio : Ubi Aristoteles ponit illam auctoritatem, « Videtur autem », et cetera, intendit ponere differentiam inter propositiones et incomplexa[89] ex quibus componuntur propositiones. Differentia igitur sua est quod omne verum vel falsum est propositio affirmativa vel negativa. Et sequitur quod nullum incomplexum est verum vel falsum[90]. Et sic salvatur prima auctoritas.

(76) secundam *C**. definitionem tertiam/ divisionem tertiam *V**
(77) falsam *V**.
(78) falsum *om. C*.
(79) significat *V**. (Emendation seems required by the sense of the argument.)
(80) quia... falsa *om. CC*V*.
(81) contra primam divisionem *C**. et primo totaliter *add. C*.
(82) See the first division, par. 2.
(83) Aristotle, *Categories* 4, 2 a 6-7.
(84) uno loco/ ultimo *V*.
(85) propositio *V**. (The reading in *CC*V* is perhaps preferable in virtue of the remainder of the paragraph.)
(86) Aristotle, *Categories* 5, 4 b 8-10.
(87) naturaliter *V**.
(88) igitur, prima divisio non est bona *add. C**.
(89) inter complexa *V**.
(90) igitur, nullum incomplexum est propositio affirmativa vel negativa *add. C**.

(31) Pro secunda est dicendum quod illa est intentio Aristotelis, quod in eo quod ita est ex parte rei sicut propositio principaliter significat et non falsificat[91] se est propositio vera, et in eo quod aliter est ex parte rei quam propositio[92] significat est falsa.

(32) Pro quo est sciendum quod omnis propositio significans principaliter[93] sicut est vel aliter quam est sive sit de praesenti sive de praeterito sive de futuro, sive de necessario sive de[94] contingenti, cujus veritas dependet a praesenti est vera vel falsa et nulla alia. Ex quo patet quod multae sunt propositiones quae nec sunt verae nec falsae cujusmodi sunt illae ' Haec significat aliter quam est ', eadem demonstrata sic principaliter significante, (*C*63v) ' Tu eris mortuus cras '[95], et universaliter omnes propositiones de futuro contingenti quarum veritas non dependet a praesenti[96].

(33) Contra aliam partem positionis[97] arguitur sic : Illa ponit aliquam propositionem fore falsam[98] quae principaliter significat sicut est ; igitur, eadem ratione habet ponere quod aliqua est vera quae principaliter significat aliter quam est ; et hoc negat illa positio[99] ; igitur, (*V**8ra) male.

(34) Ad idem, illa positio affirmat omnem propositionem falsificantem se fore falsam[1] ; igitur, a simili ratione habet ponere omnem propositionem verificantem se fore veram, quod negat illa positio[2].

(35) Ad primum dicendum quod consequentia non valet. Sed antecedens est verum. Et pro tanto : Si ex aliquibus propositionibus quarum quaelibet significat principaliter sicut est sequitur aliqua propositio, ipsa significat[3] sicut est, sed si ex aliquibus propositionibus quarum una significat[4] aliter quam est et omnes aliae[5] sicut est sequatur aliqua propositio, non sequitur quod illa significat sicut est[6]. Cum igitur propo-

(91) significat *V**.

(92) principaliter *add. C**.

(93) principaliter *om. C*.

(94) sive de necessario... de/ necessario vel de futuro (de futuro *om. C**) *CC*V*.

(95) Tu... cras/ ' Vos moriemini cras ' et ' Vos non moriemini cras ' *C*, ' Tu morieris cras ' et ' Tu non morieris cras ' *C*V*.

(96) Swyneshed thus accepts the « Aristotelian » principle that future contingents are neither true nor false. See the famous discussion of the « sea battle » in *De interpretatione*, ch. 9. *C* omits pars. 33-37.

(97) See the first conclusion, par. 25.

(98) falsam *om. V**.

(99) See the fourth supposition, par. 20.

(1) See the second supposition, par. 18.

(2) See the third supposition, par. 19.

(3) principaliter *add. C**.

(4) principaliter *add. C**.

(5) *Interl.* aliae *V**.

(6) Swyneshed rejects the principle that valid consequences must preserve truth (see the second conclusion, par. 26). In virtue of what he says here, however, they do preserve the property of signifying principally as is the case.

sitio ponens quod[7] propositio falsificans se significat sicut est[8] sequatur ex aliquibus propositionibus quarum quaelibet significat principaliter[9] sicut est[10], sequitur igitur quod ita erit quod propositio sequens ex illis significat[11] sicut est. Sed sic non potest deduci de propositione verificante se. Nam si capiatur propositio verificans se, et sit *a*[12]. Et arguitur sic : Illa significat sicut est ; igitur, vera. Dato quod concederetur[13], tunc arguitur ex alia parte (*C**79v)[14] : Illa significat aliter quam est ; igitur, illa est vera. Illa consequentia est mere impossibilis. Nam tunc non sequitur quod illa sit vera, licet sequatur quod illa sequitur ex una[15] significante aliter quam est et aliis praecise significantibus[16] sicut est, quia aliqua illorum significat aliter quam est. Ex quo patet quod[17] haec consequentia est bona : « Illa propositio (*V*156ra) falsificat se ; igitur, ipsa est falsa. » Sed non valet illa consequentia : « Propositio verificat se ; igitur, ipsa est vera. » Et sic solvitur tam prima objectio quam secunda[18].

(7) Cum... quod/ Igitur etsi *C**.

(8) significat... est/ significans etiam principaliter sicut est *C**, est falsa et *(interl.) V*.

(9) aliquibus... principaliter/ praemissis praecise significantibus *C**.

(10) *C** omits the remainder of the sentence.

(11) principaliter *add. V*.

(12) et... *a om. C***V*.

(13) Dato... concederetur/ concesso argumento *C**, dato quod illa concederetur. Sed *V*.

(14) arguitur... parte/ ex altera parte sic (79v) argumentabitur *C**.

(15) sequitur... una/ sit vera ex illamet *V*.

(16) et... significantibus/ et aliqua praecise significat *V**.

(17) est mere... quod/ non valet, sicut satis patet cum ex antecedente inferatur oppositum consequentis. Ideo quamvis propositio aliqua ex ipsamet significante aliter quam est verificat se, non tamen sequitur illam esse veram cum talis propositio non sequitur ex omnibus praemissis significantibus principaliter sicut est, ut patet. Igitur *C**.

(18) The argument in the paragraph is obscure. Perhaps Swyneshed means to argue thus: If a sentence '*p*' falsifies itself, then from '*p*' and perhaps some needed additional premisses, it follows that '*p*' is false. This by the notion of self-falsification. Again, from 'not-*p*' and perhaps some needed additional premisses, it follows that '*p*' is false. Otherwise the second supposition, par. 18, would fail. (Note that the additional premisses needed cannot be exactly the same in the two consequences. For then '*p*' would not be « pertinens ad inferendum se ipsam esse falsam ». See n. 37 to par. 3.) Hence, whether one starts from '*p*' or from 'not-*p*', it follows in any case that '*p*' is false. Some such sentences, although false, nevertheless signify principally as is the case. Now one might think that, by analogy, if a sentence '*p*' verifies itself, then whether one starts from '*p*' or from 'not-*p*', it follows in any case that '*p*' is true (par. 34). Again by analogy, one might think that some such sentences, although true, nevertheless signify principally otherwise than is the case (par. 33). But this is wrong. For such a sentence would be not only true but also false, by the third definition, par. 15. This would violate the sixth supposition, par. 22. Hence the argument in par. 33 fails. Par. 34 is sufficiently answered by par. 20. The following example may perhaps be helpful. Let the sentence 'This sentence is true' signify principally that it itself is *not* true. Then the sentence verifies itself, since "This sentence is true; therefore, this sentence is true" is an immediate consequence. Now one might argue further: if the

(36) Item, contra duas ultimas[19] conclusiones sic obicitur. Et primo contra primam per Aristotelem in primo *Priorum*[20] ubi utitur talibus regulis « Consequens est falsum ; igitur, et antecedens », et « Antecedens est verum ; igitur, et consequens ». Et per consequens non potest poni aliqua consequentia bona et[21] formalis cujus antecedens verum sit et consequens falsum, cujus oppositum ponit secunda conclusio.

(37) Pro illo est dicendum quod intentio Aristotelis per primam regulam est illa : Si consequens non significet sicut est et nec antecedens nec consequens sit pertinens ad inferendum se ipsum non significare sicut est, igitur antecedens[22] non significat sicut est. Secunda regula sic intellegitur : Si antecedens significat sicut est et nec antecedens nec consequens est pertinens ad inferendum se ipsum non significare sicut est[23], igitur consequens significat sicut est.

(38) Contra ultimam conclusionem sic arguitur per Aristotelem in primo *Periermeneias*[24] et in primo *Posteriorum*[25] et in multis aliis locis. Videtur quod Aristoteles innuat quod duo contradictoria non possunt simul esse falsa[26] ; et illa hoc ponit ; igitur, ipsa est falsa.

(39) Solutio : Conclusio est vera, sicut declaratum est. Sed intellectus Aristotelis ibidem est ille quod nulla sunt[27] duo contradictoria sibi invicem contradicentia quorum utrumque[28] significet sicut est (*V**8rb) vel quorum utrumque principaliter significet aliter quam est[29]. Et illo modo loquitur

sentence is not true, then since it principally signifies just that, it follows once again that it is true. Hence, in either case, it follows that the sentence is true. And yet it principally signifies otherwise than is the case. To this argument Swyneshed would deny the second consequence. If the sentence is not true and principally signifies just that, it does not follow that it is true, because the sentence falsifies itself. For the following is valid: "This sentence is true; therefore, it signifies principally as is the case; and it signifies principally that it is not true; therefore, it is not true ; and it principally signifies as is the case or otherwise than is the case (from step 2); therefore, it is false."

(19) duas *add V**.

(20) Aristotle, *Prior Analytics* II, 4, 57 a 36-37, and II, 2, 53 b 7-8.

(21) bona et *om. V*.

(22) antecedens *add. V**.

(23) non... est/ significare sicut non est *C**.

(24) in... *Periermeneias om. CC***V*. See Aristotle, *De interpretatione* 7, 17 b 26-28, and 9, 18 a 28-33.

(25) *Priorum CV*. See perhaps Aristotle, *Posterior Analytics* I, 11, 77 a 22-24 : « Et iterum propositione dicente quod de omni re verificatur una duarum partium contradictionis utitur demonstratio perducens ad inpossibile » (translatio Gerardi, in *Aristoteles Latinus*, L. Minio-Paluello, ed., IV, 3, [Bruges, Desclée de Brouwer, 1968]) ; and also perhaps Aristotle, *Prior Analytics* I, 46, *passim*.

(26) vera vel falsa *C*. duo... falsa/ nulla duo contradictoria sibi invicem contradicentia sunt simul vera vel falsa *C**.

(27) sunt *om. CC***V*.

(28) principaliter *add. CC***V*.

(29) sunt simul vera vel falsa *add. CC**. possunt esse simul falsa *add. V*.

Aristoteles continue dicendo id fore verum quod significat[30] sicut est[31] et illud fore falsum quod significat[32] aliter quam est — nisi in materia insolubilium ubi intellegit per ' falsum '[33] non[34] tale quod significat aliter quam est sed tale quod est destruens se, id est, falsificans, sicut per eum patet quarto *Metaphysicae*[35], ubi dicit textus sic « Accidit autem omnibus talibus destruere se ipsas », sicut est de tali oratione ' Omnia sunt falsa ', ubi intellegit Aristoteles quod talis oratio quae est pertinens ad inferendum se ipsam fore falsam destruat se, hoc est, falsificat, et quaelibet talis est falsa, ut declaratum est.

II

(40) His igitur intellectis juxta sententiam Aristotelis, consequens est insolubilium solutionem intellegere. Et primo de insolubilibus ex vocis proprietate generatis inter insolubilia simplicia a facilioribus principium mihi summam. Sit igitur haec propositio ' Falsum est ' in scripto et nulla alia praeter illam. Et significet (*C*64r) illa principaliter quod falsum est. Deinde proponatur ' Falsum est '. Si negatur vel dubitatur, contra : Propositio vera vel falsa est ; sed nulla propositio vera est ; igitur, propositio falsa est. Et ultra : Igitur, falsum est. Major est manifesta. Et minor sequitur ex casu, quod probatur sic : Oppositum minoris repugnat casui ; igitur, minor sequitur ex casu. Assumptum probatur : Nam si oppositum minoris non repugnat casui et illa est possibilis ponatur illud oppositum minoris cum casu. Tunc sequitur[36] quod propositio vera sit. Et arguitur sic : Propositio vera est ; et nulla propositio est nisi illa ' Falsum est ' ; igitur, illa est vera. Et ultra : Igitur, ita est[37] sicut ipsa principaliter significat. Consequentia patet per definitionem secundam[38]. Sed per casum illa principaliter significat quod falsum est ; igitur, ita est quod falsum est ; et nulla propositio[39] est alia ab illa ; igitur, illa est falsa[40]. Et sic sequitur illud esse verum et falsum, quod est impossibile. Si conceditur ' Falsum est ', tunc arguitur sic : Falsum est ; (*V*156rb) et omnis propositio est illa ' Falsum est ', eadem demonstrata ; igitur, illa est falsa. Et ultra[41] : Igitur, illa principaliter aliter significat quam est ; et illa principaliter

(30) principaliter *add.* *C**.
(31) est *om.* *V**.
(32) sicut... significat *om.* *C**.
(33) Illegible in *V**.
(34) nisi *V**. per... non/ quod falsum non est solum *C**.
(35) ARISTOTLE, *Metaphysics*, 4, 8, 1012 b 13-15.
(36) Tunc sequitur/ scilicet *CC** *V*.
(37) totaliter *add.* *V*.
(38) tertiam *VV**.
(39) falsa *add.* *C*.
(40) est alia... falsa/ ab illa est falsa *C**.
(41) Igitur... ultra *om.* *C**.

significat quod falsum est; igitur, non est ita quod falsum est, cujus oppositum concedebatur.

(41) Ad idem, tu concessisti falsum scitum a te fore falsum non sequens ex casu pro tempore pro quo fuit falsum; igitur, male respondisti.

(42) Ad idem, falsum est; et illa principaliter significat quod falsum est; igitur, ita est sicut illa principaliter[42] significat. Et ultra : igitur, illa est vera.

(43) Pro illo sophismate et pro similibus negatur casus tamquam impossibilis.

(44) (*C**80r) Contra : Si[43] illa propositio 'Falsum est' foret in scripto et multae propositiones forent cum illa[44], adhuc foret possibile[45] quod aliquis videret illam (*C*64v)[46]. Ponatur igitur quod multae aliae propositiones (*V**8va) sint cum illa 'Falsum est'[47] et quod ipsa principaliter significat ex impositione quod falsum est. Et sit Sortes unus homo qui[48] per totam vitam suam fuerit instructus ad concipiendum per quamcumque propositionem quam[49] videat quod falsum est. Hoc posito, pono quod Sortes videat hanc propositionem 'Falsum est' in scripto et concipiet per illam quod falsum est sicut fuerat instructus. Tunc pono quod Sortes videat continue illam propositionem. Et corrumpatur quaelibet alia ab illa ita quod nulla sit praeter illam[50]. Quo posito, Sortes concipit per illam quod[51] falsum est; igitur[52], illa sibi[53] significat quod falsum est. Consequentia patet per septimam suppositionem. Et nulli alteri a Sorte significat aliter; igitur, solum significat quod falsum est; et sic imponebatur ultimo ad significandum; ergo, illa principaliter significat[54] quod falsum est; et tantum illa est; igitur, totus casus est possibilis.

(45) Ad idem, adhuc posito[55] quod tantum illa propositio sit, ista potest principaliter significare[56] minus ex impositione et majus[57] similiter; ergo, ex impositione sic principaliter potest significare[58].

(42) principaliter *om. C**.
(43) tantum *add CC*V*.
(44) Falsum... illa/ foret in scripto et nulla alia propositio foret *CC*V*.
(45) possibile *om. C**.
(46) et si multae (*C*64v) propositiones forent (cum illa *add. CC**) *add. CC*V*.
(47) Ponatur... est *om. V*.
(48) continue *add. CV*.
(49) quam *om. V**.
(50) praeter illam/ ab illa *V**.
(51) quod *om. V**.
(52) pono... igitur *om. V*.
(53) praecise *add. V*.
(54) ergo... significat *om. C**.
(55) adhuc posito/ contra hoc *V**.
(56) illa... significare/ ista significat *V**.
(57) magis *V**.
(58) ergo... significare/ igitur, quod ex impositione significet principaliter sicut potest significare *V**. I.e., if only the sentence 'Falsum est' exists, there is no difficulty

(46) Ad idem, talis propositio ' Deus est ' potest significare principaliter quod deus est cum hoc quod tantum illa sit. Et talis propositio ' Homo est asinus ' potest principaliter significare quod homo est asinus cum hoc quod tantum illa sit. Et nulla potest causa assignari quare una potest significare principaliter cum hoc quod tantum illa sit quin[59] eadem causa vel consimili possit illa ' Falsum est ' principaliter significare quod falsum est[60] cum hoc quod[61] tantum illa est. Cum igitur, talis casus sit possibilis, quod illa ' Deus est ' principaliter significet[62] quod deus est[63] cum hoc quod tantum illa sit, sequitur quod ille casus est possibilis, quod ista propositio ' Falsum est ' (*C*65r) principaliter[64] significet quod falsum est cum hoc quod tantum illa sit.

(47) Sed hic fingitur una causa. Dicitur enim, licet talis propositio ' Deus est ' foret et nulla alia et illa principaliter significet quod deus est, ex hoc tamen non sequitur aliquod impossibile. Sed si tantum illa propositio ' Falsum est ' foret et principaliter significaret quod falsum est[65], sequitur aliquod impossibile[66]. Sed, ut posterius apparebit, illa causa nulla est nisi fatuorum protervientium qui ad insolubile aliter nesciunt respondere nisi possibile fore impossibile sustinere.

(48) Admittendus est igitur casus. Et quando[67] proponitur ' Falsum est ', concedenda est. Et concedendum est quod illa est falsa. Et negatur consequentia[68] « Igitur, illa principaliter significat aliter quam est »[69]. Sed oportet addere antecedenti quod illa non falsificat se[70]. Et hoc est falsum. Nam sequitur « Falsum est ; et omnis propositio est illa ' Falsum est ' ; igitur, illa est falsa ». Et sic illa est pertinens ad inferendum se

in its signifying "less" than that a falsehood exists, nor with its signifying "more" than that a falsehood exists. Hence, there ought to be no difficulty with its signifying exactly that a falsehood exists. It is not altogether clear what it means here to signify "more" or "less" than that a falsehood exists. Perhaps a sentence signifies "less" than that *p* if it signifies principally that *q*, where "If *q* then *p*" is not valid but "If *p* then *q*" is valid, and perhaps it signifies "more" than that *p* if it signifies principally that *q*, where "If *q* then *p*" is valid but "If *p* then *q*" is not valid.

(59) Et... quin/ quare ergo non *V*.

(60) est *om.* *V**.

(61) quod *om.* *V**.

(62) principaliter significet/ principaliter primarie significet *C*, significando primarie *C**, praecise significet *V*.

(63) est *om.* *V**.

(64) primarie *C**.

(65) quod falsum est *om.* *V**.

(66) Sed... impossibile *om.* *C**.

(67) quando *om.* *V**.

(68) illa quod consequentia haec est falsa *C**. ista est falsa *add.* *C*.

(69) See par. 40.

(70) falsificat se/ se solum falsificaret *V*.

ipsam fore falsum. Et ultra : Igitur, illa est falsa[71]. Consequentia patet per secundam suppositionem[72].

(49) Ad secundam formam[73] negatur consequentia et antecedens similiter. Consequentia enim ibi facta non valet eo quod bene respondendo (*V**8vb) in casu aliquo posito esset concedendum falsum scitum a me esse falsum et impossibile scitum a me fore impossibile, ut si poneretur quod haec propositio ' Deus est ' et quaelibet talis significet praecise[74] quod homo est asinus, et hoc bene scias. Adhuc illa foret concedenda ' Deus est ', tamen illa est falsa et impossibilis. Et antecedens similiter est negandum. Nam quod falsum est (*V*156va) sequitur ex casu. Nam cum casu non stat quod illa sit vera ; et[75] ex casu sequitur quod illa sit[76] propositio de praesenti (*C*65v) significans sicut est vel aliter quam est[77] ; igitur, ex casu sequitur quod illa sit falsa.

(50) Ad ultimam formam[78] concedenda est prima consequentia, scilicet, « Falsum est ; et illa[79] principaliter significat quod falsum est ; igitur, ita est sicut principaliter significat »[80]. Et negatur consequentia alia, scilicet, « igitur[81], illa est vera », eo quod aliqua propositio falsificans se[82] significat principaliter[83] sicut est. Consequentia patet per conclusionem primam, ut est de propositione falsificante se, ut declaratum est prius.

(51) Contra illam responsionem arguitur per Aristotelem secundo *Elenchorum*[84], capitulo de fallacia secundum quid et simpliciter[85]. Et

(71) Et sic... falsa *om. V.*
(72) divisionem (*corrected from* suppositionem) *V.*
(73) See par. 41.
(74) primarie *C.*
(75) sit... et/ significet nec *V.*
(76) quod... sit/ illa *C*.*
(77) vel... est *om. V*.*
(78) See par. 42.
(79) sic *add. V.*
(80) ita... significat/ ita est quod falsum est *C*, illa est vera *C**, quod... significat *om. V.*
(81) alia... igitur/ quia includitur quod *C*.*
(82) falsificans se/ falsa *CV.* falsificans se *om. C*.*
(83) principaliter *om. CC*.*
(84) ARISTOTLE, *Sophistic Refutations* 25, 180 b 1-7. The Vulgate text, PL 64, 1034C, is: "Similis autem ratio est et de eo quod est mentiri eumdem simul et verum dicere, sed propter id quod non est facile inspicere utrum quis assignet simpliciter veracem esse, vel mendacem difficile apparet. Prohibet autem eumdem nihil simpliciter quidem esse mendacem, qua autem veracem, vel alicujus esse veracem aliquem, veracem autem non." On this vulgate text, see L. MINIO-PALUELLO, "Note sull'Aristotele latino-medievale," V, *Rivista di filosofia neo-scolastica* 44 (1952), pp. 389-411 at p. 398. On the connection of this passage with the *insolubilia*-literature, see my "The Origins of the Mediaeval *Insolubilia*-Literature," *Franciscan Studies* 33 (1973), pp. 292-309.
(85) de... simpliciter/ de solutione paralogismorum, oportet, inquit *C*,*

ibi solvuntur insolubilia per illam formam[86] ; sed illa solutio non facit ; igitur, peccat contra solutionem Aristotelis ; igitur, non valet.

(52) Pro illo est admittendum quod[87] talis consequentia « Haec propositio significat principaliter sicut est ; igitur, haec propositio est vera » est fallacia secundum quid et simpliciter eo quod antecedens formaliter falsificat se[88]. Nam ad hoc quod aliqua propositio sit vera requiritur quod significet[89] sicut est et non falsificat se cum hoc ; sed antecedens solum ponit consequens[90] secundum unam partem sui significati[91] et secundum aliam non ; ideo arguere a tali antecedente ad tale consequens est fallacia secundum quid et simpliciter, ut si arguitur sic « Ille est albus secundum dentes ; igitur, ille est albus ».

(53) Et quod illa sit intentio Aristotelis[92] manifeste patet per eum idem[93] ubi solvit talem passum[94] fundatum super tali casu cum ponit[95] quod aliquis solum[96] juret se fore pejeratum. Tunc textus est talis : « Nam qui jurat se esse pejeratum bene jurat pejerans hoc solum quod tunc bene jurat[97]. » Ex quo textu patet quod illa propositio qua talis jurat est falsa. (*C*66r) Nam si illa propositio foret vera, et solum juraret illam, tunc solum juraret veram. Et per consequens, non foret perjurus[98]. Illis[99] igitur Aristoteles concedit[1] quod ille est perjurus[2] in hoc quod dicit in textu « bene jurat » eo quod juret propositionem significantem sicut est. Sed[3] per hoc quod in fine textus apponit illam negativam « non

(86) fallaciam secundum quid et simpliciter *CC**.
(87) si *add.* *V**. Pro... quod/ Dico quod si flat *CC**.
(88) formaliter... se/ consequens significat duo *CV*, consequens significat duo, id est, includit *C**. (The text of *C** ends here.)
(89) principaliter *add.* *CV*.
(90) ponit consequens/ ponit concedi *V*, falsificat se *V**.
(91) significati *om.* *V**.
(92) ubi aliter (?) *add.* *V*.
(93) ideo *V**.
(94) talem passum/ paralogismum *V*.
(95) talem... ponit/ secundum locum fundamenti talem casum ponens *C*.
(96) solum *om.* *CV*. The usual interpretation of this passage in Aristotle agrees with the text of *CV*; the oath-taker takes more than one oath. See my "The Origins of the Mediaeval *Insolubilia*-Literature".
(97) jurat... jurat/ jurans hoc solum dum autem pejerat *C*, jurat modo illo *V*. *Add. in marg.* Alter textus sic dicit, scilicet, ideo ubi solvit per longum passum cum super textu ponitur quod aliquis solum juret, et cetera *V**. See ARISTOTLE, *Sophistic Refutations* 25, 180 a 39-b 1. Vulgate text, PL 64, 1034C: « Nam qui jurat se pejeraturum, bene jurat perjurans hoc solum, at non bene jurat ». The last clause, « at non bene jurat », seems preferable to the text in *V**, in virtue of the remark about 'non jurat' later in par. 53.
(98) perjurius (?) *V**.
(99) perhaps deleted in *V**. Vult *V*.
(1) dicere *V*.
(2) Illis... perjurus *om.* *C*.
(3) vel *V**.

jurat » intellegitur[4] quod non jurat propositionem veram ita quod ibi est fallacia secundum quid et simpliciter « Ille jurat propositionem significantem sicut est principaliter[5] ; igitur, ille jurat veram »[6]. Illud patet per textum paulo post sequentem qui dicit « Prohibet autem eundem non simpliciter esse mendacem quoad idem »[7], ubi intendit solvere passum[8] fun- (*V**9ra) datum super tali casu : Ponatur quod Sortes sic dicat ' Sortes est mendax '. Ex quo textu sequitur quod non est inconveniens eundem simul esse mendacem et dicere propositionem significantem principaliter[9] sicut est. Ex quo patet quod non sequitur « Dico propositionem significantem sicut est ; ergo, dico verum »[10]. Sed est fallacia secundum quid et simpliciter ut prius est declaratum.

(54) Aliud sophisma : Ponatur quod illa propositio sit et nulla alia sit ' Nullum verum est ' quae principaliter significat quod nullum verum est. Deinde proponatur quod nullum verum est. Si negatur vel dubitatur, contra : Nulla propositio quae non est illa est vera ; nec illa est vera ; igitur, nullum verum est. Major patet per casum et minor est sequens ex casu. Quod probatur sic : Oppositum minoris est repugnans casui ; ergo, minor sequitur ex casu. Assumptum sic probatur : Nam si non repugnat casui, cum illa sit possibilis, ponatur quod ita sit sicut illa significat[11] cum casu. Et arguitur sic : Haec est vera ' Nullum verum est ' ; (*C*66v) igitur, ita est sicut illa[12] principaliter significat. Consequentia patet per definitionem secundam. Et illa principaliter significat quod nullum verum est ; ergo, ita est quod nullum verum est. (*V*156vb) Ex quo sequitur quod illa non est vera[13]. Si conceditur quod nullum verum est, tunc sic : Nullum verum est ; et illa sic principaliter significat ; ergo, ita est quod nullum verum est. Ex quo sequitur quod sicut illa ita principaliter significat, est verum. Et ultra[14] : igitur, illa est vera. Et ultra : igitur, aliquid est verum. Quod est oppositum praeconcessi.

(55) Solutio : Concedendum est quod nullum verum est. Et concedendum est quod ita est sicut illa principaliter significat. Et neganda est

(4) negativam.... intellegitur/ negationem ' non ', vult intellegere *CV*.
(5) principaliter *om. C.*
(6) veram *om. C.*
(7) non... idem/ et simpliciter ad menda — *(abbreviation uncertain)* est, et cetera *C*, simul simpliciter nihil esse mendacem, quid autem verum *V*. Aristotle, *Sophistic Refutations* 25, 180 b 5-7. For the Latin, see n. 84 above, to par. 51.
(8) paralogismum *CV*.
(9) principaliter *om. C.*
(10) Ex... verum/ igitur, antecedens est verum *C.*
(11) quod... significat *om. C.*
(12) conclusio *C.*
(13) bona *C.*
(14) ergo... ultra *om. C.* quod nullum... ultra/ sicut illa principaliter significat. Et ultra *V*.

consequentia « igitur, illa est vera » quia illa falsificat se quia est pertinens ad inferendum se ipsam fore falsam. Nam sequitur « Nullum verum est ; et illa propositio principaliter[15] significat sicut est vel aliter quam est ; igitur, illa est falsa. »

(56) Aliud sophisma : Ponatur quod tantum[16] sint duae propositiones, sicut *a* et *b*. Et sit *a* una propositio vera[17]. Et sit *b* illa ' Omne verum est *a*[18]. Deinde proponitur illa ' Omne verum est *a* '[19]. Si negatur vel dubitatur, contra : *a* est verum ; et nulla alia propositio ab *a* est vera ; igitur, omne verum est *a*. Major patet per casum. Et minor est sequens. Quod probatur sic : Oppositum minoris[20] est propositio possibilis ; et si illa ponatur cum casu accidit oppositum casus ; ergo, minor sequitur ex casu. Et assumptum sic probatur. Et ponatur oppositum minoris cum casu et arguitur : Aliqua est propositio vera alia ab *a* ; et nulla est alia propositio ab *a* nisi *b* ; igitur, *b* est verum ; et *b* principaliter significat quod omne verum est *a* ; igitur, ita est ; et nullum *b* est *a*, nec *a* est *b* ; igitur, *b* non est verum (*C*67r)[21], quod est oppositum unius particulae casus. Si concedatur ' Omne verum est *a* ', contra : Si omne verum sit *a*, et *b* non est *a*, et *b* est, igitur, *b* non est verum. Consequentia illa (*V**9rb) patet. Et major est concessa[22]. Et minor[23] est possibilis[24]. Igitur, conclusio est concedenda. Et tunc sic : *b* non est verum ; et *b* est propositio de praesenti principaliter[25] significans sicut est vel aliter quam est ; igitur, *b* est falsum. Et ultra : igitur, non est ita sicut *b* significat. Et *b* significat quod omne verum est *a* ; ergo, non est ita quod omne verum est *a*, cujus oppositum supra ponebatur[26].

(57) Solutio : Concedenda est hoc ' Omne[27] verum est *a* '[28]. Et concedo quod *b* est falsum. Et neganda est consequentia « igitur, *b* significat aliter quam est ». Sed[29] oportet addere antecedenti quod *b* non falsificat se. Et *b* se falsificat, ut satis patet.

(15) principaliter *om. CV.*
(16) tantum *om. C.*
(17) Et... vera/ quarum *a* est ista ' Deus est ' *C.*
(18) *Add.* et significet principaliter sicut termini communiter praetendunt *C. Add.* quae principaliter significet quod omne verum est *a V.*
(19) verum *V*.*
(20) oppositum minoris/ Minor *V*.*
(21) et per consequens nulla alia propositio ab *a* (*C*67r) est vera *add. CV.*
(22) major... concessa/ minor est concedenda *C.*
(23) major *C.*
(24) posita *CV.*
(25) principaliter *om. C.*
(26) concedebatur *CV.*
(27) Esse *V*.*
(28) *a om. C.*
(29) licet *V*.*

(58) Simile est si ponatur quod tantum[30] illae tres propositiones sint ' Deus est ' quae sit vera, ' Homo ' est[31] quae sit vera, et ' Quaelibet propositio universalis est dissimilis istis ' quae principaliter significet quod quaelibet propositio universalis est dissimilis istis[32]. Et pono quod per ly ' istis ' solum demonstrentur primae duae[33]. Deinde proponatur ' Quaelibet propositio universalis est dissimilis istis '. Si negatur vel dubitatur, contra : Illa est dissimilis istis ; et illa est quaelibet propositio universalis ; igitur, et cetera[34]. Minor patet de se. Majorem probo. Nam illa est falsa, demonstrata illa universali ; igitur, illa est dissimilis istis[35], demonstratis illis veris. Consequentia patet ex modo loquendi[36]. Assumptum probatur sic : Illa falsificat se ; ergo, (*C*67r) illa est falsa. Consequentia patet per secundam suppositionem. Et antecedens probatur. Nam sequitur : « Illa est dissimilis istis ; et illae sunt verae ; igitur, illa est falsa. » Si conceditur, tunc sic : Quaelibet propositio universalis est dissimilis istis ; et illa principaliter sic significat ; igitur, illa significat principaliter sicut est. Et ultra : igitur, illa est vera ; et illae sunt verae ; ergo, illa est similis istis. Et ultra : igitur, illa non est dissimilis istis[37], cujus contrarium concedebatur.

(59) Solutio : Concedenda est illa ' Quaelibet propositio universalis (*V*157ra) est dissimilis istis '. Et concedendum est quod illa sic[38] principaliter significat[39]. Et neganda est consequentia « ergo, illa est vera » ex eo quod illa significat se esse falsam[40], ut patet intuenti.

(60) De copulativis sit hoc exemplum : Ponatur quod illa copulativa ' Deus est et illa copulativa est falsa ' sit omnis copulativa, quae[41] principaliter significat quod deus est et quod copulativa illa est falsa[42], et quod prima pars significet quod deus est et secunda quod illa copulativa est falsa. Et ponatur quod per quodlibet tale demonstrativum ' illa ' demons-

(30) quod tantum/ tantum quod *V**.

(31) animal *add. C.*

(32) "Dissimilis istis" here means "unlike them in truth-value".

(33) quae... duae/ demonstrando per ly ' istis ' duas primas propositiones. Et significet sicut termini communiter praetendunt *C.*

(34) et cetera/ quaelibet propositio universalis est dissimilis istis, demonstrando per ly ' istam ' *(sic)* istam universalem ' Quaelibet propositio universalis est dissimilis istis ' *C.* illa est dissimilis istis *add. sed vacat V**.

(35) Si... istis *om. V.*

(36) sequendi *V.*

(37) et illa est quaelibet propositio universalis ; ergo, nulla propositio universalis est dissimilis istis *add. CV.*

(38) sic *om. C.*

(39) sicut est (sicut est *om. V*), et quod illa principaliter significat sicut est *add. CV.*

(40) illa... falsam/ falsificat se *CV.*

(41) sit... quae *om. V.*

(42) sit... falsa *om. C.*

tretur tota illa copulativa. Deinde proponitur illa. Si conceditur, tunc sic : Deus est et illa copulativa est falsa[43]. Et ultra : igitur, illa copulativa significat aliter quam est, sicut prius. Et ultra : igitur, illa est neganda[44] ' Deus est et illa copulativa est falsa '. Si negatur vel dubitatur, contra : Illa copulativa falsificat se ; ergo, illa copulativa est falsa. Antecedens patet. Nam sequitur[45] : « Deus est et illa (*V**9va) copulativa est falsa ; igitur, illa copulativa est falsa. »

(61) Solutio : Concedenda est illa copulativa. Et concedendum est (*C*68)[46] quod illa est falsa. Et neganda est consequentia « ergo, significat aliter quam est » eo quod significat sic[47] sicut prius.

(62) De disjunctivis sit hoc exemplum : Ponatur quod haec disjunctiva ' Homo est asinus[48] vel nulla disjunctiva est vera '[49] sic principaliter significet et quod prima pars principaliter significet quod homo sit asinus[50] et secunda quod nulla disjunctiva sit vera. Et non sit disjunctiva alia ab hac. Tunc dicendum est quod illa disjunctiva est falsa eo quod falsificat se. Si tamen ponatur[51] illa[52], concedendum est eo quod significat sicut est. Tunc neganda est consequentia « igitur, illa est vera », ut prius.

(63) De exclusivis sit hoc exemplum : Sit *a* illa propositio ' Deus est ' quae sit vera. Sit *b* illa exclusiva ' Tantum *a* est verum '. Et non sit propositio alia ab altera illarum. Et significet *b* principaliter[53] quod tantum *a* est verum. Hoc posito, *b* est concedendum, scilicet, illa propositio ' Tantum *a* est verum ', eo quod ita est sicut illa principaliter significat. Et tamen et dicendum est quod illa est falsa eo quod falsificat se, sicut patet consideranti.

(64) Ultimo de exceptivis sit hoc exemplum : Sit *a* illa propositio ' Nulla propositio praeter *a* est falsa '. Et non sit aliqua alia propositio ab *a*. Et sit tantum unum *a*. Et significat illa principaliter quod nulla propositio praeter *a* est falsa. Hoc posito, concedendum est *a*, scilicet, quod nulla propositio praeter *a* est falsa[54]. Et dicendum est quod *a* est falsum eo quod *a* falsificat se, ut prius[55].

(43) igitur, ista copulativa est falsa *add. CV.*
(44) illa... neganda/ non est ita quod *C.*
(45) immediate *add. CV.*
(46) On the folio numbers in *C*, see above, n. 12 to the introduction.
(47) significat sic/ falsificat se *CV.*
(48) animal *V.*
(49) quae *add V*.*
(50) animal *V.*
(51) proponatur *V.*
(52) est vera ut prius *add. sed vacat V*.*
(53) principaliter *om. V.*
(54) Hoc... falsa *om. C.*
(55) Et haec de insolubilibus ex vocis proprietate generatis sufficiant *add. CV.*

III

(65) Post haec autem consequens est solvere insolubilia ex actibus nostris nascentia. Pro quo est sciendum quod actus (*C*69) nostri ad propositum sunt duplices : quidam ex quibus sine proprietate vocis nata (*V*157rb) sunt insolubilia provenire, et alii sunt ex quibus sine proprietate vocis numquam sunt insolubilia nata provenire. Actus primi sunt sicut jurare, pejerare[56], et similia. Actus secundi sicut videre, audire, dicere[57], et similia. De quibus in particula proxima dicetur.

(66) Sit ergo hoc sophisma ' Sortes decipitur '. Ponatur quod tantum sit unus Sortes qui credit illam ' Sortes decipitur '[58] et decipiatur solum talis qui credit falsum. Deinde proponatur ' Sortes decipitur '. Si negatur vel dubitatur, contra : Oppositum ejus repugnat casui ; ergo, ipsa sequitur ex casu. Antecedens probatur. Nam si illa ponatur cum casu, ex illa sequitur suum contradictorium ; igitur, illa repugnat (*V**9vb) casui. Assumptum probatur : Ponatur illa cum casu ' Sortes non decipitur '. Et arguitur sic : Sortes non decipitur ; et omnis talis decipitur qui credit falsum ; ergo, Sortes non credit falsum. Et tunc sic : Sortes non credit falsum ; et Sortes[59] credit propositionem significantem sicut est vel aliter quam est ; igitur, Sortes credit verum ; et solum credit illam ' Sortes decipitur ' ; ergo, illa est vera ' Sortes decipitur '. Et illa principaliter significat quod Sortes decipitur ; igitur, Sortes decipitur, quod est oppositum istius propositionis positae cum casu[60].

(67) Si conceditur illa ' Sortes decipitur ', tunc sic : Sortes decipitur ; et omnis talis credit falsum ; igitur, Sortes credit falsum. Et solum credit illam ' Sortes decipitur ' ; (*C*70r) igitur, illa est falsa ' Sortes decipitur '. Et ultra : igitur, illa significat aliter quam est ; et illa solum significat quod Sortes decipitur ; ergo, non est[61] ita quod Sortes decipitur, cujus oppositum conceditur.

(68) Solutio : Concedenda est hoc quod Sortes decipitur. Et concedendum est quod illa est falsa. Et neganda est consequentia illa « ergo, significat aliter quam est ». Sed oportet addere antecedenti quod illa non falsificet se, quod non facit in proposito[62]. Sequitur enim « Sortes

(56) jurare, pejerare/ pejerare, mentiri, decipi *CV*.
(57) discere *V*.
(58) et nullam aliam, et significet illa principaliter quod Sortes decipitur *add CV*.
(59) et Sortes/ igitur *C*.
(60) istius... casu/ prius concessi *V*. positae/ positum *V**.
(61) non est *V** *interl.*
(62) quod... proposito *om. C*.

decipitur ; ergo, credit falsum ; et solum credit illam ' Sortes decipitur ' ; ergo, illa est falsa ».

(69) Simile est si ponatur quod Sortes credat illam propositionem ' Plato decipitur ' et Plato illam ' Sortes non decipitur ', et non credant alias ab istis, et quod illae propositiones sic principaliter significent. Et sit tantum unus Sortes et unus Plato. Isto posito, concedendum est quod Sortes non decipitur et quod Plato decipitur et quod illa est vera ' Plato decipitur ' et quod illa est falsa ' Sortes non decipitur ' eo quod falsificat se. Nam sequitur « Sortes non decipitur ; ergo, non credit falsum ; et credit propositionem significantem sicut est vel aliter quam est ; ergo, credit verum ; et solum credit illam ' Plato decipitur ' ; igitur, illa est vera ». Et ultra : igitur, ita est sicut illa principaliter significat. Et per casum solum illa significat quod Plato decipitur ; igitur, ita est quod Plato decipitur. Et ultra : igitur, Plato credit falsum ; et solum credit illam ' Sortes non decipitur ' ; igitur, illa est falsa ' Sortes non decipitur '. Et ita ista falsificat se. Sed illa dicta a Sorte significat principaliter sicut est et non falsificat se ; ergo, est vera[63].

(70) Simile sophisma est hoc : Ponatur quod Sortes dicat illam ' Sortes mentitur ' et solam illam et nullam aliam[64] et quod illa principaliter significat quod Sortes mentitur, et sit tantum unus Sortes, et quod omnis mentiens dicat (*C*70v) falsum. Deinde proponatur ' Sortes (*V*157va) mentitur '. Si negatur vel dubitatur, contra : Sortes dicit falsum ; igitur, mentitur Sortes. Antecedens patet ex casu. Nam (*V**10ra) sequitur « Sortes dicit illam[65] ' Sortes mentitur ' ; et illa principaliter significat quod Sortes mentitur ; et tantum unus Sortes est ; igitur, Sortes dicit falsum ; et solum dicit illam ' Sortes mentitur ' ; igitur, illa[66] est falsa. » Si conceditur, tunc sic : Sortes mentitur ; igitur, dicit falsum ; et solum dicit illam ' Sortes mentitur ; igitur, illa est falsa[67] ; et habet contradictorium ; igitur, contradictorium suum est verum, scilicet, ' Sortes non mentitur '[68]. Et arguitur sic : Sortes non mentitur ; igitur[69], illa est

(63) Note that one cannot argue that 'Plato decipitur' falsifies itself in this case. For if Plato is deceived, he believes a falsehood. And, since he believes only 'Socrates is not deceived', the latter is false. It does not follow, however, that the latter sentence signifies otherwise than is the case, so that Socrates is indeed deceived, and thus the only sentence he believes, 'Plato is deceived', is false. For 'Socrates is not deceived' is false not because it signifies otherwise than is the case, but because it falsifies itself, as par. 69 shows.

(64) et solum... aliam *om. C.*

(65) solum *add. C.*

(66) ille *V**.

(67) Si... falsa *om. C.*

(68) Si conceditur quod Sortes *(interl.)* mentitur, igitur dicit falsum. Et solam dicit istam ' Sortes mentitur ' ; igitur, ista est falsa *add. C.*

(69) Sortes... igitur *om. V.*

vera ; et igitur, ita[70] est sicut illa significat principaliter, quod Sortes non mentitur ; igitur, ita est quod[71] Sortes non mentitur, quod est oppositum concessi.

(71) Solutio : Concedendum quod Sortes mentitur. Et concedendum est quod illa est falsa. Et concedendum est quod habet[72] contradictorium. Et neganda est consequentia « igitur, ejus contradictorium est verum » eo quod suum contradictorium significat aliter quam est. Et sic duo contradictoria sunt simul falsa, ut patet per conclusionem ultimam.

(72) Aliud sophisma, quod Sortes solum juret istam ' Sortes est perjurus ' et quod tantum sit unus Sortes et illa principaliter significet quod Sortes est perjurus. Hoc posito, concedendum est quod Sortes est perjurus et quod illa ' Sortes est perjurus ' est falsa eo quod falsificat se, ut satis patet. Quia vero illa solutio in istis insolubilibus de se est satis manifesta, ideo[73] ad alia in quibus magis latet me converto[74].

IV

(73) Jam restat insolubilium ex mixtione actus nostri cum proprietate vocis nascentium solutionem narrare. Insolubile autem sic acceptum est triplex. Quoddam est in quo ponuntur signa ex impositione significativa proprietatem vocis et actus ex quo fit insolubile. Aliud est in quo ponuntur signa ex impositione significativa proprietatem vocis et[75] privationem actus ex[76] quo fit insolubile[77]. Tertium est in quo ponuntur signa ex impositione significativa proprietatem vocis et actionem vel privationem actus ex quo fit insolubile. Exemplum primi, sicut ' Sortes dicit falsum ', ' Sortes legit falsum ', ' Sortes cogitat falsum '[78], et his similia. Exemplum secundi : ' Illa (*C*71r) propositio nescitur a te ', ' Omnis propositio nescitur ', ' Aliqua propositio non creditur '[79]. Exem-

(70) ista *V**.

(71) Et arguitur... quod/ Et ultra : igitur, haec significat aliter quam est ; et solum significat quod Sortes mentitur ; igitur, non est ita quod Sortes mentitur. Tunc sic : Non est ita quod Sortes mentitur ; igitur *C*.

(72) quod habet *om. V**.

(73) leviter de istis pertranseo et *add. V*.

(74) Quia... converto *om. C*.

(75) actus... et *om. V*.

(76) actus ex/ in *C*.

(77) Hic deficit secundum membrum *add. V*.

(78) ' Sortes cogitat falsum ' *om. C*.

(79) ' Omnis... creditur '/ ' Ista propositio non creditur a te ', et cetera *C*. ' Aliqua... creditur '/ ' Ista propositio non creditur a te ', et his similia *V*.

plum tertii[80] : ' Sortes est albus ', ' Sortes est aeger '[81], ' Sortes est currens ', aliquibus casibus positis, et similia.

(74) De istis exemplis per ordinem dicetur. Et primo de primis. Sit igitur hoc sophisma ' Sortes dicit falsum ', posito illo casu quod tantum sit unus Sortes et quod dicat tantum illam propositionem ' Sortes dicit falsum ' et nullam aliam et quod illa principaliter significet quod Sortes dicit falsum. Deinde proponatur ' Sortes dicit falsum '. Si negatur vel dubitatur, contra : Contradictorium illius repugnat casui ; igitur, (*V**10rb) contradictorium ejus est negandum. Et ultra : igitur[82], illa est concedenda. Antecedens probo, quia ex contradictorio ejus cum casu sequitur contradictorium alterius partis casus ; et casus per se est possibilis ; igitur, contradictorium ejus repugnat casui. Assumptum probatur sic : Proponatur, scilicet, ' Sortes non dicit falsum ' cum casu. Et arguitur sic : Sortes non dicit falsum ; et dicit propositionem principaliter[83] significantem sicut (*V*157vb) est vel aliter quam est ; igitur, Sortes dicit verum. Tunc sic : Sortes dicit verum[84] ; et Sortes[85] dicit illam ' Sortes dicit falsum ' ; igitur, illa est vera. Et ultra : igitur, ita est sicut illa principaliter significat[86] ; et illa solum[87] significat quod Sortes dicit falsum ; igitur, ita est quod Sortes dicit falsum. Et ultra : igitur, Sortes dicit falsum, quod est oppositum propositionis positae cum casu. Si conceditur, videlicet, ' Sortes dicit falsum ', tunc sic : Sortes dicit falsam[88] ; et solum dicit illam ' Sortes dicit falsum ' ; igitur[89], illa est falsa ; et habet contradictorium ; igitur, ejus contradictorium est verum, scilicet, ' Sortes non dicit falsum '. Et ultra : igitur, ita est sicut illa principaliter significat ; et illa solum[90] significat quod Sortes non dicit falsum ; igitur, ita est quod Sortes non dicit <falsum>. Et ultra[91] : igitur, Sortes non dicit falsum, quod est oppositum prius concessi.

(75) Solutio : Concedenda est quod Sortes dicit falsum ; et concedendum est quod illa est falsa. Et concedendum est quod habetur contradictorium. Et neganda est consequentia « Igitur, ejus contradictorium est verum » quia ejus contradictorium significat aliter quam est. Et quod consequentia non valet patet[92] per conclusionem ultimam.

(80) tertii *om.* *V**.
(81) niger *C.*
(82) contradictorium... igitur *om.* *C.*
(83) principaliter *om.* *C.*
(84) Tunc... verum *om.* *C.*
(85) solum *CV.*
(86) Et... significat *om.* *V.*
(87) principaliter *C.*
(88) tunc... falsam *om.* *C.*
(89) et *C.*
(90) principaliter *V.*
(91) Et ultra... ultra *om.* *C.* igitur, ita... ultra *om.* *V.*
(92) patet *om.* *V**.

(76) Aliud sophisma : Ponatur quod tantum sint duo Sortes et quod uterque illorum[93] dicat talem propositionem 'Sortes[94] dicit falsum' et quod non dicant aliquam aliam (*C*71v) vel aliquas alias[95] et quod utraque illarum dictarum[96] principaliter significet quod Sortes dicit falsum. Deinde proponitur 'Sortes dicit falsum'. Si negatur vel dubitatur, contra : Contradictorium ejus repugnat casui ; igitur, illa est sequens ex casu. Nam ex contradictorio illius cum casu sequitur oppositum alterius partis casus ; igitur, contradictorium illius repugnat casui[97]. Assumptum probatur sic : Ponatur contradictorium illius cum casu. Et arguitur sic : Sortes non dicit falsum ; et Sortes dicit propositionem significantem principaliter[98] sicut est vel aliter quam est ; igitur, Sortes dicit verum[99] ; et qua ratione alter illorum dicit verum, uterque illorum dicit verum ; igitur, uterque illorum dicit verum ; et uterque illorum dicit illam[1] propositionem 'Sortes dicit falsum' principaliter[2] significantem quod Sortes dicit falsum ; igitur, ita est quod Sortes dicit falsum, quod est oppositum alterius partis casus. Si conceditur, tunc sic : Sortes dicit falsum ; et utraque illarum propositionum dictarum principaliter[3] sic significat ; igitur, utraque illarum principaliter significat sicut est ; et neutra falsificat se ; igitur[4], utraque illarum est vera.

(77) Solutio : Conceditur quod Sortes dicit falsum. Et conceditur quod utraque illarum significat principaliter[5] sicut est. Et dicendum quod utraque falsificat se. Et hoc illo modo : Sortes dicit falsum ; et omnis Sortes est alter (*V**10va) illorum ; igitur, alter illorum dicit falsum ; et nulla ratio potest assignari quare unus dicit falsum quin eadem vel consimili alius dicit falsum ; igitur, in tali casu posito uterque illorum dicit falsum ; et illi duo solum dicunt illas duas, scilicet, 'Sortes dicit falsum', 'Sortes dicit falsum' ; igitur, illae duae sunt falsae. Et sic utraque illarum est falsa et falsificat se.

(78) Simile sophisma est : Ponatur quod Sortes dicat illam 'Plato dicit falsum' et Plato dicat illam 'Sortes non[6] dicit falsum' et quod non dicant aliquas alias quam illas et quod illae propositiones sic principaliter

(93) simul cum alio *add. CV.*
(94) Sortes *V* interl.*
(95) aliam... alias/ propositionem (71v) nec aliquas *C.*
(96) utraque... dictarum/ uterque istorum *C.*
(97) Nam... casui *om. C.*
(98) principaliter *om. CV.*
(99) Et omnis Sortes est alter istorum ; igitur, alter istorum dicit verum *add. CV.*
(1) solum *V.*
(2) principaliter *om. C.*
(3) principaliter *om. C.*
(4) utraque... igitur *om. V.*
(5) praecise *V.*
(6) non *V* interl.*

significent et quod tantum sit (*C*72r) unus Sortes et unus Plato. Illo casu posito, dicendum est quod Sortes non dicit falsum et quod illa est falsa[7] eo quod falsificat se. Et concedendum est quod Plato dicit falsum. Et illa est vera quia[8] significat sicut est et non falsificat se[9].

(79) Simile est in parte hoc sophisma : Ponatur quod tantum unus Sortes sit et dicat solum talem propositionem ' Plato dicit falsum ' et sit tantum unus Plato qui dicat solum talem ' Sortes dicit falsum ', et quod illae propositiones principaliter sic (*V*158ra) significent. Hoc posito, dicendum est quod Sortes dicit falsum et similiter Plato et quod utraque illarum est falsa quia utraque illarum falsificat se et hoc mediate. Nam illa dicta a Sorte falsificat illam dictam a Platone et hoc immediate[10]. Et illa dicta a Platone falsificat illam dictam a Sorte et hoc immediate[11]. Et sic utraque illarum falsificat se ipsam mediate[12] sicut patet in divisione secunda particulae primae[13].

(80) Solutis insolubilibus primi membri hujus divisionis[14] jam restat solvere insolubilia secundi membri ejus divisionis. Sit hoc sophisma ' *a* propositio nescitur '. Proponatur[15] ille casus quod *a* sit illa propositio ' *a* propositio nescitur ', et sit unum *a* omne *a*, et quod illa propositio principaliter[16] significet quod *a* propositio nescitur. Deinde proponatur ' *a* propositio nescitur '. Si negatur vel dubitatur, contra : Cum casu non stat quod *a* propositio sciatur ; et *a* est una propositio ; et casus est admissus ; igitur, concedendum est quod *a* propositio nescitur. Primum antecedens probatur sic[17], quia ex illa propositione ' *a* scitur ' cum casu sequitur oppositum illius, ' *a* nescitur '[18] ; igitur, illa ' *a* scitur ' non stat cum casu. Assumptum probatur sic : Nam sequitur « *a* scitur ; igitur, scitur ita esse sicut *a* significat »[19]. Et ultra : igitur, ita est sicut *a* significat ; sed per casum *a* principaliter (*C*72v) significat quod *a* nescitur ; igitur, *a* nescitur. Et sic ex illa ' *a* scitur ' cum casu sequitur suum contradictorium. Si conceditur ' *a* nescitur ', tunc sic : Ita est quod *a* nescitur ; et tu firmiter[20] consideras de ista propositione et non dubitas an *a*

(7) ' Sortes non dicit falsum ' *add. CV*.
(8) principaliter *add. CV*.
(9) See the remarks on the similar sophism in n. 63 to par. 69, above.
(10) mediate *V*. et... immediate *om. C*.
(11) mediate *V*.
(12) Et... mediate *om. C*.
(13) secunda... primae/ secundae particulae hujus *V**.
(14) See par. 73.
(15) Ponatur *CV*.
(16) principaliter *om. C*.
(17) Primum... sic *om. C*.
(18) scitur *V*.
(19) scitur... significat/ *a (interl.)* significat sicut *C*.
(20) continue *V*.

nesciatur ; igitur, scis quod *a* nescitur. Tunc sic : (*V**10vb) Tu scis quod *a* nescitur; et tu scis quod *a* principaliter sic significat ; igitur, tu scis quod ita est sicut *a* significat principaliter ; et tu scis *a* principaliter[21] sic significare ; igitur, tu scis *a* ; igitur, *a* scitur, quod est oppositum illius ' *a* nescitur ' vel suum[22] repugnans.

(81) Solutio : Admisso casu, concedenda est illa ' *a* nescitur '[23]. Et concedendum est quod ego scio *a* sic principaliter significare. Et neganda est consequentia « igitur, scio *a* ». Sed oportet addere quod *a* non est pertinens ad inferendum se ipsum fore nescitam. Et si illud addatur, illud est negandum. Nam sequitur immediate « *a* nescitur ; igitur, *a* nescitur ».

(82) Simile sophisma est hoc : Ponatur quod tantum illa propositio sit ' Omnis propositio nescitur ' et quod illa[24] principaliter sic significet quod omnis propositio nescitur, et hoc bene sciatur. Quo posito, concedenda est hoc ' Omnis propositio nescitur '. Et concedendum est quod scitur ita esse sicut[25] illa significat[26]. Et neganda est consequentia « igitur, illa scitur » quia illa est pertinens ad inferendum se ipsum fore nescitam. Ideo est nescita. Antecedens probatur : Nam sequitur « Omnis propositio nescitur ; illamet est propositio ; igitur, illamet nescitur ». Et ultra : igitur, est nescita[27].

(83) Aliud sophisma : Ponatur quod haec propositio[28] ' Haec non creditur '[29] principaliter significet quod hoc non creditur et quod per ly ' hoc ' demonstretur illa eadem. Hoc posito (*C*73r), dicendum est quod haec non creditur. Et concedendum est quod creditur ita esse sicut illa principaliter significat et quod creditur illa sic[30] significare. Et negatur consequentia « igitur, illa est credita » quia (*V*158rb) est pertinens ad inferendum se ipsam fore[31] non creditam. Et quaelibet talis est non credita.

(84) Pro quo est notandum quod sicut quaelibet propositio pertinens ad inferendum se ipsam fore falsam est falsa ita quaelibet propositio pertinens ad inferendum se ipsam fore nescitam vel non creditam est nescita vel non credita. Et sicut non[32] omnis propositio[33] pertinens ad

(21) principaliter *om. CV.*
(22) saltem *CV.*
(23) Et concedendum est quod ego scio quod *a* nescitur *add. CV.*
(24) propositio... illa *om. V*.*
(25) principaliter *add. V.*
(26) et illa sic significare *add. C.* et quod scitur illa sic significare *add. V.*
(27) Antecedens... nescita *om. C.*
(28) sit omnis propositio *add. C.*
(29) et quod *add. C.*
(30) sic *om. C.*
(31) nescitam sive *add. C.*
(32) non *om. C.*
(33) propositio *V* interl.*

inferendum se fore veram[34] est vera ita non omnis propositio pertinens ad inferendum se ipsam scitam fore vel creditam est scita vel credita.

(85) Solutis insolubilibus secundi membri divisionis, solvenda sunt insolubilia tertii membri[35]. Sit igitur hoc sophisma ' Sortes est aeger '. Ponatur ille casus quod omnis homo aeger dicat falsum et omnis homo sanus dicat verum et solum talis et quod Sortes solum dicat illam ' Sortes est aeger ' quae principaliter sic significet. Deinde proponatur ' Sortes est aeger '. Si negatur vel dubitatur, contra : Oppositum illius repugnat casui ; igitur, casu admisso illa est concedenda. Assumptum probatur sic : Ex opposito illius cum casu[36] sequitur illa propositio ' Sortes[37] est aeger ' ; igitur, oppositum illius ' Sortes est aeger ' repugnat casui. (*V**11ra) Antecedens probatur sic : Sequitur « Sortes non est aeger ; et Sortes est homo ; igitur, Sortes est sanus ; et omnis homo sanus dicit verum ; ergo, Sortes dicit verum ; et solum dicit illam ' Sortes est aeger ' ; ergo, illa est vera ' Sortes est aeger '. Et ultra : ergo, ita est sicut illa principaliter significat ; et per casum illa principaliter significat (*C*73v) quod Sortes est aeger ; ergo, ita est quod Sortes est aeger. Et ultra : ergo, Sortes est aeger. Si conceditur, ' Sortes est aeger ', tunc sic : Sortes est aeger ; et omnis homo aeger dicit falsum ; ergo, Sortes dicit falsum ; et solum dicit illam ' Sortes est aeger ' ; ergo, haec est falsa ' Sortes est aeger ' ; et habet contradictorium ; ergo, suum contradictorium, scilicet, ' Sortes non est aeger ', est verum. Et ultra : igitur, ita est sicut illa principaliter significat ; et illa significat principaliter[38] quod Sortes non est aeger ; ergo, ita est quod Sortes non est aeger, quod est oppositum concessi.

(86) Solutio : Admisso casu, haec est concedenda ' Sortes est aeger '. Et concedendum est quod Sortes dicit falsum. Et concedendum est quod illa est falsa ' Sortes est aeger ' quia se ipsam falsificat. Et concedendum est quod habet contradictorium. Et neganda est illa consequentia « igitur, suum contradictorium est verum », sicut patet per conclusionem ultimam.

(87) Simile est si ponatur quod omnis homo albus videat falsum et nullus alius et quod Sortes videat illam solam ' Sortes est albus ' et quod illa principaliter significet quod Sortes est albus, et quod tantum sit unus homo, scilicet, Sortes. Hoc proposito[39], concedenda est haec ' Sortes est albus '. Et concedendum est quod illa est falsa ' Sortes est albus ' quia se falsificat. Nam sequitur « Omnis homo albus videt falsum ; Sortes est albus ; ergo, Sortes videt falsum ; et solum videt illam ' Sortes est albus ' ;

(34) non *add. C.*
(35) See par. 73.
(36) admisso illa est concedenda. Assumptum probatur sic : Ex opposito illius cum casu *add. V*.*
(37) non *add. C.*
(38) solum *V.*
(39) posito *CV.*

ergo, illa est falsa ' Sortes est albus '. » Et sic illa est falsa quia falsificat se. Et suum contradictorium est falsum, haec, scilicet, ' Sortes non est albus ', quia significat aliter quam est.

(88) (*V*158va) Simile est[40] si ponatur quod omnis homo currens audiat falsum et solum talis et Sortes audiat illam ' Sortes est currens ' et nullam aliam et quod illa principaliter significet quod Sortes est currens. Et sit tantum unus Sortes. Hoc proposito[41], est concedenda ' Sortes est currens '. Et concedendum est quod est falsa quia falsificat se[42]. Et est sicut in priori sophismate.

(89) Quia vero solutiones principaliter illae consistunt in hoc quod aliqua propositio se ipsam falsificat[43], jam congruit quasdam dubitationes huic repugnantes recitare et ut veritas elucescat illas solvere. Ex positione (*C*74r) praedicta sequuntur contradictoria ; ergo, ipsa est impossibilis. Assumptum probatur sic : Nam si ponatur[44] quod non omnis propositio falsa falsificat se, et tamen ex[45] illa sequitur quod[46] omnis propositio[47] falsificat (*V**11rb) se ; igitur, et cetera. Assumptum probatur sic : Nam si foret aliqua propositio falsa[48] quae non falsificat se, sit igitur, gratia exempli, haec ' Homo est asinus ', sic principaliter significando, quod, scilicet, homo est asinus. Et quod illa falsificet se probatur sic : Nam sequitur « Homo est asinus ; et numquam homo est asinus quando haec non est falsa ' Homo est asinus ' ; igitur, haec est[49] falsa ' Homo est asinus '. » Et sic ex illa propositione ' Homo est asinus ' cum alia sequitur ipsam falsam fore. Et ex illa alia sine illa ' Homo est asinus ' non sequitur illud ; igitur, illa est pertinens ad inferendum se ipsam fore falsam ; igitur, ipsa est falsificans se.

(90) Secundo sic : Aliqua propositio vera falsificat se ; ergo, multo fortius quaelibet propositio falsa[50] falsificat se. Assumptum probatur sic : Si ponatur quod haec ' Homo est asinus ' principaliter significat quod nullus homo est asinus, tunc notum est quod illa est vera. Et quod illa falsificat se probatur sic : Nam sequitur « Homo est asinus ; et illa principaliter significat quod nullus homo est asinus ; illa ' Homo est asinus ',

(40) Simile est *V** *in marg.*
(41) posito *CV*.
(42) quia... se *om. V*.
(43) Quia... falsificat/ ita quod solutio haec principaliter consistit in illo quod omnis propositio falsificans se est falsa *V*.
(44) Nam si ponitur *add. V**. Nam... ponatur/ positio illa ponit *CV*.
(45) quod *C*.
(46) et... quod/ ergo, non *V**.
(47) falsa *add. C*.
(48) falsa *om. C*.
(49) est *add. V**.
(50) falsa *om. C*.

igitur, est falsa ». Et[51] ipsa est pertinens ad inferendum se ipsam fore falsam, quare se ipsam falsificat[52].

(91) Tertio[53] ad idem sic : Sit illa propositio ' Haec est[54] propositio ' principaliter significans quod haec est propositio. Et demonstretur per ly ' haec ' illa eadem propositio ' Haec est propositio '. Hoc posito, haec est vera ' Haec est propositio '. Et illa falsificat se, quod probatur sic : Nam sequitur « Haec est propositio[55] ; et non est vera ; igitur, est falsa ». Ergo, falsificat se.

(92) Quarto[56] sic : Aliqua propositio falsificans se non falsificat se[57] ; ergo, illa propositio[58] est impossibilis. Assumptum probatur : Ponatur quod tantum sit haec propositio ' Nullum verum est ' quae (*C*74v) principaliter significet quod nullum verum est. Tunc secundum illam positionem[59] illa falsificat se. Et quod illa non falsificet se probatur sic, quia si falsificet se, tunc illo modo esset arguendum : Nullum verum est ; et illa propositio est ; igitur, illa non est vera. Et ultra sic : Illa non est vera ; et illa est propositio significans sicut est vel aliter quam est ; igitur, illa est falsa. Et ex[60] hoc non sequitur quod illa[61] falsificet se eo quod illa est impertinens ad inferendum se ipsam fore falsam. Nam ex praemissis captis in antecedente sine illa sequitur quod illa sit falsa ; ergo, summendo illam cum casu[62] superfluit. Et per consequens illa est impertinens[63]. Assumptum probatur sic : Nam sequitur sine illa « Haec non est vera ; et haec significat sicut est vel aliter quam est ; ergo, haec est falsa ». Ex quo patet quod propositio illo modo[64] non falsificat se ; sed nec alio modo[65] ; ergo, nullo modo falsificat se, cujus oppositum ponit illa opinio[66].

(93) Quinto[67] sic : Aliqua est propositio neque vera neque falsa quae falsificat se ; ergo, non omnis propositio falsificans se est (*V*158vb) falsa, cujus oppositum ponit illa opinio[68]. Antecedens probatur sic : Haec est

(51) non *V**.
(52) *V* omits all of par. 90, but replies to it in par. 96, below.
(53) Secundo *V*.
(54) est *om*. *C*.
(55) Et... propositio *om*. *C*.
(56) Tertio *V*.
(57) falsificans... se/ se non falsificat *V*.
(58) positio *V*.
(59) propositionem *C*.
(60) Et ex/ Sed *CV*.
(61) quod illa/ quia ista non *V*.
(62) illis *CV*.
(63) pertinens, et cetera *C*.
(64) illo modo *om*. *C*.
(65) sed... modo/ nec illo modo *C*, nec aliqua alia *V**.
(66) propositio *C*.
(67) Quarto *V*.
(68) propositio *C*.

hujusmodi ' Haec significat aliter quam est '[69]. Et hac posita sequitur quod illa non (V*11va) est vera nec falsa eo quod illa est pertinens ad inferendum se ipsam non significare[70] sicut est et per consequens non significat sicut est nec aliter quam est. Consequentia patet per superius dicta[71]. Et quod illa falsificet se probatur sic : Nam sequitur immediate « Haec significat aliter quam est ; ergo, haec est falsa ».

(94) Aliae objectiones multae possunt fieri quarum solutio patebit ex solutione illorum.

(95) Ideo ad primam objectionem respondetur sic, negando assumptum. Et ad argumentum negatur quod illa falsificat se ' Homo est asinus '. Et quando arguitur « Homo est asinus ; et numquam homo est asinus quando haec non[72] est falsa ; ergo, haec est falsa », neganda est haec consequentia et antecedens similiter. Consequentia non valet[73] pro tanto quia minor est una temporalis convertibilis cum hac copulativa ' Numquam homo est asinus[74] et haec non est falsa ' Homo est asinus '[75]. Et manifestum est quod haec non valet « Homo est asinus ; et numquam homo est asinus et haec non est falsa ' Homo est asinus '[76] ; ergo, haec est falsa ». Sed oportet addere quod haec propositio significat sicut est vel aliter quam est. Et si ita (C75r) addatur, ergo sequitur sine illa ' Homo est asinus ' in principio capta. Et antecedens[77] est falsum similiter. Nam illa[78] temporalis convertitur cum una copulativa falsa[79]. Nam haec est falsa ' Hoc non est falsum ', demonstrata illa ' Homo est asinus '[80].

(96) Ad secundum nego assumptum. Et ad consequentiam factam « Homo est asinus, et cetera ; ergo, illa est falsa », concedenda est conse-

(69) et demonstrando per ly ' haec ' eandem. Et ponitur quod significat aliter quam est *add. C.* igitur, ponatur quod per ly ' haec ' demonstretur illa eadem, et quod significet illa principaliter quod haec significat aliter quam est *add. V.*

(70) non significare/ fore falsam non significare principaliter *C.*

(71) See par. 2.

(72) non *om. C.*

(73) Consequentia... valet/ Neganda est consequentia *V.*

(74) asinus *om. V*.*

(75) ergo, haec est falsa *add. V.*

(76) numquam... asinus/ haec non est falsa *V*.*

(77) non *add. V.*

(78) similiter... illa/ Similiter non sequitur *V.*

(79) sed si prius declaratur *add. C.* sicut prius dicitur *add. V.*

(80) The argument seems confused. Contrary to Swyneshed, the additional premiss does not seem necessary. If one does add it, then Swyneshed is correct that one does not need to assume ' Homo est asinus ' separately. For if a man is in fact an ass, then ' Homo est asinus ' is false by the argument given. But if no man is an ass, then ' Homo est asinus ' is false since it does not signify as is the case, and yet signifies either as is the case or otherwise than is the case, by hypothesis, and so signifies otherwise than is the case, by disjunctive syllogism. Its falsehood then follows by the third definition, par. 15.

quentia et dicendum est quod consequentia non valet. Et tamen concedenda est[81] eo quod nullo casu posito illa foret concedenda. Et per consequens quocumque casu possibili posito, illa est concedenda. Quod consequentia[82] non valet manifeste patet[83] si summatur propositio convertibilis cum illa ' Homo est asinus '. Et ponatur loco illius haec, scilicet, ' Nullus homo est asinus ' sic significando. Nam notum est quod hoc argumentum non valet « Nullus homo est asinus ; et[84] illa ' Homo est asinus ' principaliter significat quod nullus homo est asinus ; ergo, illa est falsa ». Sed magis sequitur oppositum, quod ipsa sit vera. Et illa consequentia convertitur cum priori ; igitur, prior non valet[85].

(97) Ad tertiam formam similiter negatur assumptum et[86] dicendum est quod illa non falsificat se ' Haec est propositio '. Et quando arguitur « Haec est propositio[87] ; et non est vera ; ergo, est falsa », negatur consequentia. Et dato quod consequentia valeat[88], argumentum non procederet eo quod minor est falsa, scilicet, quod ista non est vera. Pro quo est sciendum quod propositio falsificat se aut, sicut praedicebatur, mediate vel immediate, mediate[89] quandocumque falsificat aliquam[90] falsificantem illam, immediate quandocumque aliqua propositio[91] significat sicut est vel aliter quam est et[92] ex illa sola[93] sequitur illam fore falsam vel ex illa cum totaliter sic esse sicut est et ex illa totaliter sic esse sine[94] illa non sequitur illam fore salsam. Ex istis patet quod haec propositio ' Haec est propositio ' non falsificat se eo quod ex ista cum aliter esse quam est (*V**11vb) sequitur illam fore faslam. Sed ex hoc non sequitur quod illa

(81) dicendum... est/ tamen consequentia non valet *C*.
(82) Quod consequentia *om. V**.
(83) oportet *V**.
(84) quod consequentia non valet ; et *add. C*.
(85) The consequence is invalid, given the stipulated signification of the first premiss, as the argument shows. Yet it is to be conceded, presumably because of a rule in Swyneshed's *Obligationes*: « Propter impositionem alicujus propositionis ad illam non est responsio varianda. » (See my "Roger Swyneshed's *Obligationes*: Edition and Comments," *Archives d'histoire doctrinale et littéraire du moyen âge*, 44 (1977), par. 21.) If consequences are thought of as single complex sentences, as they often were in mediaeval logic, and if a new imposition assigned to one part of a consequence affects the signification of the whole, which seems plausible (but contrast Robert Fland in my "Robert Fland's *Consequentiae*: An Edition", *Mediaeval Studies* 38 [1976], pp. 54-84 at pars. 9, 10, 13), then the rule justifies Swyneshed's remarks here.
(86) Tamen *V**.
(87) vera *add. C*.
(88) foret bona *C*. non foret bona *V*.
(89) mediate *om. V**.
(90) se et aliam a se *C*.
(91) principaliter *add. V*.
(92) et *om. V**.
(93) sola *om. C*.
(94) si vel *V**.

falsificat se. Sed oportet quod ex illa cum sic esse sicut est[95] sequitur illam fore falsam ad hoc[96] quod illa falsificat se. Et sic non est in proposito. Nam illa minor assumpta cum alia significat aliter quam est eo quod significat quod illa non[97] est vera.

(98) Ad quartum nego assumptum cum casu ibidem posito (*V*159ra) et admisso. Dico quod illa falsificat se, sed non[98] illo modo quo ibi arguitur. Sed sic : « Nullum verum est ; et omnis propositio significans sicut est vel aliter quam est est illa, demonstrata illa ' Nullum verum est '[99] ; ergo, illa est falsa. » Et notum est[1] quod ex minori non sequitur per se illud ; et[2] illa minor significat sicut est ; ergo, illa prima falsificat se.

(99) Ad ultimam objectionem dico negando assumptum. Et quando capitur illa propositio ' Haec significat aliter quam est ', concedo quod illa nec est vera nec falsa. Et nego quod illa falsificat se. Et concedo quod ex illa immediate sequitur quod illa sit falsa. Et nego consequentiam « igitur, illa falsificat se ». Sed oportet addere quod illa significet sicut est vel aliter quam est[3], quod non facit in proposito.

V

(100) His vero completis superest solvere quaedam sophismata quae apparent insolubilia et non sunt, sicut sint ' *a* est scitum ', ' Ista propositio significat aliter quam est ', ' Illa propositio non significat aliter quam est '[4], ' Ista propositio non significat sicut est ', et his similes. Sit ergo hoc sophisma positum ' *a* est scitum '. Ponatur ille casus quod *a* sit altera illarum ' Deus est ' quae sit scita[5], et ' *a* nescitur ' quae sic[6] principaliter significet, et[7] hoc bene scias, et sit tantum unum *a*, et lateat te quae illarum sit *a*. Deinde ponatur[8] ' *a*[9] est scitum '. Si conceditur vel dubitatur, contra : Nullo casu posito illa foret continue neganda ; et tunc illa est

(95) Et ex... est *om. C.*
(96) ad hoc/ adhuc *V**.
(97) non *om. C.*
(98) sed non/ sive (si non ?) *V**.
(99) omnis... est '/ haec propositio significat principaliter sicut est vel aliter quam est ; igitur, illa non est vera. Et (75v) ultra *C.* Sic...est '/ non est verum *V**.
(1) notum est/ non est notum *V**.
(2) quod *V**.
(3) See pars. 4-5.
(4) ' Illa... est ' *om. CV.*
(5) quae... scita/ sit vera *C.*
(6) sic *om. C.*
(7) quod *C.*
(8) proponatur *CV.*
(9) *a om. C.*

impertinens[10] ; ergo, adhuc est neganda[11]. Minor patet eo quod non sequitur « *a* est altera illarum ; ergo, *a* est scitum »[12]. Si negatur ' *a* est scitum ', contra : *a* est illa propositio ' Deus est ' quae est scita[13] ; ergo, *a* est scitum. Illa consequentia est bona ; et antecedens est dubium ; igitur, consequens non est a te negandum[14]. Item[15] negata illa ' *a* est scitum ', proponatur illa ' *a* nescitur a te '. Haec tunc est concedenda[16]. Qua concessa, arguitur sic : Ita est quod *a* nescitur a te[17] ; et de illa firme consideras et scis qualiter illa significat, et non dubitas an *a* nescitur a te[18] ; ergo, scis quod *a* nescitur a te. Et tunc sic : Tu[19] scis quod[20] *a* nescitur a te[21] ; et tu scis illam propositionem sic significare ; et illa non est pertinens ad inferendum se ipsam fore nescitam ; ergo, tu scis illam. Qua concessa, proponatur ' Utraque illarum scitur '. Si negatur vel dubitatur[22], contra : ' Deus est ' scitur a te, et ' *a* nescitur ' a te scitur[23], et (*V**12ra) illae duae tantum demonstrantur per ly ' illarum ' ; ergo, utraque illarum scitur. Si conceditur[24], tunc sic : Utraque illarum scitur ; *a* est alterum illarum ; ergo, (*C*76r) *a* scitur. Et ultra : ergo, *a* est scitum, quod erat prius negatum[25].

(101) Admisso casu, neganda est haec ' *a* est scitum '. Et ad primam formam concedenda[26] est consequentia prima, scilicet, illa « *a* est illa ' Deus est ' quae est scita ; ergo, *a* est scitum ». Et secunda consequentia est neganda, illa, scilicet, « Illa consequentia est bona ; et antecedens est tibi dubium ; igitur, consequens non est a te negandum », eo quod licet antecedens sit mihi dubium, tamen antecedens[27] est a me negandum. Et per consequens non sequitur consequens fore concedendum[28].

(10) continue... impertinens/ concedenda ; adhuc non est pertinens *C*.
(11) See the rule in "Roger Swyneshed's *Obligationes*", par. 29.
(12) nescitum *V**.
(13) quae... scita *om. C*.
(14) See the similar argument in "Roger Swyneshed's *Obligationes*", par. 82.
(15) Ideo *V*. propter *V**.
(16) Haec... concedenda *om. C*.
(17) Haec... te *om. V**.
(18) et de... te *om. C*.
(19) quod *add. V**.
(20) Tu... quod *om. C*.
(21) a te ; ergo... te *om. V*.
(22) vel dubitatur *om. C*.
(23) scitur *om. V**.
(24) et... conceditur/ igitur, istae duae sciuntur a te ; et tantum illae duae demonstrantur per ly ' istarum ' scitur et *C*.
(25) Et... negatum *om C*.
(26) neganda *V*.
(27) consequens *C*. The preferred reading here is uncertain. Neither reading seems to yield a plausible reply to par. 100.
(28) igitur, prima non valet *add. C*.

(102) Ad secundam formam similiter negatur '*a* est scitum a me '[29]. Et concedendum est totum sequens donec veniatur ad ultimum discursum (*V*159rb) factum in tertio primae figurae[30], concedendo et[31] negando antecedens, scilicet, copulativam factam ex posito falso et non pertinente[32]. Si tamen post concessionem primae partis ponatur prima pars cum secunda, tunc post positionem[33] istius concedendum est quod *a* est scitum tamquam sequens ex posito. Et tunc est negandum quod *a* sit illa '*a*[34] nescitur a te ' quia falsa et repugnans simpliciter[35].

(103) Aliud sophisma : ' Illa propositio significat aliter quam est '. Ponatur quod illa sic principaliter[36] significat. Et per ly ' ista ' demonstretur illa eadem. Deinde proponatur ' Illa propositio significat aliter quam est[37]. Si conceditur vel dubitatur, contra : Ex illa cum casu sequitur suum contradictorium ; ergo, illa est neganda. Assumptum probatur sic : Sequitur « Illa propositio significat aliter quam est ; ergo, non est ita sicut illa propositio[38] significat ; et illa propositio solum significat quod illa propositio[39] significat[40] aliter quam est ; ergo, non est ita quod illa propositio significat aliter quam est ». Et ultra : ergo, illa propositio non significat aliter quam est, quod est oppositum ipsius. Si negatur, contra : Proponatur ' Illa non significat aliter quam est '. Qua concessa, arguitur sic : Illa non significat aliter quam est ; et illa significat complexe ; ergo, illa significat sicut est. Et ultra : igitur[41], ita est sicut ipsa significat. Et illa significat quod illa significat aliter quam est ; ergo, ita est quod illa significat[42] aliter quam est, quod[43] erat negatum.

(29) Et conceditur quod *a* nescitur a me *add. CV.*

(30) primae figurae *reading uncertain in V.* The third mood of the first figure, i.e., Darii. The consequence is « Utraque illarum scitur ; *a* est alterum illarum ; ergo, *a* scitur ».

(31) non *add V.*

(32) et... pertinente/ ex imposito vero *C*, et vero impertinente *V*. I.e., since the antecedent is composed of a posited falsehood (' *a* est altera illarum ' is false in fact, although true under the supposed « casus ») and a sentence that is « impertinens » to the « casus » (' Utraque illarum scitur '), the whole antecedent is false and « impertinens », and therefore must be denied. See "Roger Swyneshed's *Obligationes*", pars. 29 and 32. There are many arguments like this in the *Obligationes.*

(33) rationem *C.* positum *V**.

(34) *a om. V**.

(35) repugnans simpliciter/ impertinens *C.*

(36) principaliter *om. C.*

(37) Sed contra *add. C.*

(38) principaliter *add. CV.*

(39) principaliter *C.*

(40) quod... significat *om. V**.

(41) illa significat cum et *add. V**.

(42) sicut est... significat *om. C.*

(43) est quod *om. C.*

(104) Solutio : Admisso casu, neganda est illa. Et neganda est[44] haec consequentia « Illa non significat aliter quam est ; et[45] significat complexe ; ergo, significat sicut[46] est ». Sed oportet addere quod illa non foret pertinens ad inferendum se ipsam[47] non significare sicut est. Et si illa addatur, illud est negandum. Nam[48] sequitur immediate ex illa « Ista[49] significat aliter quam est ; ergo, illa non significat sicut est ».

(105) Contra illam solutionem arguitur sic : Data illa solutione sequitur illa conclusio quod aliqua sunt duo contradictoria sibi invicem contradicentia et unum illorum significat sicut est et aliud (*V**12rb) non significat aliter quam est. Quod probatur sic : Nam ' Illa propositio non[50] significat aliter quam est ', demonstrata per ly (*C*76v) ' illa ' contradictoria illius, significat quod[51] illa non significat aliter quam est ; et ita est quod illa non significat aliter quam est ; et illa negativa[52] non est pertinens ad inferendum se ipsam non[53] significare[54] sicut est ; ergo, illa significat sicut est. Et tamen affirmativa sibi contradicens non significat aliter quam est eo quod illa est pertinens ad inferendum se ipsam non significare sicut est. Et sic[55] sequitur conclusio, quam concedo in quolibet[56] casu mundi ubi[57] est ita quod[58] altera pars contradicens est pertinens ad inferendum se ipsam non[59] significare sicut est, sicut est in proposito. Quare, et cetera.

(106) Simile est si ponatur quod tantum illa sit ' Omnis propositio significat aliter quam est ' et ista sic praecise[60] significet. Illo casu posito, neganda est illa ' Omnis propositio significat aliter quam est '. Et dicendum quod illa nec[61] significat sicut est nec aliter quam est, posito casu priori[62], eo quod illa est pertinens ad inferendum se ipsam non significare sicut est.

(44) illa... est *om. V.*
(45) « Illa... et *om. C.*
(46) aliter quam *C.*
(47) fore *add. C.*
(48) non *C.*
(49) alia *C.*
(50) non *om. C.*
(51) illius... quod/ scilicet *C.*
(52) negativa *om. C.*
(53) non *om. V*.*
(54) principaliter *add. C.*
(55) non *add. C.*
(56) quam... quolibet/ Dicendum est concedendo conclusionem suae a quo *C.*
(57) videlicet *V.*
(58) ubi... quod/ et generaliter ubi *C.*
(59) non *V* interl.*
(60) principaliter *C.*
(61) principaliter non *C.*
(62) posito... priori/ sicut (sicut *om. C*) in priori sophismate *CV.*

(107) Simile est in parte[63] ' Illa non significat sicut est '. Ponatur quod per ly ' illa ' demonstratur eadem et quod[64] illa sic praecise[65] significat. Deinde proponatur ' Illa non significat sicut est '. Si negatur vel dubitatur, contra : Oppositum illius non potest stare[66] cum casu. Nam si potest poni, ponatur, et arguitur sic : Illa significat sicut est ; ergo, ita est sicut illa significat. Et illa solum significat quod illa non significat sicut est ; ergo, ita est sicut illa significat[67] ' Illa non significat sicut est '[68]. Et sic sequitur contradictorium. Si conceditur ' Illa non significat sicut est ' proponatur[69] ' Illa non significat sicut est '. Qua concessa, arguitur sic : Ita est quod illa non (*V*159va) significat sicut est ; et illa sic principaliter significat ; ergo, ita est sicut[70] illa principaliter significat ; ergo, significat sicut est, cujus oppositum est concessum.

(108) Solutio : Concedenda est illa ' Illa non significat sicut est '. Et concedendum est quod ita est quod illa non significat sicut est[71]. Et concedendum est quod illa sic principaliter significat[72]. Et neganda est consequentia illa « ergo ita est sicut illa significat principaliter »[73]. Sed oportet addere antecedenti quod illa non foret pertinens ad inferendum se ipsam non significare sicut est. Et si illud addatur, illud est negandum. Nam sequitur immediate « Illa non significat sicut est ; ergo, illa non significat sicut est »[74].

(109) Simile est si ponatur illa[75] ' Non est ita sicut illa propositio principaliter significat ' et quod illa[76] principaliter sic significet, scilicet, quod non est ita sicut illa principaliter significat, et quod per ly ' ista ' demonstretur illa eadem. Hoc posito, concedenda est illa ' Non est ita sicut illa principaliter[77] significat '. Et dicendum quod illa non significat sicut est nec aliter quam est, ut in priori sophismate.

(110) (*V**12va) Simile est si ponatur quod tantum illa propositio sit ' Falsum est ' et quod illa praecise significet quod falsum est et quod quaelibet propositio quae significat sicut est sit vera[78]. Deinde proponitur

(63) si ponitur quod ista sit omnis propositio *add. C.*
(64) per ly *C.*
(65) principaliter *C.*
(66) significare *V*.*
(67) ita... significat *om V.*
(68) ergo... est *om. C.*
(69) illa ' Ita est quod *add. C.*
(70) quod *C.*
(71) Et... est *om. V.* Et... est/ et quod ita est sicut principaliter significat *C.*
(72) Et... significat *om. C.*
(73) principaliter *om. CV.*
(74) Expliciunt insolubilia *add. C.* (The text of *C* ends here.)
(75) quod ista propositio *V.*
(76) Et... illa *om. V.*
(77) principaliter *om. V.*
(78) et quaelibet quae significat aliter quam est est falsa *add. V.*

' Falsum est '. Si conceditur vel dubitatur, contra : Sequitur « Falsum est ; et omnis propositio est illa ; igitur, illa est falsa ». Et sequitur[79] : « ergo, illa significat aliter quam est ». Et ultra : ergo, non est ita sicut illa significat ; et illa solum significat quod falsum est ; ergo, non est ita quod falsum est. Et ultra : ergo, nullum falsum est. Et sic ex illa cum casu sequitur suum contradictorium. Si negatur ' Falsum est ', contra : Illa propositio est ; et non est vera ; et significat sicut est vel aliter quam est ; ergo, illa est falsa. Et ultra : ergo, falsum est.

(111) Solutio : Admittendus est casus et negandum est ' Falsum est '[80]. Et concedendum est quod illa propositio est et quod illa non est vera. Et tunc negandum[81] est quod ista significet sicut est vel aliter quam est eo quod illa est pertinens ad inferendum se ipsam non significare sicut est. Nam sequitur : Falsum est ; et omnis propositio est illa ' Falsum est ' ; ergo, illa est falsa. Et ultra : ergo, significat aliter quam est. Et ultra : ergo, illa non significat sicut est. Et per consequens illa non significat sicut est nec aliter quam est illo casu posito. Si tamen ponatur ille casus quod illa propositio sit ' Falsum est ' et nulla alia et quod illa principaliter significet quod falsum est et quod omnis propositio significans sicut est sit vera et quod omnis propositio significat sicut est vel aliter quam est[82], tunc ille casus non est admittendus eo quod includit quod eadem propositio sit vera et falsa, quod non est possibile.

(112) Et haec de insolubilibus dicta sufficiant[83]. Sed si qui contra pertractata[84] instare[85] volunt[86] non vocibus more protervientium sed sententiae[87] repugnent. In istis autem[88] si quid completum sive veritati consonum[89] repertum fuerit, ex dictis Aristotelis et aliorum reverendorum magistrorum colligitur[90]. Si quid diminutum aut veritati dissonum inveniatur, soli meae insufficientiae est impugnandum. Amen[91].

(79) illa est falsa *add.* *V*.
(80) est *om.* *V**.
(81) Abbreviation uncertain in *V**.
(82) significat... est/ significans aliter quam est sit falsa *V**. (The reading in *V* seems required by the sense of the argument.)
(83) Deo gratias. Amen *add* *V*.
(84) qui... pertractata/ quis hic determinatis *V*.
(85) instaret *V**.
(86) voluerint *V*.
(87) sententias suas *V**.
(88) autem *om.* *V**.
(89) veritati consonum/ veritatem continentem, ut fingo *V*.
(90) tolle *V*.
(91) Suiset *V*. Expliciunt insolubilia subtilissimi viri et in tota philosophia profundissimi Richardi Suiset doctoris anglici et rerum subtilissimarum atque intricatarum monarcae — immo, et ut verius dixerem, adinventoris. Deo sint laudes infinitae. Amen *add.* *V**. (On the confusion of Roger with Richard Swyneshed, see Weisheipl's paper, referred to in n. 1 to the introduction, above.)

VIII

ROGER SWYNESHED'S THEORY OF INSOLUBILIA: A STUDY OF SOME OF HIS PRELIMINARY SEMANTIC NOTIONS

One of the influential and most controversial mediaeval theories of the semantic paradoxes – *insolubilia*, as they were called then – was that of the Benedictine Roger Swyneshed, who wrote a treatise on the topic sometime probably between 1330 and 1335 (1). The Latin text of that treatise has recently been edited and published (2). Swyneshed's theory has been discussed several times in the recent secondary literature, (3) so that by now the main outlines of his view are fairly familiar. For Swyneshed, a true sentence must not only correspond to the facts ("signify as is the case", as he put it) (4); it must also not "falsify itself". A false sentence on the other hand, may be false either because it fails to correspond to the facts ("signifies otherwise than is the case") or else because it "falsifies itself". The semantic paradoxes are self-falsifying sentences, so that they are false even though they correspond to the facts. Logical consequence, on this theory, need not preserve truth although it does preserve the property of "signifying as is the case".

At this superficial level, Swyneshed's view seems fair enough. Its basic strategy is in effect to reject Tarski's so called "criterion of adequacy" by suspending semantic ascent (5) in certain instances; the notion of truth is thus distinguished from the notion of correspondence.

Nevertheless, when one looks more closely at the details of Swyneshed's theory, the picture becomes very complex indeed. In the end one wonders whether the theory is not simply incoherent. Let us begin with Swyneshed's definitions of truth and falsehood (6):

> The second (definition) is this: A true sentence is a sentence that does not falsify itself and that principally signifies as is the case, either naturally or from the imposition or impositions by which it was last imposed to signify.
> The third definition: A false sentence is an expression that falsifies itself, or else an expression that does not falsify itself and that principally signifies otherwise than is the case, either naturally or from the imposition or impositions by which it was last imposed to signify.

Two parts of these definitions deserve our attention: the notion of a sentence's signification and the notion of self-falsification.

The adverb 'principally' in the above definitions is to be explained as follows. The "principal" signification of a sentence is what is sometimes called its "total" or "adequate" signification. The sentence 'John kicked the ball over the fence', for example, principally (totally, adequately) signifies that John kicked the ball over the fence. On the other hand, it "partially" signifies that John kicked the ball, and that John kicked. In general (replacing *'p'* and *'q'* uniformly throughout), if *'p'* is a string of phonemes or letters making up a grammatically well-formed sentence, and if *'q'* is another string of phonemes or letters making up a grammatically well-formed sentence and containing *'p'* as a proper substring, then *'q' principally* (totally, adequately) signifies that *q*, but *partially* signifies that *p* (7). This notion of course presupposes that the signification of a sentence as a whole is a function of the semantic roles of all its parts, a presupposition that not all mediaeval authors accepted (8) and to which Swyneshed himself did not always adhere (9). Nevertheless, throughout his *Insolubilia* Swyneshed seems to be concerned with principal signification only; partial signification plays no role. We shall therefore omit the adverb 'principally' in the discussion below, taking it as implicit. Indeed, the manuscripts seem to include or omit the adverb quite unsystematically throughout Swyneshed's text.

For Swyneshed, sentences may get their signification in one of three ways. Thoughts or mental sentences, if there are any, (10) signify by nature; their signification is not a matter of choice or convention (11). Spoken or written sentences, on the other hand, signify "artificially", (12) and this in one of two ways. They may be "imposed" to signify; that is, they may be arbitrarily or conventionally assigned by the speakers or writers to perform certain significative tasks. In such cases, there is no guarantee that all the speakers or writers will assign a given sentence the same task, so that a sentence may signify in several different ways by several different impositions at once. On the other hand, spoken or written sentences may also be interpreted by a hearer or reader in a way they were never intended to signify by a speaker or writer. In such a case the sentence signifies (to the hearer or reader) artificially, but not by imposition. Presumably a given sentence may have different significations of this kind to different hearers or readers at the same time (13).

This last kind of signification plays no role in Swyneshed's definitions of truth and falsehood. For him, the truth value of a spoken or written sentence is to be assessed according to the speaker's or writer's intentions, not according to however the hearer or reader might happen to misinterpret those intentions. The phrase 'last imposed' in the definitions indicates that in this assessment later impositions take precedence over earlier ones. In cases where several impositions are in effect at once, truth value is presumably assessed separately relative to each imposition, although the definitions are not altogether clear about this (14).

To "signify as is the case" seems at first perhaps to be the notion of signifying in a way that "corresponds to the facts", "to reality", and to "signify otherwise than is the case" to be simply "to signify, but not as is the case". But this will not do. For if this interpretation were correct, then every significant sentence would signify either as is the case or otherwise than is the case, and so would be bivalent (15) in virtue of the above definitions. (In fact, it is easy to show from those definitions that a sentence is bivalent if and only if it signifies either as is the case or otherwise than is the case.) But Swyneshed explicitly denies that (16). He gives examples of two quite different kinds of sentences for which, he says, bivalence fails. First, there are paradoxical sentences like 'This sentence signifies otherwise than is the case' or 'This sentence does not signify as is the case' (17). Second, there are sentences about future contingents (18).

Swyneshed's inclusion of the second type of sentence suggests another way to interpret the phrases 'signify as is the case' and 'signify otherwise than is the case'. For the difficulty with assigning a truth value to sentences about future contingents arises because there appears to be as yet no "fact of the matter" one way or the other about such contingencies, no feature of the present ontology of the world that could be identified either as the contingency's being about-to-happen or as its being not-about-to-happen. If there were already such a "fact of the matter", then the issue would be settled and no longer contingent (19). This suggests that for a sentence to "signify as is the case" is for it to signify in a way that corresponds to some fact that really obtains, while for it to "signify otherwise than is the case" is for it to signify in a way that denies or contradicts some fact that really obtains. Where there is no "fact of the matter" one way or the other, the sentence signifies in a way that is neither as is the case nor otherwise than is the case.

But while this interpretation will perhaps work for Swyneshed's theory of future contingents, it conflicts with what he says about his other examples of failures of bivalence. For instance, in his discussion of the sentence (let us call it '*k*') 'This sentence signifies otherwise than is the case', Swyneshed says that indeed there is a fact of the matter; the fact is that *k* does not signify otherwise than is the case. And any sentence that signifies in a way corresponding to that fact will signify as is the case (and presumably be true). Nevertheless, *k* itself, even though it signifies in a way contradicting that actual fact of the matter, does not signify otherwise than is the case (20). Again, there is a fact of the matter about the sentence 'This sentence does not signify as is the case' (call it '*k*'). The fact is that *k* indeed does not signify as is the case. But, even though *k* signifies in a way that corresponds to that fact, it does not follow that *k* signifies as is the case (21).

In both these last two examples, Swyneshed says, the reason for the offending sentence's failure is that it is "relevant to inferring that it does not signify as is the case" (22). Some rough and ready sense of what this means can be gathered from the examples. Swyneshed attempts to define the notion more precisely as follows (23):

> For this it has to be noted that a sentence relevant to inferring that it does not signify principally as is the case is one from which, together with the case's being altogether as it is, it follows or is apt to follow that it does not signify principally as is the case.

Some of the difficulties with this notion will become apparent if we examine the idea of "relevance" in another context, in the notion of "self-falsification" that is the second of the two ingredients to merit our attention in Swyneshed's definitions of truth and falsehood (24).

A "self-falsifying" sentence is one that signifies either as is the case or otherwise than is the case and is "relevant to inferring that it is false" (25). This may happen in one of several ways. Some self-falsifying sentences falsify themselves "mediately", others do so "immediately". The former are those sentences that do not refer directly to themselves, but rather are members of a vicious many-staged referential cycle. For example, where *k* signifies that *j* is false and *j* signifies that *k* is false, each sentence falsifies the other immediately, but itself only mediately (26).

Immediately self-falsifying sentences, however, are directly self-referential sentences relevant to inferring that they are false. Some such sentences are relevant and sufficient for inferring that they are false, while others are relevant but insufficient. In the latter case, one or more additional premises are required; in the former they are not (27).

The latter case admits of one further subdivision. Some insufficient relevant sentences are relevant only to inferring that they themselves are false, others are relevant to inferring that other sentences are false as well. For example, if Socrates says only 'Socrates is speaking a falsehood', his sentence is (insufficiently) relevant to inferring only that it itself is false. (It is insufficient because one needs to add the premise that Socrates says only that sentence.) On the other hand, if there are many existing sentences, (28) then the sentence 'Every sentence is false' is (insufficiently) relevant not only to inferring that it itself is false but also to inferring that the other sentences are false too. (It is insufficient because one needs to add the premise that this or that – indicating one of the existing sentences – is a sentence.) (29)

As a first approximation we may say that in general a sentence *k* is "relevant to inferring" that *p* if and only if *k* is a premise in a valid argument that *p* (30). In some passages, Swyneshed adds the stipulation that *k* must actually be used in the argument, that it is not just an idle, extra step; the argument would be invalid if *k* were omitted (31). If there is such an argument in which *k* is the only premise, then *k* is relevant and sufficient for inferring that *p*. If not, but rather all such arguments have other premises in addition to *k*, then *k* is relevant but insufficient for inferring that *p*.

Nevertheless, although Swyneshed seems concerned only with the validity of such arguments, it is clear that validity is not enough. If validity were all that is required, then for almost any sentence *k* that is not relevant and sufficient for inferring that it is false, it is possible to construct an argument showing that *k* is at least relevant and insufficient for inferring that it is false, and indeed for inferring anything whatever. For from *k* and the contradictory or denial of *k* one can validly infer anything at all, including the falsehood of *k* (32). But one cannot in general infer the falsehood of *k* from the contradictory of *k* alone; one needs to add the premise that *k* exists (33). Hence if validity were all that is required, perfectly innocuous sentences signifying as is the case – such as 'Two plus two are four' – would turn out to be relevant to inferring that they are false and thus, since they signify as is the case, would falsify themselves (34) and so be false in virtue of Swyneshed's definition of falsehood. This clearly will not do.

If on the other hand we require not only validity but soundness, in the sense that each premise of the argument must signify as is the case, (35) then no sentence that does not signify as is the case is relevant to inferring anything whatever. But this conflicts with a claim we have already seen, that the sentences 'This sentence signifies otherwise than is the case' and 'This sentence does not signify as is the case' signify neither as is the case nor otherwise than is the case because they are "relevant to inferring that they do not signify as is the case"; on the present approach, if such sentences are relevant to inferring anything at all, they must signify as is the case.

A third possibility is to require something less than soundness but more than mere validity, to require that any premises other than *k* must signify as is the case, although if *k* is relevant to inferring that *p*, *k* itself need not signify as is the case. This would indeed conform to Swyneshed's actual wording: "from it (i.e., *k*) together with (a sentence signifying) the case's being (altogether) as (in fact) it is", it follows that *p* (36). It is only the additional premises that are specifically required to signify as is the case (37).

But such an approach would have the result that straightforwardly false sentences would be relevant to inferring that they are false, in virtue of an argument from a contradiction just as before (38). And Swyneshed denies this. In one passage he says that the sentence 'A man is an ass' does not falsify itself, (39) which since the sentence signifies otherwise than is the case, amounts to denying that it is relevant to inferring that it is false (40). But it certainly would be so relevant on this third approach. Perhaps significantly, Swyneshed's argument in this passage seems confused (41).

I do not yet know how to reconcile all these strands of Swyneshed's theory. Perhaps in the end the theory is simply incoherent. For the historians of semiotics, this illustrates a general methodological problem. To what extent must a historian give an author the benefit of the doubt? It is clearly wrong to dismiss or reject a view simply because one does not yet see how it goes. Yet at some point even the most modest historian ought to begin to suspect that the difficulties with a particularly recalcitrant theory lie not in his own failure to understand but rather in the theory itself. Where does one cross that line? Have we crossed is yet with Swyneshed? I do not know.

NOTES

1) On Swyneshed, who is not to be confused with Richard Swyneshed, the Oxford "Calculator", see James A. Weisheipl: Roger Swyneshed, O.S.B., Logician, Natural Philosopher, and Theologian, in: *Oxford Studies Presented to Daniel Callus*, ("Oxford Historical Society", new series, vol. 16; Oxford: Clarendon Press, 1964), pp. 231-252.
2) Paul Vincent Spade: Roger Swyneshed's *Insolubilia:* Edition and Comments, *Archives d'histoire doctrinale et littéraire du moyen âge* 46 (1979), pp. 177-220. References to this edition will be simply by the word *'Insolubilia'*.
3) Paul Vincent Spade: *The Mediaeval Liar: A Catalogue of the Insolubilia-Literature*, (Toronto: Pontifical Institute of Mediaeval Studies, 1975), item LXIII, pp. 102-105; Paul Vincent Spade, tr.: *William Heytesbury: On "Insoluble" Sentences. Chapter One of His Rules for Solving Sophisms*, (Toronto: Pontifical Institute of Mediaeval Studies, 1979), see index of names; Paul Vincent Spade: Insolubilia, in: Norman Kretzmann *et al., (eds.): Cambridge History of Later Medieval Philosophy*, (Cambridge: University Press, forthcoming), Ch. 12, pp. 246-253 at pp. 250-251.
4) This identification of "signifying as is the case" with correspondence is too facile, as we shall see, as is the identification below of "signifying otherwise than is the case" with failure to correspond. I adopt these identifications here only provisionally, as a first approximation.
5) The inference from *P* to the claim that *P* is true.
6) *Insolubilia*, para. 14-15: "Secunda est haec: Propositio vera est propositio non falsificans se principaliter sicut est significans naturaliter aut ex impositione vel impositionibus qua vel quibus ultimo fuit imposita ad significandum. Tertia definitio: Propositio falsa est oratio falsificans se vel oratio non falsificans se principaliter aliter quam est significans naturaliter, ex impositione, vel impositionibus qua vel quibus ultimo fuit imposita ad significandum."
7) See Paul Vincent Spade: *Peter of Ailly: Concepts and Insolubles. An Annotated Translation.* (Dordrecht: D. Reidel, 1980), p. 51 para. 168 and p. 127 n. 457; and Alfonso Maierù: *Terminologia logica della tarda scolastica*, (Rome: Ateneo, 1972), p. 490 n. 2.
8) See, for example, Paul Vincent Spade: Robert Fland's *Consequentiae:* An Edition, *Mediaeval Studies* 38 (1976), pp. 54-84 at p. 59 para. 9-10.
9) See, e.g., Paul Vincent Spade: Roger Swyneshed's *Obligationes:* Edition and Comments, *Archives d'histoire doctrinale et littéraire du moyen âge* 44 (1977), pp. 243-285 at p. 258 para. 34; *Insolubilia*, para. 90 and reply para. 96. See also the remarks on Swyneshed in Paul Vincent Spade: *Insolubilia* and Bradwardine's Theory of Signification, *Medioevo* 8 (1982), forthcoming. †
10) Swyneshed seems unsure about this. See *Insolubilia*, p. 185 n. 99.
11) This was a common view of mental language. See Spade: *Peter of Ailly*, index s.v. 'signification, natural'.
12) The manuscripts disagree on the proper term to use here. Some have 'actually' or 'accidentally'.
13) On these distinctions, see *Insolubilia*, para. 11-12.

14) There are other possible approaches consistent with the definitions. For instance, one might require that a true spoken or written sentence signify as is the case under all the impositions then in effect, while for a false sentence it is sufficient that it signify otherwise than is the case under at least one of the impositions then in effect. The opposite approach would also work. What Swyneshed will not allow, however, is that a sentence be both true and false at once. See *Insolubilia*, para. 22.
15) I.e., either true or false.
16) *Insolubilia*, para. 2-3 & 28-32.
17) *Insolubilia*, para. 2-3. If Swyneshed's strategy for handling paradoxes concerning truth and falsehood that arise when truth is identified with "correspondence" (but see n. 4 above), so that Tarski's "criterion of adequacy" is satisfied, is to distinguish the notion of truth from the notion of correspondence, it is not surprising that there still remain paradoxes concerning the notion of correspondence itself. (It is Swyneshed's consideration of these paradoxes that, as we shall see, makes the identification mentioned in n. 4 above too facile.)
18) *Insolubilia*, para. 32. Not many authors in Swyneshed's day were willing to accept failure of bivalence in the case of future contingents. See Calvin G. Normore: Future Contingents, in Kretzmann *et al.* (eds.): *Cambridge History of Later Medieval Philosophy*, Ch. 18.
19) See *ibid.* for a discussion of mediaeval responses to this apparent problem.
20) *Insolubilia*, para. 103-105.
21) *Insolubilia*, para. 107-108.
22) *Insolubilia*, para. 104-105 & 108.
23) *Insolubilia*, para. 3: "Pro quo est notandum quod propositio pertinens ad inferendum se ipsam non significare principaliter sicut est est talis ex qua cum totaliter sic esse sicut est sequitur vel natum est sequi illam non significare principaliter sicut est." See n. 27 below.
24) This notion of self-falsification in the definition of falsehood perhaps renders that definition circular. But the threat can hardly be assessed until the notion of self-falsification itself is clearly understood.
25) *Insolubilia*, para. 17. The proviso that the sentence signifies either as is the case or otherwise than is the case is not in the text, but has to be added. See the objection in para. 93 and the reply in para. 99. See also para. 18.
26) *Insolubilia*, para. 4. The example here (Swyneshed's own) is not one we should normally regard as vicious; if one of the two is true and the other false, there is no paradox. Swyneshed, however, like many mediaeval authors, regarded such cases as vicious on the grounds that there is no semantic basis for selecting one of the two sentences as the true one at the expense of the other. On such reasoning and its implications, see Paul Vincent Spade: On A Conservative Attitude toward Some Naive Semantic Principles, *Notre Dame Journal of Formal Logic* 15 (1975), pp. 597-602.
27) *Insolubilia*, para. 5-7. The presence of an additional premise is signalled in Swyneshed's text by forms of the phrase 'with the case's being as it is' *(cum sic esse sicut est)*. This seems to mean "together with a sentence signifying the case to be as in fact it is". See, e.g., *Insolubilia*, p. 181 n. 35. Sometimes the adverb 'altogether' *(totaliter)* is added: 'the case's being altogether as it is'. See e.g. para. 6-7. The role of the adverb is not clear.
28) 'Sentence' *(propositio)* for Swyneshed means sentence-token.

29) *Insolubilia*, para. 6-7.
30) *Insolubilia*, para. 5-7. This notion of "relevance" *(pertinentia)* in Swyneshed's *Insolubilia* is not the same as the notion of relevance in the mediaeval *obligationes*-literature, including Swyneshed's own treatise *Obligationes*. See *Insolubilia*, p. 181 n. 37.
31) See *Insolubilia*, p. 181 n. 37, and the references there.
32) Most authors accepted this inference in Swyneshed's day, although I have not found any passage in which Swyneshed affirms it explicitly. In any event, if valid inferences for Swyneshed are just those that preserve the property of signifying as is the case (see n. 35 below), if correspondence with the facts is a necessary, even though not a sufficient, condition for signifying as is the case, and if mutually contradictory facts never obtain simultaneously – all of which Swyneshed would appear to accept – then anything whatever follows from a contradiction.
33) See n. 28 and the discussion of the sentence 'Every sentence is false' above. There are some odd cases in which one can infer the falsehood of *k* from the contradictory of *k* alone. Let *k* be '*k* does not signify otherwise than is the case'. Then from '*k* does signify otherwise than is the case', the contradictory of *k*, it follows that *k* is false, in virtue of Swyneshed's definition of falsehood.
34) See n. 25 above.
35) Recall that for Swyneshed logical consequence need not preserve truth but does preserve the property of signifying as is the case. See *Insolubilia*, para. 35.
36) See nn. 23 & 27 above.
37) See also *Insolubilia*, para. 91 and reply para. 97.
38) There would perhaps be odd false sentences for which such an argument would not be available. If *k* is '*k* does not signify as is the case' then, as we have seen, the fact is that *k* does not signify as is the case, so that the contradictory of *k* would appear to be false. Nevertheless, the argument from the contradictory of *k* together with *k* itself is not an argument in which the additional premise, namely *k*, signifies as is the case.
39) *Insolubilia*, para. 95. See the argument in para. 89 to which this passage is a reply.
40) See n. 25 above.
41) See *Insolubilia*, p. 213 n. 80.

IX

Ockham's Rule of Supposition: Two Conflicts in His Theory

I

In his thirteenth-century *Introductiones in logicam*, William of Sherwood enunciates the following principle: "Subjects are of such sorts as their predicates may have allowed." [1] That is, the kind of supposition [2] or reference a term has in a given sentence depends at least in part on what kind of a term the predicate is. This principle I shall call the "rule of supposition". Thus, in 'A man is running' the subject 'man' has personal supposition, while in 'Man is a species' it has simple and in 'Man is a name' it has material.[3]

[1] *William of Sherwood's Introduction to Logic*, Norman Kretzmann, tr., (Minneapolis: University of Minnesota Press, 1966), p. 113. The Latin is: "talia sunt subiecta, qualia permiserint predicata." Cf. Martin Grabmann, ed., *Die Introductiones in logicam des Wilhelm von Shyreswood († nach 1267)*, (München: Verlag der Bayerischen Akademie der Wissenschaften, 1937), p. 78. I suspect it was this doctrine, in particular as it was developed by later authors, which was responsible for E. A. Moody's puzzling remarks about supposition's being a syntactical relation of term to term rather than a semantic relation of term to thing. Cf. his *Truth and Consequence in Mediaeval Logic*, (Amsterdam: North-Holland, 1953), p. 22. But contrast *ibid.*, p. 11. Moody's remarks have generated more than a little confusion in the modern literature, not least of which is the attribution to the mediaevals of a "syntactic" notion of truth. Cf., e.g., Alfonso Maierù, "Il problema della verità nelle opere di Guglielmo Heytesbury," *Studi medievali*, serie terza, 7 (1966), pp. 40-74, especially p. 46.

[2] I am concerned in this paper only with that portion of supposition theory which T. K. Scott calls "the doctrine of supposition proper", as opposed to "the doctrine of modes of personal supposition". Cf. the introduction to his *John Buridan: Sophisms on Meaning and Truth*, (New York: Appleton-Century-Crofts, 1966), pp. 29-42. I assume a minimal familiarity with at least this portion of supposition theory. Discussions may also be found in Philotheus Boehner, *Medieval Logic: An Outline of Its Development from 1250-c. 1400*, (Manchester: University Press, 1952), pp. 27-51; Boehner, "Ockham's Theory of Supposition and the Notion of Truth," in his *Collected Articles on Ockham*, (St. Bonaventure, N.Y.: The Franciscan Institute, 1958), pp. 232-267; Boehner, ed., & tr., *Ockham: Philosophical Writings*, (London: Nelson, 1957), section 4; William and Martha Kneale, *The Development of Logic* (Oxford: Clarendon Press, 1962), pp. 246-274; E. A. Moody, *op. cit.*, pp. 23-29.

[3] Kretzmann, *op. cit.*, p. 107; Grabmann, *op. cit.*, p. 75.

There are two ways in which this rule is left incomplete in Sherwood's discussion. First, is the supposition of the subject term unambiguously fixed by the kind of term the predicate is, or does the predicate merely narrow down the kinds of supposition the subject may take? Second, what features of the predicate are relevant, and how? William is silent on both counts.

In Walter Burley's longer tract *De puritate artis logicae* (1325-28),[4] the first question had been resolved. Burley maintains that any term in subject position may have personal supposition with respect to any predicate whatsoever, but it can have material or simple supposition only when it is "matched" with an appropriate predicate.[5] Hence, for instance,[6]

> ... if it be said: 'A man runs', or 'A man is white', this term 'man' determinately has personal supposition. But if it be said: 'Man is a species' or 'Man is a monosyllable', the term 'man' can suppose indifferently either personally or simply or materially. ... Hence this is not multiple: 'A man runs', or 'A man is an animal', because in these the subject supposes personally. Yet sentences of this sort: 'Man is a species' and 'Man is a

[4] Philotheus Boehner, ed., *Walter Burleigh: De puritate artis logicae tractatus longior, with a Revised Edition of the Tractatus brevior*, (St. Bonaventure, N.Y.: The Franciscan Institute, 1955), p. viii. All quotations from the *De puritate* will be from the *tractatus longior* tract 1, part 1.

[5] *Ibid.*, ca. 3, p. 9 line 34—p. 10 line 2: "Intelligendum est, quod terminus potens habere diversas suppositiones potest de virtute sermonis respectu cuiuscumque praedicati habere suppositionem personalem, quia illa est primaria acceptio vel suppositio termini. Suppositionem tamen materialem vel simplicem non potest habere nisi respectu termini sibi convenientis secundum suppositionem simplicem vel materialem."

[6] *Ibid.*, p. 10 lines 2-7, 19-34: "... si dicatur: 'Homo currit', vel: 'Homo est albus', iste terminus 'homo' determinate habet suppositionem personalem. Sed si dicatur: 'Homo est species', vel: 'Homo est disyllabum', potest iste terminus 'homo' indifferenter supponere personaliter vel simpliciter vel materialiter.... Unde haec non est multiplex: 'Homo currit', vel: 'Homo est animal', quia in istis subiectum supponit personaliter. Sed tamen huiusmodi propositiones: 'Homo est species', 'Homo est disyllabum', sunt multiplices penes secundum modum aequivocationis, ex eo quod ille terminus 'homo' potest habere suppositionem personalem vel simplicem vel materialem. Ista enim propositio: 'Homo est species', est multiplex, ex eo quod iste terminus 'homo' potest habere suppositionem personalem vel simplicem. Et ista: 'Homo est dissylabum', est distinguenda penes secundum modum aequivocationis, ex eo quod ille terminus 'homo' potest habere suppositionem personalem vel materialem, ita quod terminus potens habere istas suppositiones potest etiam habere suppositionem personalem respectu cuiuscumque, sed suppositionem simplicem vel materialem non nisi ex adjuncto, videlicet ex hoc quod comparatur alicui convenienti sibi secundum suppositionem talem, scilicet simplicem vel materialem." All translations in this paper are mine, except for the passages from William of Sherwood.

> monosyllable' are multiples with the second mode of equivocation,[7] by the fact that the term 'man' can have personal or simple or material supposition. For the sentence 'Man is a species' is multiple by the fact that the term 'man' can have personal or simple supposition. And this one 'Man is a monosyllable' is to be distinguished with the second mode of equivocation, by the fact that the term 'man' can have personal or material supposition, so that a term able to have these suppositions can also have personal supposition with respect to anything whatsoever, but simple or material supposition only from an adjunct, namely, from the fact that it is matched with something fitting it according to such supposition, namely, simple or material.

For Burley, then, sentences with certain special kinds of predicates are equivocal and must be "distinguished". Such predicates do not unambiguously fix the kind of supposition their subjects have. But it has not yet been made clear what these kinds of predicates are.

William of Ockham adopts a version of the rule of supposition that agrees with Burley's but goes beyond it with an account of the relevant features of predicates.[8] He says: [9]

[7] On the three modes of the fallacy of equivocation, cf. Aristotle, *Sophistic Refutations* 4, 166 a 14ff. The second mode is that in which we take a word "by custom" in more than one sense. Aristotle gives no example. The mediaevals took this mode to be equivocation by "transumption". William of Sherwood gives the example: 'whatever runs has feet, the Seine runs; therefore the Seine has feet' Cf. Kretzmann, *op. cit.*, p. 136; Grabmann, *op. cit.*, p. 87. It is hard to see how Burley thinks that the sentences he mentions are equivocal in this mode. † A more likely candidate is the third mode of equivocation, "when words that have a simple sense taken alone have more than one meaning in combination; e.g., 'knowing letters'. For each word, both 'knowing' and 'letters', possibly has a single meaning: but both together have more than one—either that the letters themselves have knowledge or that some one else has it of them" (Aristotle, *loc. cit.*, Oxford tr.). William of Ockham takes such sentences to be equivocal in this mode. Cf. Philotheus Boehner, ed., *William Ockham*: *Summa logicae* (St. Bonaventure, N.Y.: The Franciscan Institute, 1951-54), I, ca. 65, line 15.

[8] Burley's longer tract *De puritate* appears to have been written shortly after Ockham's *Summa logicae*. Cf. Boehner's ed. of Burley, p. viii. Thus, while Ockham's view is the more developed, his text at least is chronologically earlier than Burley's. On the relations between Ockham and Burley, cf. L. Baudry, "Les rapports de Guillaume d'Occam et de Walter Burleigh," *Archives d'histoire doctrinale et littéraire du moyen âge*, 1934, pp. 155-173, and Stephen F. Brown, "Walter Burleigh's Treatise *De Suppositionibus* and Its Influence on William of Ockham," *Franciscan Studies* 32 (1972), pp. 15-64.

[9] Ockham, *Summa logicae*, I, 65, lines 42-51: "Potest igitur ista regula dari, quod quando terminus potens habere praedictam triplicem suppositionem comparatur extremo communi incomplexis vel complexis, sive prolatis sive scriptis, semper terminus potest habere suppositionem materialem vel personalem, et est talis propositio distinguenda. Quando vero comparatur extremo significanti intentionem animae, est distinguenda, eo quod potest habere suppositionem simplicem vel personalem. Quando autem comparatur extremo communi omnibus praedictis, tunc est distinguenda, eo quod potest habere suppositionem simplicem, materialem vel personalem."

> This rule, therefore, can be given, that when a term able to have the aforesaid three kinds of supposition is matched with an extreme common to incomplex or complex <expressions>, whether spoken or written, the term can always have material or personal supposition, and such a sentence is to be distinguished. But when it is matched with an extreme signifying an intention of the soul, it is to be distinguished insofar as it can have simple or personal supposition. But when it is matched with an extreme common to all the aforesaid, then it is to be distinguished insofar as it can have simple, material or personal supposition.

Ockham thus gives a complete version of the rule of supposition which we first saw in rudimentary form in William of Sherwood. Nevertheless, I shall argue in sections II and III, below, that Ockham does not really want the rule he gives. It conflicts with the main body of his doctrine in two ways; there are pressures from two directions to revise his version of the rule. In section IV, I shall examine how some later formulations of the rule relieved these pressures.

II

The two conflicts just mentioned correspond to the two deficiencies noted above in Sherwood's discussion. The first conflict arises from Ockham's accepting the view that some sentences must be distinguished according to the kinds of supposition their subject terms may have. The second arises in addition from Ockham's own apparent contribution, namely, from his account of the relevant features of predicates. The first conflict may be brought out in the following steps:

1) The division of supposition into personal, material and simple applies to terms in the mental language (concepts) as much as to spoken or written terms in physical language.[10]
2) The kind or kinds of supposition a subject term may have is determined by the rule of supposition.
3) According to that rule, some sentences are equivocal and must be distinguished.
4) Hence, some sentences in the mental language are equivocal and must be distinguished.
5) But, on the contrary, there is no equivocation in the mental language.

[10] *Ibid.*, I, 64, lines 59-62: "Sicut autem talis diversitas suppositionis potest competere termino vocali et scripto, ita etiam potest competere termino mentali, quia intentio potest supponere pro illo quod significat, et pro se ipsa, et pro voce et scripto." On Ockham's mental language, cf. John Trentman, "Ockham on Mental," *Mind* 79 (1970), pp. 586-590.

Step 4 could of course be avoided by holding that Ockham's rule applies only to spoken and written language, and that the kind of supposition a term (concept) has in the mental language is to be decided in some other way. There is no evidence, however, that Ockham himself meant his rule of supposition to be restricted in this manner. Moreover, later writers met the above problem by revising the rule, not by restricting its applicability.

There remains the justification of my claim in step 5 that Ockham wants no equivocation in the mental language. With respect to equivocal *terms*, he is explicit: [11]

> Now it is to be known first that only an utterance, or some sign instituted by convention, is equivocal or univocal, and therefore an intention of the soul or concept is not equivocal or univocal, properly speaking.

Rather the univocity or equivocity of a spoken term is to be accounted for by the relation of "subordination" between spoken terms and concepts.[12] A univocal spoken term is subordinated to a single concept, while an equivocal one is subordinated to several concepts at once.[13]

Mental language then is what accounts for equivocation in spoken terms. There can be no equivocal terms (concepts) in mental language, since mental terms are not subordinated to anything further which could account for the equivocation.

About equivocal *sentences* Ockham is not so explicit. What he does say indicates a parallel doctrine. Each spoken sentence corresponds to a sentence in the mental language.[14] A spoken sentence is true or false according as the mental sentence corresponding to it is true or false.[15]

[11] Ockham, *op. cit.*, I, 13, lines 6-9: "Est autem primo sciendum, quod sola vox vel aliquod signum ad placitum institutum est aequivocum vel univocum, et ideo intentio animae vel conceptus non est aequivocus nec univocus proprie loquendo."

[12] On subordination, cf. *ibid.*, I, 3. Written terms are in turn subordinated to spoken terms. Cf. *ibid.*, I, 3, lines 25-46. Univocity and equivocation among written terms are explained by an obvious extension of the doctrine.

[13] *Ibid.*, I, 13, lines 10-12: "Est autem vox illa aequivoca, quae significans plura non est signum subordinatum uni conceptui, sed est signum unum pluribus conceptibus seu intentionibus animae subordinatum." Also, *ibid.*, lines 40f.: " 'Univocum' autem dicitur omne illud, quod est subordinatum uni conceptui, sive significet plura sive non."

[14] *Ibid.*, I, 3, lines 86-91: "Sed quod oporteat ponere talia nomina mentalis et verba et adverbia et coniunctiones et praepositiones, ex hoc convincitur, quod omni orationi vocali correspondeat alia mentalis in mente; et ideo sicut illae partes propositionis vocalis, quae sunt propter necessitatem significationis impositae, sunt distinctae, sic partes propositionis mentalis correspondentes sunt distinctae."

[15] Cf. e.g., William of Ockham, *Quodlibeta septem* (Strasbourg, 1491), quodlibet 5, q. 8, *passim*.

In some cases the correspondence is subject to general rules, and then the spoken sentence is said to be taken literally.[16] In other cases a spoken sentence is not taken literally, and then we must look in each case to the corresponding mental sentence to discover what the speaker meant, and how we are to evaluate his utterance. In this way are saved many of the authoritative sayings of the ancients, which are false literally but true in the sense in which they were made.[17]

The thrust of this is clear. To take a sentence in one sense or another is to correlate it (subordinate it) to one mental sentence or another. Since there are no further, supramental sentences to which mental sentences can be subordinated, no mental sentence can be equivocal.

The first pressure on Ockham's rule of supposition, then, is that it introduces equivocation into the mental language insofar as it requires that certain sentences be "distinguished". This latter feature of Ockham's rule is also found in Burley's, for whom it presented no problem. Burley, and realist logicians in general, had no vested interest in mental language.[18] But when Ockham and his followers moved the realists' extramental universals into the mind and turned them into concepts,[19] the old Aristotelian notion of a mental language [20] took on a new importance. It is only the nominalist followers of Ockham, then, who feel this first pressure on his formulation of the rule of supposition.

[16] Ockham, *Summa logicae*, II, 19, lines 41-43: "nam tales secundum proprietatem sermonis et locutionis, hoc est secundum regulas generales, per quas tales et consimiles iudicari debent, concedi possunt" Cf. also Boehner, "Ockham's Theory of Supposition," pp. 248-253.

[17] Cf. e.g., Ockham, *Summa logicae*, I, 66, lines 43-45: "Et ita est frequenter, quod propositiones authenticae et magistrales sunt falsae de virtute sermonis, et verae in sensu, in quo fiunt, hoc est, illi intendebant veras propositiones per eas."; *ibid.*, lines 51-53: ". . . et caeterae tales multae sunt simpliciter falsae de virtute sermonis, tamen illae propositiones, quas Philosophus intendebat per istas, sunt verae."; *ibid.*, I, 77, lines 10-18: "Et ideo multum est considerandum, quando terminus et propositio accipitur de virtute sermonis, et quando secundum usum loquentium vel secundum intentionem auctorum, et hoc quia vix invenitur aliquod vocabulum, quin in diversis locis librorum philosophorum, sanctorum et auctorum aequivoce accipiatur, et hoc penes aliquem modum aequivocationis. Et ideo volentes accipere semper vocabulum univoce et uno modo, frequenter errant circa intentiones auctorum et inquisitionem veritatis, cum fere omnia vocabula aequivoce accipiantur."

[18] Burley does mention it, however, in *Burlei super artem veterem Porphirii et Aristotelis* (Venice: Otinus (de Luna) Papiensis, 1497, no folio numbers) in his commentary on *De interpretatione* 1, 16 a 4ff., where he sides with Ockham and against Boethius, saying that terms do not primarily and in general signify concepts.

[19] Cf. Etienne Gilson, *History of Christian Philosophy in the Middle Ages*, L. K. Shook, tr., (New York: Random House, 1955), pp. 491f.

[20] *De interpretatione*, 1, 16 a 4ff.

III

The second pressure on Ockham's rule arises from his accepting the view that some sentences must be distinguished, and also from his own contribution, namely, from his specification of the features of the predicate relevant to determining the kind of supposition the subject has. The combination of these two, as we shall see, conflicts with his own definitions of the various kinds of supposition.

Ockham divides supposition as follows.[21] First there is the division into proper and improper supposition:[22] "Now one ought to know that just as there is proper supposition, when, namely, a term stands for that which it properly signifies, so there is improper supposition when a term is taken improperly." Proper supposition is then subdivided into personal, simple and material. Personal supposition is defined as follows:[23]

> Personal supposition in every case is that had when a term stands for its significate, whether that significate be a thing outside the soul, or whether it be an utterance or an intention of the soul, whether it be an inscription, or anything else imaginable, so that whensoever the subject or predicate of a sentence stands for its significate, so that it is taken significatively, the supposition is always personal.
>
> . . . . .
>
> ... But this is the definition, that supposition is personal when a term stands for its significate, and significatively.

On the other hand, "supposition is simple when a term stands for an intention of the soul but is not taken significatively",[24] while "supposition is material when a term does not suppose significatively, but stands for an utterance of for an inscription."[25]

Ockham's usage suggests that a term is "taken significatively" just †

[21] Cf. above, n. 2.

[22] Ockham, *Summa logicae*, I, 77, lines 1-3: "Oportet autem cognoscere, quod sicut est suppositio propria, quando scilicet terminus supponit pro eo, quod significat proprie, ita est suppositio impropria, quando terminus accipitur improprie."

[23] *Ibid.*, I, 64, lines 3-8, 24-26: "Suppositio personalis universaliter est illa, quando terminus supponit pro suo significato, sive illud significatum sit res extra animam, sive sit vox sive intentio animae, sive sit scriptum, sive quodcumque aliud imaginabile, ita quod quandocumque subiectum vel praedicatum propositionis supponit pro suo significato, ita quod significative tenetur, semper est suppositio personalis." And, "... sed ista est definitio, quod suppositio personalis est, quando terminus supponit pro suo significato et significative."

[24] *Ibid.*, lines 27f.: "Suppositio simplex est quando terminus supponit pro intentione animae, sed non tenetur significative."

[25] *Ibid.*, lines 39f.: "Suppositio materialis est, quando terminus non supponit significative, sed supponit vel pro voce vel pro scripto."

in case it stands for what it signifies.[26] But if this is so, then the definition of personal supposition quoted above is redundant, and personal supposition occurs just whenever a term stands for what it signifies. This seems to be confirmed by passages where Ockham conveniently ignores the "taken significatively" proviso, as if it added nothing to the definition.[27] We shall take this as Ockham's doctrine.

On the basis of this doctrine, the subjects of the following sentences stand for what they signify, and hence must have only personal supposition: [28]

1) Concept is a species.
2) Noun has four letters.
3) Being is a participle.

On the other hand, by Ockham's rule of supposition, the subject of 1) may have simple supposition, that of 2) material supposition, and that of 3) either. The rule of supposition, then, conflicts with Ockham's definitions of the main divisions of supposition. This is the second pressure on Ockham's rule.

IV

To the best of my knowledge, no mediaeval author ever mentioned these conflicts and pressures. But some later mediaeval nominalists in fact adopted rules of supposition that lessened the pressures or relieved

[26] Cf. e.g., his examples *ibid.*, lines 28-31, 40-42. Cf. also *ibid.*, II, 22, lines 15f., where after setting out a rule for converting sentences about the past or about the future, he says: "Et est ista regula intelligenda, quando subiectum supponit personaliter, hoc est significative."

[27] Cf. *ibid.*, I, 64, lines 9-21. A somewhat more serious problem with Ockham's account is that if "taken significatively" is redundant in the definition of personal supposition, then that definition coincides with the definition of proper supposition—unless the word 'properly' in the latter definition, quoted above, is construed very peculiarly indeed. Ockham would have done better to define proper supposition as Burley does, *op. cit.*, ca. 1, p. 2, lines 18-20: "Suppositio propria est, quando terminus supponit pro aliquo, pro quo de virtute sermonis permittitur supponere."

[28] The lack of quotation marks will perhaps bother the modern reader. Recall that the doctrine of supposition was designed in part to make the kinds of distinction we make today with quotation marks. Note also that Latin, lacking an indefinite article, would be perfectly comfortable taking the subjects of these sentences in personal supposition. They would then be "indefinite" sentences. We could in English add an indefinite article without changing the sense: '(A) concept is a species', etc. Such indefinite sentences were traditionally treated like particular sentences: 'Some concept is a species', etc.

them altogether. Richard Lavenham,[29] for instance, adopts what are essentially Ockham's definitions of the main branches of supposition,[30] and says: [31]

> But here it is to be noted as a rule that whensoever the subject of some sentence is a term of first intention and the predicate of second intention, then the subject stands simply and the predicate personally....
>
> ....
>
> ... And it is to be noted as a rule that whensoever the subject of some sentence is a term of first imposition and the predicate of second imposition, then the subject stands materially and the predicate personally.

The explication of first and second intention and of first and second imposition need not detain us, and is moreover rather problematic in Lavenham. It appears that the features of predicates that are important for Lavenham's analysis are not altogether the same as those that Ockham uses.[32] What concerns us here, however, is the fact that he does *not* view sentences of the kinds he mentions as equivocal; they do not have to be distinguished. What Lavenham does, in effect, is to eliminate Burley's and Ockham's bias in favor of personal supposition; terms can no longer have personal supposition in just any sentence. The tendency here is to avoid distinguishing sentences in Burley's and Ockham's fashion, and thereby to avoid the first conflict in Ockham's theory.

In Lavenham, however, this is as yet only a tendency. He gives only a partial account, not mentioning the cases in which both subject and predicate are of second intention or of second imposition, or in which the predicate is of first intention or first imposition. It is moreover not

[29] Died after 1399. Cf. my "The Treatises *On Modal Propositions* and *On Hypothetical Propositions* by Richard Lavenham," *Mediaeval Studies* 35 (1973), pp. 49-59, and references there.

[30] Lavenham, *Suppositiones*, paragraphs 6-11, edited in my "Five Logical Tracts by Richard Lavenham," forthcoming in a Festschrift for Anton C. Pegis, to be published by the Pontifical Institute of Mediaeval Studies. In fact, Lavenham streamlines Ockham's definitions to the extent of making explicit the role of the phrase 'taken significatively' (par. 6), and cutting it from Ockham's definition of personal supposition (par. 11). Lavenham's definition of proper supposition (par. 2), however, has the same shortcoming as Ockham's. Cf. above, n. 27, and my introduction to "Five Logical Tracts".

[31] *Suppositiones*, par. 7: "Sed hic notandum est pro regula quod quandocumque subjectum alicujus propositionis est terminus primae intentionis et praedicatum secundae intentionis, tunc subjectum supponit simpliciter et praedicatum personaliter." *Ibid.*, par. 10: ".. Et notandum est pro regula quod quandocumque subjectum alicujus propositionis est terminus primae impositionis et praedicatum secundae impositionis, tunc subjectum <supponit> materialiter et praedicatum personaliter."

[32] Cf. the discussion in my introduction to "Five Logical Tracts".

clear whether he avoids Ockham's second problem, since it is not clear just which features of predicates Lavenham takes to be relevant, and how they work.

Paul of Pergula,[33] however, adopts an account that avoids completely both of Ockham's problems. He allows only two main branches of supposition, personal and material,[34] distinguished according as the term stands for its "personal significate" or for its "material significate".[35] Now: [36]

> the personal significate is that which a term signifies for which, or a pronoun pointing to it, it can be verified affirmatively without a material sign, as: Socrates is a man. The material significate is what a term signifies for which, or a pronoun pointing to it, it cannot be verified affirmatively without a material sign, as: The term man is ly man.

Terms which are truly predicable of themselves both with and without adding the particle 'ly' have only one significate; otherwise they have two. Those of the first kind include: being, something, sign, term, noun etc.[37]

Pergula then gives his version of the rule of supposition.[38] For our purposes there are two things to note. First, Pergula nowhere allows a sentence to be "distinguished" according to the kinds of supposition

[33] Died 1451. Cf. Mary Anthony Brown, ed., *Paul of Pergula: Logica and Tractatus de sensu composito et diviso*, (St. Bonaventure, N.Y.: The Franciscan Institute, 1961), p. v.

[34] T. K. Scott, *op. cit.*, p. 31, n. 57, suggests that Buridan was alone in rejecting simple supposition as a distinct kind. Paul of Pergula is a counterexample.

[35] Paul of Pergula, *Logica*, tract 2 ("De suppositionibus"), lines 5-7: "Suppositionum personalis est acceptio termini in propositione pro suo personali significato. Materialis est acceptio termini in propositione pro suo materiali significato." The tract has been translated by Ivan Boh, "Paul of Pergula on Suppositions and Consequences," *Franciscan Studies* 25 (1965), pp. 30-89. For the passages relevant to this discussion, cf. *ibid.*, pp. 36f.

[36] Paul of Pergula, *loc. cit.*, lines 8-13: "Significatum personale est quod aliquis terminus significat pro quo vel pronomine demonstrante illud quod potest affirmative verificari sine signo materiali ut: Sortes est homo. Significatum materiale est quod aliquis terminus significat pro quo vel de pronomine demonstrante illud non potest affirmative verificari sine signo materiali ut: Iste terminus homo est ly homo." The particle 'ly' is as close as the mediaevals came to our quotation marks. Notice that its scope is ambiguous—it governs an unspecified amount of what follows it. Notice also that it is not used everywhere we should use quotation marks. See the last example in the quotation.

[37] *Ibid.*, lines 17-25.

[38] *Ibid.*, lines 26-60. The rules are complete—i.e., they cover all possible cases. Note also that whereas for Burley and Ockham, and as far as can be determined for Lavenham as well, the predicate of a sentence always has personal supposition, this is not so for Pergula.

its terms may have. In one kind of case,[39] he admits, no general rule can be given. But in that case, he says, we must look to the common idiom to determine the supposition of the terms—no mention is made of equivocation or of any need to distinguish senses. Pergula thus completes the tendency we observed in Lavenham, avoiding completely the first conflict in Ockham's theory.

The second noteworthy feature of Pergula's account concerns those terms which he says have only one significate. These seem to be just the terms responsible for the second conflict in Ockham's theory. Pergula treats them as a separate case, and says that they always have personal supposition—even when the particle 'ly' is added to them.[40] By singling out such cases for special treatment, Pergula avoids Ockham's problem. The solution is in effect a revision of Ockham's analysis of the role of the relevant features of predicates.

It appears then that at least some logicians in the Ockhamist tradition eventually managed to work themselves out of the difficulties Ockham brought upon himself by accepting the need for "distinguishing" sentences, and by his own analysis of predicates. They did this by rejecting the bias in favor of personal supposition which was responsible for the need to distinguish, and by a somewhat revised account of predicates. Although no one seems to have explicitly mentioned the pressures and conflicts in Ockham's theory, it is hard to believe that the doctrine evolved in this way by coincidence. The pressure were felt.

Bloomington, Indiana
Indiana University

[39] Rule 6, *ibid.*, lines 52-60, namely, where both subject and predicate are of second intention, are without the particle 'ly', and have two significates.
[40] Rule 1, *ibid.*, lines 26-28.

X

SOME EPISTEMOLOGICAL IMPLICATIONS OF THE BURLEY-OCKHAM DISPUTE

The dispute between Walter Burley and William of Ockham over supposition and signification has been discussed often in the literature.[1] For the most part, the philosophical — as distinguished from the textual — side of this discussion has centered on those aspects of the dispute which are based on the metaphysical disagreements between the two men. From this point of view, the main question in the debate is "For what does a common term stand when it stands in simple supposition?" Burley, the realist,[2] maintained that such a term stands for what it signifies, namely, a common nature outside the mind.[3] On the other hand, Ockham the conceptualist could not

[1] See, e.g., Philotheus Boehner, *Medieval Logic: An Outline of Its Development from 1250 – c. 1400* (Manchester: University Press, 1952), pp. 40, 48; and William and Martha Kneale, *The Development of Logic* (Oxford: Clarendon Press, 1962), pp. 265–271. On the chronology of the Burley–Ockham dispute, with references to further literature and an edition of one of the relevant texts, see Stephen F. Brown, "Walter Burleigh's Treatise *De Suppositionibus* and Its Influence on William of Ockham," *Franciscan Studies*, 32 (1972), 15–64.

[2] On Burley's realism, see Herman Shapiro, "A Note on Walter Burley's Exaggerated Realism," *Franciscan Studies*, 20 (1960), 205–214; and his "More on the 'Exaggeration' of Burley's Realism," *Manuscripta*, 6 (1962), 94–98.

[3] See Walter Burleigh, *De Puritate Artis Logicae Tractatus Longior, with a Revised Edition of the Tractatus Brevior*, Philotheus Boehner, ed. (St. Bonaventure, N.Y.: The Franciscan Institute, 1955), tract. long., tr. I, pars 1, c. 1, p. 3 lines 24 f.: "Suppositio vero simplex est, quando terminus communis vel singulare aggregatum supponit pro eo quod significat." (Henceforth, references to *De Puritate* will be to the *Tractatus Longior*, tract 1, pars 1.) The parallel passage in *De Suppositionibus* is par. 2.3 of Brown's edition. That a common term stands for a common nature is argued, *De Puritate*, c. 3, p. 8 lines 1–7: "Item, hoc nomen 'homo' significat aliquid primo, et non significat primo Sortem nec Platonem; quia sic audiens hanc vocem et sciens, quid per hanc vocem significaretur, determinate et distincte intelligeret Sortem, quod est falsum; ergo hoc nomen 'homo' non significat primo aliquod singulare; ergo significat primo commune; et illud commune est species; ergo illud, quod primo significatur hoc nomine 'homo' est species." In the lines immediately following this text (ibid., lines 8–29), Burley says that it makes no difference to the argument whether the common species

accept such a position; in his ontology there were simply no common natures outside the mind. For him, therefore, a common term in simple supposition stands for the universal concept *in* the mind.[4]

This much of the dispute then is based on the metaphysical disagreement over whether there exist common natures outside the mind. It is this metaphysical side of the dispute that is usually brought out in recent discussions.

But there is quite another question too at issue between Burley and Ockham, one the answer to which is restricted but not totally fixed by their respective metaphysical views. It is: "Disregarding the question what we are to posit at the one end of the relation of simple supposition, which kind of supposition is it in which a term stands for what it signifies?" For Burley it is simple supposition, for Ockham personal. As will be seen, this issue has epistemological implications. It is this side of the dispute that I want to explore here.

---

be a thing outside the soul or the concept in the soul. But in the next argument (ibid., lines 30–34) it is clear that Burley thinks the concept is ruled out on other grounds: "Item, haec est vera, secundum quod subiectum habet suppositionem simplicem: 'Homo est substantia secunda'. Si tamen subiectum supponeret pro intentione in anima, esset falsa, quia intentio in anima est accidens, et accidens nec est substantia prima nec secunda."

[4] William Ockham, *Summa Logicae* I, Philotheus Boehner, ed., (St. Bonaventure, N.Y.: The Franciscan Institute, 1957), c. 64, lines 27–38: "Suppositio simplex est, quando terminus supponit pro intentione animae, sed non tenetur significative. Verbi gratia sic dicendo: 'Homo est species,' iste terminus 'homo' supponit pro intentione animae, quia illa intentio est species, et tamen iste terminus 'homo' non significat proprie loquendo illam intentionem, sed illa vox et illa intentio animae sunt tantum signa subordinata in significando idem, secundum modum alibi expositum. Ex hoc patet falsitas opinionis communiter dicentium, quod suppositio simplex est, quando terminus supponit pro suo significato; quia suppositio simplex est, quando terminus supponit pro intentione animae, quae proprie non est significatum termini, quia terminus talis significat veras res et non intentiones animae." On Ockham's supposition theory in general, see John J. Swiniarski, "A New Presentation of Ockham's Theory of Supposition with an Evaluation of Some Contemporary Criticisms," *Franciscan Studies*, 30 (1970), 181–217. On the relation of Ockham's metaphysics to his philosophy of language, see also Teodoro de Andrès, *El nominalismo de Guillermo de Ockham como filosofía del lenguaje* ("Bibliotheca Hispánica de Filosofía"; Madrid: Editorial gredos, S.A., 1969). The new critical edition of Ockham's *Summa Logicae*, by Gedeon Gál and Stephen F. Brown, (St. Bonaventure, N.Y.: The Franciscan Institute, 1974), was not yet available to me at the time of writing.

I

The theory of supposition is, at least to a large extent, a *semantic* theory. It is a theory of the relation between terms and their referents.[5] Signification, insofar as it enters into this theory, is a semantic relation. But it would be a mistake to view signification solely in semantic terms. For a mediaeval, signification was primarily an *epistemological* relation. The early development of the notion of signification has been traced in some detail by De Rijk.[6] Although the details are not needed for the present paper, some elementary points will clear the way for further discussion in sections II and III, below.

Aristotle and Augustine, among others, contributed to the view of signification as an epistemological relation. In *De Interpretatione*, 3 (16b19–22), while discussing verbs, Aristotle observes that, like nouns, they too signify, "for he who uses such expressions arrests the hearer's mind, and fixes his attention" (Oxford translation). In Boethius' Latin version, the whole passage reads: "Ipsa quidem secundum se dicta nomina sunt et significant aliquid. Constituit enim qui dicit intellectum et qui audit quiescit." [7] To signify, then, is

[5] Burley, to be sure, gives a syntactic description (*De Puritate*, c. 1, p. 1 lines 25–27): "Suppositio communiter accepta est proprietas termini ad aliud terminum in propositione comparati." The parallel passage in *De Suppositionibus* occurs in par. 2.01: "Et ideo dicendum quod suppositio est proprietas extremi secundum quod unum extremum ordinatur ad aliud in propositione...." See the discussion of this text in Brown, op. cit., pp. 19–21. I suspect this description is the basis for E. A. Moody's rather confusing remarks about supposition's being a syntactic relation of term to term, rather than a semantic relation of term to thing. See his *Truth and Consequence in Mediaeval Logic* (Amsterdam: North-Holland, 1952), p. 22. Moody is not entirely self-consistent, however. See ibid., p. 11. Moody's remarks in these places are responsible for a certain confusion in the literature over what kind of a relation supposition is. One result of this confusion is the view that the mediaevals had a "syntactic" view of truth. See, e.g., Alfonso Maierù, "Il problema della verità nelle opere di Guglielmo Heytesbury," *Studi Medievali*, serie terza, 7 (1966), 40–74, especially p. 46. On the other hand, at *De Puritate*, c. 1, p. 2, lines 12 f., Burley gives a general definition of supposition that makes it clear that he thinks of it as a semantic relation: "Suppositio generaliter dicta est acceptio termini pro aliquo, scilicet pro re vel pro voce vel pro conceptu."

[6] L. M. De Rijk, *Logica Modernorum: A Contribution to the History of Early Terminist Logic*, vol. II (Assen: Van Gorcum, 1967), especially Part I, chs. 4–5.

[7] Boethius, *In Peri Hermeneias II*, Carolus Meisner, ed., (Leipzig: Teubner, 1880), I, c. 3, p. 71, lines 4–7.

"constituere intellectum" — to establish an understanding. The term is often glossed this way in the Middle Ages.[8] To take just two examples: (1) Abelard, in his *Glosses on Porphyry*, writes: "universals seem to derive no meaning [*i.e.*, *signification*] from things, particularly since they constitute no understanding of any thing" [9] ("nullam de rebus significationem contrahere videntur universalia, praesertim cum nullum de re aliqua constituant intellectum");[10] (2) John Buridan, in the opening chapter of his *Sophismata*, writes: "Signifying is described as that which establishes the understanding of a thing. So a word is said to signify that, the understanding of which it establishes for us" [11] ("Significare describitur quod est intellectum rei constituere. Ideo vox dicitur illud significare cujus intellectum nobis constituit.") [12]

A second source for the mediaeval view of signification as an epistemological relation is Augustine, especially the *De Doctrina Christiana*. There he defines a sign as follows:[13] "A sign is a thing which causes us to think of something beyond the impression the thing itself makes on the senses" ("Signum est enim res praeter speciem, quam ingerit sensibus, aliud aliquid ex se faciens in cogitationem uenire.") [14] With the exception of the additional proviso about

[8] For the early period, see De Rijk, *op. cit.*

[9] Richard McKeon, tr., in his *Selections from Medieval Philosophers*, vol. 1 (New York: Charles Scribner's Sons, 1929), p. 235. The insertion is mine.

[10] Bernard Geyer, ed., *Logica 'Ingredientibus': Die Glossen zu Porphyrius*, in *Beiträge zur Geschichte der Philosophie des Mittalalters*, Bd. 21, Ht. 1, p. 18, lines 16 f.

[11] John Buridan, *Sophisms on Meaning and Truth*, Theodore Kermit Scott, tr., (New York: Appleton-Century-Crofts, 1966), p. 67.

[12] John Buridan, *Sophismata Buridani*, ([Paris]: Jean Lambert for Denis Roce, [after 1500?]), no folio numbers (Copinger 1378). Copy at the Lilly Library, Indiana University.

[13] Augustine, *On Christian Doctrine*, D. W. Robertson, Jr., tr. ("The Library of Liberal Arts"; Indianapolis: Bobbs-Merrill, 1958), p. 34.

[14] Augustine, *De Doctrina Christiana*, Joseph Martin, ed., ("Corpus Christianorum Series Latina," v. 32; Turnholti: Typographi Brepols Editores Pontificii, 1962), II, c. 1, lines 5–7. In addition, Augustine's distinction between "thing" and "sign," in *De Doctrina Christiana*, I, 2, was quoted in Peter Lombard's influential *Sentences*, I, d. 1. Although neither Augustine's quoted text nor Lombard's discussion makes the explicit point that signification is an epistemological relation, the passage was often read this way. Thus, e.g., in Aquinas' *Scriptum super Libros Sententiarum*, I, d. 1, divisio textus (R. P. Mandonnet, ed., Paris: P. Lethielleux, 1929, p. 30), we read: "Primo ponit divisionem eorum de quibus agendum est, in res et *signa, quae ad cognitionem rerum ducunt.*" (My emphasis.)

sense impressions, this definition conforms with the Aristotelian one. A sign signifies (is a sign of) what it makes us think of or understand. Thus signification is primarily an epistemological, not a semantical, relation. To construe the 'significatio' of a term as, for instance, its Fregean "sense" only obscures this mediaeval usage.

Both Burley and Ockham make use of this epistemological notion of signification. Ockham distinguishes a broad and a narrow sense of 'signify':[15]

> ...you should know that 'sign' is taken in two ways. In one way for all that which when apprehended makes something else come into cognition, although it does not make the mind come into a first cognition of it (as is shown elsewhere), but into an actual cognition of it after a habitual one. And in this way a spoken word signifies naturally, just as every effect signifies at least its cause, and just as also the barrel-hoop over the door signifies wine in the tavern. But I am not speaking about signs in such a general way here. In another way 'sign' is taken for that which makes something come into cognition, and is apt to stand for that thing, or be added to such, in a sentence... And taking the word 'sign' in this way, a spoken word is a natural sign of nothing.

Burley, on the other hand, does not explicitly discuss signification in the readily available texts. But it is clear from one of his objections to Ockham that he too thinks of signification as an epistemological relation:[16]

---

[15] Ockham, op. cit. I, 1, lines 53–65: "...est sciendum, quod 'signum' dupliciter accipitur: Uno modo pro omni illo quod apprehensum aliquid aliud in cognitionem facit venire, quamvis non faciat mentem venire in primam cognitionem eius, sicut alibi est ostensum, sed in actualem post habitualem eiusdem. Et sic vox naturaliter significat, sicut quilibet effectus significat saltem suam causam, sicut etiam circulus significat vinum in taberna. Sed tam generaliter non loquor hic de signo. Aliter accipitur 'signum' pro illo, quod aliquid facit in cognitionem venire et natum est pro illo supponere vel tali addi in propositione... Et sic accipiendo hoc vocabulum 'signum' vox nullius est signum naturale." The translation is mine. On Ockham's theory of signification, see Philotheus Boehner, "Ockham's Theory of Signification," *Franciscan Studies*, 6 (1946), 143–170, reprinted in his *Collected Articles on Ockham*, Eligius M. Buytaert, ed. (St. Bonaventure, N.Y.: The Franciscan Institute, 1958), pp. 201–232. A more recent account may be found in Swiniarski, op. cit., pp. 183–187.

[16] Burley, *De Puritate*, c. 3, p. 8, lines 1–5. For the Latin, see above, n. 3. This and the following translation are my own.

> Again, this name 'man' signifies something first, and it does not first signify Socrates, nor Plato. For if that were so, someone who hears this word and who knows what is signified by this word would determinately and distinctly understand Socrates, which is false. Therefore, this name 'man' does not first signify any singular.

Again:[17]

> But the man who imposed signification on this name 'man' did not know me nor John who is now present, and thus this name 'man' does not signify me nor John now present.

For Ockham, the term 'man' does not signify any nature common to all men, but rather individual men–either all individual men now existing or all past, present, future and merely possible men.[18] Burley objects that he who hears the word 'man' need not thereby be made to understand this particular man, for instance, Socrates. Moreover, the man who originally imposed signification on the term did not know and was not thinking of particular men who are existing only now.[19] The force of these objections depends on taking signification as the epistemological relation described above: terms signify what they make us think of or understand.

---

[17] Ibid., lines 15–17: "Sed ille qui imposuit hoc nomen 'homo' ad significandum non cognovit me nec Joannem nunc praesentem; ergo hoc nomen 'homo' non significat me vel Joannem nunc praesentem."

[18] This is in accordance with the first two senses, respectively, of 'to signify' listed in *Summa Logicae* I, 33: " 'Significare' multipliciter accipitur apud logicos. Nam uno modo dicitur signum aliquid significare, quando supponit vel natum est supponere pro illo, ita scilicet, quod de pronomine demonstrante illud per hoc verbum 'est', illud nomen praedicatur. Et sic 'album' significat Sortem; haec enim est vera: 'Iste est albus,' demonstrando Sortem. Sic etiam 'rationale' significat hominem; haec enim est vera: 'Iste est rationalis,' demonstrando hominem. Et sic de multis aliis concretis. Aliter accipitur 'significare', quando illud signum in aliqua propositione de praeterito vel de futuro vel del praesenti vel in aliqua propositione vera de modo potest pro illo supponere. Et sic 'album' non tantum significat illud, quod nunc est album, sed illud quod potest esse album; nam in ista propositione: 'Album potest currere,' accipiendo subiectum pro eo, quod potest esse, subiectum supponit pro his, quae possunt esse alba." (lines 1–15). Note that these descriptions are given, via supposition, in purely semantic terms.

[19] This objection applies only to 'to signify' taken in the second of the two senses described above.

II

Hence for the antagonists in our dispute, the question which kind of supposition a term has when it stands for what it signifies reduces to the question which kind of supposition a term has when it stands for what it makes us think of or understand. For Burley, it is simple supposition, where a term stands for a common nature.[20] For Ockham, of course, there are no common natures; in simple supposition a term stands for a concept. This much of the dispute between the two men can be accounted for by their opposing metaphysical views. But Ockham goes further than this. He insists that it is in personal and not simple supposition that a term stands for what it signifies.

This is an epistemological point, not a metaphysical one. Ockham's conceptualism would not have been compromised in the slightest if he had said that it is in simple supposition that terms stand for what they signify. The disagreement would then have been only that for Ockham terms signify concepts, whereas for Burley they signify common natures. But Ockham does not do this. He insists that terms do not signify the concepts to which they are subordinated, but rather the individuals falling under those concepts.[21]

It would not have been at all novel for Ockham to have said that terms signify concepts. Indeed, Aristotle says (*De Interpretatione* 1, 16a3f.): "Spoken words are the symbols of mental experience" (Oxford translation).[22] Boethius interprets this as a signification relation, and takes the "mental experiences" to be concepts (*intellectus*).[23] The

---

[20] See above, n. 3.

[21] Ockham, op. cit., I, 1, lines 25–29: "Dico autem voces esse signa subordinata conceptibus seu intentionibus animae, non quia proprie accipiendo hoc vocabulum 'signa' ipsae voces semper significent ipsos conceptus animae primo et proprie, sed quia voces imponuntur ad significandum illa eadem, quae per conceptus mentis significantur." See also Ockham, *In Peri Hermeneias*, c. 1, in Philotheus Boehner, "The Realistic Conceptualism of William Ockham," *Traditio*, 4 (1946), 307–335 at p. 320: "Dicit tamen Philosophus, quod vox est nota passionis animae propter quemdam ordinem eorum in significando, quia primo passio significat res, et secundo vox significat non passionem animae, sed easdem res, quas significat passio."

[22] Boethius' Latin translation (op. cit., p. 25, lines 6 f.) is "Sunt ergo ea quae sunt in voce earum quae sunt in anima passionum notae."

[23] Ibid., p. 29 lines 13–16: "Quare recta Aristotelis sententia est: quaecumque in verbis nominibusque versantur, ea neque sensus neque imaginationes, sed

basic view here is that the role of language is to express thought. When one hears another's words, he knows what the other is thinking. In this way, then, a term serves to make us think of the speaker's concept. That is, terms signify the speaker's concepts to the hearer.[24]

This same rationale is expressed by Augustine (*De Doctrina Christiana*, II, 2):[25]

> Conventional signs are those which living creatures show to one another for the purpose of conveying, in so far as they are able, the motion of their spirits or something which they have sensed or understood. Nor is there any other reason for signifying, or for giving signs, except for bringing forth and transferring to another mind the action of the mind in the person who makes the sign.

Aquinas too upholds this position:[26]

> Now if man were by nature a solitary animal the passions of the soul by which he was conformed to things so as to have knowledge of them would be sufficient for him; but since he is by nature a political and social animal it was necessary that his conceptions be made known to others. This he does through vocal sound. Therefore there had to be significant vocal sounds in order that men might live together. Whence those who speak different languages find it difficult to live together in social unity.

---

solam significare intellectuum qualitatem." For a discussion, see De Rijk, op. cit., Part I, pp. 177–182.

[24] The plausibility of this view depends on the speaker's being distinct from the hearer. There is little if any reason to think that when a speaker hears his own words, he is made to think of his own concepts. Nor, for that matter, is there any good reason to think that a speaker's words need make *him* think of anything at all. One might hold that words express thoughts, but then the thoughts are prior to their expression, and are not caused by the utterances of the words.

[25] Robertson translation, pp. 34 f. ("Data vero signa sunt, quae sibi quaeque uiuentia inuicem dant ad demonstrandos, quantum possunt, motus animi sui uel sensa aut intellecta quaelibet. Nec ulla causa est nobis significandi, id est signi dandi, nisi ad depromendum et traiciendum in alterius animum id, quo animo gerit, qui signum dat." Martin, ed., lines 1–6.)

[26] *In Peri Hermeneias* I, c. 1, lect. II, from Jean T. Oesterle, tr., *Aristotle: On Interpretation: Commentary by St. Thomas and Cajetan* (Milwaukee: Marquette University Press, 1962), p. 24. ("Et si quidem homo esset naturaliter animal solitarium, sufficerent sibi animae passiones, quibus ipsis rebus conformaretur, ut earum notitiam in se haberet; sed quia homo est animal naturaliter *politicum* et *sociale*, necesse fuit quod conceptiones unius hominis innotescerent aliis, quod

On the other hand, by maintaining that terms do not signify the concepts to which they are subordinated (which they express) but rather extramental realities, Ockham commits himself to a somewhat different perspective on the role of language. It is thought of not so much as a tool for conveying one's thoughts to another, but as a tool for learning about extramental realities. In short, the *social* role of language is eclipsed by Ockham's view.[27] Burley held a similar position.[28]

III

But while the social aspect of language is left relatively unemphasized by both Ockham and Burley, their close interweaving of the theory of signification with the theory of supposition served to underscore another side of language. Supposition theory, I have said, is a semantic theory of reference — a theory about the relation between language and what we are talking about by means of language. On the other hand, signification is primarily an epistemological relation.

---

fit per vocem; et ideo necesse fuit esse voces significativas, ad hoc quod homines ad invicem conviverent. Unde illi, qui sunt diversarum linguarum, non possunt bene convivere ad invicem." Leonine edition, p. 11.)

[27] This is not to suggest, of course, that Ockham ever *denied* this social role of language. The matter is rather one of emphasis.

[28] *Burlei super Artem Veterem Porphirii et Aristotelis* (Venice: Otinus (de Luna) Papiensis, 11 May 1497), no folio numbers. (Goff B-1313). Copy at the Lilly Library, Indiana University. The passage is in Burley's commentary on *De Interpretatione* 1, 16a3f.: "Secundo est intellegendum quod nomen et verbum significare passiones animae dupliciter potest intellegi. Uno modo quod nomen et verbum significant passiones animae tanquam illa quae imponuntur primo ad significandum. Alio modo potest intellegi quod significent passiones animae tanquam illa mediantibus quibus imponuntur ad significandum. Primo modo non est necessarium nomen et verbum significare passiones animae...." Two arguments are given for this. Then: "Secundo modo dico quod nomina et verba significant passiones animae.... Et dico illud loquendo de nominibus primae intentionis, quod illa non imponuntur primo ad significandum passiones animae. Bene tamen est possibile quod aliquod nomen significet passionem animae, ut nomina secundae intentionis, etiam hujusmodi voces 'passio animae' 'similitudo rei in anima' et sic de similibus. Boethius tamen dicit hic quod vox non significat primo rem extra sed aliquid in anima et ex consequenti significat rem extra. Sed credo quod non sic intellegitur quod vox non primo imponitur. Si vero primo significat aliquid in anima non est necesse quod significet illud tanquam illud cui imponitur primo sed tanquam illud quod primo movet intellectum ad imponendum nomen rei intellectae."

By weaving these two theories so closely together, Burley and Ockham gave in effect not just an account of reference (the semantic side), and not just an account of knowledge (the epistemological side), but also an account of *how we can know and learn things through language.* The dispute between Burley and Ockham, then, is not just a dispute between realism and conceptualism, but also a dispute over how — in what way — language can be enlisted to do epistemological duty.

For Burley, it is the semantic relation of simple supposition that was given an epistemological role. It is only in simple supposition that a term stands for what it signifies. Hence it is only in cases of simple supposition that we are talking about what we understand by the terms.

But, pushed to its conclusion, this view seems to mean that it is only in the context of simple supposition that we know what we are talking about. It is only in cases of simple supposition that we can learn anything through language — that is, only cases of sentences such as 'Man is a species,' 'Animal is a genus.' [29] And this to the *exclusion* of such sentences as 'This cat is on the mat,' which does not teach us anything about this particular cat, since the term 'cat' does not signify particular cats but rather the common nature.

Such a doctrine reflects the Aristotelian–Arab epistemology that grew up in thirteenth-century Scholasticism, and according to which "*understanding* is of universals," that is, of common natures, "but *sensation* is of particulars." [30] In such a doctrine — Thomism, for instance — the apparent fact that we do have knowledge about individuals was a difficult point.[31]

Burley's account of the relation between signification and supposition, then, reflects well this view of knowledge. Now, as yet we know very little about Burley's epistemology, but there are some grounds nevertheless for believing that in fact he did *not* hold such a doctrine, that he allowed for intellectual knowledge of singulars.[32]

---

[29] Difficulties might perhaps — but not necessarily — arise over the predicates of these sentences, which seem to be in personal supposition, and thus not to stand for what we understand by them. The details of Burley's doctrine in this area need further study.

[30] "Intellectus est universalium, sensus autem particularium." For a valuable discussion of the issues surrounding this dictum, see Sebastian J. Day, *Intuitive Cognition: A Key to the Significance of the Later Scholastics* (St. Bonaventure, N.Y.: The Franciscan Institute, 1947).

[31] See ibid., especially Part I.

[32] See Herman Shapiro, "A Note on Walter Burley's Exaggerated Realism,"

If this should turn out to be so, it will be hard to reconcile with his views on supposition and signification.

For Ockham, on the other hand, we do have a direct knowledge of individuals — indeed, in his view there is nothing else to be known. And this fact is reflected in his account of the relation between signification and supposition. Since there are no common natures for Ockham, terms in simple supposition stand for the concepts to which they are subordinated. Thus, if, as for Burley, terms stood in *simple* supposition for what they signify, we would be back with the social view of language as a tool to convey one's thoughts to another. On the other hand, the use of words in language clearly makes us understand and think of more than utterances and inscriptions; that is the difference between knowing the language and merely hearing it. Hence, it is not *material* supposition in which terms stand for what they signify. There remains only *personal* supposition. Thus for Ockham it is the semantic relation of personal supposition that is given an epistemological role.

This has the effect of expanding the power of language to serve as a vehicle of knowledge. While for both Burley and Ockham, only certain items can be the referent of a term in material or simple supposition, in Ockham's view anything whatever can be the referent of some term in personal supposition. Thus, just as Ockham in a sense extends our power of knowing by allowing us an intellectual knowledge of singular things, so too he extends the power of language to serve as a vehicle for knowledge of anything in his ontology.

Indiana University
Bloomington, Indiana

Franciscan Studies, 20 (1960), especially pp. 212–214. Shapiro's point is perhaps confirmed by the *De Potentiis Animae*, pars. 135–136. See M. Jean Kitchel, "The 'De Potentiis Animae' of Walter Burley," *Mediaeval Studies*, 33 (1971), 85–113 at p. 111: "Istud tamen videtur falsum quia, per Philosophum, sensus est singularium et intellectus, universalium. Intellectus autem non intelligit singulare, et sic non omne ens est intelligibile ab intellectu. Ad istud dicendum quod sensus cognoscet singulare appropriate, et ibi est appropriatio a parte sensus, quia sensus cognoscit singulare et nihil nisi singulare. Sed intellectus cognoscit universale propriate, et ibi est appropriatio a parte universalis. Intellectus enim sic cognoscit universale, quod universale non cognoscitur nisi ab intellectu. Unde quod dicitur quod sensus est singularium et intellectus universalium. Hoc debet intelligi appropriate modo quo dictum est."

XI

Ockham's Distinctions between Absolute and Connotative Terms

This paper is intended as an introduction to the theory of "connotation" as developed by William of Ockham, especially as in his *Summa logicae.*[1] It is only an introduction to that theory, because it focusses on only the most rudimentary part of it, namely, the distinction between absolute and connotative terms. The paper does two things. First, it tries to clarify several crucial but obscure notions that arise in connection with this distinction, notions such as "signify the same things in the same way", "secondary signification", and "express the *quid nominis*". Second, the paper argues for the claim that connotation-theory, or at least that part of it presented here, requires no new primitive notions beyond those already required for the theory of absolute terms. I do not discuss here certain other very interesting questions in connotation-theory—for instance, its role in the theory of demonstration, and its role in reducing the number of ontological categories. These questions are discussed by Ernest A. Moody in his *The Logic of William of Ockham.*[2] They are

[1] I have used Philotheus Boehner's edition, *William Ockham: Summa logicae,* (St. Bonaventure, N.Y.: The Franciscan Institute, *pars prima,* 1957; *pars secunda et tertiae prima,* 1962) for all Latin quotations from Ockham's *Summa,* except for one passage from *pars tertiae secunda,* which is quoted from Ernest A. Moody, *The Logic of William of Ockham,* (New York: Sheed & Ward, 1935). Cf. below, n. 45. The critical edition of the complete text, by Gedeon Gál and Stephen F. Brown, from the Franciscan Institute, was not yet available to me at the time of writing. All references are to the *Summa logicae,* unless otherwise noted. For Boehner's edition, they will be given by part, chapter, and line numbers. Sections of the *Summa logicae,* including the important I, 10, have been translated by Boehner in *Ockham: Philosophical Writings,* (London: Thomas Nelson, 1957; reprinted with different pagination in "The Library of Liberal Arts", Indianapolis, Ind.: The Bobbs-Merrill Company, 1964). Nevertheless, I have used my own translations for all passages in this paper.

[2] Especially chs. 4 and 6. It may be of some help to the reader if at this point we simply list terms that Ockham explicitly says are connotative. They are: (a) all figment terms (II, 14); (b) negative terms (such as 'immaterial'), privative terms (such as 'blind') and infinite terms (such as 'non-man') (II, 12); (c) all relative terms (such as 'similar', 'father') and all quantitative terms (I, 10)—

the ones that give connotation-theory its philosophical interest. The present paper, then, presupposes for motivation that one already knows that connotation-theory is philosophically important, but finds certain obscurities in the foundations of the theory.

I

As a preliminary, several things need to be explained. The first is the notion of "signification". For Ockham, and for mediaeval logicians in general, signification, although it was incorporated into semantic theory, was primarily an epistemological notion.[3] A term—whether written, spoken, or mental (a concept)—was said to "signify" whatever it calls to mind or makes the reader (or hearer or thinker) think of. To signify was "to constitute an understanding of" (*constituere intellectum* plus genitive).[4]

A linguistic term acquires its signification in one of two ways. Mental terms (concepts) signify naturally [5]; they are natural likenesses or representations of the things they signify.[6] Spoken and written terms, on the other hand, signify by convention (*ad placitum*).[7]

indeed all terms in any category other than substance or quality (cf. I, 44-54 and I, 57-62, and Moody, *op. cit.*, ch. 4 and p. 56); (d) the terms 'true', 'good', 'one', 'power', 'act', 'intellect', 'will', 'desirable' (I, 10); (e) all concrete terms "of the first kind" (I, 10. Cf. I, 5, for an explanation.).

[3] I have discussed this in my "Some Epistemological Implications of the † Burley-Ockham Dispute", forthcoming in *Franciscan Studies* 35 (1975).

[4] Cf. Aristotle, *De interpretatione* 3, 16b19-22. In Boethius' Latin translation, the passage reads: "Ipsa quidem secundum se dicta nomina sunt et significant aliquid. Constituit enim qui dicit intellectum et qui audit quiescit." (*In Peri hermeneias II*, Carolus Meiner, ed., [Leipzig: Teubner, 1880], p. 71 lines 4-7.)

[5] I, 1, 28-34: "voces imponuntur ad significandum illa eadem, quae per conceptus mentis significantur, ita quod conceptus primo naturaliter aliquid significat, et secundario vox significat illud idem, in tantum quod voce instituta ad significandum aliquod per conceptum mentis, si conceptus ille mutaret significatum suum, eo ipso vox sine nova institutione suum significatum permutaret." Cf. also *ibid.*, lines 47-52: "conceptus sive passio animae naturaliter significat quidquid significat; terminus autem prolatus vel scriptus nihil significat nisi secundum voluntariam institutionem. Ex quo sequitur alia differentia, videlicet, quod terminus prolatus vel scriptus ad placitum potest mutare suum significatum, terminus autem conceptus non mutat suum significatum ad placitum cuiuscumque."

[6] I, 12, 12-16: "Illud autem existens in anima, quod est signum rei, ex quo propositio mentalis componitur ad modum, quo propositio vocalis componitur ex vocibus, aliquando vocatur intentio animae, aliquando passio animae, aliquando similitudo rei." Cf. also the discussion and further texts in Philotheus Boehner, "The Realistic Conceptualism of William Ockham", *Traditio* 4 (1946), pp. 207-335.

[7] Cf. the texts in n. 5, above.

Such conventions amount to the setting up of a correlation of spoken and written terms, on the one hand, with concepts on the other. Such spoken and written terms are then said to be "imposed to signify" what is signified by the concepts with which they are correlated.[8]

For purposes of semantic theory, only natural and conventional signification are important. To be sure, a term may "call to mind" and so "signify", in a very broad sense, many things by a kind of association of ideas. But if the term is neither a natural representation (concept) of those things nor imposed by linguistic conventions to signify those things, then it does not signify them in any way relevant to semantic theory.

In II, 14, Ockham seems to suggest that figment terms, such as 'chimaera', signify just what is signified by their nominal definitions.[9]

[8] Cf. the first text in n. 5, above. The picture I have sketched here is complicated somewhat, in ways irrelevant to our purposes, by the fact that *written* terms were not thought to be correlated directly with concepts, but rather with *spoken* terms, and thus only indirectly with the concepts with which the spoken terms are directly correlated. (Cf. I, 1, 43-45: "Et sicut dictum est de vocibus respectu passionum seu intentionum seu conceptuum, eodem modo proportionaliter quantum ad hoc tenendum est de his quae sunt in scripto respectu vocum.") What we have here are five relations: a relation R_1 mapping concepts into the domain of objects allowed by the ontology; a relation R_2 mapping spoken terms into concepts; a relation R_3 mapping written terms into spoken terms; a relation R_4 mapping spoken terms into the ontology; and a relation R_5 mapping written terms into the ontology. Of these five relations three, namely, R_1, R_2 and R_3, are primitive. R_1 is the relation of "natural signification" (likeness) that holds between concepts and the things conceived by them. R_2 and R_3 are conventional relations, established by imposition. R_2 determines which concepts go with which spoken words, and R_3 determines how to pronounce a written word aloud, or conversely, how to take dictation. These relations, of course, differ from language to language; that is to say, they are conventional. Relations R_4 and R_5 are derived relations. R_4 is the relative product of R_2 into R_1. (That is, a term bears R_4 to something x if and only if it bears R_2 to something which bears R_1 to x.) R_5 is the relative product of R_3 into R_4. For Ockham, relations R_1, R_4 and R_5 are "signification" relations, the first natural and the last two conventional. R_2 and R_3 are called "subordination" relations (cf. I, 1, 24-25). Thus a spoken term conventionally signifies (R_4) a thing x if and only if it is conventionally subordinated (R_2) to a mental term (concept) that naturally signifies (R_1) x. Similarly a written term conventionally signifies (R_5) a thing x if and only if it is conventionally subordinated (R_3) to a spoken term that conventionally signifies (R_4) x—i.e., if and only if it is conventionally subordinated (R_3) to a spoken term that is conventionally subordinated (R_2) to a mental term (concept) that naturally signifies (R_1) x. Thus the conventionality of the conventional signification relations R_4 and R_5 is entirely due to the conventionality of the subordination relations R_2 and R_3.

[9] lines 13-17: "ita per tales terminos fictos, cuiusmodi sunt 'chimaera', 'tragela-

The importance of this will be brought out later. For the present, however, it should be noted that, in the same lines, Ockham also seems to suggest that those nominal definitions, which are complex expressions, signify just exactly the sum total of what their constituent non-complex categorematic terms signify. Ockham does not explicitly say this, nor does he generalize it to all complex expressions,[10] but such a generalization seems plausible. Hence we may tentatively attribute to Ockham the following *Additive Principle:*

> (1) A complex expression signifies just exactly the sum total of what is signified by its constituent non-complex categorematic terms.[11]

Thus when a man hears the term 'goat-stag' (*hircocervus*), he cannot be made to think of goat-stags, since there are no such things. Rather, when he hears the first constituent of that expression, he thinks of all goats, and when he hears the second, he thinks of all stags. And so the term as a whole calls to mind, and thus signifies, all goats and all stags.[12] Similarly, when he hears the sentence 'The cat is on the mat',

phus', 'vacuum', 'infinitum', et huiusmodi, nihil significatur, nisi quod significatur per terminos alios, sicut patet ex definitionibus exprimentibus quid nominis eorum."

[10] But cf. I, 26, 87-92, where the same claim seems to be suggested for real definitions: "Verumtamen licet definitiones sint distinctae, tamen illae definitiones idem significant, et quidquid significatur per unam vel partem unius, significatur per aliam vel per partem alterius, quamvis partes differunt in modo significandi, quia aliqua pars unius est alterius casus a parte alterius." Here the phrase 'idem significant' seems to be explained in terms of the phrase 'per unam *vel partem unius*'.

[11] John Buridan is more explicit about this principle. Cf. his *Sophismata*, ca. I, conclusions 5-11 (for terms) and ca. II, conclusion 5 (for sentences). (*Sophismata Buridani*, [Paris, c. 1496-1500], *Incunabula in American Libraries*, 3rd census, B-1295, no folio numbers. Translated by Theodore Kermit Scott, *John Buridan: Sophisms on Meaning and Truth*, [New York: Appleton-Century-Crofts, 1966], pp. 72-78 and p. 89.)

[12] It calls them to mind in a "confused" way. Cf. Ockham, *Expositio super librum Perihermenias*, ca. 1, in Boehner, "Realistic Conceptualism", p. 324: "tali intellectione confusa intelliguntur res singulares extra, sicut habere intellectionem hominis confusam non est aliud quam habere unam cognitionem, qua non magis intelligitur unus homo quam alius, et tamen quod tali cognitione magis cognoscitur sive intelligitur homo quam asinus. Et hoc non est aliud quam quod talis cognitio aliquo modo assimilationis magis assimilatur homini quam asino, et non magis isti homini quam illi." (On the "confusion" of the universal concept, cf. the qualification quoted by Boehner, *op. cit.*, p. 309 n. 6.) This is Ockham's reply to objections of the kind raised by Walter Burley, that when one hears the term 'man', he is not made to think of all men, even those of whom he has no personal knowledge. (Cf. my "Some Epistemological Implications of the Burley-Ockham Dispute".)

he cannot be made to think of a "fact" or "proposition", in the modern sense (a *complexe significabile* in mediaeval terminology [13]), since there are no such "facts" or "propositions" in Ockham's ontology, but rather only individual substances and their individual qualities.[14] Instead, when the man hears the sentence 'The cat is on the mat', he is made to think of all cats by the first non-complex categorematic constituent, 'cat', and is made to think of all mats by the second, 'mat'. Thus the sentence as a whole calls to mind or signifies all cats and all mats.

II

The link between semantic theory and the epistemological notion of signification is made in I, 33. There Ockham distinguishes four "modes" of signification. In the first two modes, a term is said to signify those things of which it can be truly predicated. More precisely,

First mode: A term t signifies a thing x if and only if the sentence 'This is a t' is true, pointing to x.[15]

Second mode: A term t signifies a thing x if and only if the sentence 'This is a t' is possible, pointing to x.[16]

[13] Cf. Hubert Elie, *Le complexe significabile*, (Paris: Librairie philosophique J. Vrin, 1936).

[14] Cf. Ockham, *Expositio super librum Praedicamentorum*, in *Expositio aurea super artem veterem*, (Bologna, 1496), f. 64v: "Secundum intentionem Aristotelis nulla res extra quae non est signum nec nomen nec intentio animae, est per se in quocumque genere nisi tantum in genere substantiae vel qualitatis." These substances and qualities are individual and not universal or common. Cf., e.g., I, 14-17, and many other places.

[15] I, 33, 1-8: "'Significare' multipliciter accipitur apud logicos. Nam uno modo dicitur signum aliquid significare, quando supponit vel natum est supponere pro illo, ita scilicet, quod de pronomine demonstrante illud per hoc verbum 'est,' illud nomen praedicatur. Et sic 'album' significat Sortem; haec enim est vera: 'Iste est albus,' demonstrando Sortem. Sic etiam 'rationale' significat hominem; haec enim est vera: 'Iste est rationalis,' demonstrando hominem. Et sic de multis aliis concretis."

[16] *Ibid.*, lines 9-15: "Aliter accipitur 'significare,' quando illud signum in aliqua propositione de praeterito vel de futuro vel de praesenti vel in aliqua propositione vera de modo potest pro illo supponere. Et sic 'album' non tantum significat illud, quod nunc est album, sed illud quod potest esse album; nam in ista propositione: 'Album potest currere,' accipiendo subiectum pro eo, quod potest esse, subiectum supponit pro his, quae possunt esse alba." On the interpretation of this passage, yielding the formula above, cf. II, 7, 2-14 and II, 10, 11-18. The possible entities include past, present, and future ones. That is why Ockham can say, in the passage quoted, "non tantum significat illud, quod nunc est album, sed illud quod potest esse album", without separate mention of past or future entities. Note that Ockham seems to see no problem

In the first mode, the term 'man' signifies all and only presently existing men; in the second mode it signifies all past, present and future men, as well as merely possible ones.[17] By calling these modes of "signification", Ockham is committing himself to the view that terms make us think of the things of which they are (or can be) truly predicated.

In the third and fourth modes, terms also signify things of which they cannot be truly predicated.[18] The details of this go to the heart of connotation-theory. Only some of those details will be explored here.

In I, 10, where he is discussing the distinction between absolute and connotative terms, Ockham says [19]:

in "pointing to" (via a demonstrative pronoun) entities that are possible but do not exist.

[17] Ockham goes on to point out that the significations of terms in the first mode are constantly changing, whereas in the second mode they are fixed. Cf. I, 33, 16-21: "Accipiendo 'significare' primo modo et 'significatum' ibi correspondens, per solam mutationem rei frequenter vox et etiam conceptus cadit a suo significato, hoc est aliquid cessat significari, quod prius significabatur. Secundo modo accipiendo 'significare' et 'significatum' sibi correspondens, vox vel conceptus per solam mutationem rei extra non cadit a suo significato." The introduction of the second mode seems to be an attempt to avoid objections of the kind raised by Walter Burley, *De puritate artis logicae tractatus longior*, Philotheus Boehner, ed., (St. Bonaventure, N.Y.: The Franciscan Institute, 1955), tr. 1, pars 1, ca. 3, p. 9 lines 6-22. Both Ockham and Burley use the characteristic phrase 'vox cadere a suo significato' in this context. (Cf. the above quotation and Burley, *op. cit.*, p. 9 lines 13, 14, 20 and 22.) Nevertheless, Ockham probably did not have Burley himself in mind when he introduced the second mode of signification. For Burley's *De puritate* was written after Ockham's *Summa logicae*, and Burley's earlier *De suppositionibus*, which antedates Ockham's *Summa*, contains no passage parallel to the objections in the *De puritate*. On the chronology of the Burley-Ockham dispute, and for the text of the *De suppositionibus*, cf. Stephen F. Brown, "Walter Burleigh's Treatise *De suppositionibus* and Its Influence on William of Ockham," *Franciscan Studies* 32 (1972), pp. 15-64.

[18] I, 33, 22-37: "Aliter accipitur 'significare,' quando illud dicitur significari, a quo ipsa vox imponitur, vel illud, quod primo modo significatur per conceptum principalem vel vocem principalem. Et sic dicimus, quod 'album' significat albedinem, quia 'albedo' significat albedinem, pro qua tamen albedine non supponit hoc signum 'album'. Sic 'rationale,' si sit differentia, significat animam intellectivam. Aliter accipitur 'significare' communissime, quando aliquod signum, quod est natum esse pars propositionis vel natum est esse propositio vel oratio, aliquid importat, sive principaliter sive secundario, sive in recto sive in obliquo, sive det intelligere sive connotet illud, vel quocumque modo significet, vel significet illud affirmative vel negative, quomodo hoc nomen 'caecus' significat visum, quia negative, et hoc nomen 'immateriale' significat negative materiam, et hoc nomen 'nihil' sive 'non-aliquid' significat aliquid, sed negative, de quo modo significandi loquitur Anselmus de Casu Diaboli."

[19] lines 4-7 and 38-39: "Nomina mere absoluta sunt illa, quae non significant aliquid principaliter et aliud vel idem secundario, sed quidquid significatur per

> Purely absolute nouns are those which do not signify something principally and another thing, or even the same thing, secondarily, but rather whatever is signified by the same noun is signified equally primarily. This is clear in the case of the noun 'animal', which does not signify anything but cows and asses and men, and so on for the other animals. . . . But a connotative term is one which signifies something primarily and something secondarily.

Here 'animal' is said to be an absolute term, and so to signify only "principally" or "primarily". But what it signifies turns out, according to the passage, to be just exactly that of which it is truly predicable. Hence principal or primary signification seems to be signification in the first or second of the four modes distinguished in I, 33. Secondary signification, then, amounts to signification in one of the two remaining modes only.[20]

III

The second preliminary notion that needs to be clarified is the notion of "supposition" or reference.[21] For our purposes, it is the notion of "personal" supposition that is important. Ockham says [22]:

> . . .when a term stands in a sentence for something, so that we use that term for something of which, or of a pronoun pointing to it, the term (or the nominative of the term, if it is in an oblique case) is verified, then it supposits for it. And this is true at least when the suppositing term is taken

idem nomen, aeque primo significatur; sicut patet de hoc nomine 'animal,' quod non significat nisi boves et asinos et homines et sic de aliis animalibus. . . . Nomen autem connotativum est illud, quod significat aliquid primario et aliquid secundario."

[20] I say "only" because signification in the third mode seems to include signification in the first mode (cf. n. 18: "vel illud, quod primo modo significatur"), and signification in the fourth or broadest mode seems to include signification in all the other modes (cf. n. 18: "quocumque modo significet"). Hence a term seems to signify "secondarily" when it signifies in either the third or fourth mode but *not* in the first or second. Note that this sense of "primary" and "secondary" signification is not to be confused with the senses of those locutions in the first text quoted in n. 5, above.

[21] The literature on Ockham's supposition-theory is quite large. For a good introduction to the doctrine, cf. John J. Swiniarski, "A New Presentation of Ockham's Theory of Supposition with an Evaluation of Some Contemporary Criticisms", *Franciscan Studies* 30 (1970), pp. 181-217.

[22] I, 63, 12-17 and 35-37: "quando terminus stat in propositione pro aliquo,—ita quod utimur illo termino pro aliquo, de quo sive de pronomine demonstrante ipsum, ille terminus vel rectus illius termini, si sit obliquus, verificatur,—supponit pro illo; et hoc saltem verum est, quando terminus supponens significative accipitur. . . . . Est igitur una regula generalis, quod numquam terminus in aliqua propositione, saltem quando significative accipitur, supponit pro aliquo, nisi de quo praedicatur vere."

> significatively.[23] . . Therefore, there is a general rule, that a term in any sentence, at least when it is taken significatively, never supposits for anything except that of which it is truly predicated.

From this passage, we derive the principle:

(2) An occurrence of a term *t* in a sentence supposits (personally) for a thing *x* if and only if (a) that occurrence of *t* is "used" for *x*, and (b) the sentence 'This is a *t*' is true, pointing to *x*.

Strictly speaking, the sentence 'This is a *t*' in clause (b) need not be true at present. It will suffice also, if *t* is the subject term in a sentence about the past or about the future, or in a modal sentence, that 'This is a *t*' have been true, or will be true, or be possible, respectively.[24] From (2), so revised, it follows that

(3) A term *t* can supposit personally only for what it signifies in the first or second mode of signification—that is, only for what it primarily signifies.

It is in the light of (3) that we must read Ockham's claim in I, 64, that "Personal supposition is in general that which occurs when a term supposits for its significate".[25] We must gloss this by adding "in the first or second mode of signification". For the term 'goat-stag' has personal supposition in the (true) sentence 'No goat-stag exists'. But it does not there supposit for goats and for stags, even though by

[23] Being "taken significatively" appears to be the same as being "taken in personal supposition". Cf. my "Ockham's Rule of Supposition: Two Conflicts in His Theory" *Vivarium* 12 (1974), pp. 63-73 at pp. 69-70. Contrary to what I said in that paper, however, I am no longer confident that a term is "taken significatively" just in case it "stands for what it signifies". Rather I suggest that a term is "taken significatively" just in case it stands or supposits for *everything* it signifies (in the first or second of the four modes distinguished in I, 33). This resolves the second of the two "conflicts" in Ockham's doctrine that I discussed in that paper. But while Ockham's doctrine perhaps does not contain an outright contradiction on this point, it is still true to say that there is a "pressure" on the doctrine—if only to clarify the phrase "taken significatively". Ockham never explains clearly what he means by it. And if he in fact meant what I have suggested by the phrase, then later authors missed the point. See, besides the authors cited in my earlier paper, Walter Burley, *De puritate artis logicae tractatus longior*, tract. 1, pars 1, ca. 1, p. 3, lines 19-25. Burley's definitions there do give rise to the conflict that Ockham perhaps avoids.

[24] Cf. II, 7, and II, 9-10.

[25] lines 3-4: "Suppositio personalis universaliter est illa, quando terminus supponit pro suo significato."

(1), the Additive Principle, it signifies goats and stags.[26] The term signifies goats and stags then only in the third or fourth mode of signification (that is, only secondarily), not in the first or second mode (that is, not primarily).

IV

Finally, the last preliminary notion we need is the notion of "mental language". Mental language is the language of thought. Its terms are concepts; its sentences are judgments.[27] For our purposes, two features of mental language are relevant:

(4) Synonymy in spoken and written language is to be explained by the fact that the synonyms are correlated with the same concept, or mental expression, in the mental language.[28]

(5) There is no synonymy in mental language.

Thesis (5) can be supported in two ways. First, since there is no supra- †
mental language, one could not explain synonymy in mental language by analogy with synonymy in spoken and written language, by an appeal to the terms of some higher language, with which the synonymous concepts could be correlated.[29] Moreover, there is a stronger argument. Mental language is thought of as a stripped-down language, which lacks all features of spoken and written language that do not affect the truth or falsehood of sentences.[30] Now synonymy is one of

[26] Cf. the similar remarks about 'chimaera' in II, 14, 27-30: "Sed quidquid imaginabile significatur per hoc nomen 'chimaera', significatur per aliquem terminum, de quo in propositione de inesse vel de possibili praedicatur esse; tamen hoc nomen 'chimaera' pro illo non potest supponere." In line 25, Ockham mentions 'hircocervus' in this same context.

[27] On mental language, cf. I, 1, and I, 3, and also Ockham's *Quodlibeta septem*, (Strasbourg, 1491), quod. 5, qq. 8-9, ff. 76rb-77vb. Cf. also Peter Geach, *Mental Acts: Their Content and their Objects*, (London: Routledge and Kegan Paul, 1957), section 23, pp. 101-106; the reply by John Trentman, "Ockham on Mental", *Mind* 79 (1970), pp. 586-590; and my "Ockham's Rule of Supposition".

[28] I, 3, 20-21: "ideo multitudo conceptuum tali pluralitati synonymorum non correspondet." Cf. also *Quodlibet* 5, q. 8, f. 76vb: "nec vocibus synonymis correspondet pluralitas conceptuum."

[29] Similarly, just as equivocation in spoken and written language is explained by the fact that the equivocal terms are correlated with several concepts at once (I, 13, 10-12: "Est autem vox illa aequivoca, quae significans plura non est signum subordinatum uni conceptui, sed est signum unum pluribus conceptibus seu intentionibus animae subordinatum."), so too Ockham claims that there is no equivocation in mental language (I, 13, 6-9: "sola vox vel aliquod signum ad placitum institutum est aequivocum vel univocum, et ideo intentio animae vel conceptus non est aequivocus nec univocus proprie loquendo.").

[30] Cf. Trentman, *op. cit.*, and Ockham, *Quodlibet* 5, q. 8.

those features that do not affect truth or falsehood; synonyms are freely intersubstitutable *salva veritate*.[31] Hence there is no synonymy in mental language.

V

In I, 10, Ockham gives us the following rule for distinguishing absolute from connotative terms [32]:

> Indeed, properly speaking, such nouns [i.e., absolute nouns] do not have a definition expressing the *quid nominis*. For, properly speaking, where a noun has a definition expressing the *quid nominis*, it has *one* definition explicating the *quid nominis*, in such a way that for such a noun there are not different expressions expressing the *quid nominis* and having distinct parts, of which one part signifies something which is not conveyed in the same way by another part of the other expression. But such [absolute nouns], as far as the *quid nominis* is concerned, can be explicated in some way by *several* expressions not signifying the same thing part by part. And so none of them is properly a *definition* expressing the *quid nominis*. . . . On the other hand, a connotative noun is one which signifies something primarily and something secondarily. And such a noun properly has a definition expressing the *quid nominis*. Often one has to put one part of the definition in the nominative and another in an oblique case.

Postponing for the moment a full account of some of the notions involved here, we can extract the following principles from this passage:

(6) In general, a term may have several expressions expressing its *quid nominis*.

(7) A term has a *definition* expressing the *quid nominis* (what we more commonly call a "nominal definition") if and only if all the expressions expressing its *quid nominis* signify the same things "in the same way".[33]

[31] Note that, in virtue of the account of synonymy given in (4), this intersubstitutability holds even in so-called opaque contexts, and in particular in epistemic contexts.

[32] lines 12-21 and 38-41: "Immo proprie loquendo talia nomina non habent definitionem exprimentem quid nominis; quia proprie loquendo unius nominis habentis definitionem exprimentem quid nominis est una definitio explicans quid nominis sic, scilicet, quod talis nominis non sunt diversae orationes exprimentes quid nominis habentes partes distinctas, quarum aliqua significat aliquid, quod non eodem modo importatur per aliam partem alterius orationis. Sed talia, quantum ad quid nominis, possunt aliquo modo pluribus orationibus non easdem res secundum suas partes significantibus explicari; et ideo nulla earum est proprie definitio exprimens quid nominis. . . . Nomen autem connotativum est illud, quod significat aliquid primario et aliquid secundario. Et tale nomen proprie habet definitionem exprimentem quid nominis, et frequenter oportet ponere unum illius definitionis in recto et aliud in obliquo."

[33] And in that case presumably any one of those expressions will serve equally well as the definition.

(8) A term is connotative if and only if it has a nominal definition; otherwise, it is absolute.

Two things need to be explained here more fully—and they bring us to the main points of this paper. First, how is it determined whether a given expression expresses the *quid nominis* of a given term? Second, what does it mean to signify the same things "in the same way"? We shall find that the answer to the first question presupposes an answer to the second.

VI

When two expressions both express the *quid nominis* of a given term, when can we say that the two expressions "signify the same things in the same way"? An understanding of this is required for an understanding of (7), above. The phrase "in the same way" (*eodem modo*) suggests the distinction of four "modes" of signification in I, 33, and so suggests that two expressions signify the same things in the same way if and only if whatever is signified in one of those four modes of signification by the one expression is signified in the same mode also by the other expression.

This criterion may or may not work. I shall argue for a different criterion in section VIII, below. In any event, there is another way of looking at the matter, one which seems more enlightening and which certainly does work. In I, 6, Ockham defines his notion of synonymy [34]:

> . . .the noun 'synonym' is taken in two ways, namely, strictly and broadly. Strictly, those things are called synonyms which all users intend to use simply for the same thing. And I am not speaking in this way about synonyms here. Broadly, those things are called synonyms which simply signify the same thing in all ways, so that nothing is in any way signified by the one unless it is signified by the other in the same way, even though not all the users believe them to signify the same. . . . I intend to use the noun 'synonyms' in this second way in this chapter and in many others.

[34] lines 4-10 and 13-15: "hoc nomen 'synonymum' dupliciter accipitur, scilicet stricte et large. Stricte dicuntur illa synonyma, quibus omnes utentes intendunt uti simpliciter pro eodem; et sic non loquor hic de synonymis. Large dicuntur illa synonyma, quae simpliciter significant idem omnibus modis, ita quod nihil aliquo modo significatur per unum, quin per reliquum eodem modo significatur, quamvis non omnes utentes credant ipsa idem significare. . . . Isto secundo modo intendo uti in isto capitulo et in multis aliis hoc nomine 'synonyma'." Ockham says the same thing, in an almost identical passage, in his *Quodlibet* 5, q. 10. ff. 77vb-78ra.

Here synonymy is defined in almost exactly the same words as those used in I, 10, to characterize the expressions expressing the *quid nominis* of a connotative term.[35] Hence, however we are to take the phrase 'in the same way' there, it appears that two expressions "signify the same things in the same way" if and only if they are synonymous. And by (4), this occurs if and only if the expressions are correlated with the same concept or expression in the mental language. Thus, when all the expressions expressing the *quid nominis* of a term *t* are synonymous—i.e., correlated with the same mental expression—then *t* has a nominal definition (any of these expressions will serve equally well for this definition, since they are synonymous) and so is connotative, by (8). When not all such expressions are synonymous, *t* has no nominal definition and so is absolute, by (8).[36]

VII

We know from section VI, above, that a term *t* is connotative—that is, has a nominal definition—if and only if all the expressions expressing its *quid nominis* are synonymous. We can presumably go further, however, to say that in such a case *t* it itself synonymous with each of these expressions. Although this thesis is perhaps plausible on the face of it, Ockham nowhere explicitly asserts it. It is strongly suggested, however, by several things that he does explicitly say. In I, 26, for instance, Ockham tells us that nominal definitions signify "the same" as the terms they nominally define.[37] Now we have just seen that synonymy is not just a matter of signifying "the same", but of signifying "the same in all ways, so that nothing is in any way signified by the one unless it is signified in the same way by the other". But in I, 33, while explaining his fourth mode of signification, Ockham at least suggests that connotative terms not only signify "the same" as their nominal definitions, but also "the same in all ways". For he says that the connotative term 'blind' signifies sight, but signifies it *negatively*.[38] And this seems to be exactly the way it is signified by its nominal definition, which would presumably be something like 'animal not possessing sight'.

[35] Cf. above, n. 32.

[36] In virtue of (5), above, it follows that no connotative term in mental language has more than one mental expression expressing its *quid nominis*.

[37] lines 125-128: "Et sic 'vacuum,' 'non ens,' 'impossibile,' 'infinitum', 'hircocervus' habent definitiones, hoc est, istis nominibus correspondent aliquae orationes significantes idem quod istae dictiones."

[38] Cf. n. 18, above.

Now in the case of a nominal definition, or indeed of complex expressions generally, it is relatively clear what it might mean to signify a thing *x* "negatively". It could mean that the expression as a whole signifies *x* in virtue of some constituent non-complex categorematic term which signifies *x* [39] and which occurs within the scope of a negation-sign in that expression. This is, in part at least, a syntactic criterion. But it is not at all so clear what it can mean for a *simple* expression, like 'blind', which contains no plurality of constituent non-complex categorematic terms nor any negation-sign, to signify "negatively" like its nominal definition, unless both the simple term and its nominal definition are correlated with the same complex mental expression or complex concept which signifies negatively in the syntactic sense just described. But this, by (4), is just to say that the connotative term 'blind' is synonymous with its nominal definition.

There seems to be no reason not to generalize this to all connotative terms. We can, then, with reasonable confidence, attribute to Ockham the following principle:

(9) All the expressions expressing the *quid nominis* of a term *t* are synonymous if and only if *t* is itself synonymous with each of those expressions.

Now it is not clear whether Ockham intends his distinction between absolute and connotative terms to apply only to simple or non-complex terms, or to complex terms as well. If the former, then from (9) it follows by (5) that there are no connotative terms in mental language, since they would have to be simple, and so distinct from, yet synonymous with, the complex mental expressions giving their nominal definitions. In any case, from (9) it follows by (5) that

(10) There are no simple connotative terms in mental language; all simple or non-complex concepts are absolute mental terms.[40]

[39] Recall the Additive Principle, (1).

[40] Ockham *perhaps* denies this in *Quodlibet* 5, q. 9 (Utrum nomina mentalia distinguantur per concretum et abstractum sicut nomina vocalia ?), f. 77ra-77rb: "Et videtur quod sic, quia impossibile est quod eadem propositio simul et semel sit vera et falsa. Sed haec propositio mentalis 'Homo est albus' est vera et haec falsa 'Homo est albedo'. Ergo, non est eadem propositio in mente. Subjectum autem est idem et copula. Ergo, praedicatum est diversum. Et non nisi concretum et abstractum. Ergo, et cetera." In his determination of the question, Ockham accepts this argument and repeats it almost *verbatim* (f. 77vb). Note that the argument to the contrary (f. 77rb: "Contra, aliqua concreta et abstracta sunt synonyma, sicut 'frigus' et 'frigiditas'. Sed multitudini nominum synonymorum in voce non correspondent pluralitas in mente. Ergo, et cetera.") is

If Ockham does intend to allow his distinction to apply to complex terms as well as to simple ones, then all connotative mental terms, if indeed there are any, are complex terms and *are their own nominal definitions.*[41]

VIII

The considerations of section VII, above, indicate that when we say that two terms "signifying the same things in the same way" are synonymous, the "ways" at stake here are not the four modes of signification distinguished in I, 33, but rather *syntactic* modes of signification.[42] The most plausible way of working this out seems to be the following. A mental expression or concept naturally signifies a thing x in a given syntactic mode m if and only if x is signified by some constituent non-complex categorematic term occurring within that mental expression in the grammatical or syntactical construction m (for instance, genitively, negatively, in a prepositional phrase, in a subordinate clause, etc.). A spoken term then signifies a thing x in a given syntactic mode m if and only if it is conventionally correlated

basically an appeal to the lack of synonymy in mental language. But the synonymy mentioned there is not the synonymy of connotative terms with their nominal definitions; rather it is the synonymy of some concrete terms with their corresponding abstract terms (cf. the discussion on ff. 77rb-77va, and also I, 6-7). Ockham grants that the distinction of concrete and abstract terms of this kind does not appear in mental language, on pain of introducing synonymy there (f. 77vb). Note, however, that Ockham's main argument in this question is inconclusive. He speaks of the *mental* sentences 'Homo est albus' and 'Homo est albedo', where he ought instead to speak of the mental sentences *correlated with the spoken sentences* 'Homo est albus' and 'Homo est albedo'. The predicates of those mental sentences do differ. But Ockham gives no argument that the predicate 'white' in the first spoken sentence is correlated with a *simple* concept. It could just as well be correlated with a mental expression formulating the nominal definition of the spoken term 'white'. Indeed, this appears to be Ockham's "better doctrine". Now if Ockham would allow the mental nominal definition to be called a "concrete" term corresponding to the abstract concept of whiteness, then the argument works and the passage does not imply a denial of (10). But I doubt that Ockham would allow this. For in I, 5, 4-6, he says: "concretum et abstractum sunt nomina consimile principium secundum vocem habentia, sed non consimiliter terminantur." This seems totally inapplicable to these mental expressions. Hence I think it is best to view this passage in the *Quodlibeta* as a slip on Ockham's part, a momentary rejection of (10), supported only by a bad argument.

[41] They would be "synonymous" with their nominal definitions only in the degenerate sense of being identical with them. Synonymy in this degenerate sense is of course possible in mental language. What is ruled out by (5) is the non-degenerate case of a *plurality* of mutually synonymous expressions in mental language.

[42] These syntactic modes are referred to also in the text quoted in n. 10, above.

with a mental expression that naturally signifies x in the syntactic mode m.[43] Hence, on this approach, to say that two terms "signify the same things in the same way" is to say that they are correlated with mental expressions containing exactly the same categorematic terms in exactly the same grammatical constructions. But, since expressions containing the same categorematic terms in *exactly* the same grammatical constructions are identical, it follows that terms that "signify the same things in the same way" are correlated with identically the same mental expression, and so are synonymous, by (4), just as they should be according to I, 6.[44]

This approach thus has an advantage over that suggested in section VI, above, according to which the phrase "signify the same things in the same way" referred to the four modes of signification in I, 33. For the approach outlined here *guarantees* that expressions that signify the same things in the same way will be synonymous, as they should be according to I, 6. The approach in section VI, however, provides no clear assurance that this will be so.[45]

IX

In virtue of (9), connotative terms are synonymous with their nominal definitions. Hence, if connotative terms $t_1 \ldots t_n$ occur in the nominal definition of another connotative term t, then it is possible to replace the terms $t_1 \ldots t_n$ in the nominal definition of t by their own nominal definitions, *salva synonymitate*. Assuming, as seems plausible, that if an expression expresses the *quid nominis* of a term, then any synonymn of that expression will also express the *quid nominis* of that same term, it follows that the expression resulting from the above substitution will be a (more fully expanded) nominal definition of the original term t. If any connotative terms remain in this new expression, the process may be repeated, always *salva synonymitate*, and hence always resulting in an ever more fully expanded nominal definition of the original term t.

[43] Cf. the discussion in n. 8, above.

[44] Cf. above, n. 34.

[45] As additional evidence that Ockham has syntactic modes of signification in mind when he says that all the expressions expressing the *quid nominis* of a connotative term signify the same things "in the same way", we may cite III-II, 33: "Alia autem connotative, hoc est illa quae significant diversa vel idem *diversimode*, hoc est, affirmative vel negative, in recto vel in obliquo, vel aliquibus *talibus diversis modis...*". (Quoted in Moody, *The Logic of William of Ockham*, pp. 276-277 n. 2. Emphasis added.)

This regress of ever more fully expanded nominal definitions must terminate in a completely expanded nominal definition, each of whose constituent non-complex categorematic terms is absolute. The very possibility of scientific demonstration rests on this.[46] Thus, thesis (9) yields:

(11) Every connotative term is synonymous with a fully expanded nominal definition, each of whose constituent non-complex categorematic terms is absolute.[47]

The importance of (11) may be brought out by the following consideration. Thesis (11) suggests that there might well be parallel between the fully expanded nominal definition of a spoken connotative term *t* and the concept or mental expression with which *t* is correlated, in such a way that

(12) The fully expanded nominal definition of a spoken connotative term *t* contains an absolute categorematic constituent *t** in the syntactical construction *m* if and only if the concept or mental expression with which *t* is correlated contains an absolute categorematic concept, with which *t** is correlated, in the same syntactic construction *m*.[48]

Thesis (12) would mean that the fully expanded nominal definition of a spoken connotative term *t* completely reveals the structure of the mental expression with which *t* is correlated.

I think we should adopt (12). It allows us, for instance, to handle nicely the following text [49]:

[46] Cf. the discussion in Moody, *op. cit.*, pp. 55-57 and 267-280, especially p. 57: "If connotative terms could not be defined, or analysed, into functions of absolute terms, we would either have no means of demonstration, or else demonstration would involve infinite regress or circularity." The "infinite regress or circularity" is just another way of saying that there would be no such thing as demonstration in the usual sense. Cf. Aristotle, *Posterior Analytics* I, 3. The details of Ockham's theory of demonstration do not concern us here.
[47] Thesis (11) is already guaranteed for mental language in virtue of what was said above, in section VII, after thesis (10). If there are connotative terms at all in mental language, they are "synonymous", in the degenerate sense of being identical, with their fully expanded mental nominal definitions.
[48] Certain syntactical constructions are ruled out, namely, those that make no difference to truth or falsehood. Thus there is nothing in mental language corresponding to the four conjugations and the five declensions. And so these syntactic features of a fully expanded nominal definition would not be paralleled in the mental expression. Cf. Trentman, "Ockham on Mental" and Ockham, *Quodlibet* 5, q. 8.
[49] I, 10, 8-12 and 38-41: "non significat unum primo et aliud secundario, ita

. . . [an absolute term] does not signify one thing primarily and another secondarily, so that something has to be signified in the nominative and another in an oblique case. Nor in the definition expressing its *quid nominis* [50] does one have to posit such distinct terms in different cases or some verbal adjective [51]. . . But a connotative noun is one which signifies something primarily and something secondarily. And such a noun properly has a definition expressing the *quid nominis*. And often one has to put one term of the definition in the nominative and another in an oblique case.

The first sentence appeals to syntactic modes of signification; the oblique modes are lacking in the case of absolute terms, but presumably present (at least "often") in the case of connotative terms. Now according to the discussion in section VIII, above, these syntactic modes are determined for spoken terms by the syntactic structure of the correlated *mental* expression. The second sentence, however, speaks of an expression expressing the *quid nominis* of the term, and nothing is said there to indicate that it is a *mental* expression that is involved. But if it is a *spoken* nominal definition that is involved, how can we be sure that the syntactic modes appealed to in the first sentence, and determined by the *mental* expression, are at all reflected in the syntactic structure of the *spoken* nominal definition? The passage at least suggests that the second sentence is meant to be a restatement of the first.

The doubt is resolved if we adopt (12) and gloss "definition expressing the *quid nominis*" in the second sentence as referring to the *fully expanded* nominal definition. For then (12) guarantees that the structure of the mental expression be exactly paralleled by the structure of the fully expanded nominal definition.

X

In the passage just quoted, Ockham seems to be giving a criterion for what a term secondarily signifies:

quod oporteat aliquid significari in recto et aliud in obliquo, nec in definitione exprimente quid nominis oportet ponere talia distincta in diversis casibus vel aliquod verbum adiectivum. . . . Nomen autem connotativum est illud, quod significat aliquid primario et aliquid secundario. Et tale nomen proprie habet definitionem exprimentem quid nominis, et frequenter oportet ponere unum illius definitionis in recto et aliud in obliquo."

[50] In lines 12-21, Ockham goes on to say that "properly" speaking, absolute terms do not have *definitions* expressing the *quid nominis*. (Cf. above, n. 32.) They do, however, have *expressions* expressing the *quid nominis*.

[51] Verbs often appear in a nominal definition. (I, 10, 47-51: "Potest etiam aliquando aliquod verbum cadere in definitione exprimente quid nominis; sicut si quaeratur, quid significat hoc nomen 'causa,' potest dici, quod idem quod haec oratio 'aliquid ad cuius esse sequitur aliud,' vel 'aliquid potens producere aliud' vel aliquid huiusmodi.") 'Potens' is a verbal adjective. †

(13) A term secondarily signifies *x* if and only if it *obliquely* signifies *x*—i.e., signifies *x* in a syntactic mode involving an oblique case.

There are problems with (13). Perhaps the fully expanded nominal definition of a connotative term *t* contains no oblique cases. Then, by (13), *t* would signify nothing secondarily, in violation of the claim that connotative terms signify something primarily and something secondarily.[52] It certainly seems true that not *all* nominal definitions contain oblique cases. For it seems that 'empty place', which is presumably synonymous with 'place not filled with a body', will, like the latter, express the *quid nominis* of the figment term 'vacuum', and so formulate its nominal definition.[53] And yet, 'empty place' contains only terms in the nominative. This perhaps explains Ockham's inserting the word 'often' at the end of the passage quoted above, and gives at least some further credence to the view that he has in mind the *fully expanded* nominal definition. For 'empty' in the expression 'empty place', although it is in the nominative, is a connotative term, and so disappears in the fully expanded nominal definition. Whether such full expansions always yield oblique cases is of course still in doubt.

There is a worse problem with (13), however. For consider the figment term 'chimaera'. It can be truly predicated of nothing, and so primarily signifies nothing. Thus, whatever it signifies it signifies secondarily. It would follow from (13), then, that any categorematic term occurring in the fully expanded nominal definition of 'chimaera' must occur there at least once in an oblique case. And the same would apply also to all other figment terms. But this is most probably false.[54]

[52] Cf. the last half of n. 49. One might think that this should not be pushed. For "figment" terms, such as 'chimaera' and 'vacuum', are connotative (cf. II, 14), and yet signify nothing primarily, in violation of the same text. But if connotative terms are allowed to signify nothing secondarily, then the whole distinction Ockham is drawing in this passage collapses. Absolute terms signify nothing secondarily; connotative terms do. Primary signification should perhaps be held negotiable for connotative terms, but not secondary signification.

[53] In II, 14, Ockham says that 'vacuum' is a figment term (line 14), and therefore connotative (lines 5-6), but does not give its nominal definition. Buridan gives it as 'place not filled with a body' (*Sophismata*, ca. I, conclusion 11; Scott, tr., *John Buridan: Sophisms on Meaning and Truth*, p. 76).

[54] In I, 26, 131-132, Ockham proposes a nominal definition for 'chimaera', namely, 'animal composed of a goat and a cow' (" 'Chimaera est animal compositum ex capra et bove'—sit haec eius definitio.") The term 'animal' occurs

There is an alternative notion of secondary signification, inspired by John Buridan [55]:

(14) A term t secondarily signifies a thing x if and only if t signifies x but t cannot supposit personally for x—i.e., t does not primarily signify x.

In virtue of (9), a connotative term t signifies whatever its nominal definition signifies. And by (1), the Additive Principle, this is just the sum total of what is signified by the categorematic terms of that nominal definition. From this and (3) it follows from (14) that

(15) A connotative term t secondarily signifies a thing x if and only if x is signified by some term of the nominal definition of t but t does not primarily signify x.

But (15) too has a problem. For Ockham claims that 'one' is a connotative term.[56] And yet 'one' is truly predicable—and so primarily signifies—everything. Hence (15) would require that 'one' secondarily signify nothing at all, in violation of Ockham's claim that connotative terms signify some things primarily and some things secondarily.[57]

The best approach seems to be a compromise between (13) and (14). The result is a bit *ad hoc*, but works:

(16) A term t secondarily signifies a thing x if and only if either (a) t obliquely signifies x, or else (b) t signifies x but not primarily.

It can be easily verified that (16) avoids the problems with (13) and (14). I therefore suggest (16) as more in conformity with Ockham's "better doctrine" than (13), which seems to be what he actually intended.

XI

We are now at last in a position to answer the first question raised in section V, above: how is it determined whether a given expression expresses the *quid nominis* of a given term? We need to know this in order to understand (6), and therefore to complete our understanding

here in the nominative, but not in an oblique case. It seems highly unlikely that, if this definition is fully expanded, by replacing the connotative term 'composed' with its nominal definition, there will be an oblique occurrence of the term 'animal' in the resulting expression. It seems even less likely that this would occur in general.

[55] *Sophismata*, ca. IV, first remark; Scott, tr., *John Buridan: Sophisms on Meaning and Truth*, p. 112. I have translated Buridan's remark there into Ockham's terminology as developed in this paper.

[56] I, 10, 83. Cf. also I, 39.

[57] Cf. above, n. 52.

of Ockham's distinction between absolute and connotative terms.

In I, 10, Ockham gives us several examples of expressions expressing the *quid nominis* of the absolute term 'angel'[58]:

substance abstracted from matter
intellectual and incorruptible substance
simple substance not entering into composition with another

Each of these, he says, "explicates what the noun signifies".[59] What Ockham seems to have in mind here is some kind of "convertibility"; the expression 'substance abstracted from matter' is in some sense "convertible" with 'intellectual and incorruptible substance'. But just what this "convertibility" amounts to is not at once clear. It is not just a matter of being truly predicable of the same things, nor even of *necessarily* being truly predicable of the same things. That is, the following two alternatives fail (where 't' is replaced by a term and 't^*' by a complex term):

't^*' expresses the *quid nominis* of 't' if and only if the sentence 'For every x, x is a t if and only if x is a t^*' is true.

't^*' expresses the *quid nominis* of 't' if and only if the sentence 'For every x, x is a t if and only if x is a t^*' is necessary.

Both alternatives fail in the case of figment terms. For instance, let the expression 'place not filled with a body' express the *quid nominis* of the figment term 'vacuum',[60] and let 'animal composed of a goat and a cow' express the *quid nominis* of the figment term 'chimaera'.[61] Now chimaeras are impossible, and so are vacua.[62] It would follow, then, on either of the above alternative criteria, that 'place not filled with a body' expresses the *quid nominis* not only of 'vacuum' but also of 'chimaera', and that 'animal composed of a goat and a cow' expresses the *quid nominis* not only of 'chimaera' but also of 'vacuum'. All these terms are truly predicable of exactly the same things—namely, of nothing at all. And this is necessarily so, since chimaeras and vacua are impossible. Thus, in general, any expression expressing the *quid nominis* of any figment term would express the *quid nominis* of all figment terms alike.

One might perhaps suppose that, while this result is odd and perhaps

[58] lines 21-32.
[59] *Ibid.*, lines 24-25.
[60] Cf. above, n. 53.
[61] Cf. above, n. 54.
[62] Since both are figment terms. Cf. II, 14.

undesirable, it does not imply any outright contradiction in Ockham's theory. But that is not so. For the expressions 'place not filled with a body' and 'animal composed of a goat and a cow' are not synonymous—i.e., they do not "signify the same things in the same way". Hence, if any expression expressing the *quid nominis* of any figment term expresses the *quid nominis* of all figment terms, then no figment term is such that all the expressions expressing its *quid nominis* "signify the same things in the same way". Thus, by (7), no figment term would have a nominal definition, and so, by (8), no figment term would be connotative, in explicit violation of Ockham's doctrine.[63]

What Ockham needs then is some criterion which avoids these troublesome cases. The following criterion seems to work:

> (17) A complex expression t^* expresses the *quid nominis* of a term t if and only if either (a) t^* is synonymous with t, or else (b) t^* signifies nothing secondarily and the sentence 'For all x, x is a t if and only if x is a t^*' is necessary.

In virtue of clause (a), all complex expressions synonymous with a connotative term express its *quid nominis*, in conformity with the discussion above. All complex expressions synonymous with an absolute term express its *quid nominis* too, if indeed there are any such expressions,[64] but since absolute terms signify nothing secondarily, clause (b) applies in their case, and there are further expressions that express the *quid nominis*.

Clause (b), or something like it, is needed for absolute terms, but cannot be allowed to apply to connotative terms. It is needed for absolute terms because the examples Ockham gives of expressions expressing the *quid nominis* of the absolute term 'angel' are not synonymous with it. The phrase 'substance abstracted from matter' signifies matter in virtue of (1), the Additive Principle. But 'simple substance not entering into composition with another' does not.

[63] II, 14, 5-6: "Tales enim termini vere sunt connotativi."

[64] One might suppose that there are no such expressions. But perhaps there are. Just as 'goat-stag' is connotative, so 'goat-goat' and 'stag-stag' are absolute; they signify nothing secondarily, but do signify primarily. Whether they are correlated with the concepts with which the simple terms 'goat' and 'stag' are correlated, and so are synonymous with those simple terms, is an open question. The answer requires further insight into the syntactic modes of composition in mental language. In particular, are there mental syncategoremata in the concepts correlated with the expressions 'goat-goat' and 'stag-stag'?

Hence they cannot be correlated with the same concept, and so cannot be synonymous with one another, much less also with 'angel'. Thus a second clause is needed.

Clause (b) cannot be allowed to apply to connotative terms, because there is no guarantee that in the case of a connotative term *t*, the sentence 'For all *x*, *x* is a *t* if and only if *x* is a *t**' will be necessary only if *t* and *t** are synonymous. We have seen a particular instance of this difficulty with figment terms, above. But, since connotative terms signify secondarily, clause (b) does not apply to them.

Note finally that (17) preserves our previous sense that expressions *t** express the *quid nominis* of a term *t* only if they are in some sense "convertible" with it. The "convertibility" lies in the fact that the sentence 'For all *x*, *x* is a *t* if and only if *x* is a *t**' is necessary. This holds for connotative terms, where *t** is synonymous with *t*, as well as for absolute terms.

XII

One last point remains to be made. If secondary signification is defined as in (16), then it can ultimately be explicated in terms of primary signification and syntactic notions. For a term signifies exactly the same things as does the mental term with which it is correlated (or, if it is itself a mental term, with which it is identical). But mental terms signify just the sum total of what their non-complex categorematic constituents signify. Such constituents, however, are all absolute, and so signify only primarily. This reduction amounts to a considerable theoretical economy. Secondary signification is not a new primitive notion introduced by connotation-theory. Connotation-theory, or at least that part of it presented in this paper, adds no new primitive notions to those already needed for the theory of absolute terms.[65]

Bloomington, Indiana
Indiana University

[65] Since writing the bulk of this paper, I have had an opportunity to read Michael J. Loux's translation of the whole of part one of Ockham's *Summa*. (See *Ockham's Theory of Terms: Part 1 of the Summa logicae*, Michael J. Loux, tr., [Notre Dame, Ind.: Notre Dame Press, 1974]). Loux's introduction contains two very excellent studies of Ockham's ontology and theory of generality. I am pleased to find that Loux and I agree in interpreting many points of Ockham's connotation-theory. Nevertheless, for reasons discussed in section X, above, I think that Loux's definition of 'secondary signification', on p. 7 of his introduction, fails to capture Ockham's doctrine. Loux's definition is basically the same as my (14), above.

XII

PRIORITY OF ANALYSIS AND THE PREDICATES OF "O"-FORM SENTENCES

In 1970, John J. Swiniarski observed in this journal that there is something peculiar about Ockham's doctrine that the predicates of *O*-form sentences have confused and distributive supposition.[1] In 1973, Gareth Matthews made a similar point.[2] In brief, the problem is this: Ockham defines *confused and distributive* supposition in such a way that a given term in a sentence has confused and distributive supposition if and only if a descent to singulars under that term is possible by a *conjunctive* sentence, and the original sentence cannot be inferred from any one conjunct. Thus from 'Every man is an animal' one can descend to 'This man is an animal, and that man is an animal...', and so on for all men, but one cannot ascend from any one of the conjuncts to the original sentence. Hence the term 'man' in that sentence has confused and distributive supposition.[3] (For the record, we note here that for Ockham a given term in a sentence has *determinate* supposition if and only if a descent to singulars under that term is possible by a *disjunctive* sentence, and the original sentence can be inferred from any disjunct,[4] and that the

---

[1] John J. Swiniarski, "A New Presentation of Ockham's Theory of Supposition with an Evaluation of Some Contemporary Criticisms," *Franciscan Studies*, 30 (1970), 181–217.

[2] Gareth B. Matthews, "*Suppositio* and Quantification in Ockham," *Nous*, 7 (1973), 13–24.

[3] William of Ockham, *Summa Logicae*, critical ed. by P. Boehner, G. Gál, and S. Brown, (St. Bonaventure, N.Y.: The Franciscan Institute, 1974), pars I, ca. 70, lines 62–68: "Suppositio confusa et distributiva est quando contingit aliquo modo descendere copulative, si habeat multa contenta et ex nullo uno formaliter infertur. Sicut est in ista 'omnis homo est animal,' cuius subiectum supponit confuse et distributive: sequitur enim 'omnis homo est animal, igitur iste homo est animal et ille homo est animal,' et sic de singulis; et non sequitur formaliter 'iste homo est animal,' quocumque demonstrato, 'igitur omnis homo est animal'." (All references to Ockham will be to this edition, *pars prima*, by chapter and line numbers.)

[4] Ibid., 70, 28–31: "Est igitur regula certa, quod quando sub termino communi contingit descendere ad singularia per propositionem disiunctivam, et

term has *merely confused* supposition [what Swiniarski calls "purely confused" supposition] if and only if a descent to singulars under that term is not possible by a disjunctive sentence, but one is possible by a sentence with a disjoined *term*, and the original sentence can be inferred from any singular. Thus from 'Every man is an animal' one cannot descend to 'Every man is this animal or every man is that animal, etc.,' but one can descend to 'Every man is this animal or that animal, etc.,' and from any singular — e.g., from 'Every man is that animal' — one can infer the original sentence. Hence the term 'animal' in that sentence has merely confused supposition.[5])

From the above definition of confused and distributive supposition, it follows that the predicates of *O*–form sentences have confused and distributive supposition. For from the *O*–form sentence 'Some man is not a Greek' one can descend to 'Some man is not this Greek, and some man is not that Greek, etc.,' but one obviously cannot infer the original sentence from a single one of those conjuncts alone.

This fact, however, is incompatible with the view that descent to singulars is meant to be a kind of *analysis*, so that the original sentence is meant to be *equivalent* to the expanded sentence descended from it. For suppose that Socrates and Plato, both Greeks, are the only men. Then it is true that some man (namely, Socrates) is not this Greek (namely, Plato), and some man (namely, Plato) is not that Greek (namely, Socrates), and yet it is false that some man is not a Greek.

---

ex qualibet singulari infertur talis propositio, tunc ille terminus habet suppositionem personalem determinatam."

[5] Ibid., 70, 44–61: "Suppositio personalis confusa tantum est quando terminus communis supponit personaliter et non contingit descendere ad singularia per disiunctivam, nulla variatione facta a parte alterius extremi, sed per propositionem de disiuncto praedicato, et contingit eam inferri ex quocumque singulari. Verbi gratia in ista 'omnis homo est animal,' li animal supponit confuse tantum, quia non contingit descendere sub animali ad sua contenta per disiunctivam; quia non sequitur 'omnis homo est animal, igitur omnis homo est hoc animal, vel omnis homo est illud animal, vel omnis homo est aliud animal,' et sic de singulis. Sed bene contingit descendere ad propositionem de disiuncto praedicato ex singularibus, quia bene sequitur 'omnis homo est animal, igitur omnis homo est hoc animal vel illud,' et sic de singulis; quia consequens est una categorica, composita ex hoc subiecto 'homo' et hoc praedicato 'hoc animal vel illud vel illud,' et sic de singulis. Et manifestum est quod hoc praedicatum vere praedicatur de omni homine, ideo illa universalis est simpliciter vera. Et similiter ista infertur ex quolibet contento animalis, nam bene sequitur 'omnis homo est hoc animal quocumque animali demonstrato, 'igitur omnis homo est animal'."

Swiniarski and Matthews draw different morals from this. Matthews suggests that Ockham does not intend his descent to singulars to give a kind of analysis at all (and therefore, that supposition-theory is not a kind of quantification-theory), and correctly observes that Ockham never explicitly claims equivalence. Swiniarski, on the other hand, takes the equivalence-claim for granted, and argues that Ockham needs a "priority of analysis" rule. Such a rule would require that descent be made under subject-terms before it is made under predicate-terms. Swiniarski argues that Ockham is able to do without a "priority of analysis" rule for *A*-form sentences by his doctrine of merely confused supposition, with its peculiar descent to a disjoined term, but that he needs such a rule in order to get around the problem of the predicate of *O*-form sentences. Moreover, once such a rule is adopted, merely confused supposition becomes superfluous.[6]

I find neither of these views compelling. While Matthews is † certainly right in saying that Ockham never claims equivalence explicitly, I for one find it hard to imagine that he means anything else. For if equivalence fails, the elaborate distinction of the various kinds of personal supposition cannot be used in an account of truth-conditions. What then is the distinction for? Is it simply an idle decoration in the theory of supposition?

On the other hand, while Swiniarski's suggested "priority of analysis" rule would avoid the problem with the *O*-form sentences, it would not, as he claims it does, do away with the need for merely confused supposition entirely. Ockham, after all, uses merely confused supposition not only in his account of *A*-form sentences, but also in his account of such problem-sentences as 'I promise you a horse.'[7] A "priority of analysis" rule would eliminate the need for merely confused supposition in the case of *A*-form sentences, but not in the other cases.

It is true that Ockham says the term 'horse' in 'I promise you a horse' does not "strictly speaking" supposit at all, since it is not one of the extremes (subject or predicate) of the sentence, but only a part of an extreme.[8] This is an evasion, however, and its importance

---

[6] Swiniarski, op. cit., pp. 209–213.

[7] See Ockham, op. cit., 72, 3rd *dubium* and reply, lines 19–23 and 139–164. See also Swiniarski, op. cit., pp. 201–202 for a discussion of a similar passage in the *Elementarium Logicae*.

[8] Ockham, op. cit., 72, 155–161: "Sed numquid in ista 'promitto tibi equum'

must not be exaggerated. If only the extremes of sentences "strictly speaking" have supposition, and not their parts, this is not because only the extremes really satisfy the definition of supposition, so that the definition would have to be revised in order to accommodate the parts of extremes. For that is simply not so. Ockham defines supposition as follows:

> Now "supposition" is said to be as it were a "putting in place of another," so that when a term in a sentence stands for something in such a way that we use the term for something of which (or of a pronoun indicating which) that term (or the nominative of that term, if it is in an oblique case) is truly predicated, it supposits for it. And this is true at least when the suppositing term is taken significatively.[9]

Although Ockham goes on at once to discuss the supposition of subjects and predicates,[10] there is nothing in this definition that limits supposition to the extremes of sentences. Indeed, immediately before stating his definition, Ockham distinguishes two senses of 'supposition' and observes that, in the sense he is using, "both the subject and the predicate supposit, and in general whatever *can be* the subject or predicate of a sentence supposits."[11] The term 'horse' in 'I promise you a horse' *can be* the subject or predicate of a sentence, even if not of that one, and so has supposition in 'I promise you a

li equum supponit confuse tantum, loquendo de virtute sermonis? Dicendum quod stricte loquendo li equum non supponit confuse tantum, quia non supponit, cum sit pars extremi... Tamen extendendo nomen potest dici quod li equum supponit confuse tantum." See also Swiniarski, loc. cit. Ockham makes a similar remark, op. cit., 69, 3–4 and 16–19: "Circa quam est sciendum quod solum categorema, quod est extremum propositionis, significative acceptum, supponit personaliter... Per illam particulam 'extremum propositionis' excluditur pars extremi, quantumcumque sit nomen et categorema. Sicut hic 'homo albus est animal' nec 'homo' supponit nec 'albus' supponit sed totum extremum supponit."

[9] Ibid., 63, 11–15: "Dicitur autem suppositio quasi pro alio positio, ita quod quando terminus in propositione stat pro aliquo, ita quod utimur illo termino pro aliquo pro quo, sive de pronomine demonstrante ipsum, ille terminus vel rectus illius termini si sit obliquus verificatur, supponit pro illo. Et hoc saltem verum est quando terminus supponens significative accipitur." In fact, this definition applies only to personal supposition, as the last sentence makes clear. But that is sufficient to make my point.

[10] Ibid., 63, 16–32.

[11] Ibid., 63, 9–10: "tam subiectum quam praedicatum supponit; et universaliter quidquid potest esse subiectum propositionis vel praedicatum supponit."

horse.' Again, supposition is said to be "a property that applies to terms — but never except in a sentence."[12] The "terms" of a sentence, however, are not just its subject and predicate, but any word occurring in it which, when taken significatively, *can be* the subject or predicate of some sentence.[13]

Thus if "strictly speaking" the parts of a sentence's extremes do not have supposition, 'strictly' here can only mean "narrowly." The parts of extremes supposit just as really, just as much in conformity with the definition, as do the extremes themselves.[14] Ockham

---

[12] Ibid., 63, 1–2: "proprietas conveniens termino sed numquam nisi in propositione."

[13] Ibid., 2, 12–14: "Tertio modo accipitur 'terminus' praecise et magis stricte pro illo quod significative sumptum potest esse subiectum vel praedicatum propositionis." Contrast Swiniarski, op. cit., p. 183, who says that "in a narrower sense it is only the subject and predicate which are referred to as the terms of a proposition." Ockham does not to my knowledge ever employ such a narrow sense.

[14] As additional evidence, Ockham appeals to the supposition of parts of extremes in his resolution of the *insolubilia*. See my "Ockham on Self-Reference," *Notre Dame Journal of Formal Logic*, 15 (1974), 298–300. Indeed I suspect that † the theory of descent to singulars is included in supposition-theory *only* because the parts of extremes have supposition. For Ockham has a separate suppositional account of truth-conditions for categoricals, in *Summa Logicae*, part 2, chs. 2–4 (for the basic present-tensed forms). That account proceeds in terms of the supposition of subject and predicate alone. If only the extremes of a sentence had supposition, this account would suffice to give a full theory of the contribution suppositing terms make to the truth-conditions of categoricals. Only if the parts of extremes supposit too does the theory of descent to singulars add anything to the account in Part 2: it adds, namely, a description of what the *parts* of extremes contribute to the truth-conditions of categoricals. In short, if only the extremes had supposition, there would be no reason to have two separate accounts of truth-conditions (and I take the theory of descent to singulars to be such an account). On the other hand, if the parts of extremes supposit too, there is perhaps a reason: the account in Part 1 is the more general; the account in Part 2, although less general, is tidier. It does not, for instance, require infinite conjunctions or disjunctions, or those peculiar disjoined terms. I suspect Ockham's reason for trying to deny that parts of extremes have supposition (see above, n. 8) is that syntactical rules of the kind in ch. 71, as well as certain rules of inference, are very difficult to formulate with a generality sufficient to accommodate parts of extremes. Indeed, the context of Ockham's denial in ch. 69 concerns the fact that the rule allowing inferences from an inferior to a superior term (i.e., from a term with a narrower to a term with a broader supposition) cannot be supposed to apply to the inference 'Tu es vadens ad forum, ergo tu es existens ad forum' on the ground that 'vadens' is inferior to 'existens.'

is going to have to answer the question how 'horse' supposits in 'I promise you a horse'; he cannot in the end evade the issue, as he seems to be tempted to do, by saying that it does not supposit there at all. And since merely confused supposition is the only kind that works here, it is clear that Ockham needs merely confused supposition whether he has a "priority of analysis" rule or not.

I have dwelled at such length on this point for a reason. The predicates of *A*–form sentences have merely confused supposition; the denials of such sentences are *O*–form sentences, and their predicates are problematic. Although it has not to my knowledge previously been observed in the literature, there is an exactly similar situation with other cases of merely confused supposition. Thus the term 'horse' in 'I promise you a horse' has merely confused supposition. But what kind of supposition does it have in 'I do *not* promise you a horse'? It appears, like the predicates of *O*–form sentences, to have confused and distributive supposition. For from 'I do not promise you a horse' one can descend to 'I do not promise you this horse, and I do not promise you that horse, etc.', but one cannot ascend to the original sentence from any single conjunct. And yet, just as with *O*–form sentences, the conjunction to which one descends in this case is not equivalent to the original sentence. For I can promise you a horse and yet it might be true that for every single horse, I do not promise you *that* horse in particular.

Here then is a situation exactly like the one for the predicate of *O*–form sentences. It suggests a *general* problem: What happens to terms in merely confused supposition when they are inserted within the scope of a negation? Since Ockham needs merely confused supposition whether he has a "priority of analysis" rule or not, the adoption of such a rule will not relieve this problem. Moreover, if the general problem can be solved, the problem of the *O*–form sentences will be solved *a fortiori*. Hence a "priority of analysis" rule is *insufficient* for the general problem; and if the general problem can be handled in some other way, such a rule is *unnecessary* for the particular problem of *O*–form sentences. The "priority of analysis" rule is a red herring.

How then can the general problem be treated? Let us review the situation. Ockham defines the various kinds of personal supposition a term can have by means of two parameters: (a) the kinds of sentences to which a descent is possible under that term, and (b) whether or not one can infer ("ascend" to) the original sentence from any sentence exactly like it except that the term whose supposition is in question, together with its quantifier if it is quantified, is replaced by another term standing in discrete supposition for one of the supposita of the original term. With respect to (a), Ockham distinguishes three kinds of sentences to which a descent might be made: (1) conjunctions of categoricals, (2) disjunctions of categoricals, and (3) categoricals with disjoined terms.[15]

Let us for the moment adopt the view I think it is likely Ockham † intended: that sentences with terms in confused and distributive supposition are *equivalent* to the conjunction of categoricals one gets by descending to singulars under those terms, and that determinate supposition goes in the same way with disjunctions of categoricals and merely confused supposition with categoricals containing disjoined terms.[16] On this view, the predicate of *O*-form sentences, and 'horse' in 'I do not promise you a horse,' do not have confused and distributive supposition after all, but rather *merely confused* supposition. For 'Some man is not a Greek' is equivalent to 'Some man is not this Greek, or that Greek, etc.,' and 'I do not promise you a horse' is equivalent to 'I do not promise you this horse or that horse, etc.' Indeed, this is just what one would expect. For in general, if a sentence is equivalent to an affirmative categorical, then the denial of that sentence ought to be equivalent to the corresponding negative categorical *with the same terms.* Hence if a sentence is equivalent to an affirmative categorical with a disjoined term, the negation of that sentence ought to be equivalent to the corresponding negative

---

[15] Ockham in fact says "disjoined *predicate*" in at least one place (see n. 5, above), but this would rule out the case of 'I promise you a horse.'

[16] Such equivalence would be a sufficient condition for confused and distributive supposition and for determinate supposition. But for merely confused supposition, an additional proviso is needed: a term is in merely confused supposition in a sentence if and only if that sentence is *not* equivalent to the conjunction or disjunction descended from it under that term, but is equivalent to the descended categorical with disjoined term. (Compare the proviso in Ockham's actual definition above, n. 5.) This prevents the predicate of 'Some man is an animal,' for instance, from being in both determinate and merely confused supposition at once, even though that sentence is equivalent both to 'Some man is this animal or some man is that animal...' and to 'Some man is this animal or that animal...' Similarly, the predicate of 'No man is an island' is not both in confused and distributive and in merely confused supposition, even though the sentence is equivalent both to 'No man is this island and no man is that island...' and to 'No man is this island or that island...'

categorical with the same disjoined term. In short, *negation does not affect merely confused supposition.*

While this certainly violates Ockham's explicit doctrine, it inevitably follows from the equivalence-view I have said was probably his intention. The reason it violates his explicit doctrine is that Ockham's definitions of the various kinds of personal supposition in terms of the two parameters mentioned earlier do not exactly capture the equivalence he probably wanted.

Indeed, *no* definition in terms of these two parameters alone can exactly capture these equivalences. For in the case of the subjects of *A*-form sentences, and also the subjects and predicates of *E*-form sentences, all of which have confused and distributive supposition, one can descend to a conjunction of categoricals, to a disjunction of categoricals, to a categorical with a disjoined term, and for that matter to a categorical with a *conjoined* term (an additional possibility Swiniarski discusses).[17] And in each of these cases one cannot ascend from any one singular. But all this holds equally well for the predicates of *O*-form sentences and for 'horse' in 'I do not promise you a horse.' Thus, Ockham's parameters are simply insufficient to distinguish these cases from the others.

In sum, if Ockham did intend the kind of equivalence I have suggested, then he needs to approach the task of defining the various kinds of personal supposition in an entirely different way. The two parameters he uses will simply not suffice. Moreover, no "priority of analysis" rule is going to evade this necessity. On the other hand, if Ockham did not intend this kind of equivalence, then what was he doing?

Indiana University
Bloomington, Indiana

---

[17] Swiniarski, op. cit., pp. 212–213.

XIII

Synonymy and Equivocation in Ockham's Mental Language

IN 1957 PETER GEACH ARGUED THAT Ockham's theory of mental language was too facile, that it made the grammar of mental language look too suspiciously like that of Latin: "He merely transfers features of Latin grammar to Mental, and then regards this as explaining why such features occur in Latin—they are needed there if what we say inwardly in Mental is to be outwardly got across to others in Latin. But clearly nothing is explained at all."[1] In 1970 John Trentman responded to this charge in a short article that has since become very influential.[2] In that article Trentman makes three claims among others:

1. Ockham thought of mental language as a kind of stripped-down, "ideal" language, containing just those grammatical features that affect the truth conditions of mental sentences.[3]
2. There can be no synonymy in mental language.[4]
3. There can be no equivocation in mental language.[5]

It is the purpose of this paper to examine each of these claims in turn.[6] In so doing we

[1] *Mental Acts: Their Content and Their Objects* (London: Routledge & Kegan Paul, 1957), p. 102. See also the whole of sec. 23, pp. 101–6.

[2] "Ockham on Mental," *Mind* 79 (1970):586–90.

[3] Ibid., p. 588: "I think Ockham's Mental can in many ways be compared to the now, I suppose, slightly old-fashioned ideal languages of twentieth-century philosophers. In distinguishing Mental from Latin or any spoken language, Ockham asks us to consider what would have to be the grammatical structure of a language that was ideal for one purpose—for giving a true description of things." See also ibid., p. 589: "Ockham's real criterion, then, for admitting grammatical distinctions into Mental amounts to asking whether the distinctions in question would be necessary in an ideal language—ideal for a complete, true description of the world."

[4] Ibid., p. 588: "The existence of synonyms seems not to mark any distinction of the requisite kind so that in principle synonymous expressions can be regarded as reducible to a common mental equivalent." See also n. 5, below.

[5] Ibid.: "But just as verbal ornament gives rise to synonymy it also gives rise to equivocation, and neither can be usefully purged from a language suitable for conversation. Neither, however, serves any purpose in an ideal language of the sort envisaged. Indeed, the distinction between equivocal and univocal expressions has no point in Mental by the very nature of the case."

[6] The second and third claims are of special interest to me personally. For in my "Ockham's Distinctions between Absolute and Connotative Terms," *Vivarium* 13 (1975):55–76, I have given an account of Ockham's notion of connotative terms that relies in important respects on the claim that there is no synonymy in mental language. Again, on the basis of the third of the above claims, I have argued in my "Ockham's Rule of Supposition: Two Conflicts in His Theory," *Vivarium* 12 (1974):63–73, that there is a tension or "conflict"

shall discover that Ockham's theory of mental language is not so neat and tidy as might have been hoped. I shall argue that each of Trentman's three claims is "correct" in the sense that Ockham either explicitly holds it or else seems committed to holding it on the basis of other features of his thought. Nevertheless, I shall maintain, each of these claims also leads to difficulties for Ockham, either (with respect to the first claim) because there are certain empirical, linguistic reasons of a sort Ockham would accept for rejecting the claim as it stands, or else (with respect to the second and third claims) because it conflicts with things Ockham says elsewhere. All this suggests that Ockham had not completely thought out all the implications of what he wanted to say about mental language. And that in turn suggests that, whatever is true for other authors, the theory of mental language was perhaps not as central to Ockham's own thinking as we have come to believe.[7]

I. Perhaps Ockham's clearest general statement of his criterion for what goes into mental language occurs in *Quodlibet* 5, q. 8 ("Whether all the grammatical accidents of spoken terms are applicable to mental ones?"), the text on which Trentman bases claim 1. There Ockham puts his criterion in terms of the "needs of signification."[8] In a word, if a grammatical feature of spoken or written language can affect truth conditions, it is found in mental language; otherwise it is not. Let us call this "Ockham's Criterion." Thus the distinction between nominative and genitive case in Latin has its counterpart in mental language since the truth conditions of "Homo est homo" ("A man is a man"), which is true, differ from those of "Homo est hominis" ("A man is a man's"), which is false if there are no slaves. On the other hand, the Latin distinction between first and second declension has no counterpart in mental language since as long as grammatical well-formedness (*congruitas*) is preserved it makes no difference to the truth conditions of a sentence whether a given term occurring in it is in the first or the second declension. As Ockham points out, an indication of this may be seen in the fact that synonymous nouns, which are intersubstitutable *salva veritate* (provided well-formedness is preserved), may belong to different declensions.[9]

Ockham's Criterion may be divided into two parts: (*a*) the positive claim that all grammatical features of spoken and written language that affect truth conditions are present also in mental language, and (*b*) the negative claim that all grammatical features of spoken and written language that do not affect truth conditions are not present in mental language.

The positive part of Ockham's criterion in unacceptable. For unless Latin or some

---

in Ockham's theory of supposition. In neither paper, however, did I fully justify the claim on which my argument rested. That will be remedied here.

[7] See Trentman, "Ockham on Mental," p. 586: "Further, he thought mental language is really of prior importance to spoken or written language, and its structure is, in fact, the proper subject for the logician."

[8] William of Ockham, *Quodlibeta septem* (Strasbourg, 1491) (Hain 11941), fol. 77ra: "Ad argumentum principale dico quod omne quod accidit termino mentali accidit termini vocali sed non e converso, quia aliqua accidunt terminis vocalibus propter necessitatem significationis et expressionis et illa conveniunt terminis mentalibus, alia accidunt terminis vocalibus propter ornatum sermonis, sicut synonyma, vel propter congruitatem, et illa non conveniunt terminis mentalibus."

[9] Ibid., conclusion 2, fol. 76vb. Geach appears to have taken this observation as Ockham's guiding idea: the grammatical features with respect to which synonyms may differ are not found in mental language; all others are. (See Trentman, "Ockham on Mental,", p. 597.) In fact, although this is a consequence of Ockham's Criterion, the Criterion itself is more deeply motivated, as Trentman argues.

other spoken or written language is to be given an arbitrarily privileged status (thus opening the door to Geach's criticism), Ockham's Criterion must treat them all on a par. Hence either (i) any truth-relevant grammatical feature found in *even a single* spoken or written language is found also in mental language, or else (ii) any such feature found in *all* spoken or written languages is found also in mental language. But neither alternative is satisfactory. Since different human languages frequently adopt a variety of grammatical devices to mark a given distinction (for instance, the difference between "John loves Mary" and "Mary loves John" is marked by word order in English but by case-inflection in Latin), alternative (i) would go beyond the "needs of signification" and clutter mental language with many grammatical devices any one of which suffices to mark the given distinction, but none of which is needed to do so.

One may object that Ockham's Criterion requires less, that it requires only that the distinction marked by a truth-relevant grammatical feature in a spoken or written language be made also in mental language by *some* grammatical feature, although not necessarily by the same one, so that the needless multiplication of grammatical devices in mental language is avoided. But this is in effect to say no more than that spoken and written sentences with different truth conditions must correspond to mental sentences with different truth-relevant grammatical features—that is, with different truth conditions. That is so, but it is not what is wanted. It tells us which distinctions must be made in mental language, but it says nothing at all about how mental language makes them; it does not give us a single rule of mental grammar, but only what is to be accomplished by such rules.

If alternative (i) is unacceptable, alternative (ii) is little better. The grammatical diversity of spoken and written languages makes it very doubtful that there are any surface-level grammatical features common to them all.[10] Alternative (ii) is therefore very likely vacuous. Hence the positive part of Ockham's Criterion, on either of its two permitted readings, is either unworkable or uninformative.

Nevertheless, the negative part of Ockham's Criterion may be accepted. Grammatical features that do not affect truth conditions in a spoken or written language do not appear in mental language. They occur in spoken or written language only for "decoration" or for the sake of "well-formedness" (for instance, agreement with respect to gender).[11] Thus mental language is a minimal language; whatever the positive features of its grammar, there is nothing there that goes beyond the "needs of signification," that is not needed for the making of truth-relevant distinctions.

II. We are now in a position to argue for the second of Trentman's claims, that there is no synonymy in mental language. As far as I know, Ockham asserts this explicitly only once.[12] Several times, however, he makes a weaker claim that, if one is not careful, may be misread as saying more than it actually does. He frequently says that synonyms in spoken or written language correspond or are subordinated to the same concept or term of mental language so that the subordination relation does not map

[10] The surface-structure features must be the one that are at stake. For the closest Ockham comes to the notion of a "deep structure" is mental language itself.

[11] See above, n. 8.

[12] See the last sentence of the text quoted above in n. 8.

conventional synonyms into mental synonyms.[13] But this is not by itself sufficient to rule out mental synonymy across the board; it is only to say that mental synonyms, if there are any, are not the correlates of conventional synonyms.

On the other hand, if Ockham does not explicitly assert Trentman's second claim as often as one would like, there are at least two other reasons to think both that he *does* accept it and that philosophically he *ought* to accept it. The first reason is just the acceptable, negative part of Ockham's criterion: grammatical features of spoken or written language that do not serve the "needs of signification" by affecting truth conditions are not present in mental grammar. That this rules out all synonymy in mental language seems to be the clear intention of Ockham's whole discussion in *Quodlibet* 5, q. 8, with its repeated statement that what is in mental language is there only because of the "needs of signification," not for the sake of "decoration" or "well-formedness," and that synonymy does not serve the "needs of signification." Indeed, the intention is so clear in this text that one may regard the denial of any mental synonymy as all but explicit there.

Nevertheless, this first reason is perhaps the weaker of the two. For although the negative part of Ockham's Criterion is explicit in *Quodlibet* 5, q. 8, and is philosophically relatively unproblematic, still we must remember that the discussion there also affirms the unsatisfactory positive claim that all truth-relevant features of spoken and written language are found too in mental language. Perhaps one ought not to be entirely confident of even the acceptable parts of a text in which the philosophically unobjectionable and the philosophically objectionable are so thoroughly intertwined.

Whatever one thinks of these hesitations, the second and perhaps stronger reason for affirming Trentman's second claim is independent of these considerations. Ockham defines synonymy in the "broad" sense, which he says he will use,[14] as follows:

> Broadly, those things are called synonyms that simply signify the same thing in all ways, so that nothing is in any way signified by the one unless it is signified by the other in the same way.[15]

I have argued elsewhere[16] that the "ways" (modes) of signifying here are best interpreted syntactically, so that a mental expression or concept signifies a thing *x* in a given syntactic mode *m* if and only if *x* is signified by some constituent simple categorematic concept or mental term occurring within that expression in the grammatical or syntactical construction *m* (for instance, in the plural, in the passive voice, in a prepositional phrase, etc.).[17] It follows that synonymous mental expressions, signifying exactly the

[13] E.g., *Summa logicae*, ed. Gedeon Gál and Stephen F. Brown (St. Bonaventure, N.Y.: The Franciscan Institute, 1974), I, 3, ll. 20–22: "quia quidquid per omnia synonyma significatur posset per unum illorum exprimi sufficienter, et ideo multitudo conceptuum tali pluralitati synonymorum non correspondet." See also *Quodlibet* 5, q. 8, conclusion 2, fol. 76vb: "nec vocibus synonymis correspondet pluralitas conceptuum"; and *Quodlibet* 5, q. 9, fol. 77rb: "sed multitudini nominum synonymorum in voce non correspondet pluralitas in mente"; and fol. 77vb: "licet talis pluralitas sit in voce non tamen in conceptu, quia multitudini nominum synonymorum non correspondet multitudo conceptuum."

[14] *Summa logicae*, I, 6, ll. 15f.: "Isto secundo modo intendo uti in isto capitulo, et in multis aliis, hoc nomine 'synonyma'."

[15] Ibid., ll. 8–11: "Large dicuntur illa synonyma quae simplicter idem significant omnibus modis, ita quod nihil aliquo modo significatur per unum quin eodem modo significetur per reliquum." Ockham says the same thing, in almost the same terms, in *Quodlibet* 5, q. 10, fol. 78ra.

[16] Spade, "Ockham's Distinctions," pp. 68–69. (Although some of what is said in that article rests on the claim that there is no synonymy in mental language, the argument for the present point does not.)

[17] Spoken or written expressions, then, signify *x* in mode *m* if and only if they are subordinated to a mental expression that signifies *x* in mode *m*.

same things in exactly the same ways, would have to consist of exactly the same simple categorematic concepts in exactly the same syntactical constructions. But that is to say that they would be *identical*,[18] so that synonymy is ruled out in mental language after all.

For these two reasons, therefore, I think we ought to take Ockham at his word on the one occasion when he explicitly affirms Trentman's second claim. Nevertheless, he seems to deny it implicitly in at least one passage. In *Quodlibet* 5, q. 9 ("Whether mental names are distinguished like spoken names into concrete and abstract?"), Ockham argues that mental language possesses both the concrete term "white" and the abstract term "whiteness." The concrete term "white" is one of the paradigms of a connotative term; its nominal definition is "something having a whiteness."[19] If, therefore, mental language possesses the abstract term "whiteness," it certainly possesses the syntactic wherewithal to formulate the nominal definition of the concrete term "white." But, as I have argued elsewhere,[20] Ockham's theory of connotation seems to hold that connotative terms are synonymous with their nominal definitions. Hence if both "white" and "whiteness" are included in the vocabulary of mental language, mental synonymy will be possible after all.

Thus although the denial of synonymy is a legitimate part of Ockham's theory of mental language, he seems not to have fully realized its implications. If there is no synonymy in mental language, then mental names are not distinguished like spoken ones into concrete and abstract, despite what Ockham says in *Quodlibet* 5, q. 9.[21]

III. In order to discuss Trentman's third claim, that there can be no equivocation in mental language, some preliminary explanation of Ockham's theory of equivocation is required. Ockham, following Aristotle[22] and the tradition,[23] distinguished equivocation, which pertains to ambiguous terms, from amphiboly, which pertains to ambiguous complex expressions and especially to ambiguous sentences. I shall discuss Trentman's third claim only with respect to equivocation proper, although many of the considera-

---

[18] Or at most differ numerically. That is, they would be two tokens of the same mental type. But this kind of plurality is not what is involved in synonymy.

[19] *Summa logicae*, I, 10, ll. 41–46: "Sicut est de hoc nomine 'album', nam 'album' habet definitionem exprimentem quid nominis, in qua una dictio ponitur in recto et alia in obliquo. Unde si quaeras, quid significat hoc nomen 'album', dices quod illud idem quod ista oratio tota 'aliquid informatum albedine' vel 'aliquid habens albedinem'."

[20] Spade, "Ockham's Distinctions," secs. 7–9. The operative assumption in this argument is the principle I label Principle 9 in that paper (p. 67): "All the expressions expressing the *quid nominis* of a term *t* are synonymous if and only if *t* is itself synonymous with each of those expressions." Although Ockham never explicitly asserts that principle, I think it is legitimate to attribute it to him. See the discussion ibid.

[21] It is significant, therefore, that Ockham's argument in the passage rests on faulty reasoning. See ibid., n. 40. The issues raised by this passage are in fact more complicated, and whether it implies mental synonymy is in fact not so clear as I have suggested above. For a fuller discussion, see ibid. I refer to the matter here only to suggest that Ockham was perhaps not fully aware of the implications of his theory of mental language.

[22] Aristotle, *Sophistici elenchi*, 4, 165b30–166a23.

[23] E.g., William of Sherwood, *Die Introductiones in logicam des Wilhelm von Shyreswood († nach 1267)*, ed. Martin Grabmann (Munich: Verlag der Bayerischen Akademie der Wissenschaften, 1937), pp. 87–89; trans. Norman Kretzmann, *William of Sherwood's Introduction to Logic* (Minneapolis: University of Minnesota Press, 1966), pp. 135–40. See also Peter of Spain, *Tractatus: Called Afterwards Summule logicales*, ed L. M. De Rijk (Assen: Van Gorcum, 1972), tract VII, secs. 25–26; Lambert of Auxerre, *Logica (Summa Lamberti)*, ed. Franco Alessio (Firenze: La Nuova Italia Editrice, 1971), pp. 149–55.

tions raised below in connection with the third mode of equivocation will apply *mutatis mutandis* to amphiboly. In the end I think no ambiguity of any sort, whether of terms or of expressions, ought to be allowed in mental language.

Ockham discusses equivocation in two main places in the *Summa logicae*, in I, 13, and in III-4, 2–4.[24] The latter is the fuller treatment, although the former adds some considerations especially relevant to mental language. In III-4, 2, Ockham observes that an equivocal term is sometimes defined as one that has a diverse signfication in an expression.[25] Ockham argues that this definition will not do. First, although this is not his objection, the phrase "diverse signification" must be properly understood. For if one holds with Ockham that terms do not in general signify external natures or concepts in the mind but rather individuals, then a common term such as "man" can signify diverse things—namely, individual men—and yet be univocal. The phrase "diverse signification" must therefore be read as meaning that the term is given more than one imposition at the same time.

But even if "diverse signification" is correctly interpreted, Ockham finds the proposed definition insufficient. For, and this is his actual argument, sometimes equivocation occurs where there is no diversity of signification. His example is the sentence "Man is a noun" in which the term 'man' is imposed to signify only individual men but may refer or supposit equivocally either for those individual men or for the spoken or written term "man."[26]

As the example suggests, Ockham holds that the correct definition of equivocation must be in terms of supposition rather than signification.[27] In effect, a term is equivocal in a sentence if it can refer or stand or supposit there for diverse things in such a way that it supposits for the one and not the other. The last proviso is added because in the sentence "Every man is an animal" the term 'man' supposits for diverse individual men, but it is not equivocal there since it supposits for all such men and not for some to the exclusion of others. On the other hand, in "Man is a species" the term "man," even though it is given only a single imposition, can supposit either for individual men and not for the concept "man" or for the concept and not for the individuals.[28]

---

[24] Amphiboly is treated in III-4, 5–7. The discussion of equivocation in Ockham's *Expositio Praedicamentorum*, Ca. 1 (1 a 1–5: "Aequivoca dicuntur quorum solum") adds nothing relevant to our purposes. See his *Expositio aurea* (Bologna: Benedictus Hector Bononiensis, 1496), sign. g ii. (Hain 11950.)

[25] Lines 7–8: "Circa primum dicitur quod aequivocatio est diversa significatio alicuius termini positi in oratione." See William of Sherwood, *Introductiones in logicam*, p. 87, l. 19 (Kretzmann, p. 135); Lambert of Auxerre, *Logica*, p. 149.

[26] *Summa logicae*, III-4, 2, ll. 9–14: "Sed istud non est bene dictum, nam non semper ubi est aequivocatio ibi est diversitas significationis. Bene enim potest esse aequivocatio in pure univoco; sicut ista propositio 'homo est nomen' est distinguenda penes aequivocationem, etiam si hoc nomen 'homo' non significaret nisi unum, nec proprie nec improprie, et tamen hic non est diversa significatio."

[27] Ibid., ll. 15–18: "Et ideo dicendum est quod aequivocatio magis proprie definitur sic: aequivocatio est multorum vocatio sub eadem voce vel sub eodem signo. Ut 'vocatio' non accipiatur hic pro significatione tantum sed magis pro suppositione seu pro alicuius positione." See also n. 28, below.

[28] Ibid., ll. 30–36: "Sciendum tamen quod 'stare pro diversis' non facit aequivocationem, sed 'stare pro diversis, ita quod pro uno et non pro alio' facit aequivocationem. Sicut in ista 'omnis homo est animal', 'homo' stat pro diversis, et tamen non est aequivocatio; sed in ista 'homo est species' potest sic stare pro diversis, quia potest stare pro intentione et non pro re extra, vel potest stare pro re extra et non pro intentione, ita scilicet quod aliquis utatur hac voce pro uno et non pro alio." It seems to be intended here, although it is not explicitly said, that the term cannot be used to supposit for both the species and the individuals at once. That is, the alternatives are meant to be exclusive.

Ockham, again following Aristotle and the tradition,[29] distinguishes three modes of equivocation, which I shall call (1) equivocation by chance, (2) equivocation by analogy, and (3) equivocation by context. These are defined as follows.

A term is equivocal in the first mode (by chance) if and only if it is given more than one imposition at the same time in such a way that the impositions are independent of one another.[30] The last clause distinguishes equivocation by chance from equivocation by analogy, as we shall see. An example may be found in the term "dog," which is both imposed to signify canine animals and independently imposed to signify the constellation "the Dog."[31] Since the term has this dual imposition and signification, it may supposit in a sentence for the animals and not for the constellation or for the constellation and not for the animals. The user may have either the one or the other in mind on a given occasion. Hence the term is equivocal.[32]

A term is equivocal in the second mode (by analogy) if and only if it is given more than one imposition at the same time in such a way that the impositions are not independent of one another but rather one is primary and the rest are related in some way to it.[33] This is the familiar *pros hen* equivocity. As an example, the term "man" may be primarily imposed to signify human beings and also secondarily imposed to signify statues or images of human beings because the latter are related by resemblance to the former.[34] Just as for equivocation by chance, since the term can have this dual imposition and signification, it may supposit in a sentence for human beings and not for their images or for the images and not for the human beings. The user may have either the one or the other in mind on a given occasion. Hence the term is equivocal.[35]

---

[29] See above, nn. 22–23.

[30] *Summa logicae*, III-4, 2, ll. 48–53: "Primus modus est quando aliqua dictio est aequivoca a casu. Vocatur autem 'aequivocum a casu' quando dictio aeque primo—non semper quidem aeque primo tempore sed intentione—pluribus impositionibus, vel una aequivalenti pluribus, imponitur ad significandum, ita scilicet quod una impositione imponitur ad significandum ac si non esset prius imposita."

[31] Ibid., ll. 92–116.

[32] In ll. 53–55, Ockham allows that a term may be called equivocal in this first mode with respect to different languages. That is, the diverse impositions need not belong to a single system of impositions constituting a single spoken or written language. ("Sicut contingit quando eadem dictio est eadem in diversis idiomatibus, sicut haec dictio 'me' est Latinum et est Anglicum, ideo est aequivocum a casu.")

[33] *Summa logicae*, III-4, 3, ll. 2–8: "Circa secundum modum aequivocationis est sciendum quod tunc est secundus modus aequivocationis quando eadem dictio primo et principaliter imponitur ad significandum vel consignificandum aliquid vel aliqua, et secundario propter aliquam attributionem alterius rei ad primum significatum imponitur ad significandum aliud vel alia, ita quod in aliquibus propositionibus utimur illo vocabulo aliter quam primo erat institutum, et non in omnibus."

[34] Ibid., ll. 8–13: "Sicut est de isto nomine 'homo', quod primo erat impositum ad significandum animalia rationalia et secundo propter similitudinem statuae ad hominem utimur hoc nomine 'homo' pro statua in aliquibus propositionibus, sicut in talibus 'homo depingitur', 'homo est aureus vel argenteus', quando statua fit ex auro vel argento.

[35] Ockham stipulates another important difference between equivocation by chance and equivocation by analogy. Whereas a term that is equivocal by chance requires that every sentence in which it occurs be distinguished (at least if the equivocation occurs within a single language), a term that is equivocal by analogy requires that only certain sentences be distinguished in this way. Such a term may supposit according to its primary imposition in any sentence in which it occurs. But it may supposit according to one of its secondary impositions only if it is "matched" in a sentence with a term that is truly predicable of one of its secondary significates. See ibid., ll. 18–28: "Ex hoc oritur una regula talis, quod numquam est propositio distinguenda penes secundum modum aequivocationis nisi quando illud vocabulum quod potest sic aequivoce accipi comparatur alicui verificabili de secundario significato vel pro aliquo consimili. Et ideo ista est distinguenda 'homo depingitur' et non ista 'homo currit' nec ista 'homo est animal', et sic de aliis. Et huius ratio est quia semper terminus, ubicumque ponatur, potest stare pro suo primario significato, sed non potest semper stare pro suo

Note that a term is equivocal in one of these first two modes only if it *imposed* to signify. But only conventional, spoken or written terms are imposed to signify; mental terms or concepts signify naturally and not by imposition. It follows that only conventional terms and not mental terms can be equivocal in one of these first two modes. Already, therefore, we have at least a weak form of Trentman's third claim: there is no equivocation in mental language according to the first or second mode.

Ockham says as much in *Summa logicae*, I, 13,[36] where indeed the first two modes of equivocation are the only ones he considers.[37] There too he explains the relation between conventionally equivocal terms in these first two modes and terms or concepts of mental language. Since imposition amounts to the subordination of spoken or written terms to mental terms or concepts, an equivocal term in one of the first two modes is just a term that is subordinated to more than one concept at the same time.[38]

It is perhaps hard to see how Ockham can reconcile all the things he says about these first two modes of equivocation. If a term supposits personally for what is signifies, and if a conventional term derives its signification from the concepts to which it is subordinated, then it would seem that a conventional term that is equivocal in one of the first two modes and so is subordinated to more than one concept at the same time would supposit, whenever it is used personally, according to all its impositions at once and not, as Ockham says, according to one to the exclusion of the rest.

What Ockham has in mind seems to be this. The user of an equivocal term in one of the first two modes has adopted a certain set of subordination conventions that map the term into more than one concept. Those conventions may be thought of as dispositional or habitual in nature; they are related to what is called "linguistic competence." Now just as in the practical realm one may acquire diverse habits in such a way that on a given occasion one is disposed to adopt diverse courses of action, even though only one course is in fact adopted and so only one habit exercised on that occasion, so too with language. The user of an equivocal term has acquired diverse linguistic habits governing the use of that term, but not all such habits need to be exercised every time the term is used. The distinction that is required in order to make out Ockham's claim, then, is the distinction between dispositional and occurrent imposition or subordination, like the distinction between dispositional and occurrent knowledge and belief.

It is clear in all of this that mental language is an important part of Ockham's explanation of the mechanism by which conventional terms can come to be equivocal in one of the first two modes. Equivocation occurs in those cases in which the subordination

---

secundario significato, sed tantum in propositione ubi comparatur alicui verificabili de suo secundario significato. Et ideo tantum talis propositio est distinguenda penes secundum modum aequivocationis."

[36] Lines 10–12: "Est autem primo sciendum quod sola vox vel aliud signum ad placitum institutum est aequivocum vel univocum, et ideo intentio animae vel conceptus non est aequivocus nec univocus proprie loquendo."

[37] Ibid., ll. 25–34: "Tale autem aequivocum est duplex. Unum est aequivocum a casu, quando scilicet vox pluribus conceptibus subordinatur, et ita uni ac si non subordinaretur alteri et ita significat unum ac si non significaret alius, sicut est de hoc nomine 'Sortes', quod imponitur pluribus hominibus. Aliud est aequivocum a consilio, quando vox primo imponitur alicui vel aliquibus et subordinatur uni conceptui et postea propter aliquam similitudinem primi significati ad aliquid aliud vel propter aliquam aliam rationem imponitur illi alteri, ita quod non imponeretur illi alteri nisi quia primo imponebatur alii, sicut est de hoc nomine 'homo'."

[38] Ibid., ll. 13–15: "Est autem vox illa aequivoca quae significans plura non est signum subordinatum uni conceptui, sed est signum unum pluribus conceptibus seu intentionibus animae subordinatum."

relation is one many. Since there is no higher language to which mental language is subordinated, these kinds of equivocation cannot occur in mental language.

There is perhaps another argument for this same conclusion, an argument that does not depend on Ockham's defining the first two modes of equivocation in terms of imposition and so banishing them from mental language, as it were by *fiat*. These two modes exhaust the ways in which a term can be equivocal in virtue of "diverse signification": either the diverse significations of such a term are independent or they are not. Now since concepts are "natural likenesses" of the things they signify,[39] a concept that had a "diverse signification"—for instance, one that signified both canines and the constellation called "the Dog," or one that signified both human beings and their images—would be a natural likeness of all the things it signifies. It is hard to see how such a concept could possibly be called equivocal; rather it would be simply a *broader* concept than the concepts that signify only dogs or only the constellation "the Dog," only men or only their images. Somewhat similarly, a disjunctive term in spoken language (e.g., the term "instrument for writing or drawing with ink, or else a fenced enclosure for animals") must be sharply distinguished from a term signifying the two disjuncts equivocally (e.g., "pen").

The first two modes of equivocation fit the general definition in terms of "diverse signification" that Ockham rejects at the beginning of *Summa logicae*, III-4, 2. The third mode, however, does not fit, and it is this that leads Ockham to adopt his alternative general definition in terms of supposition. In effect Ockham defines the third mode of equivocation (equivocation by context) in such a way that a term is equivocal in this mode if and only if it is equivocal (that is, can supposit for diverse things in such a way that it can supposit for one and not the other) but not in either of the first two modes (that is, not in virtue of diverse signification or imposition). This happens when a term that is not given diverse impositions occurs in a *context* together with other words that may affect its supposition in a way that produces equivocation.[40] Ockham gives examples and rules for two main kinds of such contexts: (1) those that allow a term to supposit either simply or materially, or both, in addition to suppositing personally, and (2) tense and modal contexts, which produce what other authors called "ampliation."[41]

---

[39] There are notorious difficulties in explicating this similarity between concepts and their significates. But these difficulties do not affect the argument. The point is merely that concepts always signify the same things (in the second mode of signification distinguished in *Summa logicae*, I, 33).

[40] *Summa logicae*, III-4, 4, ll. 2–8: "Circa tertium modum aequivocationis est primo sciendum quod tunc est tertius modus aequivocationis quando dictio non accipitur pro diversis significatis, sed ex hoc solum quod alicui comparatur quod non plus pertinent ad primarium significatum quam ad secundarium. Et iste modus non accidit ex hoc quod vox potest significare diversa, sicut contingit in duobus primis modis, sed ex hoc quod eadem vox potest supponere pro diversis." The first sentence of this passage presents obvious difficulties both of syntax and of interpretation. Ought one to understand "est aequivocatio" after "sed"? Again, if, as the first halves of both sentences say, the equivocal term is not taken with diverse significations, then why does the second half of the first sentence refer to primary and secondary significates?

[41] See Alfonso Maierù, *Terminologia logica della tarda scolastica* (Rome: Edizioni dell'Ateneo, 1972), chap. 2. In *Summa logicae*, III-4, 4, ll. 106–12, Ockham also allows a third kind of context to produce this mode of equivocation. ("Alia regula est quod quando eadem dictio potest esse diversorum casuum, generum vel numerorum vel aliorum accidentium grammaticalium, illa propositio est distinguenda penes tertium modum aequivocationis. Sicut ista 'isti asini sunt episcopi', eo quod li episcopi potest esse nominativi casus vel genitivi. Verumtamen in tali paralogismo potest frequenter assignari primus modus aequivocationis; sed quando hoc habeat fieri et quando non, propter brevitatem omitto.")

The rules governing the first kind of context[42] I have elsewhere called collectively "Ockham's Rule of Supposition."[43] They are presented also in summary fashion in *Summa logicae*, I, 65:

This rule, therefore, can be given, that when a term able to have the above three kinds of supposition [namely, personal, simple, and material] is matched with an extreme common to incomplex or complex [expressions], whether spoken or written, the term can always have material or personal supposition, and such a sentence is to be distinguished. When it is matched with an extreme signifying an intention of the soul, it is to be distinguished insofar as it can have simple or personal supposition. But when it is matched with an extreme common to all the above, then it is to be distinguished insofar as it can have simple, material, or personal supposition.[44]

The rules governing the second kind of context are these:

The fourth rule is that when a common term supposits personally and is a subject with respect to a verb about the past, the sentence is to be distinguished insofar as the subject term can supposit for things that are or for things that were. Thus this is to be distinguished "Some boy was old," insofar as "boy" can supposit for him who is a boy, and then [the sentence] is equivalent to "Someone who now is a boy was old," or it can supposit for him who was a boy, and then the sense is "Someone who was a boy was old."

The fifth rule is that when a common term suppositing personally is a subject with respect to a verb about the future, the sentence is to be distinguished according to the third mode of equivocation, insofar as the subject can supposit for things that are or for things that will be.

The sixth rule is that when a common term suppositing personally is a subject with respect to a verb about the possible or about the contingent, the sentence is to be distinguished insofar as the subject term can stand for things that are or for things that can be or for things that are contingent.[45]

The rules for these two kinds of contexts present a problem for Trentman's third claim. For sentences of the kinds governed by these rules will certainly occur in mental

[42] *Summa logicae*, III-4, 4, ll. 10–86.

[43] Spade, "Ockham's Rule of Supposition."

[44] Lines 43–51: "Potest igitur dari ista regula quod quando terminus potens habere praedictam triplicem suppositionem comparatur extremo, communi incomplexis vel complexis, sive prolatis sive scriptis, semper terminus potest habere suppositionem materialem vel personalem; et est talis propositio distinguenda. Quando vero comparatur extremo significanti intentionem animae, est distinguenda, eo quod potest habere suppositionem simplicem vel personalem. Quando autem comparatur extremo communi omnibus praedictis, tunc est distinguenda, eo quod potest habere suppositionem personalem, simplicem vel materialem." See also the passages from Ockham's *Expositio in Sophisticos elenchos Aristotelis* quoted by Philotheus Boehner, "Ockham's Theory of Supposition and the Notion of Truth," in his *Collected Articles on Ockham*, ed. Eligius M. Buytaert (St. Bonaventure, N.Y.: The Franciscan Institute, 1958), pp. 232–67, nn. 19, 24–26.

[45] *Summa logicae*, III-4, ll. 4, 87–105: "Quarta regula est quando terminus communis supponit personaliter et subicitur respectu verbi de praeterito, illa propositio est distinguenda, eo quod terminus subiectus potest supponere pro his quae sunt vel pro his quae fuerunt. Sicut haec est distinguenda 'aliquis puer fuit senex', eo quod li puer potest supponere pro eo qui est puer, et tunc aequivalet isti 'aliquis, qui modo est puer, fuit senex'; vel potest supponere pro eo qui fuit puer, et tunc est sensus 'aliquis, qui fuit puer, fuit senex'. . . . Quinta regula est quod quando terminus communis supponens personaliter subicitur respectu verbi de futuro, illa propositio est distinguenda penes tertium modum aequivocationis, eo quod subiectum potest supponere pro his quae sunt vel pro his quae erunt. Sexta regula est quod quando terminus communis supponens personaliter subicitur respectu verbi de possibili vel de contingenti, illa propositio est distinguenda, eo quod terminus subiectus potest stare pro his quae sunt vel pro his quae possunt esse vel pro his quae contingunt esse." See also *Summa logicae*, I, 72, ll. 37–112; and II, 7.

language.[46] If the rules continue to apply there, they will introduce equivocation into mental language.

Indeed, Ockham explicitly allows this. In *Summa logicae*, III-4, 4, he says:

And it must be noted that this third mode of equivocation can be found in a purely mental sentence, although the first two modes have no place except among signs instituted by conven tion. Hence the mental sentence 'Man is a species' can be distinguished insofar as the subject can supposit significatively [i.e., personally] or for itself [i.e., simply]. And the same thing must be said in similar cases.[47]

Again in *Summa logicae*, I, 64, he says:

Now just as such a diversity of supposition can apply to a spoken or written term, so too it can apply to a mental term, because an intention can supposit for that which it signifies, for itself, for an utterance and for an inscription.[48]

If this claim is allowed to stand, it would of course refute Trentman's third claim. But it probably ought not to be allowed to stand. Ockham's statements here should not be regarded as his "better doctrine."

In effect, Ockham's rules provide that sentences producing the third mode of equivocation have *alternative* sets of truth conditions. When such a sentence is disambiguated in one way, it is true under one set of circumstances, and when it is disambiguated in another way, it is true under another set of circumstances. Either set of truth conditions may be applied without the other.[49] It is easy to see how this kind of situation might arise in spoken or written language. There the sentence might simply be subordinated to more than one mental sentence, although the equivocal term in that sentence is subordinated to only a single concept.[50] But it is much harder to see how such a situation could arise in mental language. One can of course have a mental sentence that is true under one set of circumstances *or* under another. But that is to have simply one *disjunctive* set of truth conditions, not *alternative* sets any one of which may be applied without the other.

In order to allow the third mode of equivocation in mental language, one would have to suppose that the truth or falsehood of some mental sentences is not determined solely by the ingredients and structures of the sentences themselves, on the one hand, and by

---

[46] Indeed, Ockham explictly says that tense is a feature of mental verbs. See *Summa logicae*, I, 3, ll. 69–72, 81–82; also *Quodlibet* 5, q. 8, 3rd conclusion, fols. 76vb–77ra.

[47] Lines 113–18: "Et est notandum quod iste tertius modus aequivocationis potest reperiri in propositione pure mentali, quamvis duo primi modi non habeant locum nisi in signis ad placitum institutis. Unde ista propositio mentalis 'homo est species' distingui potest, eo quod subiectum potest supponere significative vel pro se ipso. Et sic de consimilibus est dicendum." Professor Calvin Normore first called this passage to my attention.

[48] Lines 56–59: "Sicut autem talis diversitas suppositionis potest competere termino vocali et scripto, ita etiam potest competere termino mentali, quia intentio potest supponere pro illo quod significat et pro se ipsa et pro voce et pro scripto."

[49] This also holds for the first two modes of equivocation, and indeed for the three modes of amphiboly as well (see *Summa logicae*, III-4, 5–7). The arguments in this and the following paragraphs may also be applied *mutatis mutandis* against the possibility of there being any kind of equivocation or amphiboly in mental language.

[50] This would require that the subordination relation be able to map a whole conventional expression into something other than the sum of the mappings of its parts.

the arrangement of things in the world, on the other. Rather, a third factor is also required: some factor that determines, in cases where there are alternatives, the things for which the terms in the sentences are to supposit. What could such a factor be?

The only suggestion I have to offer is to suppose some kind of distinction between a dispositional and an occurrent assigning of supposition, to parallel the distinction between dispositional and occurrent subordination or imposition sketched above. On this view, then, a mental sentence involving equivocation in the third mode would be one the user of which has acquired a disposition to assign the equivocal term in the sentence one set of supposita, and also a disposition to assign it another set of supposita. On any given occasion either one of these sets may be actually assigned without the other. An analogous trick will not allow equivocation in the first two modes into mental language, because concepts signify naturally and always signify the same things.[51] But, as far as I know, Ockham nowhere clearly says that concepts *supposit* naturally and always for the same things. Indeed, in the passages quoted above, he explicitly denies it.[52]

It is not clear to me what it would be like to "assign" supposition to a concept in the manner required by this theory. Perhaps the notion simply makes no sense. In any case one ought not to be too eager to embrace such a theory in order to save Ockham's statements about the third mode of equivocation in mental language. For in addition to making out just how such equivocation can occur there at all, there are at least two other difficulties.

First, Ockham's rules governing the third mode of equivocation contain certain peculiar biases. The "Rule of Supposition," for instance, contains a bias in favor of personal supposition.[53] And the rules for tenses and modality contain a bias in favor of the present assertoric.[54] But why should this be so? This kind of situation looks suspiciously like the *second* mode of equivocation (by analogy), which does not occur in

[51] See the argument above, in the text to which n. 39 is appended.

[52] In *Summa logicae*, I, 1, ll. 19–21, he does say that a concept or intention of the soul is "nata" (apt by nature) to be a part of a mental sentence and "nata" to supposit there for what it naturally signifies ("Terminus conceptus est intentio seu passio animae aliquid naturaliter significans vel consignificans, nata esse pars propositionis mentalis, et pro eodem nata supponere"). But it is not clear how strongly "nata" is to be taken here. On the view sketched above, I can see no way to avoid making the dispositions to assign a certain supposition innate. If they are not innate, Ockham's ontology and psychology seem to allow no other way for the dispositions to be acquired naturally. Hence if they are not innate, then mental language, at least at the level of supposition (and so of truth), is not after all the universal language of thought, the same for everyone. Rather, it is to some extent conventional. This is certainly an unorthodox interpretation, although I can find no text to rule it out definitively. Moreover, once a degree of conventionality is allowed into mental language, it is hard to see how Ockham can confine the third mode of equivocation there to the several limited contexts allowed in III-4, 4. Why could one not, in a spirit of perversity, acquire a disposition to make the concept 'man' supposit in certain mental sentences only for asses? In order to avoid such consequences, it seems one would have to hold that the dispositions to assign supposition are innate.

[53] A term may supposit personally in any context, but simply or materially only in certain special circumstances. See above, n. 44.

[54] A term may supposit in any context for the things of which it may be truly predicted by means of a present-tensed assertoric coupla. It may supposit for the things of which it may be truly predicated by means of a past- or future-tensed or modal copula only in certain special circumstances (see *Summa logicae*, I, 72, ll. 37–112). Note that these rules appear to make sense only in the context of personal supposition. (Note the restrictions to personal supposition in the texts in n. 45, above.) Ockham does not appear to have taken account of tensed or modal sentences with terms in simple or material supposition (e.g., "Man was a species").

mental language.[55] There is nothing in the theory of the third mode of equivocation, as Ockham develops it, to explain such biases.[56]

More serious, however, is the second difficulty. It does not concern tense and modality, but rather the claim that concepts or mental terms may have simple or material supposition. Since concepts signify just what is conceived by them—that is, just what they are thoughts of—and since in general it is only in personal supposition that terms supposit for what they signify, it follows that if mental terms may have simple or material supposition, we do not always know what we are asserting in a mental sentence. If, for instance, in the mental sentence 'Man is a species' the subject has simple supposition so that the sentence asserts truly that the concept 'man' is a species, nevertheless that is not what we think when we formulate that sentence. For the subject concept 'man' signifies—and so is a thought of—men, not itself. Therefore, if mental language is to be the language of thought, so that to say in mental language that *p* is just to entertain the thought that *p*, then all supposition in mental language must be personal. There is no place there for simple or material supposition, despite what Ockham says.[57] Spoken or written sentences in which terms are equivocal with respect to personal, simple, and material supposition are then subordinated to several mental sentences at once, with distinct concepts in the place of equivocal spoken or written terms. Thus the spoken sentence "Man is a species" is subordinated to two mental sentences, one with the concept 'man' as subject and the other with the concept *of* that concept as subject.

This, then, is the theory I think Ockham *ought* to have had. It seems to me that the very notion of mental language requires that there be only personal supposition there,

---

[55] For the second mode, we have the rule (*Summa logicae*, III-4, 3, ll. 23–26): "A term always, wherever it occurs, can stand for its primary significate. On the other hand, it cannot always stand for its secondary significate, but only in a sentence where it is matched with some term truly predicable of its secondary significate." (For the Latin, see n. 35 above.) Walter Burleigh in fact treats tensed sentences, for which he gives rules essentially the same as Ockham's, as involving equivocation in the second mode. See the rules in his *De puritate artis logicae tractatus longior with a Revised Edition of the Tractatus brevior*, ed. Philotheus Boehner (St. Bonaventure, N.Y.: The Franciscan Institute, 1955), p. 49, ll. 23–31, and the remarks in "Walter Burley's *Quaestiones in librum Perihermeneias*," ed. Stephen F. Brown, *Franciscan Studies* 34 (1974), para. 5.31–5.35. He also explicitly says that it is the second mode that is involved in his "Rule of Supposition." See *De puritate*, p. 10, ll. 21–25: "Sed tamen huiusmodi propositiones: 'Homo est species', 'Homo est disyllabum', sunt muliplices penes secundum modum aequivocationis, ex eo quod ille terminus 'homo' potest habere suppositionem personalem vel simpliciem vel materialem." In "Ockham's Rule of Supposition," p. 65, n. 7, I wrote that "it is hard to see how Burley thinks that the sentences he mentions are equivocal in this mode." I no longer find it so hard to see; the second mode is the only one of the three in which the kind of bias involved in these rules is given a theoretical rationale.

[56] Recall the difficulties we had with Ockham's definition of that third mode. See above, n. 40.

[57] I have used related considerations to make a somewhat different point in my "Some Epistemological Implications of the Burley-Ockham Dispute," *Franciscan Studies* 35 (1975):212–22, at sec. 3.

[58] *Summulae dialecticae*, tract. 7, as quoted by Sten Ebbesen, "The Summulae, Tractatus VII: De fallaciis," in *The Logic of John Buridan*, ed. Jan Pinborg (Copenhagen: Museum Tusculanum, 1976), pp. 139–60, at p. 156: "Sciendum est ergo, ut mihi videtur, quod suppositio materialis non est nisi ratione vocis significativae: nullus enim terminus in propositione mentali supponit materialiter, sed semper personaliter, quia non utimur terminis mentalibus ad placitum, sicut vocibus et scripturis, numquam enim eadem oratio mentalis diversas significationes vel acceptiones habet: eaedem enim omnibus passiones animae sunt et etiam res quarum ipsae sunt similitudines, ut habetur primo Peri Hermeneias. Unde ego dico quod propositio mentalis correspondens huic propositioni prout est vera 'homo est species' non est propositio in qua subicitur conceptus specificus hominum, sed est propositio in qua subicitur conceptus quo concipitur conceptus specificus hominum, et ille iam supponit non pro se, sed pro conceptu specifico hominum; ex quo satis patet quod praedicti paralogismi secundum talem mutationem suppositionum pertinet ad fallacias in dictione." Ebbesen's paper contains much interesting information on Buridan's theory of equivocation.

contrary to what Ockham says. John Buridan realized this,[58] as did Peter of Ailly.[59] It seems to me also that Ockham ought not to have allowed equivocation in mental language in the case of tensed and modal sentences. Such a doctrine requires very dubious and perhaps untenable philosophical assumptions, as we have seen. Once again, Buridan has a view that seems preferable. Whereas Ockham holds that tensed and modal contexts *allow* a term to supposit equivocally for *alternative* sets of supposita, Buridan maintains that such contexts *make* a term supposit for the *union* of those sets.[60]

IV. We have seen that Ockham's theory of mental language runs into difficulties with respect to all three of Trentman's claims; in this regard at least Ockham appears not to have realized all the consequences of what he was saying. While it is perhaps philosophically acceptable to restrict the grammatical features of mental language to those that affect truth conditions, it is not acceptable to identify the grammatical features of mental language, as Ockham does, with *exactly* those that affect truth conditions. Ockham then still owes us a satisfactory account of mental grammar. Furthermore, although he recognizes that there can be no synonymy in mental language, Ockham appears to have forgotten this when he allowed mental names to be distinguished into concrete and abstract. Finally, although Ockham explicitly allows the "third mode" of equivocation in mental language, there appears to be no coherent and plausible way to make this out. Such equivocation with respect to simple and material supposition is simply out of place in a language that is to be the language of thought, while with respect to tense and modality it involves a tampering with mental supposition in ways that are not very plausible or even very clear.

All this indicates that Ockham's notion of mental language was not very thoroughly worked out. However interesting, suggestive, or even important we may find the theory today, it was perhaps not the center and focus of Ockham's own logical thought to the extent that it has been of much of our own thinking about Ockham.[61]

Indiana University

---

[59] *Conceptus et insolubilia* (Paris: Pierre le Dru for Durland Gerlier, [ca. 1495], Copinger 391), fol. 5vb: "Infertur etiam quod quia terminus mentalis proprie dictus in propositione mentali semper naturaliter accipitur pro re quam ultimate significat naturaliter proprie, ideo semper supponit pro suo significato ultimato, semper personaliter supponit et numquam materialiter." Peter of Mantua even appears to have said that all supposition is personal in any language (including spoken or written language?), although his reasoning is a bit obscure. See Peter (Alboinus) of Mantua, *Logica* (Venice: Simon Bevilaqua, 1 Dec. 1492, Goff P-501), fol. 2rb: "Et quia nulla est suppositio nisi personalis, ideo potest dici pro regula quod omnis terminus supponens supponit personaliter."

[60] Thus whereas for Ockham the sentence "*B* will be *A*" is true in one sense if and only if what is now *B* will be *A*, and true in another sense if and only if what will be *B* will be *A*, for Buridan the sentence "*B* will be *A*" is true (*simpliciter*) if and only if what is or will be *B* will be *A*. See *Iohannis Buridani Tractatus de consequentiis*, ed. Hubert Hubien (Louvain: Publications universitaires, 1976), I, 8, 11. 363–69: "Notandum est quod propositio de subiecto ampliato per praedicatum expondenda est per disiunctionem in subiecto temporis praesentis ad tempus vel tempora ad quod vel ad quae fit ampliatio, ut 'B erit A' 'quod est vel erit B erit A', et 'homo est mortuus' 'qui est vel fuit homo est mortuus', et 'antichristus potest esse homo' 'qui est vel potest esse antichristus potest esse homo', et 'rosa intelligitur' 'quod est vel fuit vel erit vel potest esse rosa intelligitur'." See also *Johannes Buridanus: Sophismata*, ed. T. K. Scott (Stuttgart: Fromman-Holzboog, 1977), Ca. 5; trans. in T. K. Scott, *John Buridan: Sophisms on Meaning and Truth* (New York: Appleton-Century-Crofts, 1966), pp. 144–57.

[61] See above, n. 7.

XIV

Ockham on Terms of First and Second Imposition and Intention, with Remarks on the Liar Paradox

Chapter 11 of the first part of Ockham's *Summa logicae* presents a doctrine that is deceptively simple. In the preceding chapters (Chs. 4-10), Ockham drew some distinctions that apply to terms of all kinds—spoken, written, and mental ones. Now, in Ch. 11, he turns to a new set of distinctions, ones that apply only to spoken and written terms, not to mental terms.[1] We shall henceforth group spoken and written terms together and speak of them as "conventional" terms, since they signify *ad placitum* whereas concepts or mental terms signify naturally.[2]

Conventional terms, Ockham tells us, may be divided first into terms of first imposition and terms of second imposition. Each alternative may be taken in a broad or a strict sense. Terms of first imposition in the strict sense may be further divided into terms of first intention and terms of second intention. Again, each alternative may be taken in a broad or a strict sense.[3] In Ch. 12 Ockham goes on to discuss first and second intentions themselves, each alternative again in a broad and a strict sense. Whereas terms *of* first or second intention are conventional terms, first and second intentions themselves are concepts. And although Ockham does not explicitly say so, it appears at first that terms *of* first intention are meant to be exactly those subordinated to first intentions, and terms *of* second intention exactly those subordinated to second intentions.[4]

[1] "Positis divisionibus quae possunt competere tam terminis naturaliter significantibus quam etiam terminis ad placitum institutis, dicendum est de quibusdam divisionibus competentibus terminis ad placitum institutis." (*Summa logicae*, I, 11, lines 4-6) All references to the *Summa logicae* will be to the critical edition by Gedeon Gál and Stephen F. Brown, St. Bonaventure, N.Y.: The Franciscan Institute 1974.

[2] See *Summa logicae*, I, 1.

[3] For a fairly clear presentation of these divisions, see John J. Swiniarski, *A New Presentation of Ockham's Theory of Supposition with an Evaluation of Some Contemporary Criticisms*, in: Franciscan Studies, 30 (1970), 181-217 at pp. 185-187.

[4] On subordination, see *Summa logicae* I, 3, and my *Ockham's Distinctions between Absolute and Connotative Terms*, in: Vivarium, 13 (1975), 55-76 at p. 57 n. 8.

So far so good. The terminology of first and second imposition and intention is more or less familiar, and at least the main outlines of Ockham's doctrine are quite clear. Terms of first imposition signify things, whereas terms of second imposition signify conventional terms. Similarly, first intentions signify things, whereas second intentions signify concepts. And finally, terms *of* first and terms *of* second intention are presumably subordinated to first and second intentions, respectively. Everyone recognizes that further refinements must be made, but the details seem tedious and unimportant.

I

When one looks more closely, however, at least three problems emerge. First, it is not so clear after all that Ockham meant terms *of* first and second intention to be exactly those subordinated to first and second intentions, respectively. For (a) Ockham tells us in Ch. 12 that intentions or concepts are "of two kinds".[5] The two kinds turn out to be first and second intentions. It seems therefore that every concept is either a first intention or a second intention. Hence, if terms *of* first and second intention were correlated with the first and second intentions themselves in the way supposed, it would follow that every conventional term is either of first intention or of second intention. But this does not seem to be so. The division in Ch. 11 seems to be such that only terms of first imposition in the strict sense are of first or second intention; other terms are of neither.[6]

Moreover (b) in Ch. 12 Ockham includes mental syncategoremata among first intentions in the broad sense. Hence conventional syncategoremata ought to be included among terms *of* first intention in the broad sense. But it seems they are not. Conventional syncategoremata are terms of first imposition in the broad sense, and it is terms of first imposition in the strict sense, excluding syncategoremata, that are divided into terms of first and of second intention.

Furthermore (c) in Ch. 12 Ockham says that second intentions are signs of first intentions (and perhaps of other signs as well).[7] Hence

[5] *Summa logicae* I, 12, line 44: "Tale autem signum duplex est."

[6] *Summa logicae* I, 11, lines 46-49: "Nomina autem primae impositionis, stricte accipiendo 'nomen primae impositionis', sunt in duplici differentia, quia quaedam sunt nomina primae intentionis et quaedam sunt nomina secundae intentionis." See also the diagram in Swiniarski, *op. cit.*, p. 187.

[7] *Summa logicae* I, 12, lines 59-60: "Intentio autem secunda est illa quae est signum talium intentionum primarum." *Ibid.*, lines 74-77: "Protest etiam dici quod intentio secunda potest accipi stricte pro intentione quae significat

terms *of* second intention ought to be likewise signs of first intentions. And indeed some of them are—e.g., the conventional terms 'genus', 'species', 'universal', etc. But there is nothing in the definition given in Ch. 11 that requires this. According to that definition [8] names of second intention signify concepts (and perhaps other signs), but not necessarily concepts that are first intentions. The spoken term 'second intention' is a case in point.

Toward the end of Ch. 12, Ockham tells us that "just as names of second imposition conventionally signify names of first imposition, so a second intention naturally signifies a first one."[9] This misrepresents the doctrine of Ch. 11, according to which names of second .mposition signify conventional signs, but not necessarily conventional signs of first imposition.[10] The conventional term 'name of second imposition' is a case in point.

Reasons (a)-(c) give good grounds for doubting that Ockham meant terms of first and of second intention to be subordinated to the first and second intentions themselves in the way suggested. Reason (c) is perhaps the weakest. One might suppose that Ockham did intend this kind of correlation, but was simply careless and misrepresented in Ch. 12 the doctrine of Ch. 11. His remarks in Ch. 12 about terms of second imposition perhaps support this conjecture. Nevertheless, reasons (a) and (b) seem to me to be stronger. Although I shall argue that Ockham's divisions in Ch. 11 are not exactly what they seem to be and are assumed to be in reasons (a) and (b), the revisions I shall suggest will not affect the main points of (a) and (b). I shall therefore not assume that Ockham intended the kind of exact correlation in question, and shall treat the doctrine of terms *of* first and second intention in Ch. 11 without regard for the discussion of first and second intentions themselves in Ch. 12.

The second main problem one finds in the discussion in Ch. 11 is

praecise primas intentiones, vel large pro intentione quae significat intentiones et signa ad placitum instituta, si tamen sit aliqua talis."

[8] *Summa logicae* I, 11, lines 49-52: "Nomina secundae intentionis vocantur illa nomina quae praecise imposita sunt ad significandum intentiones animae, vel praecise intentiones animae quae sunt signa naturalia, et alia signa ad placitum instituta vel consequentia talia signa."

[9] *Summa logicae* I, 12, lines 70-72: "Et ideo sicut nomina secundae impositionis significant ad placitum nomina primae impositionis, ita secunda intentio naturaliter significat primam."

[10] *Summa logicae* I, 11, lines 9-11: "Nomina secundae impositionis sunt nomina imposita ad significandum signa ad placitum instituta et illa quae consequuntur talia signa, sed nonnisi dum sunt signa."

the presence of phrases the precise sense of which is unclear. Thus, terms of second imposition are said to signify conventional signs, "but not except as long as they are signs".[11] Similar phrases occur throughout the chapter.[12] It is more or less clear what such phrases are intended to do. The conventional term 'thing', for instance, signifies conventional signs among other things. But since it would signify those same utterances and inscriptions whether they were conventional signs or not, 'thing' is not a term of second imposition. The problem is to capture the force of such phrases *exactly*.

Again, one finds in Ch. 11 phrases such as 'what follows such signs' or 'the consequences of such signs'.[13] In each case the "such signs" appear to be conventional signs,[14] and Ockham seems to mean by "consequences" the grammatical accidents such as tense, case, mood, number, etc.[15] Such "consequences" are said to be signified by certain terms. It is hard to know what to make of this. For (a) Ockham is not entirely consistent about it. He defines names of second intention, for instance, as "those names that are (i) precisely imposed to signify intentions of the soul, or else (ii) precisely [imposed to signify] intentions of the soul, which are natural signs, and other signs instituted by convention, or the consequences of such signs".[16] Yet a few lines later he says, "In the broad sense that is called a name of second intention which signifies intentions of the soul, which are natural signs, whether it also signifies signs instituted by convention (only as long as they are signs) or not."[17] The strict sense is narrower.[18] Note that nothing is said here about "the consequences of such signs";

[11] See above, n. 10.

[12] See e.g., line 15 "nonnisi quando sunt ad placitum institutae", and lines 19-24: "Et vocantur ista nomina 'nomina nominum', quia non imponuntur nisi ad significandum partes orationis, et hoc nonnisi dum istae partes sunt significativae. Illa enim nomina quae praedicantur de vocibus ita quando non sunt significativae sicut quando sunt significativae, non vocantur nomina secundae impositionis."

[13] See above, nn. 8 and 10.

[14] In line 52 (see above, n. 8), the reference is strictly speaking ambiguous. It may refer to natural as well as to conventional signs.

[15] See Swiniarski, *op. cit.*, p. 185.

[16] See above, n. 8.

[17] *Summa logicae* I, 11, lines 57-60: "Large illud dicitur nomen secundae intentionis quod significat intentiones animae quae sunt naturalia signa sive etiam significet signa ad placitum instituta tantum dum sunt signa sive non."

[18] *Summa logicae* I, 11, lines 61-63: "Stricte autem illud solum dicitur nomen secundae intentionis quod praecise significat intentiones animae quae sunt naturalia signa."

they seem here to be signified by terms of second intention in neither the broad nor the narrow sense.

Moreover (b), the ontology of such "consequences" is rather dubious. Grammatical accidents such as tense and number are not real entities in the categories of substance or quality, so that it is hard to see how Ockham can say they are "signified" at all. Rather, the *terms* 'tense', 'number', etc., seem to be connotative terms that no more signify tense and number than 'blindness' signifies blindness as a real entity.[19] In the end I suspect Ockham wanted the *terms* for such grammatical accidents to be counted as terms of second imposition (or of second intention), but his official ontology does not allow such accidents as entities to be signified, despite what he says on some occasions.

The third main problem in Ch. 11 concerns one very surprising sentence. After describing terms of second intention in the broad sense, Ockham says, "And in this sense some name of second intention and first imposition is also a name of second imposition." [20] But how can a term be of both first and second imposition? Was that division not meant to be exclusive? [21] And was not the division of terms into those of first and those of second intention meant to be a division confined to terms of first imposition in the strict sense? How then can a term of second intention be also a term of second imposition?

II

In this section I shall set out some definitions that I hope will capture the doctrine in Ockham's Ch. 11 while doing the least possible violence to the text. In accordance with the discussion of the first main problem, above, I shall not try to make the definitions of terms of first and second intention parallel what Ockham says in Ch. 12

[19] On connotative terms, see my *Ockham's Distinctions between Absolute and Connotative Terms*, in: Vivarium, 13 (1975), 55-76.

[20] *Summa logicae* I, 11, lines 60-61: "Et sic aliquod nomen secundae intentionis et primae impositionis est etiam nomen secundae impositionis."

[21] In *Summa logicae* I, 11, lines 36-38, Ockham says only that all terms not of second imposition in either the broad or the strict sense are terms of first imposition; he does not say that *only* such terms are of first imposition. ("Omnia autem alia nomina ab istis, quae scilicet non sunt nomina secundae impositionis nec uno modo nec alio, vocantur nomina primae impositionis.") Nevertheless, in lines 43-45 Ockham says that *only* categoremata that are not of second imposition are of first imposition in the strict sense. ("Aliter potest accipi stricte, et tunc sola nomina categorematica, quae non sunt nomina secundae impositionis, vocantur nomina primae impositionis, et non nomina syncategorematica.") The broad sense adds only syncategoremata to the strict sense. Hence it appears that the division is meant to be exclusive after all.

about first and second intentions themselves. In accordance with the discussion of the second main problem, I shall confine myself to terms other than the names of grammatical accidents. I think Ockham wanted the doctrine of terms of first and second imposition and intention to apply to such names too, but I do not know how to make it apply there and, in view of the second main problem discussed above, I do not think Ockham knew how either. I shall simply disregard Ockham's occasional claims that grammatical accidents are signified by certain terms. I thereby violate the text to a degree (although, as we have seen, the text is not consistent), but in so doing I preserve Ockham's ontology. Finally, with respect to the third main problem discussed above, I shall claim that some terms of second intention may indeed be also of second imposition, as Ockham says. But no term of first imposition is also of second imposition, contrary to what Ockham says.

Let S be a subordination-function, between spoken and written expressions on the one hand and concepts on the other. (Since we take S to be a function, we are in effect ignoring equivocal terms.) Then, where t is a conventional term, we shall say that with respect to S:

(1) t is of first imposition (broad sense) if and only if, for all x and for all subordination-functions S^* like S for t but with a domain not necessarily the same as the domain of S, t signifies x under S^* if and only if t signifies x under S.

(2) t is of first imposition (strict sense) if and only if t is of first imposition (broad sense) and t signifies some x.

(3) t is of second imposition (broad sense) if and only if t is not of first imposition (broad sense).

(4) t is of second imposition (strict sense) if and only if t is of second imposition (broad sense) and t signifies no mental sign.

(5) t is of first intention (broad sense) if and only if t signifies something that is not a sign.

(6) t is of first intention (strict sense) if and only if t signifies something, but nothing that is a sign.

(7) t is of second intention (broad sense) if and only if t signifies only signs and at least one mental sign (a natural sign).

(8) t is of second intention (strict sense) if and only if t is of second intention (broad sense) and t signifies only conventional signs.

The reader should compare these definitions with what Ockham actually says in Ch. 11. The fit is fairly close. Here I shall make only a few observations.

First, *t* may satisfy definition (1) and yet signify nothing at all with respect to *S*.[22] In such a case *t* is syncategorematic. Hence conventional syncategoremata are of first imposition in the broad sense, as Ockham says.[23] The additional clause in definition (2) requires that *t* be categorematic there.[24]

Second, *t* satisfies definition (1) if and only if its signification is completely independent of all subordination conventions for expressions other than *t*. Hence, *t* satisfies definition (3) if and only if its signification is not so independent, that is, its signification depends at least in part on whether and what other spoken or written expressions signify. Thus conventional terms like 'noun' will be terms of second imposition in the broad sense. That term, for instance, will signify not only mental nouns, but also spoken and written ones—but the latter "not except as long as they are signs". This is as it should be. On the other hand, according to definition (3), the conventional term 'syncategorema' is also of second imposition in the broad sense, although it signifies conventional syncategoremata even when they are not signs at all in the sense of "signifying something". Again, a conventional term like 'non-sign' is a term of second imposition in the broad sense on definition (3), even though it signifies spoken and written expressions *not* so long as they are signs, but rather as long as they are *not* signs.

Definition (3) thus violates Ockham's proviso: "not except as long as they are signs". But it does so only in rather exotic cases. For the rest, it fits quite closely what Ockham says. Indeed, I suspect Ockham *would* want to call the conventional terms 'non-sign' and 'syncategorema' terms of second imposition in the broad sense, had he explicitly faced the question. I therefore suggest definition (3) as *ad mentem* if not *ad literam Ockham*.

Third, note that some terms of second intention in the broad sense are also of second imposition in the broad sense, as Ockham says.[25] Terms such as 'sign 'will be like this.

[22] I.e., signify nothing at all either primarily or secondarily. On primary and secondary signification, see my *Ockham's Distinctions between Absolute and Connotative Terms*.

[23] *Summa logicae* I, 11, lines 39-43: "Verumtamen nomen primae impositionis dupliciter accipi potest, scilicet large, et sic omnia nomina quae non sunt nomina secundae impositionis sunt nomina primae impositionis. Et sic talia signa syncategoremata 'omnis', 'nullus', 'aliquis', 'quilibet' et huiusmodi sunt nomina primae impositionis."

[24] See *Summa logicae* I, 11, lines 43-45, quoted above in n. 21.

[25] See above, n. 20.

Fourth, note that every conventional term is either of first or of second imposition in the broad senses, but not of both. Yet not every conventional term is of first or of second intention in either sense, although none is of both. The terms that are neither of first nor of second intention are exactly the syncategoremata, together with terms, such as 'spoken name', that signify only conventional signs. Unless such a term is a proper name of itself (and we shall ignore this possibility, as Ockham did), it will be of second imposition in the broad sense. Hence among terms of first imposition in the strict sense (i.e., excluding syncategoremata), the division into terms of first and terms of second intention is both exclusive and exhaustive. This is the only group among those we are considering for which this can be said.

It does not follow, however, that all terms of first or of second intention are also of first imposition in the strict sense. Ockham's presentation seems to lead him to think it does follow. Hence when he finds that some terms of second intention are also of second imposition in the broad senses, he wrongly says that some terms of first imposition are also of second imposition.[26]

Ockham's text in Ch. 11 is, I have argued, obscure at several points and simply contradictory at others. No consistent account of Ockham's theory, therefore, can hope to conform entirely to the text. The definitions I have offered above provide, I think, a good reconstruction, one that departs minimally from Ockham's actual words.

III

Finally, I should like to comment briefly on one application—or rather misapplication—of the doctrine in Ch. 11. There is a persistent claim in modern secondary literature that Ockham's distinctions in Ch. 11 provide the key to understanding his attempt to solve the Liar paradox.[27] The claim seems to have originated with Philotheus Boehner, who wrote:[28] "Since the predicates *verum* and *falsum*, being

[26] *Ibid.*

[27] See, e.g., Philotheus Boehner, *Ockham's Theory of Supposition and the Notion of Truth*, in: *Collected Articles on Ockham*, ed., Eligius M. Buytaert, St. Bonaventure, N.Y. 1958, pp. 232-267 at pp. 254-260; E. J. Ashworth, *Language and Logic in the Post-Medieval Period*, Dordrecht 1974, p. 104; Francesco Bottin, *Le antinomie semantiche nella logica medievale*, Padua 1976, pp. 173-175.

[28] Boehner, *op. cit.*, p. 257.

second intentions, are predicated about propositions or names of propositions, it follows that they cannot be predicated about themselves or about any proposition in which they are contained without reference to other prepositions. The famous *Insolubile* is solved by Ockham on the ground of this impossibility."The time has come to set the record straight: *Ockham's distinctions in Ch. 11 have nothing whatever to do with his "solution" to the Liar,*

A glance at what Ockham actually says about the Liar should suffice to settle the point.[29] He nowhere appeals to the doctrine of first and second impositions and intentions. Why then did Boehner say that he does? What appears to have happened is this. Boehner seems to have seen in Ockham's doctrine of impositions and intentions an anticipation of the theory of types or of Tarski's theory of "levels of language". Just as the latter were used in recent times to prevent the emergence of the Liar paradox, so too, the reasoning seems to have gone, Ockham's distinctions could be used to the same end.[30] Whatever the plausibility of that, the fact remains, of course, that Ockham did not so use it.

But is it even plausible? I think not. Boehner's discussion here is extremely obscure, and in my opinion confused. But it seems to start with the observation that the terms 'true' and 'false' are of second intention. (Indeed, they are of second intention and second imposition, both in the broad sense.) From this Boehner somehow draws the conclusion that self-reference is to be ruled out across the board. That conclusion does not in fact follow. Indeed, Ockham explicitly denies it and, although he does reject self-reference in paradoxical cases,[31] he does not do so because of any considerations about terms of second intention.[32]

Bloomington, Indiana
Indiana University

[29] *Summa logicae* III-3,'46. Boehner, *op. cit.*, p. 259n., quotes another text, from *Ockham's Commentary on the Sophistici Elenchi*. See also my *Ockham on Self-Reference*, in: Notre Dame Journal of Formal Logic, 15 (1974), 298-300.
[30] Boehner, *op. cit.*, especially pp. 259-260.
[31] See the discussion in my *Ockham on Self-Reference*.
[32] For a further discussion, see my review of Ashworth, *op. cit.*, in: Dialogue, 15 (1976), 333-340.

XV

LES MODALITES ALETHIQUES SELON OCKHAM

Dans la seconde partie de sa *Summa logicae* [1], Guillaume d'Ockham donne une théorie de la modalité qui a les caractères suivants. Tout d'abord, les propositions [2] contenant des termes modaux sont syntaxiquement divisées en deux types :

(1) Celles qui ont un *dictum*, c'est-à-dire celles qui sont formées avec l'une des constructions à l'accusatif plus infinitif que le latin emploie dans l'*oratio obliqua*. En pareil cas, le terme modal est grammaticalement un adjectif ou un participe. On a donc, *Sortem currere est possibile* "Pour Socrate courir est possible".

(2) Celles qui sont formées sans *dictum*. Dans ce cas le terme modal est habituellement un verbe ou un adverbe. On a ainsi, *Sortes potest currere* "Socrate peut courir", *Sortes possibiliter currit* "Socrate possiblement court".

En second lieu, une proposition modale du type (1) peut en général être prise en deux sens distincts :

(a) Selon le *sensus divisionis* une telle proposition est équivalente à la proposition correspondante de type (2). Dans les propositions du type (1) prises en ce sens et dans toutes les propositions du type (2), le terme modal – quelle que soit sa forme grammaticale – est logiquement un *opérateur* prenant une proposition comme argument. C'est là ce que l'on appellerait aujourd'hui "propositions modales *de re*".

(b) Selon le *sensus compositionis* une telle proposition modale de type (1) n'est pas équivalente à la proposition correspondante de type (2). Dans ce cas le terme modal – quelle que soit sa position grammaticale dans la proposition – est logiquement un *prédicat* prenant le nom d'une proposition comme argument. C'est là ce que l'on appellerait aujourd'hui "propositions modales *de dicto*" [3]

---

* Traduit de l'anglais par A. de Libera. Titre original : "Ockham's Account of Alethic Modalities"

1 Guillaume d'Ockham, *Summa logicae*, II, 9-10 in G. Gál & S. Brown (1974). †

2 Cette division fonctionne en général seulement comme une division entre propositions *catégoriques*, bien qu'Ockham ne s'y limite pas explicitement.

3 Sur l'importance de traiter la modalité comme un prédicat et comme un opérateur, voir Richard Montague, "Syntactical Treatments of Modality, with Corollaries on Reflexion Principles and Finite Axiomatizability", *Acta Philosophica Fennica* 16 (1973), pp. 153-167, repris dans R.H. Thomason, ed., *Formal Philosophy : Selected Papers of Richard Montague*, (New Haven, Connecticut : Yale University Press, 1974), pp. 286-302. Pour une réplique, voir R.K. Meyer, "Syntactical Treatment of Negation", *Analysis* 40 (1980), pp. 74-78.

En troisième lieu, Z étant une proposition, soit $D(Z)$ le *dictum* de Z. M étant un prédicat modal, soit m l'opérateur modal correspondant. Dans ces conditions une proposition modale '$D(Z)$ est M' de type (1b) est vraie si et seulement si Z est l'un des *supposita* (c'est-à-dire référents) de M. D'autre part, Z étant une proposition modale de type (2), avec un sujet S, un prédicat P et un opérateur modal m, on considère toutes les propositions Y de la forme 'Ceci est un P', où le pronom 'ceci' indique à son tour chacun des *supposita* de S. Dans ces conditions, Z est vraie si et seulement si

(i) si Z est une universelle affirmative, *tout* Y est un *suppositum* de M.
(ii) si Z est une particulière affirmative, *au moins un* Y est un *suppositum* de M.
(iii) si Z est une universelle négative, *aucun* Y n'est un *suppositum* de M.
(iv) si Z est une particulière négative, *non tout* Y est un *suppositum* de M.

On notera que n'importe quel Y donné est un *suppositum* de M si et seulement si '$D(Y)$ est M' est vraie. Par conséquent, dans la théorie d'Ockham la modalité *de dicto* est fondamentale ; les conditions de vérité des propositions modales *de re* peuvent être ramenées à celles des propositions modales *de dicto*, mais non l'inverse.

Pour cette raison on pouvait certainement s'attendre qu'Ockham fournirait une explication approfondie de la modalité *de dicto* – c'est-à-dire du fait qu'une proposition soit le *suppositum* ou le référent d'un prédicat modal M. On pouvait s'attendre qu'il expliquerait soigneusement ce que signifie exactement le fait de dire qu'une proposition donnée est nécessaire ou contingente, possible ou impossible. Et de fait, Ockham essaie bien de donner une telle explication. Voiçi ce qu'il dit [4] :

"Tamen de propositione necessaria est sciendum quod propositio non propter hoc dicitur necessaria quia semper sit vera, sed quia est vera si sit et non potest esse falsa. Sicut haec propositio in mente 'Deus est' necessaria est, non quia semper sit vera, – quia si non est, non est vera –, sed si sit, est vera et non potest esse falsa. Similiter haec propositio in voce 'Deus est' est necessaria, et tamen non semper est vera, quia quando non est, tunc non est vera nec falsa ; sed si sit prolata, est vera et non potest esse falsa nisi termini aliter instituerentur ad significandum.

4 Ockham, *op. cit.*, II, 9, 72-84. Trad. P.V. Spade : "Nevertheless, in the case of a necessary sentence you have to know that a sentence is not called necessary because it is always true, but because it is true if it exists, and cannot be false. For instance, the sentence in the mind "God exists" is necessary, not because it is always true – for if it does not exist it is not true – but rather because if it exists it is true, and it cannot be false. Likewise the spoken sentence "God exists" is necessary, and yet it is not always true. For when it does not exist, it is then not true or false. But if it is spoken it is true, and it cannot be false unless the terms were to be instituted to signify in some other way.

It ought to be said analogously in the case of an impossible sentence, that it is one that is false if it exists. Yet it is not false unless it is a sentence. And so analogously in the case of a contingent sentence. But in order for a sentence to be known or believed, and so on, more is required. But *what* is required, that is a matter for the book *Posterior Analytics* and for other books".

"Proportionaliter debet dici de propositione impossibili, quod est illa quae si sit, est falsa, non tamen est falsa nisi sit propositio. Et ita, proportionaliter, est de propositione contingenti. Sed ad hoc quod propositio sit scita vel credita, et sic de aliis, plus requiritur. Sed *quid* requiritur, pertinet ad librum *Posteriorum* et ad alios libros".

Considérons ce texte avec soin. Dans le premier paragraphe, Ockham dit qu'une proposition est nécessaire si et seulement si "elle est vraie si elle existe, et ne peut être fausse". C'est là une très curieuse affirmation. Son fondement est, bien entendu, la notion que le porteur de la vérité et de la fausseté est la proposition-*token*, l'énoncé individuel ou l'inscription ou la pensée momentanée, et non quelque espèce de proposition-*type* ou de "proposition" extra-linguistique, au sens philosophique moderne du terme, quelque chose qui serait "exprimé" par la proposition. Cet aspect des vues d'Ockham est de saine et courante doctrine nominaliste au XIVe siècle. C'est également doctrine nominaliste courante que d'affirmer que ces propositions-tokens ne peuvent remplir leur fonction de porteurs de valeurs de vérité à moins d'exister. Les énoncés individuels s'envolent à peine ont-ils été prononcés, les inscriptions individuelles peuvent être écrites puis effacées et nos pensées du moment sont choses fugitives. L'existence de tels porteurs des valeurs de vérité est par conséquent passablement contingente. Comme le dit Ockham dans le passage cité plus haut, "si elle n'existe pas, elle n'est pas vraie".

La motivation d'Ockham dans l'analyse de la modalité que l'on vient de voir est claire. Nous voulons dire, par exemple, que 'Dieu existe' est nécessaire. Cette proposition n'est pas nécessaire parce que toujours vraie – car une telle proposition-token n'a pas du tout besoin d'exister, auquel cas elle n'a pas la moindre valeur de vérité, ni vérité ni fausseté. Bien plutôt, elle est nécessaire "parce qu'elle est vraie si elle existe, et ne peut être fausse". De la même façon, la proposition "Un homme est un âne" est une proposition impossible, non parce que toujours fausse – car une telle proposition-token n'a pas besoin d'exister, auquel cas elle n'est pas fausse – mais plutôt parce qu'"elle est fausse si elle existe".

Comme le contingent est ce qui n'est ni nécessaire ni impossible, l'analyse ockhamiste de la nécessité et de l'impossibilité dans le passage cité, va nous permettre de construire aussi bien une analyse de la contingence. Vers la fin du passage Ockham dit explicitement que la contingence peut être traitée par analogie avec le traitement de la nécessité et de l'impossibilité. Dans le même passage, il reconnaît qu'il y a un réquisit supplémentaire pour donner une analyse des modalités épistémiques et doxastiques. Mais il n'en paraît pas moins penser que l'analyse qu'il donne dans ce passage est adéquate aux modalités aléthiques. Et là, à ce qu'il me semble, Ockham a tort.

Selon le passage cité plus haut, les relations suivantes tiennent pour n'importe quelle proposition Z :

(I) Z est nécessaire si et seulement si (a) si Z existe, Z est vraie, et (b) il n'est pas possible à Z d'être fausse.

(II) Z est impossible si et seulement si, si Z existe, Z est fausse.

Les conditionnels placés à droite de (I) et (II) ne doivent pas être lus comme des implications matérielles mais probablement comme des implications strictes, ou ce qu'Ockham appelle des "conséquences simples" [5]. On pourrait donc penser que la clause (b) dans (I) est redondante, dans la mesure où elle est d'ores et déjà garantie par (a) et par le fait que si *Z* est fausse elle existe. Mais c'est peut-être aller trop vite en besogne. On peut en effet arguer que si *Z* est fausse elle existe, et que, comme (par la clause (a)) si *Z* existe elle est vraie, si *Z* est fausse elle est, par conséquent, *à la fois* vraie et fausse, ce qui est impossible. D'où *Z* n'est pas fausse. Et véritablement, à interpréter les conditionnels comme des implications strictes, l'on peut peut-être tirer la conclusion plus forte qu'il est *nécessaire* que *Z* ne soit pas fausse. Mais, inférer de cela qu'il est *possible* à *Z* d'être fausse, c'est présupposer un certain rapport entre les notions de possibilité et de nécessité qui, comme nous le verrons, ne peut être considéré comme allant de soi dans la théorie d'Ockham.

Considérons maintenant les principes suivants, qui mettent en relation la possibilité à l'impossibilité et à la nécessité :

(III) *Z* est possible si et seulement si *Z* n'est pas impossible.

(IV) *Z* est possible si et seulement si la contradictoire de *Z* n'est pas nécessaire [6].

Les principes (III) et (IV) sont des lois modales tout à fait standard. Ockham les admet [7], et de fait on peut en remonter la trace jusqu'à Aristote [8]. Il ne fait pas de doute que nous voudrions pouvoir affirmer ces principes dans une logique modale ockhamiste. Pourtant, chacun d'entre eux, une fois combiné avec (I) et (II), donne naissance à des anomalies. Et leur conjonction mutuelle avec (I) et (II) engendre une franche contradiction.

Conformément à (III), dire que *Z* est possible c'est dire qu'elle n'est pas impossible. Par (II), ceci revient à dire que *Z* pourrait exister et pourtant n'être pas fausse. Mais si *Z* existe et qu'elle n'est pas fausse, elle est vraie. D'où, dire que *Z* est possible revient à dire, en vertu de (III), que *Z* pourrait être vraie. Mais, conformément à (IV), dire que *Z* est possible c'est dire quelque chose d'assez différent, non que *Z* pourrait être vraie mais plutôt que la contradictoire opposée à *Z* n'est pas nécessaire. Et ceci, en vertu de (I), revient à dire que la contradictoire opposée à *Z* pourrait être fausse.

L'anomalie de (III) peut être mise en évidence de la manière suivante. Soit *A* la proposition "Aucune proposition n'est affirmative" et soit *B* sa contradictoire, en l'occurrence, "Quelque proposition est affirmative". Comme l'existence de propositions-tokens est une matière contingente, il est parfaitement possible que *A* puisse être la seule proposition-token existante. Dans ce cas, *A* sera vraie et non fausse. D'où, par (II), *A* n'est pas impossible. Par conséquent, par (III), *A* est

5 Pour cette identification, voir Marilyn McCord Adams, "Did Ockham Know of Material and Strict Implication ? A Reconsideration", *Franciscan Studies* 33 (1973), pp. 5-37.

6 Le principe (IV) est ce qui est présupposé par l'inférence (au paragraphe précédent) de 'il est *nécessaire* que *Z* ne soit pas fausse' à 'il n'est pas *possible* à *Z* d'être fausse'.

7 Cf. par ex., Ockham, *op. cit.*, III-3, 14-16.

8 Aristote, *De interpretatione*, 13.

possible. Néanmoins, on peut aussi bien montrer que *B*, la contradictoire de *A*, est nécessaire. Tout d'abord, il faut observer que si *B* existe elle est vraie, puisqu'elle est elle-même une proposition affirmative. D'où la clause (a) de (I) est satisfaite. Pour ce qui est de la clause (b), considérons la proposition '*B* est fausse'. Si cette proposition existe elle est ou vraie ou fausse. Mais elle n'est pas vraie, car sinon *B* serait effectivement fausse et ainsi existerait. D'où, par la clause (a), *B* serait vraie, et ainsi *B* serait à la fois vraie et fausse. Il s'ensuit par conséquent que, si la proposition '*B* est fausse' existe, elle est fausse. Donc, par (II), cette proposition est impossible. D'où, par (III), elle n'est pas possible. Ceci nous donne la clause (b) de (I). D'où, *B* est nécessaire.

Nous avons ainsi une proposition possible *A* dont la contradictoire ne laisse pas néanmoins d'être nécessaire. Cette situation étrange et non orthodoxe engendre une contradiction pure et simple si l'on accepte le principe (IV).

L'anomalie de (IV) est analogue à la précédente. Soit *C* la proposition "Aucune proposition n'est négative" et soit *D* sa contradictoire, en l'occurrence, "Quelque proposition est négative" Comme l'existence de propositions-tokens est une matière contingente, il est parfaitement possible que *D* puisse être la seule proposition-token existante. Dans ce cas, *D* sera fausse. Ceci viole la clause (a) de (I). D'où, *D* n'est pas nécessaire. Par conséquent, par (IV), la contradictoire de *D*, en l'occurrence *C*, est possible. Toutefois, *C* est impossible par (II), car si *C* existe elle est fausse, dans la mesure où elle est elle-même une proposition négative.

Nous avons ainsi une proposition *C* qui est à la fois possible et impossible. Cette situation bizarre engendre une franche contradiction si l'on admet le principe (III).

Il y a pourtant encore d'autres conséquences étranges de l'analyse des modalités aléthiques chez Ockham. La proposition 'Quelque proposition existe' s'y révèle être nécessaire. Et aussi bien, c'est là ce que fait la proposition 'Cette proposition existe', se référant elle-même. Ce sont là des résultats surprenants pour une théorie motivée au premier chef par la reconnaissance du fait qu'une proposition créaturelle – *i.e.*, une proposition-token – quelle qu'elle soit n'est pas nécessaire mais radicalement contingente. On pourrait certes penser, au premier regard, que cette difficulté est plus apparente que réelle, mais à la réflexion, on ne voit absolument pas comment Ockham pourrait en vérité exprimer dans sa propre théorie la contingence même qui la motive.

Le lecteur attentif aura sans aucun doute remarqué que toutes les difficultés dégagées plus haut font intervenir des propositions qui, d'une manière ou d'une autre, sont sui-référentielles. On pourrait, par conséquent, objecter que le véritable problème réside ici dans la sui-référence et non dans la théorie de la modalité selon Ockham. Pourtant, le genre de sui-référence qui est à l'oeuvre dans ces exemples ne fait pas intervenir de prédicats sémantiques et, normalement, il ne devrait pas soulever de difficultés. C'est ainsi, notamment, que tous les exemples donnés plus haut, peuvent être abordés de front dans les systèmes modernes de logique modale. Ils peuvent également être traités sans difficulté par la théorie modale nominaliste de Jean Buridan qui, comme Ockham, reconnaît que les porteurs des valeurs sémantiques comme la vérité et la fausseté sont des créatures qui existent de manière contingente [9].

Il semble donc bien que le problème réside dans la théorie même d'Ockham. En fin de compte, il ne nous donne pas une explication cohérente de ce que cela veut dire pour une proposition d'être nécessaire ou possible, contingente ou impossible. Sa théorie de la modalité *de dicto* – et par conséquent la totalité de sa théorie modale – en est menacée dans ses fondations mêmes.

Indiana University

† 9 Johannes Buridanus, *Sophismata*, ca. 8, conclusion 3 in Scott (1977), pp. 124-125. Pour une très élégante étude de la doctrine de Buridan sur ce point, voir A.N. Prior, "The Possibly-True and the Possible", *Mind* 78 (1979), pp. 481-492, repris dans A.N. Prior, *Papers in Logic and Ethics*, P.T. Geach and J.-P. Kenny, eds., (Amherst : University of Massachusetts Press, 1976), pp. 202-214.

XVI

ROGER SWYNESHED'S *OBLIGATIONES*: Edition and Comments

The mediaeval literature on *obligationes* has never been fully studied by modern scholars, although at least three articles on the topic have appeared in recent years: Ignacio Angelelli, "The Techniques of Disputation in the History of Logic," *The Journal of Philosophy* 67 (1970), pp. 800-815; Mary Anthony Brown, "The Role of the *Tractatus de obligationibus* in Mediaeval Logic," *Franciscan Studies* 26 (1966), pp. 26-35; and L. M. De Rijk, "Some Thirteenth Century Tracts on The Game of Obligation," *Vivarium* 12 (1974), pp. 94-123. Angelelli's article deals with Paul of Venice's tract,[1] while Brown's deals with Paul of Pergula's.[2] Both, therefore, concern relatively late examples of the literature. De Rijk's paper, on the other hand, publishes two early thirteenth century texts, on *falsi positio* and *impossibilis positio*, from a Munich Ms. These texts probably date no later than the 1220's, before William of Sherwood's tract.[3] †

(1) Paul of Venice, *Logica magna* II, 14 (Venice: Albertinus [Rubeus] Vercellensis, for Octavianus Scotus, 1499 [Hain 12505]), ff. 177ra-192rb. Angelelli (*op. cit.*, p. 803 n. 12) also cites the Venice, 1552, edition of Paul's *Summa totius dialecticae (=Logica parva).*

(2) Paul of Pergula, *Logica*, tract. 5, in Mary Anthony Brown, ed., *Paul of Pergula: Logica and Tractatus de sensu composito et diviso* ("Franciscan Institute Publications," Text Series, no. 13; St. Bonaventure, N.Y.: The Franciscan Institute, 1961), pp. 102-133.

(3) De Rijk (*op. cit.*, p. 94, n. 2) also cites Romuald Green's unpublished 1963 Louvain thesis, "An Introduction to the Logical Treatise *De obligationibus*, with critical texts of William of Sherwood (?) and Walter Burley," vol. 1: "Introduction"; vol. 2: "Critical Texts of William of Sherwood (?) and Walter Burley". There is also a discussion of the *obligationes* in C. L. Hamblin, *Fallacies* (London: Methuen, 1970), see index. In addition to Swyneshed's text edited below, I have prepared an edition of the *Obligationes* of the mid-fourteenth century logician Robert Fland (forthcoming), † and of the late fourteenth century logician, natural philosopher and theologian Richard Lavenham ("Richard Lavenham's *Obligationes*: Edition and Comments," forthcoming in *Rivista critica di storia della filosofia*. Cf. also my "The Treatises *On Modal Propositions* and *On Hypothetical Propositions* by Richard Lavenham," *Mediaeval Studies* 35 (1973), pp. 49-59 at p. 51.) Since this paper was first written, De Rijk has published two further studies of the *obligationes*, in *Vivarium* 13 (1975), pp. 22-54,

The exact purpose of the *obligationes* has not been determined. Angelelli treats the *disputatio de obligationibus* as a kind of game played by an "opponent" *(opponens)* and a "respondent" *(respondens)*, the purpose of which is to see if the respondent can be forced (by the rules of the game) to concede a contradiction.[4] But although this viewpoint is useful for setting out and understanding the rules of *obligatio*, it is doubtful, to say the least, that the mediaevals themselves thought of such disputations as games.

An *obligatio*, in the sense in which the term is used in this literature, has nothing directly to do with ethics or moral obligation. Rather, "an *obligatio* is an expression by means of which someone is bound to reply affirmatively or negatively to the *obligatum*."[5] Thus, for instance, if the opponent should say "I posit that *(pono quod)* every man runs", and if that *positio* is admitted by the respondent, then the respondent is obliged to reply affirmatively to the sentence 'Every man runs' (the *obligatum*) throughout the disputation. He replies affirmatively by saying "I concede" *(concedo)*.[6] On the other hand, if the opponent says "I give it up that *(depono quod)* every man runs", and if that *depositio* is admitted by the respondent, then the respondent is obliged to reply negatively to the sentence 'Every man runs' throughout the disputation. He replies negatively by saying "I deny" *(nego)*.[7] The disputation lasts until the opponent says "Let the time of *obligatio* lapse" *(Cedat tempus obligationis)*.[8]

After the *obligatio* has been made and admitted,[9] certain sentences are "proposed"[10] by the opponent. The respondent must reply to each of the proposed sentences in turn. He has three replies open to him: he may

and *Vivarium* 14 (1976), pp. 26-49. Green's thesis is currently in press at the Franciscan
† Institute.)

(4) Angelelli, *op. cit.*, especially p. 803. Cf. also Hamblin, *op. cit.*, pp. 125-126.

(5) Cf. below, par. 6. The definition is quoted *verbatim* by Richard Lavenham. (Cf. par. 1 of the edition mentioned above in n. 3.)

(6) Angelelli, *op. cit.*, p. 803. Cf. also Robert Fland's *Obligationes*, pars. 1-3.

(7) Angelelli, *loc. cit.*, and Fland, *op. cit.*, par. 38.

(8) Cf. below, par. 75, and Fland, *op. cit.*, par. 2.

(9) It seems that there is at least an implicit distinction between "admitting" and "conceding" in the context of *obligationes*. The initial *obligatio* is said to be "admitted". It is not said to be "conceded". The subsequent steps of the disputation may, subject to the rules, be "conceded". They are not said to be "admitted". (Contrast Angelelli, *loc. cit.*) In many authors, this distinction is not always rigorously observed.

(10) Angelelli, *op. cit.*, *passim*, takes Paul of Venice as having each subsequent step of the disputation constitute a new and added *obligatio*. This does not seem to be the case for many authors, among them Swyneshed and Fland. For them, the *obligatio* is made at the outset of the disputation, and although there may perhaps also be subordinate *obligationes* introduced in later steps (as in pars. 98 and 102 below — Fland does not discuss this possibility), this is not the norm. Subsequent steps are said to be "proposed". "Proposing" is not one of the recognized species of *obligatio*. (Cf. pars. 3 and 16, below.) The distinction in terminology is not always rigorously observed. In this connection, it is interesting to note the variant readings, *passim*, in manuscripts *V* and *V'* of Swyneshed's text.

concede the proposed sentence, he may deny it, or he may doubt it (by replying "dubito"). In general, the tracts on *obligationes* are more or less systematic presentations of the rules governing which kinds of *obligationes* are to be admitted and which of the three replies to the subsequent proposed sentences the respondent is allowed to make.

Curiously, except for the disputations given solely for illustrative purposes in these tracts, not a single *disputatio de obligationibus* seems to have been preserved. If one contrasts the *disputatio de obligationibus* with a disputation-form such as the *quaestio*, the reason for this fact becomes apparent. The *quaestio* was primarily a learning device. It always had a *topic* ("Whether such and such is the case?"). By contrast, the *disputatio de obligationibus* did not have a topic. At the end of a *disputatio de obligationibus*, no questions have been answered, no issues have been aired, no subject matter has been pursued. As a learning device, therefore, it would be hard to see the point of conducting a *disputatio de obligationibus*.

Accordingly, one would not expect what is said in a *disputatio de obligationibus* to be of much interest to anyone in its own right. And in fact, it appears from the literature that this is so. Interest in such a *disputatio* centers not on the content, but rather on the *rules the disputatio illustrates*.

This suggests that the mediaeval tracts on *obligationes* ought perhaps be viewed as attempts to formulate rules for "hypothetical reasoning". †
I say "hypothetical reasoning" for lack of a better term. For the rules of *obligationes* mix epistemological with purely logical considerations. The kind of reasoning involved is the kind used in cases such as the following:

> What if P were true? In that case, Q would also be true, since it follows from P. Furthermore, we know that R, though contingent, is in fact true. And that would not change if we supposed P, since R is independent of P. So we would still have R. On the other hand, even though we know that S is in fact true, it conflicts with P, and so we would have to reject S. Finally, we do not know whether T is in fact true or false. And, like R, it is independent of P. So assuming P still leaves T in doubt.

This little sketch illustrates somewhat colloquially the kind of reasoning that, translated into a more technical and stylized format, would come under the heading of that species of *obligatio* known as *positio*.[11] It is not simply reasoning deductively from a hypothesis. It is somewhat closer to what goes on in counterfactual reasoning ("What would have happened if Caesar had not crossed the Rubicon, but the world were in other respects as much as possible the same?") Even counterfactual reasoning, however, does not normally rest on epistemological considerations. Note, for instance, the reasoning concerning R and T in the example. This illustrates suppositions 10-12 of Swyneshed's tract,[12] the rules governing

(11) Cf. below, pars. 62-122. (12) Cf. below, pars. 25 & 29-30.

one's replies to sentences which are "irrelevant" *(impertinentes)* to the *obligatum*. These rules are the ones which introduce epistemological considerations into the *disputatio de obligationibus*. For the species *positio*, one might try to express the import of these rules in terms of Leibnizian possible worlds as follows: when P is posited and admitted, one's replies to the subsequent proposed sentences must be such that one concedes (or denies the contradictory of) a sentence if and only if it conforms to all possible worlds in which P is true and which are otherwise as much as possible like what, *for all one knows*, the actual world is like. *Positio*, it seems, is the basic species of *obligatio*. The others may be construed in terms of it.

This brief account of *obligationes* will suffice for the present. More detailed comments on Swyneshed's tract in particular may be found in the notes to the text edited below. A fuller study of the *obligationes*-literature in general will have to await the publication of further texts.[13]

The text edited below is the *obligationes* of Roger Swyneshed (died before May 12, 1365).[14] It was written after roughly 1330 and certainly before 1335,[15] and therefore comes from the middle period of the literature. The tract often appears in the MSS together with a companion tract *De insolubilibus*.[16] Indeed, in the MS used as the basis for the edition below, the two tracts have a common prologue.[17]

Together, Swyneshed's *Obligationes* and *De insolubilibus* were very influential.[18] The *De insolubilibus* was used by William Heytesbury to provide the first of four previous views discussed in the opening chapter, "De insolubilibus", of his immensely famous *Regulae solvendi sophismata*.[19] Swyneshed's view thus shared in the latter's circulation. Despite Heytesbury's criticisms, however, Swyneshed's position was adopted, sometimes in an amplified and somewhat revised form, by a number of

(13) Cf. above, n. 3.

(14) James A. WEISHEIPL, "Roger Swyneshed, O.S.B., Logician, Natural Philosopher, and Theologian," in *Oxford Studies presented to Daniel Callus* ("Oxford Historical Society," new series, vol. 16; Oxford: Clarendon Press for the Oxford Historical Society, 1964 for 1959-60), pp. 231-252 at p. 241. This article is still the most complete and authoritative source for Roger's life. As Weisheipl argues in this article, Roger is not to be confused with Richard Swyneshed, the famous Merton "Calculator".

(15) *Ibid.*, p. 247. Cf. supporting arguments, *ibid.*, pp. 244-247.

(16) Cf. my *The Mediaeval Liar: A Catalogue of the Insolubilia-Literature*, ("Subsidia Mediaevalia", vol. 5; Toronto: Pontifical Institute of Mediaeval Studies, 1975),
† item LXIII. I have prepared an edition of Swyneshed's *De insolubilibus* (forthcoming).

(17) But contrast the *V* text for par. 1.

(18) Cf. WEISHEIPL, *op. cit.*, pp. 235 & 243.

(19) *Tractatus gulielmi Hentisberi de sensu composito et diviso, Regulae ejusdem cum sophismatibus, Declaratio Gaetani supra easdem...*, (Venice: Bonetus Locatellus for Octavianus Scotus, 1494 [Hain 8437]), ff. 4va-7rb. Copy at University of Chicago Library.

later authors.[20] The influence of his *Obligationes* is somewhat less clear, largely because the history of the *obligationes*-literature in general is not yet well researched. Nevertheless, it appears that Swyneshed's position was adopted more or less intact by the late 14th century logician, natural philosopher, and theologian, Richard Lavenham. Robert Fland, in the mid-14th century, described two distinct traditions in the *obligationes*-literature, which he calls the "antiqua responsio" and the "nova responsio". The latter appears to be basically Swyneshed's view.[21]

Weisheipl lists the known MSS of Swyneshed's *Obligationes*[22]. Of these, I have examined eight:

Bruges, Bibl. publ. MS 500, ff. 143vb-150rb (mid-14c).
Paris, Bibl. nat. lat. 14715, ff. 86ra-90rb (c. 1378).[23]
Vatican, Vat. lat. 950, f. 117va-b (15c), fragment only.
Vatican, Vat. lat. 2130, ff. 152ra-154va (15c).
Vatican, Vat. lat. 2154, ff. 1ra-6rb (15c).[24]
Vatican, Vat. lat. 2185, f. 78ra-vb (1355-1357).

(20) Perhaps most notably by Paul of Venice. Cf. my *The Mediaeval Liar*, item L. Cf. also the anonymous item III. Item XVII, in two MSS, which I listed there as anonymous but bearing a close relation to Swyneshed's text, turns out on closer examination to be Swyneshed's text itself. Weisheipl, *op. cit.*, p. 240 n. 1, also cites Bodl., MS 676 (S.C. 2593), ff. 126-131, as containing an additional copy. I had overlooked this MS in my *The Mediaeval Liar*. John of Celaya's text also appears to have been influenced by Swyneshed. The text is edited, with a study, in Marie-Louise Roure, « Le traité ' Des propositions insolubles ' de Jean de Celaya », *Archives d'histoire doctrinale et littéraire du moyen âge*, 1962, pp. 235-338.

(21) The former view was held by Peter of Ailly, Albert of Saxony, and Paul of Pergula. Cf. the edition of Fland's text mentioned above in n. 3. The designations "antiqua" and "nova", therefore, should not be taken to suggest that the new view in any sense overcame or replaced the old one. †

(22) Weisheipl, *op. cit.*, p. 243. I have not examined: Oxford, Bodl., Canon. Lat. 278, ff. 78v-80 (c. 1391), incomplete; Prague, Metropol. 1645 [O. LXI], ff. 138-153v (early 14c), with Swyneshed's *Insolubilia*; or Vatican, Vat. lat. 3065, ff. 123v-126 (15c). Prof. d'Alverny has forwarded to me from Prof. De Rijk the information that there is another copy, not listed by Weisheipl, in Toledo, 94-28, ff. 59-68. I have not seen this MS. Rome, Casanatense, MS 85 (D. IV. 3), ff. 22va-23va, contains an anonymous tract tentatively identified as Swyneshed's *Obligationes* in *Catalogo dei manoscritti della Biblioteca Casanatense*, ("Ministero della pubblica istruzione, Indici e cataloghi," nuova serie II), vol. 1, (Rome: La libreria dello stato, 1949), p. 154. The text is not in fact Swyneshed's, but rather a discussion of three views on *obligationes*, the first of which is "magistri Riccardi Suinesecht anglici".

(23) Explicit "Et in hoc terminantur obligationes reverendi magistri Jo. Swinsed de Anglia doctoris in sacra theologia." Cf. Weisheipl, *op. cit.*, pp. 238, 243-244, on this attribution and on the claim that Swyneshed was a doctor of theology.

(24) On the date, cf. *Codices vaticani latini : codices* 2118-2192, Anneliese Maier, ed., (Vatican: In Bibliotheca Vaticana, 1961). Weisheipl, *op. cit.*, p. 243, says this MS is 14c.

Venice, San Marco Z301 (1576), ff. 41va-44rb (14c).
Vienna, Dominikanerkloster 160 (130), ff. 124rb-125va (early 14c).[25]

On the basis of these MSS, it is clear that there were at least two redactions of Swyneshed's *Obligationes* in circulation shortly after it was written. The one version was an abbreviated form of the other. The most important and obvious distinction between these two redactions is in the number of "suppositions" employed.[26] The longer version has twelve suppositions, including two forms of the eighth. This tradition is represented by the 14c. Bruges and Paris MSS, and by Vat. lat. 2154. On the other hand, the shorter version of the text has only eight suppositions, corresponding to numbers 3-4, 6, 8 (second form), 9-12 of the longer text. It is represented by Vat. lat. 2185, the Venice and Vienna MSS (all 14c.), and by Vat. lat. 2130. Some MS copies in this tradition leave out more than others, but all of them, in addition to abbreviating the list of suppositions, also omit other large sections of the longer version.[27]

After examining the MSS, I have chosen Vat. lat. 2154 as the basis for the edition below (with the sign "*V**"). This copy represents the longer redaction, and is for the most part quite reliable. Against this I have collated Vat. lat. 2130 (with the sign "*V*"), representing the shorter, more abbreviated redaction. Although both MSS are 15c., and therefore not the earliest of those examined, they contain a reasonably firm text.

I have not noted marginalia, except where they affect the text. Nor, for the most part, have I noted trivial variants that do not affect the sense. The orthography has been normalized according to Lewis and Short, *A Latin Dictionary*. Both MSS occasionally use the first-conjugation perfect forms 'negasti', 'dubitasti', etc., which I have retained. Square brackets signal editorial deletions, pointed brackets editorial additions. Divisions of the text have been made in accordance with the prologue in par. 1.

I have included among the notes some comments designed to help the reader through this rather difficult text. These are for the most part cross-

(25) With an anonymous commentary, ff. 109va-122vb. Between the commentary and the text proper, there are two other texts, a *De suppositionibus*, f. 123ra-b, and a *De consequentiis*, ff. 123rb-124rb. The latter is not Swyneshed's text mentioned by Weisheipl, *op. cit.*, p. 245. On the contrary, both texts are by William of Sutton. Cf. James A. Weisheipl, "Repertorium Mertonense," *Mediaeval Studies* 31 (1969), pp. 174-244 at p. 219. Following the text of Swyneshed's *Obligationes* in the MS, there is part of a copy of Walter Burley's *Insolubilia*, ff. 125va-126vb. The first part of this tract is found on f. 60rv. Cf. Weisheipl, "Repertorium...", p. 196, and my *The Mediaeval Liar*, item LXVII.

(26) Cf. pars. 13-30, below.

(27) Of the MSS I have examined in this tradition, Vat. lat. 2130 seems to present the fullest text. Even so, it lacks most or all of the following paragraphs of the edition: 10, 12-14, 17, 19, 20, 22-23, 26-27, 42-52, 63-66, 70-71, 78-79, 85-88, 95, 98-104, 106-116, 120-122, 124, 132, 135, 137-138.

references, elaborations of a particular argument, references to discussions by other mediaeval authors, etc. They in no sense constitute a full commentary. That will have to wait until additional texts are published, and the nature and history of the *obligationes*-literature in general becomes clearer.

The edition follows below.

* * *

<*Obligationes*>[28]

I

(1) (*V*152ra, *V**1ra) Cum in singulis scientiis secundum subjectam materiam sit certitudo quaerenda,[29] primo *Ethicorum*,[30] et materia artis dialecticae est vox significativa quae apud diversos diversificatur,[31] primo *Periermenias*,[32] inde[33] est quod in hac arte non demonstrationes sed persuasiones et evidentiae quodammodo probabiles expectantur.[34] Hujus autem artis ab Aristotele traditae duae sunt partes spectantes ad propositum.[35] In quarum una de obligationibus, in alia vero de insolubilibus obscure et intricate determinatur, quod translatori magis quam Aristoteli est impugnandum.[36] De quibus ut sermo vel sententia Aristotelis plenius pateat atque levius juxta modum legendi consuetum, primo de obligationibus, secundo de insolubilibus in praesenti determinabitur.[37] Et ut facilior[38] fiat processus, illud opus particulatim dividetur.[39] Prima particula prohemialis est. Secunda vero quasdam divisiones, definitiones, suppositiones, conclusiones solutionem obligationum concernentes[40] continet. Tertia de impositione tamquam de prima specie obligationis

(28) Richardi Suiset Angli Obligationes *V**. On the confusion of Roger with Richard Swyneshed, cf. Weisheipl, "Roger Swyneshed", *passim*.

(29) secundum... quaerenda/ sit certitudo quaerenda secundum materiam subjectivam, ut *V*.

(30) Aristotle, *Nicomachean Ethics* I, 3, 1094b12-14.

(31) diversa significat, ut *V*. (32) Aristotle, *De interpretatione* 1, 16a3-7.

(33) consequens V.

(34) et... expectantur/ evidentia probabili excitentur vel provocentur *V*.

(35) ab... propositum/ traditae sunt ab Aristotele duae partes ad propositum spectantes *V*.

(36) obscure...impugnandum/ quod translatori est impugnandum, non quod Aristoteles obscure determinaverit *V*.

(37) sermo... determinabitur/ sententia plenior [pateflat] pateat atque brevior juvenibus juxta modos loquendi consuetos, primo ergo de obligationibus in praesenti determinabitur, deinde de insolubilibus *V*.

(38) facilius *V*. (39) in quinque partes dividamus *V*.

(40) solutionem... concernentes/ et solutiones obligationum *V*.

considerat. Quarta vero de positione.[41] Quinta de depositione tamquam de ultima specie determinat.[42] Post haec de veritate insolubilium est consideratio quae in quinque partes consimiliter dividetur. In prima continentur quaedam divisiones, definitiones, conclusiones ad insolubilium solutionem pertinentes. In secunda de insolubilibus ex proprietate[43] vocis nascentibus prosequitur. In tertia de insolubilibus ex actibus nostris orientibus discutietur. In quarta de insolubilibus ex mixtione actus nostri cum proprietate vocis generantis determinabitur. In quinta de quibusdam sophismatibus quae apparent insolubilia et non sunt considerabitur. Et sic erit finis negotii praesentis.

II

(2) Divisiones vero proposito pertinentes sunt quattuor. Et prima est haec : Propositionum alia probabilis simpliciter alia improbabilis simpliciter.[44] Probabilis simpliciter[45] est propositio demonstrabilis a[46] causa. Et improbabilis simpliciter[47] est propositio repugnans probabili[48] simpliciter. Sed est sciendum quod non omne probabile vel improbabile (*V**1rb) est simpliciter probabile vel improbabile.[49] Pro quo sciendum quod probabile est illud ad quod probandum evidentias veras vel apparentes facere contingit.[50] Improbabile est illud ad quod improbandum evidentias veras vel apparentes contingit facere.[51] Ex quo patet quod idem[52] est probabile vel improbabile sicut est de tali propositione 'Sol est major tota terra'.[53]

(3) Secunda divisio est ista : Omnis obligatio vel concernit complexa tantum vel partim complexa et partim incomplexa. Obligatio concernens complexa tantum dividitur, quia[54] quaedam obligat ad concedendum, sicut positio,[55] et quaedam ad negandum, sicut depositio. Sed obligatio concernens partim complexa et partim incomplexa est illa mediante qua complexum vel incomplexum imponitur[56] ad significandum,[57] et illa dicitur impositio.

(41) *Add.* determinabit. In *V*.
(42) obligationum determinabit *V*. (*V* lacks the remainder of par. 1.)
(43) parte *V**. (Emendation taken from description of 4th *particula*.)
(44) probabilis... simpliciter/ simplex probabilis, alia simplex improbabilis *V*.
(45) Probabilis simpliciter/ Propositio simplex probabilis *V*.
(46) *Add.* causis vel a *V*.
(47) Et... simpliciter/ Propositio simplex improbabilis *V*. (48) improbabili *V**.
(49) vel... improbabile/ est simplex probabile nec omne improbabile est simplex improbabile *V*.
(50) ad... contingit/ pro quo probando contingit adducere evidentias veras vel apparentes. Et *V*.
(51) ad... facere/ pro quo probando non contingit dare evidentias veras vel apparentes *V*.
(52) illud *V**. (53) sicut... terra'/ vel quod idem est probabile vel improbabile *V*.
(54) Obligatio... quia/ Obligationum concernentium complexa tantum *V*.
(55) *Add.* et impositio *V*. (56) ponitur *V*. (57) *Add.* aliquid *V*.

(4) Tertia divisio est haec . Propositionum alia est pertinens obligato, alia est impertinens obligato. Et pertinentium obligato (V152rb) alia est sequens ex obligato, alia repugnans obligato. Circa quod notandum quod secundum aliam et aliam speciem obligationis aliud et aliud est obligatum. Nam in[58] impositione totum praeter signa dicitur[59] obligatum, et in positione positum, et in depositione depositum vel contradictorium[60] depositi. Exemplum primi : « Impono quod '*a*' significet praecise[61] quod deus est. » Tunc totum praeter hoc verbum 'impono' est obligatum.[62] Exemplum secundi, ut « Pono tibi istam 'Sortes currit'. » Tunc totum est obligatum praeter hoc 'pono'. Exemplum tertii, ut « Depono tibi istam 'Sortes currit'. » Tunc totum hoc est depositum[63] 'Sortes currit'. Et hoc verbum 'depono' est signum depositionis. Et 'Sortes[64] non currit' est etiam obligatum, quia est depositi contradictorium.

(5) Quarta et ultima[65] divisio est haec : Impertinentium obligato aliud ad quod et extra tempus obligationis non est varianda responsio propter variationem ex parte rei, et aliquod ad quod sic.[66] Exemplum primi : Haec propositio[67] 'Deus est' et haec propositio[68] 'Homo est asinus' sunt impertinentes alicui obligationi,[69] et his similes. Exemplum secundi, ut 'Rex sedet' vel 'Rex[70] non sedet', et his similes. De impertinentibus primo modo est[71] sciendum quod ad impertinens simili modo est[72] respondendum intra[73] tempus obligationis sicut extra. De impertinentibus secundo modo hoc non tenet universaliter, sed solum[74] ubi non est aliqua variatio facta ex parte[75] rei sive[76] significationis propositionis propter obligationem.

(6) Ex jam dictis patent definitiones, quae sunt tres.[77] Prima est haec : Obligatio est oratio mediante qua quis[78] affirmative vel negative tenetur respondere ad obligatum.

(7) Secunda definitio est haec : Propositio pertinens est propositio[79] non obligata quae, qualitercumque significet, propter (V^*1va) obligatum[80] est concedenda vel neganda.

(58) *Interl.* in *V*. (59) signa dicitur/ signum obligationis dicitur esse *V*.
(60) vel contradictorium/ et oppositum *V*. (61) *Add.* idem *V*.
(62) Roger's practice indicates that it would have been more correct to say here "totum praeter hoc 'impono quod' est obligatum." So too, in the second example below, the *obligatum* is everything besides the words 'pono tibi istam'.
(63) hoc... depositum/ depositum est *V*. (64) Si V^* (65) *Om.* et ultima *V*.
(66) *Interl.* et... sic V^*. aliud... sic/ alia est ad quam non est varianda responsio extra tempus obligationis propter mutationem factam ex parte rei, et alia est ad quam est responsio varianda *V*.
(67) propositiones *V*. (68) *Om.* haec propositio *V*.
(69) alicui obligationi/ alicujus obligationis *V*. (70) *Om.* Rex V^*.
(71) *Om.* modo est *V*. (72) simili... est/ primo modo est eodem modo *V*.
(73) infra *V*. (74) *Om.* solum *V* (75) aliqua... parte/ facta variatio *V*.
(76) vel ex parte rei sed solum *V*. (77) definitiones... tres/ tres definitiones *V*.
(78) pars V^*. *Add.* obligatus *V*. (79) *Add.* mediata, id est *V*.
(80) *Om.* propter obligatum *V*.

(8) Tertia definitio est haec : Propositio impertinens est propositio non[81] obligata, et[82] propter obligatum[83] nec est concedenda nec neganda.[84]

(9) Contra primam definitionem sic obicitur : Obligatio non est aliud nec alia quam propositio obligata. Sed mediante illa sola non[85] tenetur aliquis affirmative vel negative respondere.[86] Igitur, prima definitio non valet.[87]

(10) Contra secundam definitionem et tertiam conjunctim sic obicitur : Aliqua est propositio non obligata nec pertinens nec impertinens. Igitur, illae definitiones sunt insufficientes. Assumptum sic probatur si ponatur ista 'Tu es Romae' : Qua admissa, si proponitur statim 'Tu es obligatus' ista est concedenda. Tamen ista nec est pertinens nec impertinens. Nam impertinens non est ex eo quod propter obligatum illa est concedenda qualitercumque significet,[88] nec pertinens ex eo quod nec sequitur ex obligato nec sibi repugnat.[89]

(11) Solutio primi : Negatur primum assumptum[90] pro tanto quia obligatio non est tantum obligatum, sed obligatio est[91] totum aggregatum ex signis obligationis et obligato.[92]

(12) Ad aliam objectionem dicendum quod quaelibet propositio non obligata est pertinens vel impertinens. Et cum ponitur 'Tu es Romae' admittenda est. Et concedenda est haec 'Tu es obligatus'. Et dicendum quod ista est impertinens. Et negatur quod propter obligatum est ista concedenda vel neganda, sed propter obligationem est concedenda vel neganda.

(13) Consequenter sequuntur duodecim[93] suppositiones.[94] Prima est haec : Omnis propositio est probabilis vel improbabilis. Hoc patet ex definitione istorum terminorum 'probabile' vel 'improbabile' supradicta.[95]

(14) Secunda suppositio est haec : In omni consequentia bona pro significatis consequentis et antecedentis, ubi consequens est in plus quam antecedens est magis improbabile antecedens quam consequens. Ista satis patet. Nam in omni consequentia tali consequens pluribus modis potest probari quam antecedens. Ergo, consequens est probabilius antecedente.

(81) est... non/ non est propositio *V'*. (82) *Om.* et *V'*. (83) obligata *V.*

(84) The sense is that, although a *propositio impertinens* may be *concedenda* or *neganda* (cf. pars. 25, 29), this is not because of the *obligatum*.

(85) ratio (?) *V'*. (86) responderi *V'*. (87) *V* lacks all of par. 10.

(88) Cf. 2nd definition, par. 7.

(89) Cf. the 2nd part of the 3rd division, par. 4. Despite the opening words of this paragraph, the argument does not constitute an objection against the sufficiency of definitions 2 and 3, but rather against the consistency of definition 2 with the 3rd division, in par. 4.

(90) *Add.* vel argumentum *V.* (91) *Om.* obligatio est *V.*

(92) *V* lacks all of par. 12. (93) octo *V.*

(94) *Add.* obligationum *V. V* lacks the remainder of par. 13 and all of par. 14.

(95) supradictis *V'*. Cf. 1st division, par. 2.

Et ultra : ergo, antecedens est improbabilius consequente. Primum assumptum patet in tali consequentia 'Homo sedet ; ergo, animal sedet'.

(15) Tertia est quod[96] obligato improbabili non est aliquid[97] improbabilius illo concedendum. Ista patet sic : Propter minus[98] inconveniens non est[99] majus inconveniens concedendum. Ergo, obligato improbabili non est aliquid improbabilius illo concedendum.[1]

(16) Quarta est quod[2] sunt tantum tres species obligationis. Hoc patet ex divisione[3] secunda hujus particulae.

(17) Quinta est ista : Omnis terminus in voce vel in scripto est ad placitum significativus. Hoc sic probatur : Omnis intentio[4] significat naturaliter et non ad placitum, vel naturaliter et[5] ad placitum. Sed nulli termini in scripto vel in voce significant naturaliter (*V**1vb) ita quod non ad placitum. Igitur, omnes tales termini ad placitum <et>[6] naturaliter sunt significativi. Pro quo sciendum quod intentiones in conceptibus non ad placitum sed naturaliter significant, in cujus signum laici sciunt quod dies est, quod sol lucet, sicut litterati. Sed intentiones in scripto vel in voce ad placitum et naturaliter significant, quia naturaliter visui vel auditui repraesentant, ad placitum quia ex impositione qualitercumque imponens voluerit nati sunt significare.

(18) Sexta[7] : Omnis propositio[8] ad quam extra tempus obligationis propter mutationem ex parte rei est varianda responsio est ponenda vel deponenda. Haec patet. Nam omnis propositio est concedenda vel neganda qua concessa propter istam non est improbabilior concedenda deducta impositione.[9] Sed omne propositio ad quam extra tempus obligationis propter mutationem ex parte rei est varianda responsio est hujusmodi. Igitur, et cetera.

(19) Septima : Nulla propositio ad quam extra tempus obligationis propter mutationem factam ex parte rei non est varianda responsio est ponenda vel deponenda. Hoc patet ex probatione sextae. Nam nulla propositio est ponenda vel deponenda qua concessa est propter illam improbabilior concedenda. Sed omnis propositio ad quam extra tempus

(96) Tertia est quod/ Prima est haec *V*. (97) aliud *V*. (98) unum *V*.

(99) *Add.* aliud vel *V*.

(1) *Om.* Ergo... concedendum *V*. (2) Quarta... quod/ Secunda est haec *V*.

(3) definitione *V*. *V* lacks the remainder of par. 16 and all of par. 17.

(4) In this par., 'intentio' seems to be used not only for concepts, but for spoken and written terms as well.

(5) vel *V**. (6) For the emendation, cf. par. 37. (7) Tertia est haec *V*.

(8) *Add.* et solum talis V.

(9) Haec... impositione/ Probatur quia tali propositione concessa non contingit propter illam improbabiliorem concedere deducta propositione et cetera *V*. « Deducta impositione » here refers to the new or secondary imposition a proposition acquires in an *obligatio per impositionem*. *V* lacks the remainder of par. 18 and all of par. 19-20.

obligationis non est varianda responsio propter mutationem ex parte rei est hujusmodi.[10] Igitur, et cetera.

(20) Octava : Ad propositionem necessariam vel impossibilem non est varianda responsio intra tempus nec extra propter impositionem alicujus termini ad significandum. Sed ad propositionem contingentem est responsio varianda propter impositionem termini ad significandum et propter mutationem ex parte rei. Ubi igitur pono quod haec propositio[11] 'Homo est asinus' significet Sortem currere, tunc proposita ista 'Homo est asinus' patet quod propter impositionem non est concedenda, quia non est sequens. Nec etiam sequitur : « 'Homo est asinus' significat Sortem currere ; igitur, Sortes currit » vel « homo est asinus », quod idem est pro nunc.

(21) Vel octava[12] : Propter impositionem alicujus propositionis ad illam[13] non est responsio varianda. Hoc patet. Nam quaecumque propositio[14] imponatur[15] ad significandum, propositio[16] illa erit impertinens impositioni[17] quae[18] tunc imponetur.[19] Igitur, propter talem impositionem non est responsio ad illam varianda.[20]

(22) Contra : Ponatur ista 'Hoc est falsum' ad significandum praecise quod deus est. Tunc ista est concedenda. Sed si illa eadem imponitur ad significandum quod homo est asinus, tunc est neganda, quia impossibilis. Ergo, propter impositionem propositionis responsio ad illam est varianda.

(23) Solutio : Licet ista imponatur ad significandum quod deus (V^*2ra)

(10) The reasoning here is not entirely clear. First of all, a *propositio deponenda* ought not be *concessa* (cf. par. 3, 123). The arguments here and in par. 18 are plainly meant to be based on par. 15. But in the light of par. 20, the argument here amounts to an attempt to prove that no necessary or impossible proposition is *ponenda* or *deponenda*. It is not clear, however, how this follows from par. 15. On these difficulties, cf. note 29 to par. 88.

(11) The statement of the supposition earlier in the par. requires the imposition of a *term*, not, as here, of a *proposition*. Cf. the alternative form of the 8th supposition, par. 21.

(12) Vel octava/ Quarta est ista quod *V*. (13) significandum, ad eam *V*.

(14) *Om.* propositio *V*. (15) ponatur *V*. (16) *Om.* propositio *V*.

(17) positioni *V*.

(18) quia V^*. The antecedent of 'quae' here seems to be 'propositio illa', not 'impositioni'.

(19) ponetur *V*. *V* lacks the remainder of par. 21 and all of pars. 22-23.

(20) Par. 21 is not meant to be a *restatement* of par. 20, but rather an alternative supposition. In fact, it is this second version that is usually referred to as « suppositio octava ». Cf., e.g., par. 39, 47. The force of the *suppositio* in this par. seems to be that *impositio* is a "metalinguistic" *obligatio*, whereas *positio* and *depositio* are "object-linguistic" ones, and that the two levels must not be confused. (Cf. n. 41 to par. 63.) On the distinction between object-language and metalanguage, cf. Alfred Tarski, "The Concept of Truth in Formalized Languages," in Alfred Tarski, *Logic, Semantics, Metamathematics: Papers from 1923 to 1938*, J. H. Woodger, tr., (Oxford: Clarendon Press, 1969), pp. 152-278, and Alfred Tarski, "The Semantic Conception of Truth and the Foundations of Semantics," in *Philosophy and Phenomenological Research* 4 (1944), pp. 341-376.

est, non propter hoc est concedenda vel neganda. Sed si ponitur simul cum hoc quod pro instanti[21] illius propositionis denotetur illa eadem, tunc propter positionem et impositionem simul est illa neganda 'Hoc est falsum'. Sed propter solam impositionem non.

(24) (*V*152va) Nona[22] : Ad propositionem pertinentem et non ad impertinentem propter obligatum[23] est responsio varianda. Hoc patet. Nam propter obligatum non est varianda responsio nisi ad sequens vel ad repugnans. Sed pertinens est sequens vel repugnans et impertinens non. Igitur, et cetera.[24]

(25) Decima est quod propositio[25] impertinens scita ab aliquo principaliter significare[26] sicut est sine obligatione ad hoc pertinente[27] est concedenda. Exemplum : Si ponatur 'Homo currit', deinde[28] proponitur 'Tu es homo'. Ista est concedenda, hoc supposito. Probatur[29] quia tale impertinens foret concedendum extra tempus obligationis. Et quia responsio ad illud non est varianda propter obligatum,[30] ergo si obligatio non sit pertinens ad illud, sequitur quod infra tempus obligationis ad illud non est varianda responsio.[31]

(26) Vel potest probari haec suppositio sic : Ad impertinens non est varianda responsio propter obligatum.[32] Ergo, si obligatio non sit pertinens ad illud, sequitur quod ad tale impertinens non est responsio varianda propter obligatum nec propter obligationem. Ergo, ad tale impertinens sic est respondendum infra sicut extra. Sed extra quaelibet talis foret

(21) 'Pro instanti' here seems to indicate the referent of the demonstrative 'hoc' in 'Hoc est falsum'.

(22) Quinta suppositio est haec quod *V*.

(23) Contrast par. 21. There it was « propter impositionem », here « propter obligatum ». Note that an *obligatum* is never a *propositio pertinens* nor a *propositio impertinens* (cf. « non obligata » in the 2nd and 3rd definitions, par. 7-8).

(24) Hoc... cetera/ Probatur quia pertinens est sequens vel repugnans obligato et non impertinens *V*.

(25) Decima... propositio/ Sexta est ista *V*.

(26) principaliter significare/ sibi significare simpliciter *V*.

(27) The phrase « obligatio ad hoc pertinens », or a variant of it, appears frequently throughout this text. In each case, one must ask what is the antecedent of the pronoun. In general, it seems that, where the term *T* is the antecedent and *p* is a proposition denoted by *T*, the *obligatio* is « ad hoc pertinens » if and only if the proposition "*p* is a *T*" (or perhaps, "*p* is not a *T*") follows from the *obligatum*. (Cf. par. 124 for an explicit statement of this where the antecedent is 'depositum'. On the other hand, cf. par. 63 for a different, and perhaps confused, reading where 'positum' is the antecedent. The parenthetical phrase is included above because Roger's practice sometimes seems to demand it. Cf., e.g., par. 27-28.

(28) *Add.* si *V*. (29) hoc... Probatur/ propter hoc *V*.

(30) since it is *impertinens*. Cf. par. 24.

(31) infra... responsio/ etiam est concedendum infra tempus obligationis *V*. *V* lacks all of par. 26-27 and the first two sentences of par. 28.

(32) From the 9th supposition, par. 24.

concedenda a quocumque sciente principaliter sibi significare sicut est. Igitur, et infra.

(27) Contra : Ponatur quod haec 'Homo est asinus' sit impertinens scita a te tibi principaliter significare sicut est, et quod nulla obligatio fiat tibi. Adhuc secundum illam suppositionem haec 'Homo est asinus' foret concedenda.[33]

(28) Solutio : Negatur ista 'Homo est asinus'. Et negatur quod illa sit impertinens scita a te tibi principaliter significare sicut est. Pro quo est sciendum[34] quod quandocumque ex obligato sequitur oppositum obligationis vel e contra, respondendum est ad illud obligatum tamquam ad impertinens. Verbi gratia, ponatur quod nihil est tibi[35] positum. Deinde si[36] proponatur eadem,[37] respondendum est ad illam ac si nulla obligatio tibi fieret,[38] quia ex posito[39] sequitur oppositum obligationis. Nam sequitur : 'Nihil est tibi positum ; ergo, non ponitur quod nihil sit tibi positum',[40] quod est oppositum obligationis.[41] Et sic est in priori copulativa.[42]

(29) Undecima[43] : Propositio impertinens scita ab aliquo sibi principaliter significare aliter quam est sine obligatione ad hoc pertinente est neganda.[44] Exemplum : Si ponitur illa 'Omnis homo currit', deinde si ponitur 'Tu non es homo', neganda est quia impertinens et cetera.

(30) Duodecima[45] : Propositio impertinens scita ab aliquo sibi[46] significare dubie[47] sine (*V**2rb) obligatione et cetera[48] est dubitanda. Exemplum : Ponitur illa 'Omnis homo sedet'. Deinde si ponitur 'Rex sedet' illa est dubitanda, quia est impertinens scita principaliter tibi significare dubie sine obligatione et cetera.[49] Patent illae ultimae ex sexta et ejus probatione.[50]

(31) Ultimo[51] ex praedictis sequuntur duae conclusiones. Prima : Quacumque propositione posita vel deposita, ponenda vel deponenda, nulla[52] propositio impertinens scita ab aliquo sibi principaliter significare

(33) In violation of suppositions 7 and 8 (first form), pars. 19-20.

(34) Pro... sciendum/ Et nota *V*. (35) *Om.* tibi *V*. (36) *Om.* si *V*.

(37) illa 'Nihil est tibi positum' *V*.

(38) ac... fieret/ tamquam si nulla esset obligatio *V*. That is, it is *dubitanda*. Cf. par. 92.

(39) opposito *V*. (40) *V* lacks the remainder of par. 28.

(41) The same example is discussed in pars. 64, 91-92.

(42) I.e., the copulative *positio* of par. 27. (43) Septima suppositio est ista *V*.

(44) ad hoc... neganda/ adhuc est et cetera neganda *V**. *V* lacks the remainder of par. 29.

(45) Octava est ista *V*. (46) *Add.* principaliter *V*. (47) *Om.* dubie *V**.

(48) et cetera/ ad hoc pertinente *V*. (49) *Om.* Exemplum... cetera *V*.

(50) Patent... probatione/ Istae duae suppositiones patent ex probatione sextae suppositionis *V*.

(51) *Om.* Ultimo *V*. (52) *Om.* nulla *V*.

sicut est est neganda sine obligatione ad hoc pertinente,[53] nec scita[54] significare principaliter aliter quam est est concedenda, nec scita[55] significare principaliter dubie est neganda vel concedenda.[56] Patet ex tribus[57] ultimis suppositionibus.

(32) Secunda conclusio : Propter concessionem partium copulativae non est[58] copulativa concedenda[59] nec propter concessionem disjunctivae est aliqua pars ejus concedenda.[60] Prima pars conclusionis probatur sic[61] : Sit *a* una copulativa facta ex obligato falso et impertinente[62] significante principaliter sicut est. Sit *b* illud obligatum. Tunc concessis istis[63] partibus[64] tota copulativa est impertinens obligato[65] scita principaliter significare aliter quam est. Igitur, neganda. Consequentia patet per secundam[66] suppositionem.[67] Secunda pars conclusionis probatur sic : Sit *c* oppositum talis copulativae, *b* existente obligato[68] sicut prius. Et arguitur sic : *c* disjunctiva est oppositum copulativae negatae.[69] Igitur, illa est concedenda. Et quod utraque pars sit neganda patet. Nam una pars est opposita *b* obligato.[70] Igitur, illa est neganda. Et alia[71] est impertinens significans principaliter aliter quam est. Igitur, est neganda. Sequitur de speciebus obligationis.[72]

(53) sicut... pertinente/ praecise sicut est sine obligatione ad hoc pertinente est neganda ab illo *V*.
(54) *Add.* sibi *V*. (55) *Add.* sibi *V*.
(56) neganda... concedenda/ dubitanda vel concedenda vel neganda ab illo. Haec conclusio *V*.
(57) duabus *V*. (58) *Add.* propter hoc *V*.
(59) Part of the rationale for this is discussed in par. 43.
(60) On disjunction, cf. the exception mentioned in pars. 96-97. Robert Fland takes this second conclusion to be characteristic of what he calls the "new" school of thought on *obligationes*: « Unde illa responsio ponit tales duas regulas. Prima est : Utraque pars copulativae est concedenda, quae copulativa est neganda. Secunda est quod disjunctiva est concedenda cujus utraque pars est neganda. » Cf. my forthcoming edition of Fland's *Obligationes*, par. 17.
(61) Prima... sic/ Hoc probatur quantum ad primam partem *V*.
(62) *Add.* non *V*. (63) his duabus *V*. (64) *Add.* copulativae *V*.
(65) *Add.* falso *V*. (66) primam regulam sive *V*.
(67) Better, the 3rd supposition, par. 15. This is the first supposition in the numbering according to *V*.
(68) *Add.* composito ex obligato *V*.
(69) negandae. Ergo, ista disjunctiva est concedenda quia illius disjunctivae altera pars est vera, scilicet, illius disjunctivae pars opposita parti falsae copulativae quae pars disjunctivae est vera. Et ipsa disjunctiva est impertinens. *V*.
(70) Nam... obligato/ Nam illa est opposita obligati positi *V*.
(71) *Add.* pars *V*. (72) *Om.* Sequitur... obligationis *V*.

III

(33) (*V*152vb) Impositio est obligatio mediante qua complexum vel incomplexum[73] imponitur ad significandum. In impositione autem sumendae[74] sunt regulae. Prima est ista[75] : Omne obligatum per impositionem sine obligatione[76] ad hoc pertinente[77] est concedendum.[78] Exemplum : Ponitur quod '*a*' praecise significet quod deus est. Tunc haec est concedenda « '*a*' significat praecise quod deus est » quia est obligatum per impositionem et cetera.

(34) Secunda regula : Omne sequens ex obligato[79] per impositionem sine obligatione ad hoc pertinente est concedendum.[80] Exemplum : Ponitur quod haec propositio 'Homo est asinus'[81] praecise significet quod deus <est>. Tunc haec est concedenda « 'Homo est asinus' est vera » quia sequitur ex obligato per impositionem et cetera.[82]

(35) Tertia regula : Omne repugnans obligato per impositionem sine obligatione et cetera,[83] est negandum,[84] ut in proximo exemplo haec est neganda « Nulla talis 'Homo est asinus' est vera » quia repugnat obligato et cetera.

(36) Quarta regula : Ad impertinens[85] sine obligatione ad hoc pertinente respondendum est velut per illud[86] concipitur. Exemplum : Si[87] ponitur[88] quod haec 'Homo est asinus' praecise significet quod[89] homo est asinus (*V**2va), deinde si[90] ponitur « 'Homo est asinus' et 'Deus est' sunt[91] similes », dubitanda est quia dubitatur quid vel quomodo haec significet 'Deus est', cum posset inst<it>ui vel non, <et>[92] quia impertinens scita ab aliquo[93] principaliter significare dubie. Ideo est

(73) « complexum vel incomplexum ». Cf. the description of *impositio* in the 2nd division, par. 3.

(74) subjungendae *V*. (75) *Om.* Prima... ista *V*.

(76) sine obligatione/ sive per obligationem *V*. (77) pertinentem *V*.

(78) *V* lacks the remainder of par. 33. (79) *Add.* sive per obligationem *V*.

(80) negandum et repugnans obligato per impositionem *V*. *V* lacks the remainder of par. 34.

(81) *Add. sed vacat* est vera quia sequitur ex obligato per impositionem et cetera. Tertia regula *V**.

(82) Cf. the remarks on the distinction between object-language and metalanguage in n. 20 to par. 21. Here the conclusion, like the *obligatum*, is metalinguistic. Note that, while « 'Homo est asinus' est vera » is *concedenda*, 'Homo est asinus' is not, since that would involve an illicit move from metalanguage to object-language and would violate par. 21.

(83) et cetera/ ad hoc pertinente *V*. (84) *V* lacks the remainder of par. 35.

(85) omne simile *V*. (86) *Add.* principaliter *V*. (87) Sine *V**.

(88) imponatur *V*. (89) *Om.* haec... quod *V*. (90) *Om.* si *V*.

(91) *Add.* propositiones *V*. (92) *Om.* quia... <et> *V*. (93) *Add.* sibi *V*.

dubitanda.[94] Et nota quod[95] propositio impertinens[96] in omni specie obligationis est illa quae nec sequitur nec repugnat obligato.

(37) Consequenter est videndum qualiter in ista specie obligationis et mediantibus quibus signis est obligandum, et quae habent obligari. Pro quo est intellegendum quod[97] mediantibus istis signis 'pono' vel 'suppono' vel 'impono'[98] in hac specie obligationis habet quis obligari et hoc illo modo : « Pono », vel « Ponitur quod '*a*' praecise significet quod deus est. »[99] Illa habent etiam obligari in hac specie obligationis in voce vel in scripto. Sed mediantibus terminis in intellectu non contingit haec obligari,[1] quia tales[2] naturaliter et non ad placitum significant,[3] sicut est supra in quinta suppositione.[4]

(38) Ulterius, in hac specie notanda est haec divisio[5] : Omnis impositio vel consistit circa orationem vel terminum.[6] Si circa orationem,[7] hoc est[8] dupliciter, vel circa orationem[9] congruam vel incongruam. Si circa congruam, hoc dupliciter,[10] vel circa congruam quae est propositio vel circa orationem quae non est propositio.[11] De membris[12] divisionis dicetur infra per ordinem.[13]

(39) De primo, ponatur[14] quod '*a*' solum[15] significet hominem in propositione falsa[16] in qua ponitur, et solum asinum in propositione vera in qua ponitur,[17] et[18] solum idem quod hoc[19] disjunctum 'homo vel non homo' in propositione dubia in qua ponitur.[20] Deinde proponitur hoc[21] 'Homo est *a*'. Si conceditur vel dubitatur, contra : Nulla obligatione tibi facta vel impositione,[22] illa foret a te[23] neganda. Sed propter impositionem propositionis[24] non est responsio ad eam varianda, per suppositionem

(94) *Om.* Ideo... dubitanda *V.*
(95) *V* lacks the remainder of par. 36 and the beginning of par. 37. Cf. n. 97 to par. 37.
(96) *Interl.* im- *V**. (97) *Om.* Consequenter... quod *V**.
(98) signis... 'impono'/ membris 'impono', 'imponatur', 'suppono', 'supponatur' *V.*
(99) habet... est »/ fit impositio *V.*
(1) Illa... obligari/ Et nota quod in hac <specie> obligationis sumuntur termini vocales vel scripti et non termini concepti *V.*
(2) sunt *V.* (3) significativi *V.* (4) *Om.* sicut... suppositione *V.*
(5) in... divisio/ circa hanc speciem *V.*
(6) vel... terminum/ circa terminum vel circa orationem consistit *V.*
(7) *Add.* consistit *V.* (8) potest esse *V.* (9) *Om.* orationem *V.*
(10) *Om.* hoc dupliciter *V.*
(11) circa congruam... propositio/ ipsa est propositio vel non *V.*
(12) *Add.* autem hujus *V.*
(13) dicetur... ordinem/ ponenda sunt aliqua sophismata. Et primum *V.*
(14) imponatur *V.* (15) *Om.* solum *V.* (16) *In marg.* in... falsa *V.*
(17) *Om.* in qua... ponitur *V.* (18) *Add.* significet hoc *V.* (19) *Om.* idem... hoc V.
(20) *Om.* in... ponitur *V.* (21) proponitur hoc/ ponatur *V.*
(22) obligatione... impositione/ impositione facta *V.*
(23) a te/ concedenda vel *V.* (24) *Add.* ad significandum *V.*

octavam.[25] Igitur, adhuc est a te[26] neganda. Similiter posset deduci per communes processus, sed causa brevitatis omitto. Si negetur 'Homo est *a*', tunc sic : Tu negas illam pro instanti prolationis. Et tunc[27] bene respondisti. Et pro tunc illa fuit impertinens. Igitur, pro tunc illa fuit falsa.[28] Et pro tunc '*a*' ponebatur in propositione falsa. Et ultra[29] : igitur, tunc solum significavit hominem. Et per consequens tunc haec[30] fuit falsa 'Homo est[31] homo'.

(40) Solutio : Admittatur casus et negatur quod homo sit *a*, quia impertinens scita non[32] significare sicut est.[33] Et negatur consequentia[34] « Tu negasti illam pro instanti prolationis ; igitur,[35] illa fuit falsa » quia respondens non semper tenetur respondere[36] penes veritatem et falsi- (*V**2vb) tatem propositionis,[37] sed penes hoc quod scit ita esse[38] sicut illa principaliter[39] significat vel non ita esse,[40] et hoc si illa sit impertinens. Sed concesso quod illa[41] est falsa, concedendum est quod '*a*' po- (*V*153ra) nitur[42] in illa propositione. Et negatur consequentia : « igitur, solum significat hominem in illa », nec consequentia ex casu valet.

(41) Si tamen sic respondeatur[43] contra : « In quacumque propositione falsa in qua ponitur '*a*', '*a*' solum[44] significat hominem ; haec est propositio falsa in qua ponitur '*a*'[45] ; igitur, in illa[46] '*a*' solum significat hominem, » concedenda est consequentia et negandum est antecedens pro majore et minore,[47] quia[48] falsum et non sequens ex posito. Nam antecedens est una copulativa cujus utraque pars est concessa, et ex hoc non sequitur quod illa[49] sit concedenda, sicut patet per secundam conclusionem.[50]

(42) Contra : Inter majorem et minorem non est nota conjunctionis media. Igitur, ibi non est copulativa.

(43) Dicendum est quod consequentia non valet, quia licet non sit ibi nota conjunctionis media, tamen major et minor sumantur copulative, et ideo ibi est copulativa. Unde notandum quod ex duabus propositionibus

(25) quartam *V*. Cf. par. 21 (2nd version of supposition 8). (26) *Om.* a te *V*.
(27) negas... tunc/ negasti istam partem positionis. Et per te *V*.
(28) By suppositions 10-12, pars. 25, 29-30. (29) *Om.* Et ultra *V*.
(30) consequens... haec/ hoc *V*.
(31) *Add.* est *V*.
(32) scita non/ non scita *V*, *V**. (Emend to conform to suppositions 10-12, par. 25, 29-30.) *Add.* sicut principaliter significat, non scita principaliter *V*.
(33) principaliter significat *V**. (34) *Add.* facta, scilicet *V*.
(35) illam... igitur/ istam. Et pro tunc bene negasti. Et pro tunc illa fuit impertinens. Ergo, pro tunc *V*.
(36) *Om.* non... respondere *V*. (37) *Add.* non semper habet respondere *V*.
(38) scit... esse/ scitur esse vel non esse *V* (39) *Add.* sibi *V*.
(40) *Om.* vel... esse *V*. (41) I.e., 'Homo est *a*'. (42) ponebatur *V*.
(43) *Om.* in... respondeatur *V*. (44) *Om.* '*a*' solum *V*. (45) *Add.* ponitur *V**.
(46) hac propositione *V*. (47) *Add.* parte *V*. (48) *Add.* ipsum est *V*.
(49) tota copulativa *V*. (50) *V* lacks par. 42-52.

non copulative acceptis numquam sequitur tertia nisi sequatur ex altera illarum per se. Inde est quod ex tribus propositionibus non dispositis in materia et forma semper vel pro majori parte accipitur nota conjunctionis apparenter tenendo majorem cum minore ut quod deficit ex evidentia ex defectu modi et figurae ad conclusionem inferendam suppleatur per apparentem conjunctionem majoris cum minore. Sed in argumento syllogistico major cum minore copulative sumuntur demissa nota conjunctionis eo quod evidentia ex modo et figura est satis manifesta.[51]

(44) Et ulterius, non sequitur, licet in illa propositione 'Homo est *a*' '*a*' significat hominem, quod illa[52] sit falsa.

(45) Contra : In istis duabus propositionibus 'Homo est *a*' et 'Homo est homo', praedicata idem significant praecise et subjecta et copulae similiter. Et propositiones sunt ejusdem qualitatis et quantitatis. Igitur, consequentia bona.

(46) Solutio : Negatur consequentia, et quia[53] manifeste patet : quod non sequitur [non sequitur] « Quilibet homo est masculus ; ergo, omnis homo est masculus, » et tamen subjecta et copulae et praedicata convertuntur et propositiones sunt ejusdem quantitatis et qualitatis.[54] Antecedens[55] similiter est negandum, quia est una copulativa cujus una pars est falsa[56] et tota copulativa est impertinens. Igitur, neganda.

(47) Similiter et si imponitur [quod] quilibet talis terminus 'homo' ad significandum asinum tantum, et quilibet talis terminus 'asinus' ad significandum asinum tantum. Deinde proponitur illa 'Homo est asinus' Si conceditur vel dubitatur, contra : Continue ante[57] istam[58] impositionem fuit neganda ista 'Homo est asinus'. Et propter impositionem propositionis non est responsio ad illam varianda.[59] Igitur, adhuc est illa neganda 'Homo est asinus'.

(48) Ad idem : 'Homo (*V**3ra) est asinus' est propositio ad quam propter mutationem factam ex parte rei non est responsio varianda extra tempus obligationis. Talis propositio nec ponenda nec deponenda. Consequentia patet per septimam suppositionem. Igitur, ad illam propositionem 'Homo est asinus' respondendum est infra tempus sicut extra. Sed extra foret neganda. Igitur, et infra.

(51) With this par., cf. the first part of the second conclusion, par. 32.

(52) I.e., 'Homo est homo'. at the end of par. 39.

(53) Understand « ratio quia negatur ».

(54) The force of this example rests on gender. Cf. my "Robert Fland's *Consequentiae*: An Edition" *Mediaeval Studies* 38 (1976), pp. 54-84, par. 15. Gender of course is not at stake in the consequence in par. 45, above. The point of the argument here seems to be simply to show that, for whatever reason, consequences of the kind in par. 45 are not *in general* to be conceded.

(55) I.e., of the consequence in par. 45.

(56) Presumably the part « praedicata idem significant ». Cf. the end of par. 40

(57) contra *V**. (Emend for sense.) (58) *In marg.* si... istam *V**.

(59) By supposition 8 (2nd form), par. 21.

(49) Si negatur illa 'Homo est asinus', contra : 'Homo est asinus' est una propositio affirmativa cujus quaelibet res significata per subjectum est res significata per praedicatum, et e contra. Igitur, illa propositio est vera. Et nulla positio tibi fit vel depositio.[60] Igitur, per nullam obligationem factam tibi est responsio ad illam varianda. Et illa est vera scita a te. Igitur, illam habes concedere.

(50) Solutio : Negatur 'Homo est asinus'. Et negatur quod 'Homo est asinus' est propositio affirmativa et cetera,[61] quia illa non sequitur ex impositione facta et significat aliter quam est.

(51) Contra : Quilibet talis terminus 'homo' significat asinum tantum. Et nihil est subjectum istius propositionis 'Homo est asinus'[62] nisi talis terminus 'homo', nec praedicatum nisi talis terminus 'asinus'. Et aliquid significatum per subjectum et aliquid per praedicatum. Igitur, quaelibet res significata per subjectum illius propositionis est res significata per praedicatum ejusdem, et e converso, quod fuit negandum.

(52) Responsio : Concedo, et nego antecedens, scilicet, illam copulativam factam ex duabus categoricis [consequentiam] quia est impertinens et significat aliter quam est, sicut in priori sophismate.

(53) De secundo membro divisionis[63] sit hoc sophisma : Imponatur quaelibet talis oratio 'hominem esse' ad significandum praecise quod[64] homo est. Deinde proponatur 'hominem esse'. Si conceditur vel negatur vel dubitatur, contra : 'Hominem esse' est oratio incongrua.[65] Igitur, nec concedenda nec neganda nec dubitanda.[66] Et alterum illorum fecisti. Igitur, male respondisti. Si non conceditur, contra[67] : Illa est oratio[68] necessaria. Igitur, concedenda.[69] Antecedens probo[70] : Illa oratio significat sicut continue ante hoc fuit, et nunc[71] est, et continue[72] post hoc erit ; igitur, necessaria.[73]

(60) And so, *a fortiori*, there is no *obligatio ad hoc pertinens*. The case of *impositio* is covered by supposition 8 (2nd form), par. 21.

(61) Cf. par. 49.

(62) *Add. sed vacat* et aliquid significatum per subjectum nisi talis terminus 'asinus' ac aliquid significatum per subjectum *V**.

(63) *Om.* divisionis *V*. (I.e., « impositio circa orationem incongruam ». Cf. par. 38.)

(64) praecise quod/ illam *V*.

(65) It is not clear why this should be *incongrua*. Contrast par. 56, where the accusative-infinitive construction 'deum esse' is said to be *congrua*. Better examples are to be found in par. 55.

(66) *Om.* nec dubitanda *V**.

(67) Et... contra/ Consequentia patet de se. Et antecedens est notum. Sed quod ipsa sit concedenda probatur *V*.

(68) *Om.* oratio *V*. (69) ipsa est concedenda. Consequentia patet et *V*.

(70) declaratur quia *V*. (71) continue sicut *V*. (72) *Add.* sicut *V*.

(73) ipsa est necessaria et per consequens est concedenda *V*. Note the temporal notion of necessity here. Roger does not reject this notion in par. 54.

(54) Solutio : Non est respondendum ad illam nisi excusatorie, dicendo[74] quod ipsa est oratio[75] incongrua, et per consequens nec vera nec falsa. Et concedendum est quod illa significat sicut continue ante hoc fuit et nunc[76] est et[77] continue post hoc erit, et negatur consequentia : « igitur, est necessaria ». Sed oportet addere quod illa foret propositio eo quod nihil est verum vel falsum, necessarium, possibile, impossibile, contingens,[78] nisi propositio.

(55) Simile est omnino[79] si ponitur quod talis oratio 'homo asinus bos' praecise[80] significat[81] quod deus est, vel si ponitur quod talis oratio 'amat legit'[82] significat praecise[83] quod deus est,[84] homo est asinus. Similis est responsio.[85]

(56) (*V**3rb) De tertio membro divisionis,[86] videlicet, de impositione orationis congruae quae non est propositio, sit[87] hoc sophisma : Ponatur quod quaelibet[88] talis oratio 'deum esse' significat praecise[89] quod deus est. Deinde proponitur « 'Deum esse' est verum ». Si conceditur vel dubitatur,[90] contra : Propter impositionem tibi factam concessisti vel dubitasti[91] impertinens significans principaliter[92] aliter quam est. Igitur, male respondisti. Antecedens probo : Nam haec propositio « 'Deum esse' est verum » est impertinens impositioni tibi factae,[93] et illa significat aliter quam est. Quod patet, quia significat quod 'deum esse' est verum, ex quo sequitur quod 'deum esse' est propositio, quod non est possibile. Ergo, male. Si negatur,[94] contra : Negasti sequens[95] ex impositione tibi[96] facta. Ergo, male respondisti.[97] Nam sequitur : «'Deum esse' est[98] necessarium;

(74) eo *V*. (75) *Om.* oratio *V*. (76) sicut *V*. (77) *Add.* sicut *V*.
(78) necessarium... contingens/ vel contingens vel impossibile vel necessarium *V*.
(79) *Om.* omnino *V*. (80) 'homo... praecise/ 'Homo est asinus' *V*.
(81) *Add.* principaliter *V*. (82) *Add.* docet *V*. (83) principaliter *V*.
(84) *Om.* Deus est *V*.
(85) Similis... responsio/ et his similes. Et hujusmodi ut in prioribus dictum est deinde est responsio *V*.
(86) Cf. par. 38. (87) divisionis... sit/ soluit poni *V*. (88) *Om.* quaelibet *V*.
(89) principaliter *V*. (90) *Add.* vel negatur *V*. (91) *Om.* vel dubitasti *V*.
(92) *Om.* principaliter *V*.
(93) impositioni... factae/ positioni *V*. Contrast par. 34. The difference is to be accounted for by the fact that 'Homo est asinus' there, unlike 'deum esse' here, is a proposition. Other authors sometimes use the accusative-infinitive construction (called a *dictum*) to stand in material supposition for the corresponding proposition. (Thus cf. William of Ockham, *Summa logicae* I, ca. 67, lines 23-33 ["Opera philosophica, vol. 1"; St. Bonaventure, N. Y.: The Franciscan Institute, 1974]; and Walter Burleigh, *De puritate artis logicae tractatus longior, with a Revised Edition of the Tractatus brevior*, Philotheus Boehner, ed., ["Franciscan Institute Publications," Text Series, no. 9; St. Bonaventure N. Y. The Franciscan Institute, 1955], p. 3 lines 31-32 and p. 4 lines 16-28.) Roger is in effect ruling out this usage. The *dictum* here is used to stand in material supposition for itself.
(94) *Add.* « 'Deum esse' est verum » *V*. (95) necessarium *V*. (96) *Om.* tibi *V*.
(97) *Om.* respondisti *V*. (98) *Om* est *V**.

igitur, 'deum esse' est verum. Et antecedens sequitur ex impositione. Nam sequitur : 'Deum esse' significat quod deus est. Et aliqua propositio necessaria sic significat et naturaliter.[99] Et 'deum esse'[1] convertitur cum propositione necessaria.[2] Igitur, 'deum esse' est necessarium.

(57) Solutio : Negatur quod 'deum esse' est verum.[3] Et negatur quod 'deum esse' est necessarium. Et negatur consequentia : « 'Deum esse' significat sicut[4] propositio necessaria significat ; igitur,[5] convertitur cum propositione necessaria » quia nihil[6] convertitur cum propositione necessaria[7] nisi propositio. Sed 'deum esse' non est propositio eo quod est oratio infinitiva, et nulla oratio est propositio nisi indicativa oratio.[8]

(58) (*V*153rb) De ultimo membro divisionis,[9] videlicet, de impositione orationis congruae[10] quae est propositio, sit[11] hoc sophisma : Imponitur quod quaelibet talis oratio[12] 'Deus est' significet praecise[13] quod homo est asinus, et hoc bene scitis, et[14] quod quaelibet talis oratio 'Homo est asinus'[15] praecise sic significet. Deinde proponitur 'Deus est'. Si negatur vel dubitatur, contra : Nulla impositione tibi facta, ipsa foret a te concedenda. Sed propter impositionem propositionis ad significandum non est ad illam varianda responsio.[16] Ergo, adhuc est a te concedenda. Si[17] conceditur, contra : Tu concessisti impossibile infra tempus obligationis facta impositione[18] possibili. Ergo, male respondisti.[19] Ad idem, hoc 'Homo est asinus' est a te neganda. Et illa 'Deus est' convertitur cum illa 'Homo est asinus'[20], et hoc bene scias. Igitur, et illa 'Deus est' est a te neganda.

(59) Solutio : Conceditur 'Deus est'[21]. Et negatur quod tu[22] concessisti impossibile.

(60) Contra : Tu concessisti 'Deus est'. Et illa[23] est impossibilis. Igitur, concessisti impossibile.

(61) Solutio[24] : Conceditur consequentia et negatur antecedens quia est una[25] copulativa falsa et[26] impertinens quae significat aliter quam est.

(99) *Om.* et naturaliter *V*. (1) *Add.* est verum *V**.
(2) Et... necessaria/ ergo, hoc 'deum esse' sic significat sicut propositio necessaria significat. Et ultra *V*.
(3) *Add.* Et negatur « 'Deum esse' est propositio. » *V*.
(4) *Add.* sicut *V**. (5) ergo, et cetera. Et negatur quod 'deum esse' *V*.
(6) vel *V**. (7) *Om.* cum... necessaria *V*.
(8) est oratio... oratio/ non est oratio de verbo finito sed infinito *V*.
(9) Cf par. 38. (10) complexae *V*. (11) solvitur *V*. (12) propositio *V*.
(13) idem *V*. (14) hoc... et/ tamen scias *V*.
(15) oratio... asinus'/ 'Deus est' *V*.
(16) By supposition 8 (2nd form), par. 21. (17) *Om* Si... Si *V**.
(18) Tu... impositione/ Impossibile infra tempus obligationis concessisti impositione tibi facta *V*.
(19) *V* lacks the remainder of par. 58.
(20) 'Homo est asinus'/ 'Homo est *a*' *V**. (21) *Add.* est impossibile *V*.
(22) quod tu/ ergo *V*. (23) hoc 'Deus est' *V*. (24) *Om.* Solutio *V*.
(25) *Om.* una *V*. (26) *Om.* falsa et *V*.

Ad aliam formam[27] conceditur hoc « 'Homo est asinus' est neganda ». Et conceditur quod 'Deus est' convertitur cum illa et hoc bene scio. Et negatur consequentia : « igitur, illa est a te neganda ».[28] Et haec de impositione sufficiant.[29]

IV

(62) Positio est obligatio mediante qua quis obligatus[30] tenetur affirmative[31] respondere ad positum.[32] Regulae positionis[33] (V*3va) sunt quattuor. Prima[34] : Omne positum sine obligatione ad hoc pertinente non repugnans positioni in tempore positionis[35] est concedendum.[36] Exemplum : Si ponitur quod homo currit,[37] haec propositio 'Homo currit' est concedenda quandocumque proponitur[38] in tempore positionis.[39]

(63) Circa illam regulam est notandum quod positum sine obligatione ad hoc pertinente est tale quod fatendum est fore positum ubi non obligatur quod illud sit positum,[40] sicut est in exemplo regulae. Si tamen obligatur quod haec sit posita 'Homo currit', non foret illa concedenda propter obligationem, sed respondendum foret ad illam sicut ad impertinens.[41]

(64) Ulterius sciendum pro regula quod positum non repugnans positioni est ex quo non sequitur oppositum positionis sicut est in exemplo regulae. Si tamen positum repugnat positioni respondendum est ad illud sicut ad impertinens. Exemplum : Si ponitur 'Nihil est tibi positum' respondendum est ad illam sicut ad impertinens[42] quia repugnat positioni. Nam ex obligato sequitur oppositum obligationis seu positionis.[43]

(27) aliam formam/ secundam *V*. Cf. the end of par. 58 (« Ad idem. »).

(28) Because of the first part of conclusion 2, par. 32. The conclusion does not follow from the conceded conjuncts alone, although it would presumably follow from their conjunction.

(29) conceditur... sufficiant/ cum dicitur « Ista 'Deus est' est impossibilis ; et bene scis illud ; ergo, est a te neganda » negatur consequentia et cetera. *V*.

(30) *Om.* obligatus *V*. (31) *Add.* vel negative *V*. (32) propositum *V*.

(33) in hac specie obligationis principaliter subjungendae *V*.

(34) *Add.* regula est haec *V*. (35) obligationis *V*.

(36) a te admittendum *V*. *Add. interl.* vel concedendum *V*.

(37) *Om.* quod... currit *V*.

(38) quandocumque proponitur/ pro tunc homo currit *V*.

(39) obligationis *V*. *V* lacks pars. 63-66.

(40) Cf. n. 27 to par. 25. A better wording would have been « ubi non sequitur ex obligato quod illud sit positum ».

(41) For then the *positio* would be a metalinguistic one, from which the object-linguistic 'Homo currit' does not follow. Cf. n. 20 to par. 21. Not every metalinguistic *positio* is an *impositio*.

(42) I.e., it is *dubitanda*. Cf. par. 92.

(43) The same example is used in pars. 28, 91-92.

(65) Contra illam regulam obicitur sic : Ponatur quod 'Omnis homo est asinus' sit positum sine obligatione ad hoc pertinente non repugnans positioni. Tunc juxta illam regulam illa 'Homo est asinus' foret concedenda.[44]

(66) Solutio : Negatur 'Homo est asinus'. Et negatur quod illa est posita sine obligatione ad hoc pertinente non repugnans positioni quia in hac specie obligationis positum repugnat positioni, quod manifeste patet. Nam est obligatio pertinens ad hoc quod 'Homo est asinus' sit posita. Igitur, non ponitur quod 'Homo est asinus' sit positum sine obligatione ad hoc pertinente et cetera, quod est oppositum positionis. Et quandocumque ita est respondendum est ad positum sicut ad impertinens.

(67) Secunda regula : Omne sequens ex posito sine obligatione ad hoc pertinente non repugnans positioni in tempore obligationis[45] est concedendum. Exemplum : Si ponatur haec 'Omnis homo currit', deinde proponitur haec 'Omnis homo movetur'. Est concedenda quia sequitur ex posito sine obligatione[46] ad hoc pertinente.

(68) Tertia regula : Omne repugnans posito sine obligatione ad hoc pertinente non repugnans[47] positioni in tempore positionis[48] est negandum.[49] Exemplum : Si in exemplo proximae[50] regulae proponitur illa 'Aliquis[51] homo sedet' neganda est quia repugnat posito.

(69) Quarta regula : Ad impertinens[52] sine obligatione ad hoc pertinente velut[53] per illud quod[54] principaliter concipitur[55] respondendum est.[56] Exemplum : Si ponatur 'Omnis homo sedet', et postea[57] proponitur ista 'Rex sedet', dubitanda est quia principaliter[58] per illam concipitur quod rex sedet. Et dubium est an rex sedeat an non.[59] Et ista est impertinens et cetera.[60]

(44) In violation of suppositions 7 and 8 (1st form), par. 19-20.
(45) positionis *V*. (46) positio... obligatione/ positione *V**.
(47) repugnante *V**. (48) *Om.* non... positionis *V*.
(49) *Add.* in tempore obligationis *V*.
(50) primae *V**. (Emend for sense. See also *V* in n. 51 immediately below.)
(51) Si... 'Aliquis/ Exemplo proximo posito manifeste si proponatur 'Omnis *V*.
(52) Ad impertinens/ Impertinenti posito *V*. (53) respondendum est sicut *V*.
(54) *Om.* quod *V*. (55) *Add.* significare *V*. (56) *Om.* respondendum est *V*.
(57) et postea/ deinde *V*. (58) *Om.* principaliter *V*. (59) *Om.* Et... non *V*.
(60) *Om.* et cetera *V*. *V* lacks par. 70-71. Note how these four rules for *positio* are virtual duplicates of the four for *impositio*, par. 33-36. This illustrates my claim that *impositio* is a metalinguistic *positio*. Cf. n. 20 to par. 21. Perhaps because of this, † authors such as Peter of Ailly (*Tractatus de arte obligandi*, [Paris: Georg Mittelhus, 1489. *Incunabula in American Libraries*, 3rd census, A-484. Copy at Walters Art Gallery, Baltimore], f. 6rb), Paul of Venice (Angelelli, *op. cit.*, p. 803), and Paul of Pergula (*Logica*, tract. 5, *ed. cit.*, p. 102, lines 9-11) do not treat *impositio* as a separate species of *obligatio*.

(70) Contra : Ponatur quod 'Homo est asinus' sit impertinens sine obligatione ad hoc pertinente significans (*V**3vb) sicut est. Tunc per illam regulam sequitur quod illa 'Homo est asinus' foret concedenda.

(71) Solutio : Negatur quod homo est asinus. Et negatur quod illa est concedenda. Et negatur quod illa est impertinens significans sicut est sine obligatione ad hoc pertinente eo quod obligatur quod illa sit impertinens. Ideo respondendum est infra tempus obligationis ad illam sicut extra. Consequentia patet per dicta in quarta definitione.

(72) Positis regulis videndum est quibus signis et per quas propositiones et qualiter in hac specie obligationis contingit obligare et quando et per quantum tempus respondens erit obligatus. Pro primo est sciendum quod mediantibus istis signis 'pono' vel 'ponitur', 'suppono' vel 'supponitur' contingit hic obligare.[61]

(73) Pro secundo est sciendum quod[62] omnis propositio[63] ad quam extra tempus obligationis per mutationem ex parte rei est varianda responsio et nulla alia est hic obliganda.[64]

(74) Pro tertio est notandum quod in hac specie obligationis [obligare] contingit sic obligare : « Pono » vel « Ponitur » quod omnis homo sit Romae » vel « quod omnis <homo> currit, » et sic de singulis.[65]

(75) Pro quarto et quinto conjunctim est sciendum[66] quod dicto aliquo illorum signorum[67] cum obligato,[68] si respondens assentiat statim obligatur,[69] et aliquo tempore[70] quousque[71] dicatur illa oratio[72] 'Cedat tempus obligationis' continue erit respondens[73] obligatus. Et dicta illa oratione 'Cedat tempus obligationis' non est respondens obligatus amplius. Sed tunc rei veritas fatenda est.[74]

(76) (*V*153va) Istis praemissis pro processu in hac specie obligationis est haec divisio[75] : Omnis positio est simplex vel composita. Positio simplex est quando tantum[76] catogorica ponitur. Et illa est duplex : Quaedam est

(61) Positis... obligare/ Obligandum est alicui per ista signa in hac specie obligationis : 'pono', 'suppono', 'ponatur' et 'supponatur'. *V*.

(62) *Om.* Pro... quod *V*. (63) *Add.* et solum talis est hic obliganda *V*.

(64) *Om.* et... obliganda *V*. Cf. supposition 6, par. 18.

(65) Pro... singulis/ ut « Pono quod omnis homo sit Romae. » *V*.

(66) Pro... sciendum/ Et nota *V*.

(67) *Add.* 'impono', 'suppono', 'ponatur', et 'supponatur' *V*.

(68) *Add.* sequente *V*. (69) erit obligatus *V*. (70) *Om.* et... tempore *V*.

(71) *Add.* non *V**. (72) dicatur illa oratio/ dicat *V*. (73) *Om.* respondens *V*

(74) Et... est/ nisi conveniat ad invicem disputantes inter se *V*. *Add.* Istis praemissis pro et cetera *V**. (Cf. par. 76.) The discussion of *impositio*, above, contains no corresponding rule governing the duration of the *obligatio* (cf. par. 37), but presumably the rule in this par. will apply there as well. It certainly applies to *depositio* (cf. par. 130), and is perhaps covered by the very general remarks in par. 129.

(75) Istis... divisio/ His habitis prosequendum est illam divisionem quae est *V*.

(76) aliqua *V*.

ubi positum[77] repugnat positioni, quaedam ubi positum[78] non repugnat.[79] Et illa est duplex : Quaedam ex cujus obligato non[80] sequitur aliquid fore positum, quaedam ex cujus obligato[81] sequitur aliquid fore positum.

(77) Positio composita est quando hypothetica ponitur. Et illa est triplex secundum tres species hypotheticae. Prima, quando copulativa ponitur. Secunda, quando disjunctiva ponitur. Tertia, quando ponitur temporalis.[82] Et quaelibet[83] illarum est multiplex, ut dicetur in sequentibus.[84]

(78) Et secundum membra hujus divisionis singulatim sophismata proponuntur. Et primo de positione simplici, deinde de positione composita.

(79) Sed videtur quod haec divisio sit insufficiens quoad secundum partem ejus, cum aliquas species hypotheticae assignet et aliquas non, sicut causalis et conditionalis.

(80) Solutio : Hoc non obstante quod non assumat omnes species hypotheticae, haec est divisio sufficiens. Pro quo sciendum[85] quod in hac divisione solum[86] assumuntur[87] species hypotheticae ponibiles[88] et deponibiles. Et species dimissae nec sunt ponibiles (*V**4ra) nec deponibiles, quod ex septima suppositione satis patet, eo quod nec ad conditionalem nec ad causalem est mutanda responsio propter mutationem ex parte rei et extra tempus obligationis. Sed ad copulativam et alias est mutanda responsio extra tempus obligationis propter mutationem ex parte rei. Igitur, illae sunt ponibiles et deponibiles, sicut per sextam <et> septimam suppositionem.[89]

(81) Istis visis redeo ad propositum, Et primo[90] de positione[91] simplici in qua positum non repugnat positioni. Et sit[92] hoc sophisma : Ponatur

(77) ubi positum/ simplex positio quae *V*.
(78) ubi positum/ quae *V*. (79) *Add.* positioni *V*.
(80) ex... non/ est ex qua extra tempus obligationis *V*.
(81) ex... obligato/ est ex qua extra tempus obligationis non *V*.
(82) *Om.* Tertia... temporalis *V**. Roger treats temporals like copulatives. Cf., e.g., pars. 93, 95. Cf. also my "Robert Fland's *Consequentiae*: An Edition", par. 20, and contrast Ockham's fuller and more adequate analysis in his *Summa logicae* II, ca. 35 ("Opera philosophica, vol. 1"; St. Bonaventure, N. Y.: The Franciscan Institute, 1974).
(83) quilibet *V**.
(84) *V* lacks pars. 78-79. (85) Solutio... sciendum/ Et nota *V*.
(86) semper V. (87) accipiuntur *V*. (88) principales *V*.
(89) suppositiones *V**. Et species... suppositionem/ propositiones. In positione autem specierum admissarum non sunt principales ut deponibiles propositiones ut potest haberi ex tertia suppositione. Ergo, divisum est sufficienter. *V*.
(90) Istis... primo/ De partibus illius divisionis nunc ponenda sunt sophismata per ordinem *V*.
(91) *Add.* autem *V*. (92) Et sit/ solvitur *V*.

quod *a* sit altera illarum 'Deus est' vel 'Homo est asinus',[93] et lateat te quae illarum sit *a*. Deinde ponatur[94] quod *a* est verum. Si conceditur vel dubitatur,[95] contra : Illa est impertinens ad quam extra tempus obligationis non est responsio varianda. Igitur, ad illam est respondendum infra[96] sicut extra. Consequentia[97] patet per dicta in quarta divisione.[98] Sed extra foret neganda. Igitur, et infra.[99] Si negatur '*a* est verum',[1] proponitur illa '*a* est falsum'. Si conceditur vel dubitatur, contra[2] arguitur sicut prius. Si negatur illa,[3] cedat tempus obligationis[4] et arguitur sic : *a* est verum vel *a* est falsum. Sed *a* non est verum. Igitur, *a* est falsum. Major sequitur ex posito. Et minor est concessa. Igitur, conclusio est concedenda. Et illam negasti. Igitur, male.

(82) Aliter arguitur contra responsionem qua negatur[5] quod *a* est verum. Arguitur : *a* est illa 'Deus est'. Igitur, *a* est verum.[6] Illa consequentia bona. Et antecedens est tibi dubium. Igitur, consequens non est a te negandum.

(83) Solutio : Admittatur casus et neganda est haec '*a* est verum' et haec similiter '*a* est falsum'. Et ad primam formam in oppositum[7] concedenda est[8] consequentia et negandum est antecedens. Nam antecedens est una copulativa impertinens posito[9] scita principaliter significare aliter quam est. Ideo est negandum. Consequentia patet per propositionem undecimam[10] et conclusionem[11] primam. Et tamen utraque ejus[12] pars[13] est concedenda. Prima, quia sequens[14] ex posito. Secunda, quia impertinens significans principaliter[15] sicut est. Et ex hoc non sequitur copulativam[16] fore concedendam,[17] sicut patet per conclusionem secundam.

(93) 'Deus...asinus'/ 'Homo est asinus' et 'Deus est' *V*. (94) proponatur *V*. (95) *Add.* vel negetur *V*. (96) *Om.* infra *V*. (97) *Om.* Consequentia *V*. (98) dicta... divisione/ divisionem quartam *V*.
(99) nunc ipsa est neganda *V*.
(1) '*a* est verum'/ ergo, *a* est falsum. Si conceditur vel dubitatur, contra *(Si... contra, perhaps deleted)* : Deinde *V*.
(2) tu *V**. (3) *Add.* scilicet, '*a* est falsum', dicatur *V*.
(4) Cf. par. 75. The terminating of the *obligatio* is appropriate here, since the argument which follows switches to the metalanguage for a discussion of the *obligatio* (« Major sequitur ex posito », etc.). Cf. the similar situation in par. 93. Roger does not, however, *always* signal these switches with « Cedat tempus obligationis ». Cf., *e.g.*, the argument earlier in this paragraph.
(5) responsionem... negatur/ respondentem qui negat *V*.
(6) *Om.* Arguitur... verum *V*. (7) Cf. the end of par. 81 (« Si negatur illa. »).
(8) concedenda est/ est dicendum quod conceditur *V*. (9) *Om.* posito *V*.
(10) propositionem undecimam/ suppositionem tertiam *(tertiam, perhaps deleted)* sextam *V*. Supposition 6 in the *V* tradition is supposition 10 in the *V** text, par. 25. This supposition is irrelevant in the present context. What is wanted is supposition 7 (11 in the *V** text), par. 29.
(11) *Add.* et conclusionem *V**. (12) *Om.* ejus *V*.
(13) *Add.* illius copulativae *V*. (14) quia sequens/ patet *V*.
(15) *Om.* principaliter *V*. (16) copulativa *V**. (17) concedenda *V**.

(84) Ad aliam[18] formam[19] negatur illa consequentia : « *a* est illa 'Deus est' ; igitur, *a* est verum, » et antecedens similiter. Consequentia non valet, quia *a* potest esse 'Deus est' et tamen[20] 'Deus est' sit falsum.[21] Et antecedens est negandum, quia impertinens falsum[22] significans principaliter[23] aliter quam est.[24]

(85) Contra : Antecedens est dubium. Et tu negasti. Igitur, male.

(86) Solutio : Negatur consequentia. Sed oportet addere quod antecedens[25] sit mihi dubium sine obligatione ad hoc pertinente. Et illud est negandum.[26] Si tamen ponatur quod antecedens sit mihi dubium sine obligatione ad hoc pertinente, dicendum quod obligatio ibi obligat aliquid obligari. Et ideo respondendum est ad obligatum sicut ad impertinens, ut dicitur in declaratione primae regulae hujus particulae.[27]

(87) Contra positum (*V**4rb) in se sic arguitur : Positum est una propositio ad quam extra tempus obligationis non est varianda responsio. Igitur, talis propositio nec est ponenda nec deponenda. Consequentia patet per septimam suppositionem.[28]

(88) Solutio : Prima suppositio[29] verificatur de propositionibus quibus concessis forent multa inconvenientia concedenda. Sed illo casu admisso non oportet inopinabile, nec inconveniens magis posito est concedenda.

(89) (*V*153vb) De positione simplici in qua positum non repugnat positioni ex cujus posito sequitur aliquid fore positum[30] sit[31] hoc sophis-

(18) secundam *V*. (19) Cf. par. 82. (20) *Add.* quod *V**.

(21) *Add.* et hoc per impositionem propositionis ad significandum *V*.

(22) impertinens falsum/ est *V*. (23) *Om.* principaliter *V*.

(24) *V* lacks pars. 85-88.

(25) I.e., « *a* est illa 'Deus est' », the antecedent of the consequence in pars. 82 and 84, not of the consequence in par. 85.

(26) From the *positio* in par. 81, it follows that « *a* est illa 'Deus est' » is doubtful, and so the *obligatio* is indeed « ad hoc pertinens ».

(27) Cf. par. 64, and the example in par. 66. The last part of this par. (from « Si tamen ») is unclear. Is the *positio* here meant to be added to that in par. 81, so that both *positiones* are in force at once? In any case, why does « obligatio ibi obligat aliquid obligari » ?

(28) septimam suppositionem *abbreviation uncertain in V**. *Perhaps read* aliam superiorem.

(29) The *prima suppositio*, par. 13, is irrelevant. Better perhaps is the 3rd *suppositio*, par. 15, which is the 1st in the *V* tradition, and which is implicitly used in the argument for *suppositio* 7 (the basis for par. 87). Cf. n. 10 to par. 19. Note, however, that *V* lacks the 7th *suppositio*, par. 19, as well as pars. 85-88. In any case, the argument in par. 88, in order to be a « solutio » to par. 87, must bear on the 7th supposition. Note the form of this « solutio ». It does not deny that the consequence in par. 87 is governed by *suppositio* 7. Rather, the *rationale* for *suppositio* 7 (given implicitly in terms of *suppositio* 3 in par. 19) does not bear on this case. But this means that the 7th supposition is too strongly worded to be justified by the reason given in par. 19. Cf. the difficulties mentioned above in n. 10 to par. 19.

(30) Cf. par. 76. (31) solvitur *V*.

ma : Ponatur[32] quod 'Tu curris' sit tibi[33] positum. Deinde proponitur 'Tu curris'. Si negatur vel dubitatur, contra : 'Tu curris' est tibi positum.[34] Igitur, 'Tu curris' est concedendum.[35] Si conceditur, contra : Eadem ratione haec[36] foret concedenda[37] 'Homo est asinus' si ponatur[38] quod illa est positum.[39]

(90) Solutio : Negatur quod tu curris. Et conceditur quod illa est tibi posita. Et non[40] sequitur : Igitur, est a te[41] concedenda. Sed oporteret addere quod illa foret posita sine obligatione ad hoc pertinente.[42] Et si illud additur, illud est negandum.

(91) De positioni simplici in qua positum repugnat positioni[43] sit[44] hoc sophisma[45] : Nihil est tibi positum. Deinde proponitur illa 'Nihil est tibi positum'. Si negatur vel dubitatur, contra : Tu negasti tibi[46] positum in tempore positionis.[47] Ergo, male respondisti. Si conceditur, contra : Positum repugnat positioni.[48] Igitur, respondendum est ad positum sicut ad[49] impertinens.[50] Consequentia[51] patet per improbationem decimae suppositionis.[52]

(92) Solutio : Dubitanda est illa 'Nihil est tibi positum' eo quod sic[53] foret respondendum ad illam sine obligatione. Et concedendum est quod tu negasti[54] dubium positum[55] in tempore positionis. Et non sequitur : Ideo male respondisti. Sed oportet addere[56] quod sit positum[57] dubium scitum a me fore dubium[58] positum sine obligatione ad hoc pertinente non repugnans positioni. Et si illud additur,[59] est negandum.

(93) Sequitur[60] de positione composita.[61] Et primo de copulativa vel

(32) *Om.* Ponatur *V.* (33) *Om.* tibi *V.*
(34) *Om.* Deinde... positum *V.* (35) *Add.* si proponatur *V.*
(36) quae (?) *V**. *Om.* haec *V.* (37) *Add.* ista *V.* (38) proponatur *V.*
(39) posita. Sed haec est neganda. Ergo, et cetera. Si negatur vel dubitatur, contra : 'Tu curris' est tibi positum. Ergo, 'Tu curris' est a te concedendum. *V.*
(40) tamen *V**. (41) *Om.* a te *V.*
(42) sine... pertinente/ secundum obligationem ad hoc pertinentem non repugnans positioni *V.*
(43) Cf. par. 76. (44) solvitur *V.*
(45) *Add.* Ponatur quod *V.* This sophism is discussed also in pars. 28 and 64.
(46) *Om.* tibi *V.* (47) obligationis *V.*
(48) positum... positioni/ cedat tempus obligationis. Hoc est repugnans obligationi *V.*
(49) ad... ad/ ac si foret *V.*
(50) *Add.* Sed si sic foret esset neganda *V.*
(51) *Om.* Consequentia *V.*
(52) improbationem... suppositionis/ dictas suppositiones *V.* Cf. par. 28.
(53) sicut *V.*
(54) The argument in this par. is obscure. The *dubium positum* has not been denied at all, but rather doubted.
(55) tu... positum/ dubitatio ponitur *V.* (56) *Om.* addere *V.*
(57) *Om.* positum *V.* (58) fore dubium/ extra *V.* (59) si... addatur/ tunc *V.*
(60) *Om.* sequitur *V.* (61) *Add.* modo sequitur. Et solvitur hoc sophisma *V.*

temporali. Si ponitur copulativa, hoc potest esse dupliciter : vel quod illa ponatur absolute vel sub conditione. Et similiter de temporali. De copulativa posita absolute sit illud sophisma[62] : Ponatur haec 'Omnis homo currit[63] et nulla obligatio tibi fit'. Deinde proponitur 'Omnis homo currit'. Se negatur vel dubitatur, dicitur 'Cedat tempus obligationis'[64] et arguitur sic[65] : Illa est tibi posita.[66] Igitur, illa est a te concedenda. Si conceditur, contra : Hoc obligatum repugnat positioni.[67] Igitur, ad positum respondendum est sicut ad impertinens. Consequentia patet ex praedictis. Et per consequens haec 'Omnis homo currit'[68] non est concedenda.

(94) Solutio : Negatur illa 'Omnis homo currit'. Et conceditur quod positum negatur. Et non sequitur : « ideo[69] male respondetur », quia positum repugnat positioni.

(95) (*V**4va) Ulterius est notandum pro copulativis quod si ponitur aliqua copulativa et sit admissa, utraque pars ejus est concedenda. Exemplum : Si ponitur illa copulativa 'Omnis homo currit et tu es homo', concedenda est illa copulativa cum utraque ejus parte.[70] Et consimiliter[71] de temporali, ut si ponitur illa temporalis : 'Dum omnis homo sedet, rex sedet', illa est concedenda et utraque ejus pars.[72]

(96) Si autem ponitur disjunctiva hoc potest esse dupliciter : vel sic quod nulla pars sequitur ad disjunctivam vel sic quod ponitur disjunctiva cujus altera pars vel utraque pars[73] sequitur ad disjunctivam.[74] Si ponitur disjunctiva cujus nulla pars sequitur ad disjunctivam,[75] concedenda est disjunctiva et respondendum est ad utramque partem sicut ad[76] impertinens.[77] Exemplum : Si ponitur illa disjunctiva[78] 'Omnis homo currit vel tu sedes', tunc illa disjunctiva est concedenda et prima pars est neganda quia impertinens et significans aliter quam est. Secunda[79] concedenda quia impertinens significans[80] sicut est. Si autem ponitur disjunctiva cujus utraque pars sequitur ad disjunctivam,[81] quaelibet[82] pars[83] est concedenda. Exemplum : Si ponatur haec disjunctiva[84] 'Sortes est movens

(62) *Om.* Et primo... sophisma *V.*
(63) *Add.* Si negatur vel dubitatur, contra : Haec est tibi posita *V.*
(64) Cf. n. 4 to par. 81. (65) dicitur... sic/ contra *V.* (66) ponitur *V**.
(67) obligationi *V.*
(68) Igitur... currit'/ Ergo, illud obligatum est negandum si foret pertinens. Ergo *V.*
(69) ergo, tu *V. Abbrev. uncertain in V*.* (70) *Om.* Ulterius... parte *V.*
(71) *Add.* fiat *V.* (72) *Om.* ut... pars *V.* (73) *Interl.* vel... pars *V**.
(74) Si... disjunctivam/ De disjunctiva vero *V.* (75) aliam *V.*
(76) concedenda... ad/ illa est concedenda. Et ad utra<m>que partem respondendum est ac si foret *V.*
(77) *Add.* significans aliter quam est. Et ista disjunctiva proposita est concedenda quia impertinens significans sicut est. Si autem ponatur disjunctiva cujus quaelibet pars est sequens ad aliam, quaelibet ejus pars est concedenda *V.*
(78) *Om.* illa disjunctiva *V.* (79) *Add.* pars est *V.*
(80) impertinens significans/ significat *V.* (81) illam *V.* (82) *Add.* ejus *V.*
(83) *Add.* sequitur *V**. (84) *Om.* haec disjunctiva *V.*

vel Sortes non[85] est quiescens' hujus utraque pars est concedenda quia utraque pars sequitur ad disjunctivam.[86]

(97) De disjunctiva cujus altera pars sequitur ad disjunctivam sit hoc exemplum : Ponatur quod omnis homo currit vel omnis homo movetur. Tunc illa pars 'Omnis homo movetur' est concedenda quia sequens disjunctivam. Patet : Prima pars est neganda quia impertinens significans aliter quam est.[87]

(98) Sed adhuc est dubium de disjunctiva ad cujus utramque partem varianda est responsio extra tempus obligationis propter mutationem ex parte rei. Sit igitur hoc sophisma : Ponitur illa disjunctiva 'Tu es Romae vel tu curris'. Deinde proponitur illa : 'Tu es Romae'. Si negatur,[88] proponitur illa 'Tu curris'. Si negatur,[89] proponitur ejus contradictorium, videlicet, 'Tu non curris'. Haec est concedenda quia ejus oppositum negatur.[90] Qua concessa, ponitur illa.[91] Et proponitur illa 'Tu es Romae'. Si conceditur, cedat tempus obligationis. Idem concessisti et negasti infra tempus obligationis. Igitur, male respondisti eo quod non est mutatio facta ex parte rei.[92] Si negatur, cedat tempus obligationis. Illa sequitur ex posito.[93] Igitur, concedenda. Quia sequitur 'Tu es Romae vel tu curris ; sed tu non curris ; igitur, tu es Romae'. Illa consequentia est bona et utraque pars est posita.[94] Igitur, conclusio concedenda.

(85) *Om.* non *V.* (86) *Om.* hujus... disjunctivam *V.*

(87) De... est/ Deinde si ponatur disjunctiva cujus alia pars solum ad illam sequitur, pars sequens est concedenda. Et alia potest negatur *(sic)* quia est impertinens significans aliter quam est. Exemplum : Si ponatur 'Omnis homo currit vel omnis homo movetur', haec est neganda 'Omnis homo <currit>' eo quod ipsa est impertinens et cetera. Alia autem est concedenda sed falsa *V. V* lacks par. 98-104.

(88) It presumably cannot be conceded, since it is *impertinens* and false.

(89) This presumably cannot be conceded, for the same reason. Note that the previous denial of 'Tu es Romae' does not affect the proper reply to 'Tu curris'. One is bound only by the *obligatum*, not by the *obligatum* together with subsequently conceded or denied propositions (but cf. below, n. 90 to par. 98 and n. 98 to par. 101). Robert Fland takes this as another characteristic of the "new" school of thought on *obligationes* (cf. my forthcoming edition of Fland's *Obligationes*, cited above in n. 3 to the introduction, and also n. 60 to par. 32).

(90) "Proposing" a proposition *(proponatur)* is not the same as "positing" it *(ponatur)*. Hence one's replies to proposed propositions do not add to the *positio* by which one is *obligatus*. Cf. n. 89 to par. 98, above. Nevertheless, one is bound by one's replies to proposed propositions to this extent at least, that one must concede a proposition whose (contradictory, and perhaps subcontrary) "opposite" one has already denied, and presumably also to the extent that one must deny a proposition whose (contradictory, and perhaps contrary) "opposite" one has already conceded. But cf. n. 98 to par. 101.

(91) This is a new *positio*, added to that set out earlier in the paragraph. One is now bound by both *positiones*.

(92) Note the « eo... rei » clause. Cf. note 98 to par. 101.

(93) I.e., from the new, combined *positum*. Cf. n. 91 to par. 98, above.

(94) I.e., both parts of the antecedent. Since both parts are *posita*, and not just *concessa*, a reply like that in par. 83 is ruled out. Cf. also n. 5 to par. 102, below.

(99) Solutio : Admittatur disjunctiva et utraque ejus pars per se est neganda. Et concedendum est contradictorium secundae partis. Et quando ponitur illa debet admitti, et cum postea proponitur prima pars quae negatur ante positionem contradictorii secundae partis, (V^*4vb) tunc debet concedi quia tunc erit sequens ex positis et prius nec sequebat ex posito nec ex positis.

(100) Contra illam responsionem arguitur sic : Nulla repugnantia sunt concedenda infra tempus obligationis. Sed illa responsio concedit repugnantia infra tempus obligationis. Igitur, male. Minor probatur : Si ponitur prima,[95] tunc ista est concedenda infra tempus obligationis. Et si[96] postea proponitur 'Tu non es Romae' illa est concedenda infra tempus obligationis. Et si post proponatur 'Tu non curris' ista est concedenda simpliciter secundum illam responsionem. Et ista tria repugnant manifeste.

(101) Solutio : Concedenda est conclusio quod tria repugnantia sunt concedenda et quattuor et sic deinceps. Et duo contradictoria similiter sunt concedenda propter mutationem rei ut si illa 'Tu es Romae' poneretur,[97] et postea proponatur 'Tu sedes', illa est concedenda. Si postea durante tempore obligationis tu stares, et tibi proponeretur illa 'Tu non sedes', illa foret concedenda. Et sic contradictoria infra tempus obligationis forent concedenda. Et hoc est verum dum tamen nullum contradictorium repugnans posito concedatur infra tempus obligationis.[98]

(95) I.e., the disjunction 'Tu es Romae vel tu curris' of par. 98.

(96) *Interl.* si V^*.

(97) It is not clear whether this is to be a *positio* replacing the one in par. 98, or a *positio* in addition to it, as in the latter part of par. 98. In either case, 'Tu sedes' and 'Tu non sedes' are both to be conceded—at different times—because they are *impertinentes* and true. Perhaps the point of what Robert Fland calls the "new" way (cf. n. 60 to par. 32 and n. 89 to par. 98) is to allow for just this kind of case, to recognize that a *disputatio de obligationibus* is not an instantaneous event, but rather "takes time". This would explain, for instance, the first half of conclusion 2. Suppose a proposition *p* is *impertinens*, and true at one time during the disputation but false at another. Then both *p* and its negation will be *concedenda*—at different times. But at no time will the contradictory conjunction of *p* and its negation be *concedenda*. Cf. the similar reasoning in John Buridan's *Sophismata Buridani*, (Paris: Antoine Denidel and Nicole de la Barre [c. 1496-1500], *Incunabula in American Libraries*, 3rd census, B-1295, copy at Harvard College Library, incunabula 8325.5), ca. 7, translated in Theodore Kermit Scott, *John Buridan: Sophisms on Meaning and Truth*, ("Century Philosophy Sourcebooks"; New York: Appleton-Century-Crofts, 1966), pp. 169-179.

(98) It is not clear how much of this paragraph is meant to be a reply to par. 100. The example of 'Tu sedes' involves a « mutatio rei » which is lacking in par. 100 (and in the original argument in par. 98). Perhaps the most satisfactory reading takes only the first sentence as the reply to par. 100, and the rest of the paragraph as an observation concerning a different kind of case in which *repugnantia* are to be conceded. Note that the example with 'Tu sedes' constitutes an exception to the claim, in n. 90 to par. 98, that one must concede a proposition whose opposite one has already denied. The stipulation should be understood that this is so only where there is « nulla mutatio facta ex parte rei ». Cf. also n. 92 to par. 98.

(102) Sed adhuc est dubium de illa disjunctiva ad cujus unam partem varianda est responsio et ad aliam non. Sit ergo hoc sophisma : Ponitur illa disjunctiva 'Tu es Romae vel homo est asinus'. Deinde proponitur 'Tu es Romae'. Si conceditur, cedat tempus. Illa est impertinens significans aliter quam est. Ergo, est neganda. Antecedens probo. Nam arguitur : A tota positione ad aliquam[99] ejus partem est fallacia consequentis, cum arguendo enim a disjunctiva ad alteram ejus partem sit fallacia consequentis. Si negatur 'Tu es Romae', proponitur illa 'Tu non es Romae'. Haec tunc est concedenda.[1] Qua concessa, ponatur illa cum primo posito.[2] Et postea proponitur illa 'Tu es asinus'.[3] Si negatur,[4] cedat tempus obligationis. Consequentia sequitur ex positis. Igitur, concedenda. Nam sequitur : Tu es Romae vel tu es asinus. Sed tu non es Romae. Igitur, tu es asinus. Nec potest hic negari antecedens tamquam copulativa impertinens falsa eo quod utraque pars est posita.[5]

(103) Solutio : Concedenda est hoc 'Tu es Romae'. Et dicendum quod illa est sequens ex disjunctiva posita. Et in consequentia necessaria, non tamen formali.[6]

(104) Unde sciendum : Quandocumque ponitur disjunctiva ad cujus unam partem est varianda responsio et ad aliam non, concedenda est illa pars ad quam est varianda responsio si proponitur in tempore obligationis tamquam sequens ex posito in consequentia necessaria.[7]

(99) aliam *V**. (1) Cf. n. 90 to par. 98. (2) Cf. n. 91 to par. 98.

(3) Roger seems to have forgotten his example, which had 'Homo est asinus' instead. The difference is important, since 'Homo est asinus' is impossible, while 'Tu es asinus' may or may not be, depending on one's doctrine about pronouns. The remainder of the argument may be read with 'Homo est asinus' understood throughout.

(4) It presumably cannot be conceded, since it is impossible. Cf. n. 3 to par. 102, above.

(5) Cf. n. 94 to par. 98. Note that the explanation of the first half of conclusion 2, given above in n. 97 to par. 101, accounts for this difference. Once admitted, a *positum* is assumed to be so to the end of the disputation. (In this connection, cf. the end of par. 101.) One's reply to it is not affected by a « mutatio rei », unlike one's reply to a *propositio impertinens*. Hence, once two *posita* are both admitted, they are both assumed to be so until the end of the disputation. It follows from such an assumption that their conjunction is so until the end of the disputation. The kind of situation described in n. 97 to par. 101 cannot arise. Note that, according to suppositions 7 and 8 (first form), par. 19-20, an impossible proposition is not *ponenda*. In virtue of these last several paragraphs, this should perhaps be understood in a broader sense: mutually inconsistent propositions may not be jointly posited.

(6) Cf. my "Five Logical Tracts by Richard Lavenham", in J. Reginald O'Donnell, ed., *Essays in Honour of Anton Charles Pegis*, (Toronto: Pontifical Institute of Mediaeval Studies, 1974), pp. 70-124 at pp. 76-81. Roger's remark here suggests that his terminology is closer to that of Buridan and Albert of Saxony than to that of Lavenham and Paul of Pergula.

(7) This in fact only works if the second disjunct is impossible—not, as the paragraph allows, if it is necessary.

(105) (V154ra, V*5ra) Adhuc est dubium de quibusdam copulativis[8] quae contradictiones videntur includere.[9] Sit ergo illud sophisma[10] : Ponatur[11] talis copulativa 'Hoc est homo et hoc est asinus'. Et omne demonstratum per ly 'hoc' est[12] homo. Deinde proponitur illa 'Hoc[13] est asinus'. Si negatur vel dubitatur, cedat tempus.[14] Contra : Illa est[15] pars copulativae positae.[16] Igitur, concedenda.[17] Qua concessa proponitur illa 'Hoc[18] demonstratum est asinus'. Si conceditur proponatur illa 'Asinus est homo'[19]. Si negatur, cedat tempus.[20] Contra : Illud sequitur[21] ex posito. Igitur, concedenda.[22] Assumptum probatur. Nam sequitur : Omne demonstratum est homo[23] ; hoc demonstratum est asinus ; igitur, asinus est homo.[24] Ideo[25] si negatur illa 'Hoc demonstratum est asinus', proponitur illa 'Hoc est homo'.[26] Haec est concedenda. Qua concessa proponitur 'Hoc non est aliud quam hoc demonstratum'. Si conceditur, proponatur illa 'Hoc est hoc demonstratum'. Illud est sequens. Nam sequitur : 'Hoc est hoc ; et hoc[27] non est aliud quam hoc demonstratum[28] ; igitur, hoc est hoc demonstratum'. Si conceditur,[29] tunc sequitur quod hoc demonstra-

(8) *Add.* absolute positis *V*.

(9) This paragraph returns to the discussion of (absolute) copulatives begun in par. 93 and interrupted by the discussion of disjunctives in par. 96-104.

(10) *Om. Sit...* sophisma *V*. (11) *Add.* enim *V*. (12) per... est/ sit *V*.

(13) 'Omnis homo *V*. (14) *Add.* obligationis *V*. (15) *Add.* altera *V*.

(16) posito *V**. (17) Cf. par. 95. (18) 'Omne *V*.

(19) 'Asinus... homo'/ 'Homo est asinus' *V*. (20) *Add.* obligationis *V*.

(21) Contra... sequitur/ Hoc sequebatur *V*. (22) hoc fuit concedendum *V*.

(23) asinus *V*.

(24) Hence 'Asinus est homo' cannot be denied. On the other hand, since it is impossible, it cannot be conceded, in virtue of supposition 3, par. 15. (This presumes, of course, that the *positum* is possible, and therefore less *improbabile* than 'Asinus est homo'. Cf. par. 106.) Hence 'Asinus est homo' can be neither conceded nor denied, once 'Hoc demonstratum est asinus' is conceded. Note however that the conclusion here, 'Asinus est homo', does not follow from the *positum* alone, but from the *positum* together with the conceded 'Hoc demonstratum est asinus'. Cf. n. 89 to par. 98, and n. 30 to par. 105.

(25) hoc... ideo/ ergo, homo est asinus si demonstretur homo. Item *V*.

(26) hoc *V*. The preferred reading is uncertain. 'Hoc est hoc', following *V*, conforms better to the argument in the immediately following lines. On the other hand, par. 106 (the bulk of which is missing in *V*) refers again to 'Hoc est homo'. Moreover, while it is obvious why 'Hoc est homo' should be conceded (cf. par. 95), one might have expected some explanation why 'Hoc est hoc' should be conceded (presumably because it is « sequens ex posito »). The role of the proposition in the argument which follows is to provide an existence-clause, a guarantee that 'hoc' has a referent, so that from 'Hoc non est aliud quam hoc demonstratum' one can infer 'Hoc est hoc demonstratum' (cf. my "Five Logical Tracts by Richard Lavenham", pp. 86-87). For this purpose, 'Hoc est homo', 'Hoc est hoc', or even 'Hoc est', would do equally well.

(27) *Om.* et hoc *V**. (28) *In marg.* demonstratum *V*.

(29) *Add.* proponatur hoc *V*.

tum est asinus,[30] quod prius erat negatum. Ideo[31] si negatur illa 'Hoc non[32] est aliud quam[33] hoc demonstratum', proponitur ejus contradictorium 'Hoc est aliud quam hoc demonstratum'. Tunc sequitur quod hoc demonstratum est.[34] Qua concessa,[35] proponitur 'Hoc demonstratum est asinus'. Si conceditur, contra[36] : Idem conceditur et negatur infra tempus.[37] Igitur, male respondetur.[38] Si negatur illa 'Hoc demonstratum est asinus', cedat tempus.[39] Illa sequitur ex[40] concessis. Nam[41] sequitur : 'Hoc est asinus ; hoc est[42] hoc demonstratum ; igitur, hoc demonstratum est asinus'.[43]

(106) Solutio : Copulativa est possibilis. Et quando ponitur est admittenda. Et conceditur 'Hoc est asinus'. Et negatur 'Hoc demonstratum est asinus'.[44] Et conceditur 'Hoc est homo'[45] et 'Hoc non est aliud quam hoc demonstratum'. Et conceditur quod hoc demonstratum est.[46] Et quando arguitur : « Hoc est asinus ; et hoc est <hoc>[47] demonstratum ; igitur, hoc demonstratum est asinus »,[48] dubitatur consequentia.[49]

(30) Presumably because 'Hoc est asinus' was conceded, and now 'Hoc est hoc demonstratum' is conceded. *Cf.* the end of par. 105. But note that the conclusion does not follow from the *positum* alone—and for that matter, neither does 'Hoc est hoc demonstratum'. *Cf.* n. 89 to par. 98 and n. 24 to par. 105.

(31) Item *V*. (32) *Interl.* non *V*. (33) *In marg.* aliud quam *V*.

(34) *Om.* Tunc... est *V*. The role of this sentence is unclear. It is referred to, however, in par. 106.

(35) Qua concessa/ Quo concesso *V*. (36) cedat tempus obligationis. Tu *V*.

(37) conceditur... tempus/ concessisti et negasti *V*. (38) *Om.* respondetur *V*.

(39) *Add.* obligationis *V*. (40) Illa... ex/ Illis *V*. (41) non *V*.

(42) asinus... est/ hoc ; et hoc non est aliud quam *V*.

(43) Hence one cannot concede 'Hoc demonstratum est asinus' even though it follows *ex concessis*. Note that in virtue of n. 89 to par. 98, this should pose no problem. The final consequence here is problematic. The minor, 'Hoc est hoc demonstratum', has not been conceded. The argument in this and the next several paragraphs is very obscure. For these passages I have consulted also the other MSS listed in the introduction, above.

(44) But presumably not for the reason given in par. 105. *Cf.* the end of n. 24 to par. 105. One might argue as in par. 107 that it is to be denied because it is *repugnans posito* (cf. par. 105: « Et omne demonstratum per ly 'hoc' est homo. ») But then why should par. 105 resort to such an elaborate, and ultimately unsatisfactory, argument to the same conclusion?

(45) *Cf.* n. 26 to par. 105.

(46) This seems to refer to the passage « Tunc sequitur quod hoc demonstratum est' in par. 105. (*Cf.* n. 34 to par. 105.) If so, it is out of place. For the passage occurs in par. 105 on the alternative that 'Hoc non est aliud quam hoc demonstratum' is *denied*. If the sentence here is emended to « Et conceditur quod hoc est hoc demonstratum », the argument agrees better with the text of par. 105. Then for the « quando arguitur » passage, cf. n. 30 to par. 105. Another alternative is to delete the 'non' in 'Hoc non est aliud quam hoc demonstratum'. Then it is the last consequence of par. 105 that is doubted.

(47) For the emendation, cf. par. 108.

(48) *Om.* Solutio... asinus' *V*. (49) *V* lacks par. 107-116.

(107) Contra : Consequens[50] repugnat positis. Igitur, consequens est negandum. Et antecedens est una copulativa cujus utramque partem concessisti. Igitur, habuisti antecedens concedere et consequentiam negare.[51]

(108) Solutio : Si arguitur ex praemissis a me concessis, nego quod consequentia non valet 'Hoc est asinus ; hoc est hoc demonstratum ; igitur, hoc demonstratum est asinus'. Si tamen ponatur quod arguitur ex illis praemissis concessis, concedenda est consequentia quia est bona, et dubitanda est copulativa.[52]

(109) Pro quo sciendum quod tales copulativae sunt possibiles 'Hoc est homo et hoc non est homo', et tantum asinus demonstretur per ly 'hoc'. Et similiter illa 'Aliquis illorum est homo et nullus illorum est homo'. Et haec similiter 'Uterque illorum (*V**5rb) sedet et neuter illorum sedet', et etiam omne demonstratum per ly 'illorum' sedet. Et consimiles.[53] Tamen tales copulativae omnino sunt impossibiles 'Hoc est et hoc non est' pro secunda parte, quia quaelibet talis propositio ut est secunda pars copulativae est impossibilis per se, 'Hoc non est', pro eo, scilicet, quod convertitur cum tali propositione 'Hoc quod est non est' quae semper sic significando est falsa et impossibilis. Et similiter quaelibet talis 'Chimaera <non>[54] est', 'Sortes non est', 'Antichristus non est', et sic de consimilibus.

(110) Contra : Si quaelibet talis foret impossibilis et aliqua illarum haberet contradictorium, illud foret necessarium. Igitur, aliqua talis foret necessaria 'Homo est' et 'Sortes est', et sic de aliis, quod non est verum. Et quod illa[55] contradicunt patet per regulam communem quodin singularibus non refet praeponere vel postponere negationem.[56]

(111) Solutio : Conceditur quod cujuslibet contradictorium est necessarium. Et negatur quod haec 'Sortes est' est necessaria. Et haec 'Chimaera est', et sic de aliis, non sunt contradictoria[57] primarum.

(112) Pro quo sciendum est quod illa propositio 'Sortes non est' aequi-

(50) antecedens *V**. (Emend for sense.) (51) And not doubt it, as in par. 106.

(52) Contrary to par. 107, the consequence is valid and is to be conceded, although its antecedent is to be doubted in virtue of the first half of conclusion 2. This seems to be a clarification and correction of par. 106. It is not the *consequence* that is to be doubted, as par. 106 says. Rather it is to be *conceded*, and its *antecedent* is to be doubted. Nevertheless, there is still a problem. If the consequent is to be denied, as par. 107 says, and if the consequence is conceded, as in par. 108, then the antecedent cannot be doubted as in par. 108, in virtue of par. 82. The reply to par. 82 in par. 84 does not deny this principle.

(53) This is presumably meant to be a generalization of the situation argued in par. 105-108. The copulatives are such that « contradictiones videntur includere ». The reasoning inherits the obscurity of the argument in par. 105-108. Cf. also par. 113-114.

(54) For the emendation, cf. par. 111. (55) illud *V**.

(56) Cf. my "Robert Fland's *Consequentiae*: An Edition", par. 16.

(57) contradictorio *V**.

valet tali copulativae 'Sortes est et non Sortes est'. Ideo contradictorium illius est una disjunctiva facta ex oppositis partibus talis copulativae. Et quaelibet talis disjunctiva est necessaria. Et quaelibet talis copulativa est impossibilis.

(113) Et tunc ad regulam[58] dico quod [est] intellegitur de propositionibus quarum res significatae per praedicata possunt inesse rebus et non inesse per subjecta,[59] utrisque rebus existentibus, ut hic 'Sortes sedet et Sortes non sedet' et 'Sortes currit et Sortes non currit' et sic de aliis.[60]

(114) Aliter potest dici ad quamcumque talem copulativam 'Hoc est homo et hoc non est homo' et sic de aliis, dubitando quamcumque talem et concedendo quod aliqua talis est possibilis, nulla tamen prolata ab opponente[61] est concedenda vel neganda a respondente, sed dubitanda. Et si ponitur talis copulativa possibilis, non debet admitti. Et negatur haec consequentia : 'Hoc est possibilis ; igitur,[62] est ponibilis', eo quod nulla propositio est ponibilis nisi talis ad quam extra tempus obligationis [non] est varianda responsio propter mutationem ex parte <rei>, sicut patet per septimam suppositionem secundae particulae. Prima responsio est facilior, secunda famosior.

(115) Adhuc est dubium de copulativis non includentibus repugnantiam. Ponatur quod non respondisti dubie nec respondes dubie ad aliquam propositionem ubi propositam. Deinde proponitur 'Rex sedet'. Si negatur vel conceditur,[63] cedat tempus. Contra : Illa est impertinens scita a te principaliter significare dubie. Igitur (V^*5va) non est neganda nec concedenda. Consequentia patet per ultimam partem secundae divisionis.[64] Si dubitatur, proponitur illa 'Tu respondisti dubie ad illam'. Si conceditur vel dubitatur, cedat tempus. Illa est oppositum positi. Igitur, neganda. Si negatur, cedat tempus. Respondisti ad illam nec negando nec concedendo nec dubitando. Igitur, et cetera.

(116) Solutio : Dubitanda est illa 'Rex sedet'. Et negatur quod respondisti dubie ad illam, quia repugnat posito. Ad secundam,[65] concedo consequentiam et nego antecedens, scilicet, copulativam propositam repugnan-

(58) This presumably refers back to the beginning of par. 109.

(59) Understand this passage as « possunt inesse rebus significatis per subjecta et possunt non inesse eisdem ».

(60) This paragraph seems to suggest that if a proposition p is possible, and if its negation is likewise possible, then the conjunction of p and its negation is possible. But it was presumably to avoid situations much like this that conclusion 2 was set out. Cf. n. 97 to par. 101.

(61) Abbreviation uncertain in V^*. (62) Abbreviation uncertain in V^*.

(63) dubitatur V^*. (Emend for sense.)

(64) This seems irrelevant. Cf. rather suppositions 10-12, par. 25 and 29-30.

(65) There appears to be a lacuna in the text of V^*. There is no « secundam ».

tem. Quaelibet tamen pars est concedenda, quia impertinens significans sicut[66] est.

(117) Ultimo[67] de copulativis sub conditione positis[68] sit[69] hoc sophisma : Ponatur illa[70] copulativa[71] 'Sortes dabit Platoni[72] denarium sub tali conditione quod Plato obviabit homini qui non dat[73] sibi denarium'. Et obviet Plato[74] Sorti. Deinde proponitur illa 'Sortes dabit Platoni denarium'. Si negatur vel dubitatur, contra : Illa sequitur ex posito. Igitur, fuit concedenda. Nam sequitur : « Sortes dabit Platoni denarium sub tali conditione et cetera ; igitur, Sortes dabit Platoni denarium. »[75] Si conceditur, tunc sic : Sortes dabit Platoni denarium[76] sub conditione quod Plato obviabit homini qui non dabit sibi denarium.[77] Et Plato[78] obviabit Sorti. Igitur, Sortes non dabit Platoni denarium, quod est oppositum prius[79] concessi.

(118) Similiter si dicatur quod casus est impossibilis,[80] contra : Sortes est[81] liberae voluntatis. Et habet denarium ad dandum.[82] Et non impeditur. Igitur, potest dare illum[83] cuicumque voluerit sub aliqua[84] conditione.[85] Et Plato est homo. Igitur, Sortes potest dare Platoni denarium sub tali conditione quod obviabit homini qui non dabit denarium sive impleatur sive non. Igitur, totus casus est possibilis.

(119) Solutio : Admittendus est casus. Et conceditur quod Sortes dabit Platoni denarium[86] sub tali[87] conditione quod[88] obviabit homini[89] qui non dabit sibi denarium. Et negatur consequentia « igitur, obviabit homini qui non dabit sibi denarium, » quia Sortes potest dare denarium sub aliqua conditione quae non adimpletur nec unquam implebitur. Et sic est ibi. Si tamen ponatur quod nisi contradictio impleatur non dabit Platoni denarium, tunc non est positio admittenda.[90]

(66) aliter quam *V**. (Emend for sense.) (67) *Om.* Ultimo *V*.
(68) *Om.* positis *V*. (69) solvitur *V*. (70) Ponatur illa/ Ponatur haec *in marg.* *V*.
(71) *Om.* copulativa *V*. The proposition is not syntactically a copulative. The argument rests on an implicit copulative force. To bring this out, the proposition should perhaps be translated "Socrates will give Plato a denarius, *and* he will do this under the condition, etc."
(72) *Interl.* Platoni *V*. (73) dabit *V*. (74) obviet Plato/ Plato obviat soli *V*.
(75) *Om.* Si... denarium » *V*. (76) *Add.* et solum *V*.
(77) *Add.* Ergo, Plato obviabit homini qui non dabit sibi denarium *V*.
(78) *Add.* solum *V*. (79) *Om.* prius *V*.
(80) Similiter... impossibilis/ Si negatur *V*. (81) *Add.* homo *V*.
(82) *Om.* ad dandum *V*. (83) denarium *V*. (84) sub aliqua/ de ista *V*.
(85) *Add.* sive impleret sive non *V*. *V* lacks the remainder of par. 118.
(86) *Add.* Et conceditur quod solum dabit sibi denarium *V*.
(87) ista *V*. (88) *Add.* Plato *V*.
(89) Sorti et cetera *V*. *V* lacks the remainder of par. 119 and all of pars 120-122.
(90) The argument is over an ambiguity in the notion of a condition. In the conditional proposition "If *p* then *q*", which is the condition? Grammatically, it is *p*. On the other hand, one might argue that in a sense it is *q*, on the grounds that *p* is so

(120) Similiter in parte est hoc sophisma : Ponatur quod Sortes erit servus Platonis sub tali conditione quod Plato non erit dominus Sortis, et aliter non. Deinde proponitur 'Sortes erit servus Platonis'. Si negatur, contra : Illa sequitur ex posito. Igitur, est concedenda. Nam sequitur 'Sortes erit servus Platonis sub tali conditione. Igitur, Sortes erit servus Platonis'. Si dubitatur, arguitur consimiliter. Si conceditur, tunc Sortes (*V**5vb) erit servus Platonis et solum sub ista conditione quod Plato non erit dominus Sortis. Et ultra : Igitur, sequitur quod Sortes non erit servus Platonis.

(121) Solutio : Distinguendo de termino 'non aliter' quia dupliciter potest exponi : primo modo non aliter, id est, sub alia conditione, Sortes erit servus Platonis nisi quod Plato non erit dominus Sortis. Alio modo potest sic exponi : Non aliter, scilicet, si Plato [non] erit dominus Sortis, Sortes non erit servus Platonis.

(122) Unde sciendum quod nulla obligatio est obliganda ad quam extra tempus obligationis non est varianda responsio propter mutationem ex parte rei ut patet per septimam suppositionem. Et quaelibet contra<dictio> est hujusmodi. Igitur, et cetera.

V

(123) Depositio est obligatio mediante qua quis obligatus tenetur negative respondere ad depositum. Regulae principales[91] sustinendae[92] sunt tres. Prima est haec : Omne depositum[93] sine (*V*154rb) obligatione ad hoc pertinente in tempore obligationis[94] est negandum.[95] Exemplum: Si deponitur illa 'Tu non stas' et postea proponitur illa, tunc illa est neganda quia deposita sine obligatione ad hoc pertinente.

(124) Intellectus regulae est : Si aliqua propositio deponatur et ex obligato non sequitur quod illa sit deposita, tunc in tempore depositionis illa est neganda, sicut in proximo exemplo.

(125) Secunda regula est haec : Omne antecedens ad depositum sine obligatione ad hoc pertinente in tempore depositionis[96] est negandum.[97]

only if (only under the condition that) q is so. The question is a terminological one. Par. 117 relies on the latter interpretation: "Socrates will give Plato a denarius, *and* he will do this *only if (only under the condition that)* Plato etc." (Cf. n. 71 to par. 117.) On the other hand, par. 118 rests on the former reading: "Socrates will give Plato a denarius, *and* he will do this *if* (but not necessarily only if) Plato etc." The reply in par. 119 opts for the interpretation given in par. 118.

(91) Regulae principales/ Principaliter hic sunt istae regulae *V*.

(92) *Add.* quae *V*. (93) *Add.* in tempore depositionis *V*.

(94) *Om.* in... obligationis *V*.

(95) *V* lacks the remainder of par. 123 and all of par. 124.

(96) obligationis *V*. (97) *V* lacks the remainder of par. 125.

282

Exemplum : Si deponatur illa quae prius proponatur, tunc illa 'Tu sedes' [illa] est neganda, quia antecedit ad depositum et ex obligato non sequitur illud fore antecedens ad depositum.

(126) Tertia regula : Omne contradictorium depositi sine obligatione ad hoc pertinente in tempore depositionis[98] est concedendum[99] ut si in exemplo prius posito, si proponatur illa 'Tu stas' illa est concedenda, quia contradictorium depositi et[1] ex obligato non sequitur illud contradicere deposito.

(127) Consequenter est videndum cum quibus signis et qualiter et ex quibus in hac specie obligationis contingit obligari. Pro quibus est sciendum quod sicut in secunda specie contingit obligari ita in depositione est obligandum solis signis hic et ibi variatis. Nam in hac specie mediantibus istis signis 'depono' vel 'deponitur' obligari contingit.[2]

(128) Consequenter pro processu illius speciei est haec divisio : Omnis depositio est simplex vel composita. Simplex quando categorica deponitur, composita quando hypothetica deponitur. Et illa est duplex, sicut in positione,[3] ut in sequentibus patebit.[4]

(129) Circa (*V**6ra) depositionem est sciendum quod deposita aliqua propositione consimiliter respondendum est et proponendae sunt sicut si proponeretur contradictorium depositi, ut satis patet intuenti.[5]

(130) De depositione simplici sit hoc sophisma[6] : Deponatur illa 'Aliquae[7] propositiones non sunt similes'. Deinde proponatur illa « 'Deus est' et 'Homo est asinus' sunt propositiones. »[8] Si negatur vel dubitatur, cedat tempus.[9] Illa est impertinens significans principaliter sicut est. Igitur, est concedenda. Consequentia patet per decimam suppositionem.[10] Si conceditur,[11] proponitur illa « 'Deus est' et 'Homo est asinus' sunt propositiones similes. » Si conceditur vel negatur, contra : Illa est impertinens significans principaliter dubie ; ergo, est dubitanda. Si dubitatur, contra[12] : Illa sequitur ex obligato et[13] concesso. Nam sequitur : Omnes

(98) obligationis *V*. (99) *V* lacks the remainder of par. 126.

(1) *Interl.* et *V**.

(2) Consequenter... contingit/ Est autem sciendum quod haec obligatio sit per haec signa 'depono', 'deponitur', et eodem modo sicut in positione solum signo variato. *V*.

(3) *Positio* uses a threefold division of hypotheticals. Cf. n. 82 to par. 77.

(4) Consequenter... patebit/ Depositionum itaque alia simplex alia composita. Simplex est quando illud quod deponitur consimiliter est sicut in positione dictum est, ut patebit. Composita est quando deponitur hypothetica. *V*.

(5) Circa... intuenti/ Et nota quod deposita aliqua hypothetica et similiter de positione simplici et respondendum est sicut contradictorium depositi deponeretur. *V*.

(6) *Om*. De... sophisma *V*. (7) aut quia *V**. (8) *Om*. sunt propositiones *V*.

(9) *Add*. obligationis. Tunc *V*.

(10) decimam suppositionem/ suppositionem sextam *V*. (11) negatur *V*.

(12) contra... contra/ cedat tempus *V**.

(13) non *V**. *Om* et *V*. (Emend for sense.)

propositiones sunt similes. 'Deus est' et 'Homo est asinus' sunt propositiones. Igitur, illae[14] sunt[15] similes. Hic[16] major est obliganda[17] et minor est concessa. Igitur, conclusio est concedenda.

(131) Solutio : Admittenda est depositio. Et conceditur[18] « 'Deus est' et 'Homo est asinus' sunt propositiones. »[19] Et dubitatur an sint similes. Et conceditur quod sequitur ex obligato et bene concesso quod istae sunt similes. Et negatur consequentia « igitur, concedendum est quod illae sunt similes ». Nec est illa regula in omnibus[20] sustinenda.[21] Nam si[22] propositio significans aliter quam est sequatur ex copulativa facta ex obligato et[23] concesso non sequitur tamen quod illa sit concedenda, quia copulativa est neganda ex qua sequitur sicut patet per conclusionem secundam.[24]

(132) Simile est huic : Deponatur illa 'Aliquis[25] homo currit'. Deinde proponitur 'Tu es homo'. Illa est concedenda quia impertinens significans principaliter sicut est. Deinde proponitur illa 'Tu curris'. Illa est neganda quia impertinens significans principaliter aliter quam est. Et si arguitur « ex concesso vero et obligato », concedenda est consequentia et negandum est antecedens, scilicet, copulativa facta ex obligato <et> concesso tamquam impertinens significans principaliter aliter quam est.

(133) Sequitur de depositione composita.[26] Deponatur illa copulativa 'Tu sedes et tu[27] non stas'.[28] Deinde proponatur 'Tu sedes'. Et si negatur vel dubitatur, cedat tempus.[29] Illa est impertinens significans principaliter[30] sicut est. Igitur, est concedenda. Qua concessa, proponitur 'Tu non stas'.[31] Si negatur vel dubitatur, contra : Illa sequitur ex bene concessis.[32] Igitur, concedenda. Si conceditur,[33] cedat tempus.[34] Illa[35] copulativa est a te neganda. Igitur, altera[36] pars est a te neganda[37] vel dubitanda. Sed nulla est dubitanda. Igitur, altera pars est a te neganda. Praeterea,[38] concessa utraque parte copulativae, proponatur ejus contradictorium, scilicet, 'Tu non sedes vel tu stas'. Haec est concedenda. Deinde proponitur illa 'Tu non stas'. Illa est concedenda, quia prius fuit concessa. Et illa sicut prius significavit. Qua concessa arguitur sic : Tu non sedes vel tu stas. Sed[39] tu non stas. Igitur, tu non sedes, cujus oppositum concedebatur.

(134) Solutio : Conceditur quod tu[40] sedes, et similiter tu non (*V**6rb)

(14) 'Deus est', 'Homo est asinus' *V*. (15) *Add.* propositiones *V*.
(16) *Om.* Hic *V*. (17) *Add.* eo quod contradicit deposito *V*.
(18) concedenda est haec propositio *V*. (19) *Add.* similes *V (but perhaps deleted)*.
(20) obligatione *V*. (21) *Add.* vera *V*. (22) *Add.* talis *V*. (23) *Om.* et *V**.
(24) tertiam. Et similiter facit in aliis. *V*. *V* lacks all of par. 132.
(25) Omnis *V**. (Emend for sense.)
(26) Sequitur... composita/ De depositione composita solvitur hoc sophisma *V*.
(27) *Om.* tu *V*. (28) sedes *V*. (29) cedat tempus/ contra *V*.
(30) *Om.* principaliter *V*. (31) sedes *V*. (32) concesso *V*. (33) non *V*.
(34) *Add.* obligationis *V*. (35) Ista tota *V*. (36) *Om.* altera *V*.
(37) *V* lacks the remainder of par. 133. (38) Abbreviation uncertain in *V**.
(39) Abbreviation uncertain in *V**. (40) non *V**. (Emend for sense.)

stas.[41] Et[42] conceditur quod[43] copulativa est neganda. Et negatur consequentia : « igitur, altera[44] ejus[45] pars est[46] neganda vel dubitanda. » Nam utraque parte copulativae concessa, copulativa est neganda, sicut satis[47] patet per conclusionem secundam.[48]

(135) Ad secundam formam[49] quando proponitur contradictorium concedendum est. Et quando postea ponitur 'Tu non stas' est concedendum. Et quando arguitur ex obligato cum illo concesso inferendo oppositum concessi concedenda est consequentia et negandum est antecedens sicut prius de copulativa facta ex obligato et concesso, quia impertinens significans principaliter aliter quam est.

(136) Similiter arguendum est et[50] respondendum[51] si deponatur temporalis. Si deponatur disjunctiva utraque pars ejus est neganda quia antecedit[52] ad depositum ut hic : Si deponatur illa 'Antichristus erit[53] vel Antichristus erit (*V*154va) albus'[54] utraque pars ejus est neganda[55] tamquam antecedens ad depositum.[56]

(137) Sed dubium est si deponatur disjunctiva cujus altera pars sequitur ad ipsam. Verbi gratia, deponatur haec disjunctiva : 'Sortes currit vel Sortes movetur'. Deinde proponitur 'Sortes movetur'. Si conceditur vel dubitatur, cedat tempus. Illa antecedit ad depositum. Igitur, neganda. Qua negata proponitur 'Sortes currit'. Si conceditur vel dubitatur consimiliter arguitur. Si negatur, proponatur ejus contradictorium 'Sortes non currit'. Illa tunc est concedenda eo quod suum oppositum negatur. Qua concessa, proponitur 'Sortes movetur'. Si conceditur, contra : Idem concessisti et negasti. Igitur, male respondisti. Similiter, illa antecedit depositum. Igitur, neganda. Si negatur, contra : Illa sequitur ex bene concesso. Igitur, concedenda. Antecedens patet. Nam sequitur : « Sortes currit aut Sortes movetur. »[57]

(138) Solutio : Depositio non est admittenda eo quod deponitur disjunctiva ad quam non est varianda responsio extra tempus obligationis propter

(41) Conceditur... stas/ Quando dicitur 'Tu sedes et tu non sedes' conceditur *V*.
(42) *Add.* similiter *V*. (43) *Add.* tota *V*. (44) aliqua *V*. (45) *Om.* ejus *V*.
(46) *Add.* a te *V*. (47) sicut satis/ ut *V*.
(48) teriam *V**. *V* lacks all of par. 135.
(49) Cf. par. 133 (« Praeterea »). (50) Similiter... et/ Consimiliter est *V*.
(51) *Add.* ad argumentum *V*.
(52) Si... antecedit/ Si autem disjunctiva deponatur neganda est utraque ejus pars tamquam antecedens *V*.
(53) est *V*. (54) *Om.* albus *V*.
(55) utraque... neganda/ neganda est utraque pars *V*.
(56) *V* lacks all of par. 137-138.
(57) Understand the addition « Sed Sortes non currit. Igitur, Sortes movetur. » But note that the major is not « bene concesso », since it is *depositum*. Curiously, Roger does not point this out in his reply.

mutationem ex parte rei.[58] Similiter de tali disjunctiva 'Antichristus erit vel Antichristus erit albus' et sic de singulis.

(139) Sed dubium est de mixtione[59] positionis cum depositione, ut si fiat hoc sophisma : Ponatur illa 'Sortes currit'[60] et deponatur illa 'Sortes non quiescit'. Deinde proponatur illa 'Sortes[61] movetur'. Si conceditur, cedat tempus.[62] Illa antecedit[63] ad depositum.[64] Igitur, est neganda. Si negatur,[65] cedat tempus.[66] Illa sequitur ex posito. Igitur, est concedenda.

(140) Solutio : Admissa positione non est depositio admittenda. Pro quo est notandum quod quandocumque obligatur mediante positione simul[67] et depositione si obligatum unius repugnat obligato alterius admissa una obligatione alia[68] non est admittenda.[69] Et haec de obligationibus sufficiant.[70]

(58) This is not so. The reply in this paragraph seems to be addressed to a different argument. Perhaps there is a lacuna in the text. Cf. also the end of n. 57 to par. 137, above.

(59) institutione *V*. (60) *Om*. illa... currit' *V*. (61) *Add*. non *V*.

(62) *Add*. obligationis *V*. (63) Illa antecedet/ Illud est sequens *V*.

(64) *Add*. *in marg*. vel antecedens *V*. (65) *Add*. consimiliter *V*.

(66) *Add*. obligationis *V*. (67) mediante... simul/ simul positione *V*.

(68) altera *V*. (69) est admittenda/ debet admitti et cetera *V*.

(70) Et... sufficiant/ Et sic est finis de obligationibus Suiset. Amen. Deo gratias. *V*. *Add*. Expliciunt obligationes Reverendi doctoris Suiset. Incipiunt insolubilia ejusdem. *V*. *Add*. Expliciunt obligationes Richardi Suiset Anglici doctoris Artium et in hac arte subtilissimi. Sequuntur insolubilia ejusdem. *V**. On the confusion of Roger with Richard Swyneshed (the Merton "Calculator"), and on the various forms of Swyneshed's name, cf. Weisheipl, "Roger Swyneshed...", cited above, n. 14 to the introduction.

XVII

Three Theories of *Obligationes*: Burley, Kilvington and Swyneshed on Counterfactual Reasoning

This paper defends the thesis that the mediaeval genre of logical treatises *De obligationibus* contained a theoretical account of counterfacutal reasoning, perhaps the first such account in the history of philosophy. This interpretation helps to explain some of the theoretical disputes in the obligationes literature in the first half of the fourteenth century. Section 1 is introductory. Section 2 presents Walter Burley's theory, while section 3 argues for the counterfactual interpretation of obligationes and section 4 discusses difficulties with Burley's theory. Section 5 presents the textual basis for Richard Kilvington's theory, and section 6 outlines that theory. Section 7 discusses Roger Swyneshed's theory. Section 8 contains a summary and conclusion.

1. Introduction: obligational reasoning

Mediaeval treatises *De obligationibus* have only recently begun to be investigated in detail.[1] Despite the name, such treatises have nothing especially to do with morality or ethics. Rather, they concern a peculiar form of disputation between two parties. What is 'obligatory' in such a disputation is simply that the rules of the form obliged one party, the so called 'respondent', to reply in certain ways at the various steps of the disputation.

It is still not entirely clear just what the purpose of such disputations was. Unlike the *quaestio*-form of disputation, in which substantive matters of controversy are argued and a decision reached, a *disputatio de obligationibus* is a 'disputation' without anything really in dispute. For while the format requires two opposing participants, it does not involve opposing doctrines.[2]

It has been suggested that what we have in the treatises *De obligationibus* is a

1 In addition to items mentioned in the following footnotes, the relevant bibliography includes: Ignacio Angelelli, 'The techniques of disputation in the history of logic', *J. philos.*, **67** (1970), 800–815; Mary Anthony Brown, 'The role of the *Tractatus de obligationibus* in mediaeval logic', *Franciscan studies*, **26** (1966), 26–35; C.L. Hamblin, *Fallacies* (1970, London), see the index; Eleonore Stump, 'William of Sherwood's treatise on obligations', *Historiographia linguistica*, **7** (1980), 249–264; and her *Boethius's In Ciceronis Topica* (forthcoming). This last contains chapters 'Obligations according to Walter Burley' and 'Topics, consequences and obligations in Ockham's *Summa logicae*'. †

2 Paul Vincent Spade, 'Roger Swyneshed's *Obligationes:* edition and comments', *Archives d'hist. doctr. et litt. du moyen âge*, **44** (1977), 243–285 (p.245). But see footnote 55 below.

rudimentary attempt to articulate a theory of logical deduction.[3] But this seems to be wrong for two reasons. First, principles of logical deduction are not formulated in these treatises; they are presupposed there and are formulated instead in treatises *De consequentiis*. But second, even apart from this, the suggestion conflicts with one of the most characteristic features of obligational disputation, that the respondent is sometimes obliged to affirm certain sentences that *cannot* be deduced from what has gone before.

It has also been suggested that the real purpose of the treatises *De obligationibus* was pedagogical rather than theoretical; that they codified the methods used to exercise students' logical skills,[4] or perhaps to examine their mastery of such skills.[5] But while it is certainly true that some of the more complicated and subtle obligational disputations would make effective exercises or examinations, it is not so clear what it is that would be exercised or examined in that way. The characteristic feature mentioned in the preceding paragraph suggests that it would not be the student's strictly logical skills. More importantly, the pedagogical interpretation conflicts with one of the facts to be investigated in this paper, that in the development of the obligationes literature there occurred a certain controversy that appears entirely unmotivated if one thinks of obligational disputations merely as exercises or examinations and that suggests instead that the focus of this literature was on theoretical matters, not exclusively on pedagogical ones.

In this paper I shall explore and argue in favour of the view that what we have in

3 Philotheus Boehner, *Medieval logic: an outline of its development from 1250 to c. 1400* (1952, Manchester), 14: 'It would, however, be incorrect to see in these tracts only a collection of rules for such school exercises, since they contain a nucleus of rules for an axiomatic method, though in a rather crude form'. I say 'logical deduction' instead of Boehner's 'axiomatic method', since in fact there is nothing like an axiomatic proof theory in mediaeval logical literature except for certain presentations of the syllogistic.

4 James A. Weisheipl, 'Developments in the arts curriculum at Oxford in the early fourteenth century', *Mediaeval studies*, **28** (1966), 151–175 (pp.163–164): 'These were strictly ingenious exercises among † school boys and had little objective value, ...'. Also Romuald Green, *The logical treatise 'De obligationibus': an introduction with critical texts of William of Sherwood and Walter Burley* (forthcoming, St. Bonaventure, N.Y.), Introduction: 'In general terms, *De obligationibus* is a medieval logical treatise designed to initiate students into the practice of logical reasoning, especially with a view to taking part in disputations'; Ch.2.1: '*De obligationibus* is a logical treatise that was designed to give beginners a series of exercises in the use of the logical rules of inference, particularly in view of disputation'. Green's view is quoted with approval in L.M. De Rijk, 'Some thirteenth century tracts on the game of obligation, I', *Vivarium*, **12** (1974), 94–123 (p.94). There is some textual evidence for this 'pedagogical' view. Indeed the early *Obligationes Parisienses* contains a passage saying explicitly that the purpose of these disputations is ***exercitatio sive esse exercitatum***, 'exercise or being exercised' (edited in L.M. De Rijk, 'Some thirteenth century tracts on the game of obligation, II', *Vivarium*, **13** (1975), 22–54 (p.27.2). Nevertheless, the material to be presented in the following pages shows that the situation must have been more complicated than this.

5 Alan R. Perreiah, 'Insolubilia in the *Logica parva* of Paul of Venice', *Medioevo*, **4** (1978), 145–171 † (pp.152-156); and his 'What obligations really are', *Medioevo*, **5** (1979) (forthcoming).

the obligationes literature is in fact an attempt to give a theoretical account of counterfactual reasoning.[6] If this view is correct then the mediaeval obligationes literature is probably the first such attempt in the history of philosophy.

Robert Fland, writing sometime between 1335 and 1370, distinguished two schools of thought in the obligationes-literature, what he called the 'old reply' and the 'new reply'.[7] The 'old reply' was the view held for instance by Walter Burley, who wrote an *Obligationes* in 1302.[8] But Burley by no means had a monopoly on this view;

6 I here use the term 'counterfactual' in the rather broad sense now common in philosophical literature, to include all subjunctive conditionals whether their antecedents are actually 'contrary to fact' or not (see e.g., David K. Lewis, *Counterfactuals* (1973, Cambridge, Mass.)). In Spade (footnote 2), 245–246, I considered the possibility that counterfactual reasoning could provide a rough model for obligational disputations, but I did not suggest that the theory of obligations or any part of it was ever actually intended as an account of counterfactual reasoning. To the best of my knowledge, that suggestion was first made in connection with Richard Kilvington in Norman Kretzmann, 'Obligations and counterfactuals', unpublished lecture delivered to the 1980 Summer Institute on Medieval Philosophy, Cornell University. That seminal and exciting lecture prompted many of the thoughts that led to the present paper and called my attention to the texts of Kilvington discussed below. Eleonore Stump, 'Obligations: From the beginnings to the early fourteenth century', in *Cambridge history of later medieval philosophy* (forthcoming, Cambridge), 315–334, suggests that Kilvington in those texts 'shifts the emphasis of obligations away from a consideration of scattered paradoxes arising from difficulties in evaluating certain inferences in disputational contexts and towards a logic of counterfactuals' (p.332). On this view, obligationes were not originally a theory of counterfactuals, but *became* one (or something very like one) with Kilvington. The difficulty with this view lies in specifying what those pre-Kilvingtonian 'disputational contexts' could have been, for which obligationes helped in 'evaluating certain inferences', if they were not already instances of counterfactual reasoning much like those discussed in the modern literature. I know of no other way to account for the evidence presented in section 3 below. That evidence leads me to think that obligationes were a theory of counterfactuals from the very beginning, and that what we find in Kilvington is not a transformation of something else into a theory of counterfactuals but rather a substitution of one theory of counterfactuals for another—a substitution that may have been prompted by difficulties with the original theory but, as I shall argue, was in any event no improvement. But even if this 'counterfactual' interpretation of obligationes is correct, it is surely not the whole story; certain species of obligatio that are not discussed in this paper—for instance, 'petitio'—seem to be something else altogether. †

7 Paul Vincent Spade, 'Robert Fland's *Obligationes:* an edition', *Mediaeval studies*, **42** (1980), 41–60. For more on the differences between these two replies, see Spade, 'Obligations: developments in the fourteenth century', in *Cambridge history of later medieval philosophy* (forthcoming, Cambridge), 335–341. †

8 Edited by Green (footnote 4). Burley was born in 1274 or 1275 and died not before 1344. The most complete study of Burley to date is Augustin Uña Juarez, *La filosofia del siglo XIV: Contexto cultural de Walter Burley* (1978, Madrid).

indeed, it appears to have been more or less the 'standard' theory of obligationes throughout the entire subsequent history of the literature.[9]

The 'new reply', on the other hand, seems to have originated with Roger Swyneshed, whose *Obligationes* was written probably between 1330 and 1335.[10] The differences between those two views are striking, as we shall see. Recently, Norman Kretzmann has called attention to some passages in Richard Kilvington's *Sophismata*, written around 1325 and therefore between Burley's treatise and Swyneshed's, that seem to present yet a third view on obligationes, a view that may be regarded as a transition between the 'old' and the 'new' responses.[11] These three theories of obligationes will be the focus of this paper.

2. Outline of Walter Burley's theory

An obligational disputation is a 'disputation' between two parties, the 'opponent' and the 'respondent'. If one takes the pedagogical and practical aspects of obligationes seriously and supposes that such disputations actually took place, then the two parties represent two real people. Otherwise one may regard the distinction between 'opponent' and 'respondent' as simply a convenient fiction useful in describing the rules of a certain kind of reasoning. In any case, the burden of the rules falls mainly on the respondent; the opponent is free to make any move he wants in the disputation.[12]

9 See Spade (forthcoming, footnote 7). Before Burley, the situation is not so clear. De Rijk has edited some early treatises that maintain views not nearly so developed and articulated as Burley's, but otherwise in the same line of development. See the *Tractatus Emmeranus de falsi positione* in De Rijk 1974 (footnote 4), and the *Oblig. Paris.* (footnote 4). (Significant doctrinal similarities and differences between these treatises and Burley's will be noted below.) There is another and much longer treatise, however, attributed to William of Sherwood and edited by Green (footnote 4), that maintains a theory in all important respects identical with Burley's. If the treatise is indeed by Sherwood, then Burley's theory is by no means original with him, but rather goes back at least to Sherwood in the middle thirteenth century. In fact, however, I think the attribution of the treatise to Sherwood is almost certainly mistaken. Instead I think the work very probably dates from the very last years of the thirteenth century and is perhaps even an early treatise by Burley himself. Reasons for this view will be † presented in Paul Vincent Spade and Eleonore Stump, 'Walter Burley and the Obligationes attributed to William of Sherwood: a question of authorship' (forthcoming). If the view is correct, then Burley is perhaps not only a representative of Fland's 'old reply' but its originator as well.

10 Edited in Spade (footnote 2). It is not known when Swyneshed was born, but he died probably before 12 May 1365. On the identity of Roger Swyneshed (who is not to be confused with Richard Swyneshed, the so called Mertonian 'Calculator') see James A. Weisheipl, 'Roger Swyneshed, O.S.B., logician, natural philosopher, and theologian, *Oxford studies presented to Daniel Callus* (1964, Oxford), 231–252. Swyneshed's 'new' theory of obligationes was later maintained by Richard Lavenham (see Paul Vincent Spade, 'Richard Lavenham's *Obligationes*: edition and comments', *Riv. crit. di stor. della filos.*, 33 (1978), 225–242).

11 Kretzmann (footnote 6). On Kilvington, see A.B. Emden, *A biographical register of the University of Oxford to a.d. 1500* (3 vols., 1957–59, Oxford), vol.2, 1050–1051. See also below (footnote 57). The date of Kilvington's birth is unknown, but he was dead by March 1362.

12 E.g., William of Ockham, *Summa logicae* (1974, St. Bonaventure, N.Y.), III–3, 41.28–32: 'Et consistit ars ista in hoc quod in principio debet aliqua propositio poni, deinde debent propositiones proponi *secundum quod placet opponenti*, ad quas debent respondere concedendo vel negando vel dubitando vel distinguendo' (emphasis added).

There were several different kinds or 'species' of obligatio; the list varied from author to author.[13] But the most basic species, to which perhaps others could be reduced, was one called *positio* or 'positing'. For simplicity I shall confine myself to this species.

In a positio the opponent begins the disputation by saying 'I posit that *p*'. That is, for the duration of the disputation we are to suppose it is the case that *p*, we are 'obligated' to uphold it as true. The sentence '*p*' in such a positio is called the *positum*. The respondent must either 'admit' or 'deny' the positio by saying either 'I admit it' or 'I deny it'. Some treatises stipulate that the respondent must admit the positio only if it posits a contingent sentence,[14] while others admit a special kind of positio in which the positum is an impossible sentence that is nevertheless not 'manifestly' impossible, so that its opposite can be entertained and believed.[15] We shall ignore cases of the latter kind in this paper.

After a positio is admitted, the disputation proceeds as follows. The opponent 'proposes' or sets forth a series of sentences, to each of which the respondent must reply 'I concede it',[16] 'I deny it', or 'I doubt it',[17] according to the rules below. Some authors also allow the respondent to reply 'I distinguish' and then to isolate various senses of an ambiguous proposed sentence.[18] But this maneuver seems to be simply a

13 *Oblig. Paris.* (footnote 4), 27.28–28.10, Burley (ed. Green (footnote 4), par. 0.02), Ockham ((footnote 12), III–3, 39.12–13) and Albert of Saxony (*Perutilis logica* (1522, Venice), VI.2, fol. 48rb) all give six species: positio, depositio, dubitatio (*Oblig. Paris.* calls this 'dubitetur'), instituio, sit verum (*Oblig. Paris.* calls this 'rei veritas') and petitio. Marsilius of Inghen, *Tractatus de arte obligandi* (1489, Paris, falsely attributed to Peter of Ailly), fol. 6rb, mentions these same six species, but accepts only the first three. (The third he calls 'dubie positio'.) Putative-Sherwood, ed. Green (footnote 4), par. 0.01, lists three species, of which the first is divided into positio and petitio; the other two are depositio and dubitatio. Swyneshed ((footnote 2), par. 3), Fland ((footnote 7) *passim*) and Lavenham ((footnote 10), par. 1) all accept only positio, depositio and impositio. Paul of Venice (*Logica* (= *Logica parva*; no date, Venice: photoreprint 1970, Hildesheim), 118, and *Logica magna* (1489, Venice), II.14, fol. 177 rb) and Paul of Pergula (*Logica and tractatus de sensu composito et diviso* (1961, St. Bonaventure, N.Y.), 102.9–11) give only two species: positio and depositio.

14 Swyneshead (footnote 2), par. 18–20; Lavenham, (footnote 10), par. 5; Fland (footnote 7), par. 3.

15 *Tractatus Emmeranus de impossibili positione*, ed. De Rijk 1974 (footnote 4); putative-Sherwood, ed. Green (footnote 4), par. 1.82–1.87; Burley, ed. Green (footnote 4), par. 3.179–3.186; Ockham, (footnote 12), III–3, 42. For some reason, this species of obligatio seems to have disappeared from the literature after Ockham.

16 Note that conceding is not admitting, just as positing is not proposing. One admits the positio, but concedes only subsequently proposed sentences. Note also that the positio is not the positum. One admits the positio, but must concede the positum if it should happen to be one of the sentences subsequently proposed.

17 The earlier treatises edited by De Rijk do not seem to have systematically recognised doubting as an appropriate response in a positio. They do, however, allow the response 'Prove it!' (*proba*). In the *Tract. Emm. de falsi pos.*, ed. De Rijk 1974 (footnote 4), 106.22–29, this seems to be something like a request for further information and to be only a preliminary to conceding or denying. In the *Oblig. Paris.* (footnote 4) 'Prove it!' is recognised as an appropriate response in a dubitatio. But dubitatio is a separate species of obligatio, distinct from positio. The response does not appear to have been used in a positio. The systematic role given to doubting in the context of a positio is one of the major differences between Burley's theory and the views of these early treatises. See also footnote 22.

18 E.g., Ockham in footnote 12. Compare also the role of 'Prove it!' in the *Tract. Emm. de falsi pos.* as discussed in footnote 17.

preliminary to one of the three other allowed responses, so that we shall ignore the complication. The first sentence is proposed after the positio is admitted is said to be proposed 'in the first step' (*primo loco*), and similarly for subsequent steps. That is, the numbering of the steps of thc disputation begins with the first proposed sentence, not with the original stating and admitting of the positio.

The respondent's correct reply to a proposed sentence is determined in part by whether that sentence is 'relevant' (*pertinens*) or 'irrelevant' (*impertinens*).[19] The specification of these notions is the most visible point of controversy among the three theories of obligationes we are considering. On Burley's theory, it goes like this. Where A is the i-th proposed sentence and X_i is as in (2) below,

(1) A is *relevant* at step i if and only if either
  (a) X_i implies A, in which case A is said to be 'sequentially relevant' (*pertinens sequens*) at i or
  (b) X_i implies $\sim A$, in which case A is said to be 'incompatibly relevant' (*pertinens repugnans*) at i.[20]

  A is *irrelevant* at i if and only if it is not relevant at i.[21]

(2) X_i is the smallest set containing the positum such that, for all sentences B and for all $j<i$,
  (a) if B was proposed at step j and had to be conceded there according to the rules in (3) below, then $B \varepsilon X_i$, and
  (b) if B was proposed at j and had to be denied there according to (3), then $\sim B \varepsilon X_i$.

(3) A is to be conceded, denied or doubted at step i according to the following rules:
  (a) if A is sequentially relevant at i, it is to be conceded there;
  (b) if A is incompatibly relevant at i, it is to be denied there;
  (c) if A is irrelevant at i and
    (i) the respondent knows A to be true, it is to be conceded at i;
    (ii) the respondent knows A to be false, it is to be denied at i;
    (iii) otherwise A is to be doubted at i.[22]

19 Although the notions of relevance and irrelevance are present in the *Tract. Emm. de falsi pos.* and *Oblig. Paris.*, the actual terms 'pertinens' and 'impertinens' are not used systematically there. *Oblig. Paris.* (footnote 4), 28.4, does use the term 'impertinens' but does not define it, and it is not a regular term in the vocabulary of that treatise. The explicit definition of these notions and their systematic use seem to be another characteristic difference between Burley's theory and the views of the earlier treatises.

20 The logical relations in (a) and (b) are probably most appropriately interpreted in terms of semantic entailment rather than formal derivability. A set of sentences is said to imply exactly what is jointly implied by all the sentences in that set. In terms of semantic entailment, a set of sentences is said to imply exactly what is true in all models in which every sentence in the set is true.

21 Ed. Green (footnote 4), par. 3.14.

22 Ed. Green (footnote 4), par. 3.14–3.16. In *Oblig. Paris.* (footnote 4), 29.1–9, the correct responses to proposed sentences do not depend in any way on the state of the respondent's knowledge. An irrelevant true sentence is to be conceded, and an irrelevant false sentence is to be denied, whether the respondent knows their truth values or not. (The treatise does not explicitly used the term 'irrelevant' here; see footnote 19.) The *Tract. Emm. de falsi pos.*, ed. De Rijk 1974 (footnote 4), 103.3 and 9, gives no explicit general rules at all for what were later called 'irrelevant' sentences, but does appeal to particular cases of rules like those in *Oblig. Paris.*

In virtue of (1)–(3) the relevance or irrelevance of any later step, and the proper response to it, may be determined recursively on the basis of the proper response to the previous steps. The relevance or irrelevance of the first step, and the proper response to it, are determined on the basis of the positum alone.

Since we are not considering that special kind of obligatio in which the positum is impossible, X_1 will be a consistent set. Moreover in general if A is proposed at step i and X_i is consistent, then (1)–(3) guarantee that if A is to be conceded at i then $X_i \cup \{A\}$ is consistent, and if A is to be denied at i then $X_i \cup \{\sim A\}$ is consistent. Hence by induction Burley's theory of obligationes as set out in (1)–(3) is 'consistent' in each of the following, progressively stronger senses:

(4a) no one disputation requires the respondent to concede an impossible sentence at any step;

(4b) no one disputation requires the respondent to concede sentences of the form A and $\sim A$ at different steps;

This conforms to what was said in footnote 17 about doubting as an appropriate response in a positio. The incorporation of such epistemic considerations into the theory of positio appears to have been a later innovation. Indeed, I suspect it occurred around the time of Burley and the putative Sherwood (footnote 9). Some evidence of this may be seen in the rather unsettled and indecisive use of epistemic qualifications in obligationes-treatises from this period. In Burley, for instance, the textual situation is somewhat more complicated than (1)–(3) would suggest. In Green (footnote 4), par. 3.15–3.16, Burley adds epistemic clauses even to the rules for sequentially and incompatibly relevant sentences. There a sentence that follows from the positum alone must be conceded, and a sentence that is incompatible with the positum alone must be denied, whether the respondent is aware of these logical relationships or not. But other sequentially or incompatibly relevant sentences—i.e., those the relevance of which depends not on the positum alone but also on the correct responses to previously proposed sentences—must be conceded or denied respectively only if the respondent recognises their relevance. (See the phrases 'scitum esse tale' in par. 3.15–3.16.)

Nevertheless, I think the rules as formulated in (1)–(3) give a more accurate picture of Burley's intentions, because (a) the epistemic clauses for relevant sentences are contradicted by the rules in par. 3.14, (b) if those epistemic clauses are included the rules are no longer exhaustive (they fail to specify a correct response when the proposed sentence is in fact relevant but is not recognised as relevant), and (c) Burley himself generally ignores the clauses in those rules elsewhere. (Sometimes, although not so regularly, he also ignores the epistemic clauses in (3ci) and (3cii). But the fact that doubting is a recognised response to irrelevant sentences shows that the clauses must be included there and that Burley is being elliptical or careless in these cases). For the putative-Sherwood, ed. Green (footnote 4), par. 1.03, the respondent must concede the positum whenever it is proposed, but must concede all other sequentially relevant sentences and deny all incompatibly relevant sentences only if he knows they are sequentially or incompatibly relevant (par. 1.05–1.06, 1.09). But the author does not always rigorously observe these epistemic considerations. Ockham (footnote 12), III–3, 41.48–50, adds such a clause even to the rule for conceding the positum itself when it is later proposed. But while, like the putative-Sherwood, Ockham includes a similar clause in his rule for sequentially relevant sentences (41.63–65) he curiously omits the qualification in his rule for incompatibly relevant sentences (41.70–73). Ockham does not adhere to these clauses in practice any more than Burley or the putative-Sherwood does. I suspect therefore that these variations of wording should not be given much weight; they do not indicate any ultimate differences in theory but rather reflect only a tentativeness and hesitation caused by what was still the novelty of incorporating epistemic considerations into the theory of positio. See also footnote 42.

(4c) no one disputation requires the respondent to concede at different steps each member of an inconsistent set of sentences.

Nevertheless consider the following sense of 'consistency':

(4d) no one disputation requires the respondent to give different responses to the same sentence proposed at different steps.

Burley's theory violates (4d) and so is 'inconsistent' in that sense. Burley recognises this kind of inconsistency and apparently regards it as harmless.[23] Because his theory is (4b)-consistent, it will be (4d)-inconsistent only if there are cases in which a sentence is doubted at an earlier step but conceded or denied at a later step.[24] Burley gives an example. Let *A* and *B* be contingent sentences, neither of which implies the other, and let *A* be doubtful while *B* is known to be false.[25] Then

Positum:	$A \vee B$	
1.	*A*	(doubted)
2.	*B*	(denied)
3.	*A*	(conceded)

In step 1 *A* is doubted because it is irrelevant there and is in fact doubtful. Step 2 is denied because it is also irrelevant and is in fact known to be false. In step 3, however, *A* is conceded even though it was doubted in step 1, because in step 3 it is no longer irrelevant but rather sequentially relevant.

This illustrates an important fact about Burley's theory of obligationes, namely that the order or position of the proposed sentences in a disputation may affect the correct responses to them. Indeed, this is true not only in the sense that the theory violates (4d), so that the same sentence may require different responses at different steps of the *same* disputation, but also in the sense that the theory violates:

(4e) no *two* disputations constructed from the same positum and differing only with respect to the order in which sentences are proposed are such that the respondent is required to give one response to a sentence in the one disputation and a different response to the same sentence in the other disputation.

23 Ed. Green (footnote 4), par. 1.136–1.137.

24 Once a sentence has been conceded (although it may have been doubted earlier), it must thereafter always be conceded whenever it is proposed at any subsequent step. See Burley, ed. Green (footnote 4), par. 3.56: 'si aliquid sit concessum, semper est concedendum, durante tempore obligationis'. The same holds for denial, although Burley does not explicitly say so.

25 In fact Burley, ed. Green (footnote 4), par. 1.136, stipulates only that *B is* false, not that it is *known* to be false. In virtue of (3), however, this must be corrected if Burley is to make his point. Burley frequently makes this slip. See footnote 22.

Burley's (4e)-inconsistency is a trivial corollary of his (4d)-inconsistency. If different disputations are formed from the one just above by inserting $A \vee B$ at various steps, that sentence has to be conceded in every case because it is sequentially relevant. But this does not affect the responses to the other steps. Hence any two such disputations illustrate (4e)-inconsistency: they differ only with respect to order, and yet A is to be doubted in the first of the two and conceded in the second.[26]

Not all cases of (4e)-inconsistency are so trivial. An important special case emerges if we consider:

(4f) no two disputations constructed from the same positum and differing only with respect to the order in which sentences are proposed are such that the respondent is required to concede a sentence in the one disputation and to deny the same sentence in the other disputation.

Since (4e) implies (4f) but not conversely, (4e)-consistency is the stronger kind of *consistency*. Hence (4f)-inconsistency is the stronger kind of *inconsistency*. Burley's theory, as it turns out, is inconsistent even in that stronger sense.

Just as he recognised the (4d)-inconsistency of his theory, so too Burley recognises its (4f)-inconsistency. He gives the following illustration.[27] Where both Socrates and Plato are known to be black,[28] let it nevertheless be posited that Socrates is white. Then

(5)	Positum:	Socrates is white.	
	1.	Socrates and Plato are alike in color.	(conceded)
	2.	Plato is white.	(conceded)
	Positum:	Socrates is white.	
	1.	Plato is white.	(denied)
	2.	Socrates and Plato are alike in color.	(denied)

Step 1 of the first disputation is conceded because it is irrelevant and known to be true. Step 2 is then conceded as sequentially relevant. In the second disputation, however, step 1 is denied because it is irrelevant and known to be false. Hence step 2 is denied as incompatibly relevant.

3. Obligationes as a theory of counterfactuals

Richard Kilvington, as we shall see, seems to have regarded its (4f)-inconsistency as a decisive difficulty for Burley's theory of obligationes, one that prompted Kilvington to revise that theory. But why should this feature be regarded as a difficulty at all? It will only be regarded that way if one has some antecedent view about the purpose of obligational disputation in general.

26 The fact that the converse also holds, so that A is to be conceded in the first disputation and doubted in the second, does not spoil the point but only reinforces it by illustrating (4e)-inconsistency once again.

27 Ed. Green (footnote 4), par. 3.34.

28 In fact Burley says only that they *are* black, not that they are *known* to be black. See footnotes 22 and 25.

Fifteenth-century authors sometimes cite two passages, in Aristotle's *Prior analytics* and in the *Metaphysics*,[29] as forming the theoretical basis for obligationes.[30] According to those passages, when the possible is posited nothing impossible will thereby happen. Historically, the connection of obligationes with these texts seems dubious, both because the obligationes-literature predated the ready availability of the Latin *Metaphysics* and also because the earlier literature seems to make no mention of either passage.[31] Nevertheless there is a conceptual even if not a historical link. The passages can be applied to obligationes if and only if the conceded sentences in an obligational disputation, and the contradictories of the denied sentences, are viewed as expressing what 'happens' given the positum. And while the early literature cites neither passage, it does in fact view obligational disputation in this way. The early-thirteenth-century *Tractatus Emmeranus de falsi positione*, for instance, says that in order to concede truths one does not need to posit anything, but in order to concede falsehoods one does need to posit something 'so that it may be seen *what happens then*'.[32] And the *Obligationes Parisienses*, probably somewhat later, says: 'Hence the participants in this kind of disputation do not follow the truth of things absolutely, but rather the truth of things that they have *under a condition*'.[33]

Thus the conceded sentences in an obligational disputation, and the contradictories of the denied sentences, are from the very beginnings of the literature viewed as somehow 'following' from the positum, as expressing what 'happens' given the positum. This 'following', however, cannot be a matter of logical implication, in the sense of formal deducibility or semantic entailment, since one of the

29 *Prior analytics* I, 13, 32a18–20; *Metaphysics* IX, 4, 1047b10–12. The former passage has '*tethentos*', quite literally 'positing'. (The *Metaphysics* has '*hypothoimetha*'.) Note also that although the Latin *Prior analytics* has 'contingens' in this passage, mediaeval authors sometimes took this as 'possibile' See, e.g, Edward A. Synan, *The works of Richard of Campsall*, vol.1: *Quaestiones super librum Priorum analeticorum* (1968, Toronto), q.15, p.225: 'Quaerantur: an, posito possibili in esse (*Synan*: inesse), accidat inpossibile, et generaliter, utrum diffinicio contingentis sit bene data?' The discussion here concerns the passage cited.

30 E.g., the *Copulata tractatuum parvorum logicalium*, quoted in English in Boehner (footnote 3), 18, and the *Obligationes* appended to editions by the Cologne Thomists of Peter of Spain's *Syncategoremata*, as translated in Joseph P. Mullally, *Peter of Spain: Tractatus Syncategorematum and selected anonymous treatises* (1964, Milwaukee), 117. Both passages are quoted in Green (footnote 4), Ch. 3.1.

31 See the early treatises in De Rijk 1974 and 1975 (footnote 4), and in L.M. De Rijk, 'Some thirteenth century tracts on the game of obligation, III', *Vivarium*, **14** (1976), 26–49; Burley and the putative Sherwood in Green (footnote 4); Ockham (footnote 12), III–3, 39–45. The *Copulata tractatuum parvorum logicalium* (footnote 30) goes on to cite *Metaphysics* IV, 8, 1012b13–14, as the basis for the mediaeval discussion of semantic paradoxes or *insolubilia*. This too seems historically wrong. See Paul Vincent Spade, 'The origins of the mediaeval *Insolubilia*-literature', *Franciscan studies*, **33** (1973), 292–309.

32 Ed. De Rijk 1974 (footnote 4), 103.16–23: 'Et notandum quod hec obligatio non dicitur *falsi positio* propter hoc quod tantummodo falsa ponantur, sed quia sepius ponantur quam vera. Cum enim omnis positio fiat propter concessionem et vera propter sui veritatem habea<n>t concedi non indigent positione. Sed cum falsa non in se causam concessionis <habeant>, indigent positione ut concedantur et videatur quid inde accidat'.

33 Ed. De Rijk 1975 (footnote 4), 27.4–6: 'Unde disputantes hoc genere disputationis non secuntur veritatem rerum simpliciter sed veritatem rerum quam habent sub conditione'.

most characteristic features of obligational disputations is that some sentences (irrelevant known truths) must be conceded that are *not* implied in these ways by the positum or indeed by anything that has gone on earlier in the disputation.[34] Instead it appears that what we have is a kind of counterfactual reasoning. What other kind of reasoning is there in which, in order to see what happens given a certain contrary-to-fact hypothesis, we must take into account various contingent facts about the way things actually are?[35]

If one looks at obligational disputations that conform to Burley's rules from the admittedly anachronistic point of view of modern possible-world semantics, one might describe such a disputation as incompletely specifying—but more and more completely as the disputation progresses—a class of possible worlds in which the positum is true but that otherwise differ as little as possible from what, for all the respondent knows, the actual world is like; the specification proceeds by considering sentences one by one, and departing from what the respondent knows about their truth only if necessary for the sake of consistency with what has been decided already. The remarks about the respondent's knowledge accommodate the epistemic elements in (3) above, and the fact that it is a class of worlds rather than a single world that is specified accommodates the fact that the respondent must doubt an irrelevant sentence *A* proposed at step *i* if he does not know its truth value, so that *A* will be true in some worlds consistent with what he has responded through step *i* and false in others. In virtue of the failure of (4d), such doubts may in some cases be resolved in later steps. But there is no guarantee that all such doubts will be so resolved.

These epistemic considerations would drop out if the respondent were omniscient.[36] In that case the disputation could be described as incompletely but progressively specifying a *single* possible world in which the positum is true but that otherwise differs as little as possible from the actual world. From this point of view, the (4f)-inconsistency of Burley's theory reflects the fact that there may be more than one way to construct such a minimally different world on the basis of a given positum.

This approach is reminiscent of certain modern possible-worlds semantics in which counterfactual conditionals are evaluated by looking to possible worlds in which the counterfactual antecedent is true and that are otherwise 'closest' or 'most similar' to the actual world.[37] And this in turn conforms to the earlier suggestion that what we have in obligational disputation is a kind of counterfactual reasoning, a kind that mixes in certain epistemological factors as found in (3).

34 See clause (ci) of (3).

35 Lewis (footnote 6), Ch. 5, does discuss three other kinds of reasoning that have this property, but none of them is even a remotely plausible candidate here. In particular, the fact that such reasoning is often employed in considerations of morality and ethics (where what one *ought* to do if such and such happens is decided in part by other contingent features of the way things actually are) should not lead one to make a superficial connection with the mediaeval term 'obligatio'. (See section 1 above.) Thus in (5), if Socrates were white, it would not follow that Plato would be morally obliged to be white too, or that Socrates and Plato would be morally obliged to be different in color.

36 Or if one adopted the rules in *Oblig. Paris.* discussed in footnote 22.

37 See Lewis (footnote 6).

I think there is strong evidence for this 'counterfactual' interpretation of obligationes. First, in accordance with the above quotations from the *Tractatus Emmeranus de falsi positione* and the *Obligationes Parisienses*, it provides a way in which both the conceded steps of disputation and the contradictories of the denied steps may be viewed as 'following' from the positum, as expressing what would 'happen' given the positum, even though they need not be logically implied by the positum: they 'follow' in the sense in which the consequent of a true counterfactual may be said to follow from its antecedent.

Second, the 'counterfactual' interpretation provides an explanation for the otherwise apparently pointless treatment of 'irrelevant' sentences in obligational disputation. It is hard to see what else could have motivated the rules for such sentences. Obligational disputations are meant to explore what would happen if the positum were true but everything else stayed as much as possible the same.

Third, this interpretation provides a rationale for the fact that Burley and others allow one to posit certain kinds of *impossible* sentences,[38] and for Burley's statement that when we posit a possible sentence that sentence should either be false, or true but doubtful, or 'sometimes a truth that is known to be true, for instance as against quibblers, who sometimes deny a truth that is known to be true. For a truth that is known to be true is not always *held* to be true'.[39] In all these cases, the point seems to be that in practice we sometimes do reason counterfactually from such hypotheses, hypotheses that may be actually impossible or on the other hand may be known to be not contrary to fact at all. On any other interpretation, why should Burley take such trouble to explain how we might have occasion to reason obligationally from a known truth? It would be better to explain why it is more typical, and apparently less in need of explanation, to reason deliberately from known falsehoods.[40]

Fourth, obligational disputations have many of the characteristic properties of counterfactuals. For example:

(a) Strengthening the antecedent fails. Where B is known to be true but neither follows from nor is incompatible with A, posit A and propose B at the first step; B must then be conceded as irrelevant and known to be true. But there is no disputation in which $A \,\&\, {\sim} B$ is posited and B is to be conceded; B must be denied as incompatibly relevant whenever it is proposed in such a disputation. (Since B does not follow from A, $A \,\&\, {\sim} B$ is a possible positum.)

(b) Transitivity fails. Where B is subalternate to the possible sentence A and A is known to be false, posit A and propose B at the first step; B must be conceded as sequentially relevant. Again, posit B and propose ${\sim} A$ at the

38 Ed. Green (footnote 4), par. 3.179–3.186.

39 Ed. Green (footnote 4), par. 3.02: 'Et sciendum quod in positione possibili debet poni falsum contingens et verum dubium et aliquando, verum scitum esse verum, verbi gratia, ut contra protervientes, qui aliquando verum negant scitum esse verum; non enim semper verum scitum esse verum habetur pro vero'.

40 See footnote 32.

first step; $\sim A$ must be conceded there as irrelevant and known to be true. But there is no disputation in which the possible A is posited and $\sim A$ is to be conceded; $\sim A$ must be denied as incompatibly relevant whenever it is proposed in such a disputation.

(c) Contraposition fails. Where A and B are contingent subcontraries and B is known to be true, posit A and propose B at the first step; B must then be conceded as irrelevant and known to be true. But there is no disputation in which $\sim B$ is posited and $\sim A$ is to be conceded; since A and B are subcontraries, $\sim A$ must be denied as incompatibly relevant whenever it is proposed in such a disputation.

There is of course no generally agreed upon list of formal properties a theory must have before it counts as a theory of counterfactuals. Nevertheless, if one compares the theory of obligationes with Sobel's list of valid inference patterns and fallacious inference patterns for his own theory of counterfactuals, it is apparent that the fit is very close indeed.[41]

Fifth and finally, the 'counterfactual' interpretation of obligationes, as we shall see, yields a plausible account of the transition from Burley's theory to Kilvington's, and from Kilvington's to Swyneshed's.

All these factors together add up to strong evidence for the 'counterfactual' interpretation. In the sections below we shall accept that interpretation and maintain that the following capture the intention of the mediaeval authors:

(6) For every true (or assertable[42]) counterfactual 'Were A then B'—we shall write this $A \,\square\!\!\rightarrow B$[43]—there is an obligational disputation with positum A in which B is conceded or $\sim B$ denied.

41 J. Howard Sobel, 'Utilitarianisms: simple and general', *Inquiry*, 13 (1970), 394–449 (pp.433–438). Assuming (6) and (7) below, and assuming omniscience on the part of the respondent, all three of the theories of obligationes considered in this paper—Burley's, Kilvington's and Swyneshed's—validate Sobel's valid inference patterns $V_1 - V_9$ and $V_{12} - V_{13}$ for counterfactuals, with the exception that, in the case of Kilvington's theory, one needs to assume also that the sets X described in (18) below are consistent in order to validate V_3, V_7, V_{12} and V_{13}, and with the further exception that Burley's theory violates Sobel's V_7 in virtue of (4f)-inconsistency: sometimes both $A \,\square\!\!\rightarrow B$ and $A \,\square\!\!\rightarrow \sim B$. (Sobel's $V_{10} - V_{11}$ and V_{14} have nothing especially to do with counterfactuals. Note that on the 'relativised' interpretation described below, Burley's violation of V_7 is innocuous.) Again, assuming (6) and (7), all three of the theories discussed in this paper invalidate Sobel's invalid inference patterns $F_1 - F_8$ for counterfactuals; all three, however, *validate* his invalid F_9: the necessity of the counterfactual follows from the corresponding strict implication. For Sobel's invalid patterns there is no need to assume consistency in the case of Kilvington's theory, and there is no need to assume omniscience. Indeed, Sobel's F_7 (conditional excluded middle) would be *valid* on each of the three theories if one did assume omniscience. There are other recognised theories of counterfactuals for which conditional excluded middle is valid (e.g., Robert C. Stalnaker, 'A theory of conditionals', in Nicholas Rescher (ed.), *Studies in logical theory* (1968, Oxford), 98–112 (pp.106–107).

42 The epistemic clauses in the rules of obligationes make it unclear whether we are dealing with the conditions for the *truth* of the counterfactual or for the respondent's being epistemically in a position to *assert* the counterfactual. The rules for relevant sentences favour the former; those for irrelevant sentences favour the latter. (Compare footnote 22.) This ambiguity allows for both the 'relativised' and the 'non-relativised' interpretations of Burley described in §4.

43 Following Sobel (footnote 41) and Lewis (footnote 6).

(7) For every obligational disputation with positum A in which B is conceded or $\sim B$ denied, there is a true (and assertable) counterfactual $A \Box\!\!\rightarrow B$, and for every such disputation in which B is denied or $\sim B$ conceded, there is a true (and assertable) counterfactual $A \Box\!\!\rightarrow \sim B$.

Let us now explore how this interpretation accounts for some of the developments and changes in the theory of obligationes between Burley and Swyneshed.

4. Difficulties with Burley's theory

Some mediaeval authors—for instance Peter of Spain and Richard Lavenham—held that true conditionals are necessary,[44] and while they did not explicitly apply this to counterfactual conditionals in particular, neither did they explicitly restrict it to non-counterfactual ones. Nevertheless the fact that Burley's theory of obligationes is (4f)-inconsistent means—via (6) and (7)—that he is at least implicitly committed to saying that some true counterfactuals are only contingent.[45] For in virtue of (7), (4f)-inconsistency means that in some cases both $A \Box\!\!\rightarrow B$ and $A \Box\!\!\rightarrow \sim B$ are true, where A is possible. It follows that in such cases both counterfactuals are contingent. For if $A \Box\!\!\rightarrow B$ were necessary then, since (6) guarantees *modus ponens* for counterfactuals,[46] $\sim B$ would be incompatibly relevant at any step in any disputation with positum A. Hence there would be no disputation with positum A in which $\sim B$ is conceded, so that by (6) $A \Box\!\!\rightarrow \sim B$ would be false, contrary to the assumption. Similarly, if $A \Box\!\!\rightarrow \sim B$ were necessary then $A \Box\!\!\rightarrow B$ would be false.

44 Peter of Spain, *Tractatus, called afterwards summule logicales* (ed. L.M. De Rijk: 1972, Assen), treatise 1, par.17, p.9.17–18: 'Unde omnis conditionalis vera est necessaria, et omnis conditionalis falsa est impossibilis'. The same claim was made in the section on hypotheticals in Lavenham's *Summulae logicales* edited in Paul Vincent Spade, 'The treatises *On modal propositions* and *On hypothetical propositions* by Richard Lavenham', *Mediaeval studies*, 35 (1973), 49–59, par. 2. (On the place of this text in Lavenham's *Summulae logicales*, see Paul Vincent Spade, 'Notes on Richard Lavenham's so called *Summulae logicales*, with a partial edition of the text', *Franciscan studies* (forthcoming).) Robert Fland, both in his *Obligationes* (footnote 7), par. 35, and in his *Consequentiae* (edited in Paul Vincent Spade, 'Robert Fland's *Consequentiae*: an edition', *Mediaeval studies*, 38 (1976), 54–84, par. 20) states that 'quaelibet conditionalis quae non valet est impossibilis'. (By a conditional that 'non valet', he appears to mean a false conditional.) Since Fland's statement is (intended as) a logical law, it is necessary and hence so is its contrapositive 'Every possible conditional is true (valid)'. Thus by distribution every necessarily possible conditional is necessary, so that by Brouwer's Axiom every true (valid) conditional is necessary. Fland of course never heard of Brouwer, but the modal assumptions here are probably not too strong for him.

45 In this connection, it is interesting to observe that Thomas Bradwardine, a contemporary of Kilvington at Merton College, explicitly allows that some true conditionals are contingent, and lists among his examples Christ's counterfactual statement (Matthew 12: 21), 'for if the mighty works, which were done in you, had been done in Tyre and Sidon, they would have repented long ago in sackcloth and ashes'. See Thomas Bradwardine, *De causa dei contra Pelagium et de virtute causarum* (1618, London, photoreprint 1964, Frankfurt a.M.), III, 5, 604D. In the modern literature it is generally recognised that counterfactuals are usually contingent. See Lewis (footnote 6), 68.

46 Assume A and $A \Box\!\!\rightarrow B$ are true. Then by (6), there is a disputation with positum A in which B is conceded. But (1)-(3) provide that in a disputation with a true positum, only truths will be conceded.

This fact is what prevents the following (4a)-inconsistency in Burley's theory. Let A be a possible sentence and let both $A \Box\!\!\rightarrow B$ and $A \Box\!\!\rightarrow \sim B$ be true. Then

Positum: A

1. $A \Box\!\!\rightarrow B$
2. $A \Box\!\!\rightarrow \sim B$
3. B
4. $\sim B$
5. $B \& \sim B$

If steps 1 and 2 were necessary truths, they would have to be conceded insofar as any necessary truth is always sequentially relevant.[47] But then steps 3 and 4 would follow by modus ponens, and so would be sequentially relevant and have to be conceded. Likewise, step 5 would be sequentially relevant and have to be conceded, so that Burley's theory would be (4a)-inconsistent. But we have seen in section 2 that Burley's theory is not (4a)-inconsistent. it is saved from such inconsistency here because steps 1 and 2 are contingent.[48]

This is perhaps just as it should be. Nevertheless, the disputation illustrates an important feature of Burley's theory as interpreted by (6) and (7), a feature that is very odd for an account of the truth of counterfactuals. Since in virtue of (7) it sometimes happens that for possible A both $A \Box\!\!\rightarrow B$ and $A \Box\!\!\rightarrow \sim B$ are true, the consequent of a true counterfactual is not always to be conceded in all obligational disputations with the counterfactual's antecedent as the positum. This sounds perhaps as though one were saying that a counterfactual is true but then refusing to grant that its consequent would be true if its antecedents were true, so that one would be taking back with one hand what had just been given with the other. But that is not what is going on. By (6) and (7), the counterfactual is true if and only if its consequent must be conceded in *some* disputation with its antecedent as the positum. But all that one has refused to grant is that the consequent must be conceded in *all* such disputations. Nevertheless this feature certainly does violate our sense of how counterfactuals operate in practice. It implies, for instance, that if $A \Box\!\!\rightarrow B$ and $A \Box\!\!\rightarrow C$, it does not in general follow that $A \Box\!\!\rightarrow B \& C$.

It might be supposed that this odd feature is not a consequence of Burley's theory

47 Burley does not explicitly state this as a general principle. But he does say that anything follows from the impossible. (Walter Burley, *De puritate artis logicae tractatus longior, with a revised edition of the Tractatus brevior* (ed. Philotheus Boehner: 1955, St. Bonaventure, N.Y.), tract. long., 61.12.) By contraposition, the necessary follows from anything and so is always sequentially relevant. In his *Obligationes*, ed. Green (footnote 4), par. 3.50–3.52, Burley gives several examples in which he says that 'God exists' must be conceded 'because it is necessary'. Furthermore, in his discussion of cases in which the positum is impossible (ed. Green (footnote 4), par. 3.180), Burley says that one must not there use the rule 'the necessary follows from anything'. But he does not deny that the rule is valid, and indeed the context suggests that he otherwise accepts it.

48 The correct responses in the above disputation are these. Step 1 must be conceded as irrelevant and (known to be) true. Step 2 must then be denied as incompatibly relevant. Step 3 must be conceded as sequentially relevant, and steps 4 and 5 denied as incompatibly relevant.

but of our interpretation of it and that, still within an overall 'counterfactual' interpretation, (6) should be replaced by what one previously refused to grant, by the stronger

(8) for every true counterfactual $A \Box\!\!\rightarrow B$, B must be conceded or $\sim B$ denied in *every* obligational disputation with positum A.

Since Burley's theory is (4b)-consistent, and since in virtue of (7) there are cases in which both $A \Box\!\!\rightarrow B$ and $A \Box\!\!\rightarrow \sim B$, (8) is inconsistent with (7), so that this approach would have to make some adjustments at (7) too. But no matter what those adjustments might be, such an approach will not work. First, there are disputations with positum A in which B and $\sim B$ are not even proposed, so that (8) would make every counterfactual false. Second, even if we ignore this difficulty and think of disputations as implicitly running on so that every sentence or its negation is proposed at some step or other, (8) has the effect of making $A \Box\!\!\rightarrow B$ true only if B logically follows from A or else both A and B are true in fact.[49] Thus in the cases for which the theory was primarily designed, namely those in which the antecedent is contrary to fact, (8) would reduce counterfactuals to strict implications. This violates our sense of how counterfactuals operate in practice just as much as (6) and (7) do. Moreover, Burley's theory of obligationes, with its characteristic treatment of irrelevant sentences, would be a tremendously overcomplicated device to express a theory of counterfactuals that amounted to no more than this.

A somewhat more attractive approach is to suppose that Burley regarded counterfactuals as true or assertable *relative* to a given obligational disputation. Thus it might be that $A \Box\!\!\rightarrow B$ is true or assertable relative to one disputation while $A \Box\!\!\rightarrow \sim B$ is true or assertable relative to a different disputation. The two disputations can be thought of as specifying different classes of possible worlds in which the positum is true but that otherwise depart as little as possible from what, for all the respondent knows, the actual world is like. The two classes differ depending on which features of the actual world are held fixed and which are allowed to vary in those other worlds. This is determined by the *order* in which one proposes sentences in the two disputations. In general, a given disputation is more 'conservative' about the sentences proposed earlier than it is about the sentences proposed later; the former stand a greater chance of being irrelevant and so judged according to the respondent's knowledge of the facts. If one wants to choose among competing

49 Assume $A \Box\!\!\rightarrow B$. Then $\sim B$ does not logically follow from A. For simplicity we will treat the denial of $\sim B$ as the conceding of B. Then if A is true, B is true and conceded in all disputations with positum A. If A is false, there are two cases. If (a) B logically follows from A, then B is conceded in all disputations with positum A. If (b) B does not follow from A, there are two subcases. If (i) B is true, then since $\sim B$ is a falsehood compossible with A, there are disputations with positum A, following the pattern of (9) below, in which $\sim B$ is conceded. In such disputations B is not conceded. Hence it is not the case that B is conceded in all disputations with positum A. If (ii) B is false, $\sim B$ is irrelevant and conceded when it is proposed at the first step of a disputation with positum A. In such cases B is not conceded. Hence again it is not the case that B is conceded in all disputations with positum A. In short (8) implies that $A \Box\!\!\rightarrow B$ is true only if both A and B are true or else B logically follows from A.

counterfactuals and their supporting disputations, if one wants to know what would 'really' happen given the positum, then on this interpretation one must designate a certain disputation, with its particular order of proposing sentences, as the 'preferred' one for that positum. This amounts to selecting a ranking of sentences in the order in which one must be prepared to allow their truth values to depart from the actual world given the positum; the later sentences one must be more prepared to allow to vary.

One can accommodate this interpretation by reading (6) and (7) in terms of the *truth* of counterfactuals and recognising that nevertheless some true counterfactuals are to be 'preferred' to others. Perhaps a more plausible interpretation would read (6) and (7) in terms of the *assertability* of counterfactuals, in such a way that $A \Box\!\!\rightarrow B$ is assertable *relative* to exactly those disputations in which A is posited and B conceded or $\sim B$ denied.[50] Then for each positum a single 'preferred' disputation would be designated. *True* counterfactuals would be those assertable with respect to a 'preferred' disputation.

This 'relativised' approach, with its preference for certain orderings of sentences, goes a long way toward removing the oddity of Burley's theory. And indeed Burley does say in one place that 'one must pay most attention to the order'.[51] Perhaps this is no more than an observation that order affects the responses. But it sounds like advice. If it is advice addressed to the respondent, it seems misplaced. For while the order of the proposed sentences affects the replies the respondent must give to them, the respondent does not have to pay any special heed to that order. All he has to do is to remember how he has replied to the previous steps; he can forget their order. On the other hand, if the quotation is advice addressed to the opponent, it likewise seems misplaced unless the opponent is trying to do more than just fulfill his part in a disputation that conforms to the rules; the rules allow him to propose anything he wants in any order he pleases.[52] What more might he be trying to do? On the 'relativised' interpretation, he might be trying to conduct a disputation to determine what 'really' happens given the positum. In that case, just as Burley advises, he must indeed 'pay most attention to the order'.

This 'relativised' interpretation also removes the difficulty from the following odd feature of Burley's theory. Burley gives an example in which A and B are compossible known falsehoods such that A does not logically imply B.[53] Then:

(9) Positum: A

1. A and B have the same truth value. (conceded)
2. B (conceded)

50 See footnote 42.

51 Ed. Green (footnote 4), par. 3.34: 'Ordo est maxime attendendus'. Note that this is the passage in which Burley recognises the (4f)-inconsistency of his theory. See above at footnote 27.

52 See footnote 12.

53 Burley gives the example of 'You are in Rome' and 'You are a bishop' (ed. Green (footnote 4), par. 3.61 – 3.63). See also putative-Sherwood, ed. Green (footnote 4), par. 1.14. The illustration was a standard one, although the details of the argument varied. Indeed, Burley gives three different versions of the argument. I have used his second (par. 3.63) since it is in that form that Kilvington discusses the issue. (See §5.) A somewhat different illustration is used to make the same point as (9) in the *Tract. Emm. de falsi pos.*, ed. De Rijk 1974 (footnote 4), 107.29 – 108.10, and in the *Oblig. Paris.* (footnote 4), 31.13 – 27.

Step 1 is irrelevant and known to be true, since both *A* and *B* are known to be false even though *A* is counterfactually posited to be true. Hence step 1 is to be conceded. But then step 2 is to be conceded as sequentially relevant.[54] (The responses would have been exactly the same if *A* had logically implied *B*, although it does not in Burley's example.)

The point here is to show that once a falsehood has been posited, one can be forced to concede any other compossible falsehood whatever. If (6) and (7) are read in terms of the truth of counterfactuals, then Burley's point departs just as surely as (4f)-inconsistency does from our ordinary sense of how counterfactual reasoning ought to go. It means that $A \mathrel{\Box\!\!\rightarrow} B$ is true whenever *A* is false and does not logically imply $\sim B$. But the difficulty disappears on the 'relativised' interpretation of Burley's theory.

Nevertheless, it must be admitted that there is no evidence whatever for this 'relativised' interpretation apart from the inconclusive observation that 'one must pay most attention to the order'. Not only is there no evidence in Burley himself, but as far as I have been able to determine, there is no evidence in any other author who held in effect the same theory before or after Burley. If this is what Burley intended, he certainly did not make his intention very plain.

The situation then is this. If we view obligationes as a theory of the truth of counterfactuals, then Burley's theory has properties that violate our sense of how counterfactuals behave in practice. And while we can prevent those violations by viewing obligationes as a theory of the assertability of counterfactuals and by relativising counterfactuals to particular disputations, there is really very little historical evidence to support such an interpretation.[55] It might be argued that this situation shows that Burley did not intend his theory as an account of counterfactuals at all. But in virtue of the evidence presented in section 3, I think it more likely that he did so intend it, and that what we have is a theory of counterfactuals *that has problems*. Either Burley intended his theory in the non-relativised form, in which case it departs from ordinary usage, or if he intended the relativised interpretation, he seems to have been unable or unwilling to say exactly what he meant—and so do his predecessors and successors. I suspect they were simply unclear which they intended. In any case, if we interpret Burley's theory as a theory of counterfactuals *with problems*, it is easy to see how other authors felt that the theory needed to be revised. And that happened with Kilvington and Swyneshed.

It should be pointed out that departure from ordinary usage would probably not be as strong an objection for a mediaeval author as it is for a modern one. Mediaeval logicians did not often think of themselves as codifying the practices of natural

54 Note the similarity between this disputation and the first of the two disputations Burley used to illustrate the (4f)-inconsistency of his theory. See (5).

55 In fact it might be argued (see footnote 42) that the rules for relevant sentences count against such an interpretation. In this connection it would perhaps be fruitful to investigate the use of the vocabulary of obligationes in the sophismata-literature. There one regularly finds two mutually contradictory conclusions drawn from a counterfactual hypothesis. The resolution of the sophisma, if it does not point out a simple fallacy, might in effect consist of stipulating a preference for one order over another.

language. First of all Latin, the language of academic discourse, was not a natural language for them any more than Esperanto is for us. By Burley's day, anyone who spoke or wrote Latin did so as a second language, a highly technical language for use in special contexts: academic, ecclesiastical, legal or medical. Second, mediaeval logicians did not generally attempt to capture or represent ordinary Latin usage, but rather to *regiment* it in the interests of precision; if such regimentation violated ordinary usage, that would not by itself be a decisive objection as long as the regimentation was clear. Many authors, for instance, cheerfully adopted a rule of scope that flagrantly violated conventional usage in some cases.[56]

Burley gives no real evidence for anything but the non-relativised interpretation of his theory. The fact that, so interpreted, his theory departs from our sense of how counterfactuals actually behave would not for a mediaeval be an especially critical point. Still, it is easy to understand how some authors would have regarded such a departure as sufficient grounds for considering a different theory of obligationes. And that seems to have happened first with Richard Kilvington.

5. The textual basis of Richard Kilvington's theory

Richard Kilvington, in the forty-seventh of his sophismata,[57] considers the positum 'If the king is sitting you know the king is sitting, and if the king is not sitting you know the king is not sitting'. This is of course logically equivalent to 'Either you know the king is sitting or you know the king is not sitting', and it is in the latter form that Kilvington actually uses it. Both disjuncts are known to be false in fact (you recognise that you do not know what the king is doing), although their disjunction is counterfactually posited to be true. We shall abbreviate this positum:

(10) $Ks \vee K{\sim}s.$

On the basis of (10), Kilvington argues obligationally that both Ks and ${\sim}Ks$ must be conceded. His arguments are these:[58]

56 See Paul Vincent Spade, 'Five logical tracts by Richard Lavenham', in J. Reginald O'Donnell (ed.), *Essays in honour of Anton Charles Pegis* (1974, Toronto), 70–124 (p.86).

57 Richard Kilvington, *Sophismata*, edited with introduction, translation and commentary by Norman Kretzmann and Barbara Ensign Kretzmann (forthcoming). References will be to the line numbers in the typescript of the edition of sophisma 47. †

58 Kilvington (footnote 57), 1–14:

TU SCIS REGEM SEDERE. Supposito isto casu, quod si rex sedeat, tu scias regem sedere; et si rex non sedeat, tu scias regem non sedere. Tunc probatur sophisma sic. Tu scias regem sedere vel tu scis regem non sedere, sed tu non scis regem non sedere; igitur tu scis regem sedere. Maior patet per casum, et minor patet quia est vera non repugnans. Quod patet, nam ista non repugnant: 'Si rex sedet, tu scis regem sedere; et si rex non sedet, tu scis regem non sedere' et 'Tu non scis regem non sedere' Ad oppositum arguitur sic. Tu scis regem non sedere; igitur tu non scis regem sedere. Antecedens patet, quia tu scis regem sedere vel tu scis regem non sedere, sed tu non scis regem sedere; igitur tu scis regem non sedere. Et per consequens sophisma est falsum. Et minor patet ut prius, quia est vera et impertinens.

(11a) Positum: $Ks \vee K{\sim}s$

1. ${\sim}K{\sim}s$ (conceded)
2. Ks (conceded)

(11b) Positum: $Ks \vee K{\sim}s$

1. ${\sim}Ks$ (conceded)
2. $K{\sim}s$ (conceded)

Step 1 of each argument is conceded because it is irrelevant and known to be true; step 2 is then conceded because it is sequentially relevant.[59] With the inessential differences that step 1 proposes a negative sentence that must be conceded rather than the corresponding affirmative that would have to be denied, these two arguments illustrate the (4f)-inconsistency that generated much of the difficulty discussion in section 4. Kilvington seems to regard the situation as undesirable, and in his discussion of it takes the opportunity to revise the theory of obligationes. In the course of that discussion he digresses to consider the case of (9) above, which he also seems to regard as undesirable.

Since Kilvington apparently objects to the (4f)-inconsistency of Burley's theory, we might expect him to deny that the order of the proposed sentences in a disputation affects the correct responses to them. For it is this feature of Burley's view that is responsible for his (4f)-inconsistency. The same feature is also responsible for (9), since if the sentences had been proposed there in reverse order the responses to them would have been just the opposite. Indeed in one passage Kilvington does seem to deny that order counts and to recognise that in this respect he is departing from accepted theory.[60] Nevertheless the situation is more complicated than that.

59 In the second argument (footnote 58) Kilvington adds a third step ${\sim}Ks$, which follows from step 2 and must therefore be conceded as sequentially relevant. This step is of course redundant in virtue of step 1.

60 Kilvington (footnote 57), 119–131 (with emphases added):

> Item, si te esse episcopum foret concedendum propter hoc quod sequitur ex isto posito 'Tu es Romae' et ex isto concesso '"Tu es Romae" et "Tu es episcopus" sunt similia', igitur a multo fortiori immediate post positum proposita ista propositione 'Tu es episcopus', ista foret concedenda, quia sequitur ex posito et alio vero impertinenti. Nam in principio sequebatur 'Tu es Romae, et, "Tu es Romae" et "Tu es episcopus" sunt similia; igitur tu es episcopus'. *Cum igitur propositio sequens ex vero et posito sit tantum concedenda sicut propositio sequens ex posito et concesso, ceteris paribus*, sequitur quod in principio, post positum immediate, foret haec concedenda: 'Tu es episcopus'—quod est falsum *secundum istam responsionem*, quia immediate post positum, proposita ista 'Tu es episcopus', foret haec falsa et impertinens, et per consequens neganda.

See also footnote 69. The words 'secundum istam reponsionem' and the context of the passage as a whole indicate that Kilvington recognises that this view is distinct from the usual one. Note that this passage explicitly contradicts Burley, ed. Green (footnote 4), par. 3.47:

> Sed non omne sequens ex posito cum vero impertinente est concedendum, quia posito isto 'tu es Romae', tunc ista 'tu es episcopus' sequitur ex posito cum isto vero impertinente 'te esse Romae et te esse episcopum sunt similia'. Et tamen ista 'tu es episcopus' non est concedenda primo loco, quia non sequitur: praemissae erant concedendae, igitur conclusio erat concedenda; sed sequitur: praemissae erant concessae, igitur conclusio erat concedenda.

Kilvington's theory is not altogether clear. He nowhere gives a systematic account of obligationes, but only piecemeal comments. Moreover, there are theoretical and textual difficulties in certain crucial passages. We must therefore proceed with caution.

One puzzling passage occurs in Kilvington's digression about (9). Where *A* and *B* are compossible known falsehoods such that *A* does not logically imply *B*, Kilvington says that

(12) if we posit that *A* were true, then step 1 of (9) would not be conceded unless *B* were true. But in that case the respondent would be no more obligated because of the positum than he would be if *A* were actually true. Therefore, *B* is not to be conceded because of the positum *A*.[61]

There is a second puzzling passage later in the same digression, and it will help shed some light on (12). There Kilvington says not just that step 1 of (9) would not have to be conceded unless *B* were true, but that in fact

(13) Step 1 must be denied, not conceded as on Burley's theory.[62]

But his reason for this is obscure. For, he says,

(14) If *A* and ~*B* were so, step 1 would not have to be conceded. Therefore it ought to be denied now.[63]

These passages are hardly persuasive as they stand. First, in (14) Kilvington presumably means not only that step 1 would not have to be conceded if *A* and ~*B* were so, but in particular, that it would have to be denied in that case. Second, there is the suggestion in (14) that the response to a sentence in the actual world depends on the response to it in some other possible worlds. This may sound like the way to an infinite regress, but I think that can be avoided. What Kilvington is saying here is in effect: If disputation (9) were conducted in a world in which *A* and ~*B* are so, step 1

61 Kilvington (footnote 57), 111–118:

> Unde dico—in communi exemplo, ut facilius intelligatur—quod posita ista 'Tu es Romae', non contingit probare aliquod falsum sibi compossible, ut istam: 'Tu es episcopus', et similia. Et causa est quia posito quod tu esses Romae, non concederes istam '"Tu es Romae" et "Tu es episcopus" sunt similia' nisi fores episcopus. Sed tunc non plus obligaris propter aliquid positum quam si tu esses Romae actualiter. Igitur propter istud positum—quod tu es Romae—non est concedendum te esse episcopum.

62 Kilvington (footnote 57), 222–224: 'Aliter tamen dicendum est in talibus quando ponitur "Tu es Romae" et deinde proponitur "'Tu es Romae' et 'Tu es episcopus' sunt similia", neganda est haec propositio proposita' Immediately before this passage (132–221), Kilvington considers another response to (9), based on the observation that inferences of the form '*p*, therefore *P* is true' are invalid even if '*P*' is a name of the sentence replacing '*p*', because '*P*' is not *necessarily* a name of that sentence. The point can perhaps be argued, but in any case does not go to the heart of the matter. It can be sidestepped by replacing step 1 of (9) by ~*A* v *B*. Kilvington's definitive response to (9) seems to be different.

63 Kilvington (footnote 57), 224–227: 'Quia te existente Romae et te non existente episcopo, not foret haec concedenda: "'Tu es Romae' et 'Tu es episcopus' sunt similia"; et ideo nunc est eadem propositio neganda a te'.

would not have to be conceded—and would in fact have to be denied—because in that world the positum *A* is true and step 1 is false, and where the positum is true one responds to relevant and irrelevant sentences alike according to the fact of the matter.[64] There is no infinite regress; the point is only that the response to a sentence in a disputation in the actual world, where responses may depart from the truth, depends on the response that would have to be given to that sentence if the disputation were conducted in certain other possible worlds where responses in that disputation would not depart from the truth. This is a roundabout but quite intelligible way of saying simply that the response to that sentence in the actual world depends on its *truth value* in certain other possible worlds. But the question then is: Why in particular are the possible worlds in which *A* and $\sim B$ are true the right ones to pick in this case—rather than, for instance, worlds in which *A* and step 1 of (9) are true?

A somewhat similar account can be given for (12). There Kilvington is saying in effect: Pick a world in which *A* is true. If disputation (9) were conducted in that world, then step 1 would not be conceded unless *B* is also true in that world, because when the positum is true one concedes only truths. In such a world the respondent would be no more obligated 'because of the positum' to concede a given sentence than he would be in the actual world if *A* were actually true. Therefore in the actual world *B* is not to be conceded because of *A*.

The passage is still obscure. For instance, the detour through worlds in which *A* is true seems unnecessary to make the point. And the last step seems particularly unrelated to what precedes it. But the upshot of the passage seems to be that, since *A* does not imply *B* in the actual world (or for that matter in worlds in which *A* is true), therefore if *B* is to be conceded at all in the actual world, it is not 'because of *A*'. But this is not yet an answer to Burley. Burley does not say that *B* in (9) is to be conceded because of the positum *A* alone, but rather because of the positum and step 1 together.

The context of this entire digression is (10) and the arguments (11a) and (11b). Kilvington responds to this sophisma by saying that *Ks* is to be doubted, and he offers the additional information that the simple sentence *s* ('The king is sitting') is to be doubted as well.[65] But this last poses a third puzzle. For *s* is not proposed in either (11a) or (11b). Does Kilvington mean that it *would* have to be doubted if it *were* proposed? And if so, is this true of both (11a) and (11b) or of one of them only?[66]

Kilvington's reason for saying that *Ks* is to be doubted presents a fourth difficulty. Because this claim disagrees with both (11a) and (11b), we should perhaps expect Kilvington to respond to both of those arguments. In fact, however, he responds only to (11a). For, he says, it is true by the hypothesis (10) that

64 This is certainly true for Burley's theory in virtue of (1)–(3), and for Swyneshed's theory as described in section 7. There is no special reason to suppose that Kilvington did not intend this feature to be true of his own theory too. If he did not, then I do not know what to make of (14).

65 Kilvington (footnote 57), 240–241: 'His visis, respondeo aliter ad sophisma, dubitando istud sophisma 'Tu scis regem sedere' et dubitando istam similiter: "Rex sedet"'. Kilvington takes great pains (242–257) to point out that although *s* is to be doubted in the actual world, it is not at all doubtful in worlds in which (10) is true.

66 Since order does not count for Kilvington, it would make no difference where *s* were inserted into (11a) or (11b). See footnote 69.

(15) s only if $\sim K \sim s$.

But in fact (10) has nothing to do with this; (15) is true simply because knowledge implies truth, so that $K \sim s$ only if $\sim s$, from which (15) follows by contraposition. What Kilvington probably intends here is not so much the conditional (15) as the biconditional

(16) s if and only if $\sim K \sim s$,

which would indeed be true 'by the hypothesis' (10).[67] In any case since, Kilvington continues, s is to be doubted it follows that $\sim K \sim s$—that is, step 1 of (11a)—is to be doubted too, not conceded as on Burley's theory.[68] Presumably a similar response is meant to apply to (11b), but Kilvington does not say so.

Kilvington's remarks here indicate that his theory of obligationes, unlike Burley's, will be (4d)-consistent. For, since Burley's theory is not (4d)-consistent, it is simply not true that in general one cannot concede the antecedent or deny the consequent of a sentence A that has to be doubted. What is true instead is that, once its antecedent is conceded or its consequent denied, A cannot be doubted in any *subsequent* step, although it may have had to be doubted earlier. Hence, it appears that Kilvington's theory of obligationes will not only insist on (4f)-consistency, as suggested above, but also insist on (4d)-consistency. In short, on Kilvington's theory, the position or order of the proposed sentences in a disputation will in no way affect the correct responses to them.[69]

67 Mediaeval logicians were notoriously lax about this, frequently stating only a conditional where a biconditional was clearly intended.

68 Kilvington (footnote 57), 258–262: 'Ad argumentum concedendum est quod tu scis regem sedere vel tu scis regem non sedere. Sed minor coassumpta est dubitanda—scilicet, haec: "Tu non scis regem non sedere". Quia si rex sedet, tu non scis regem non sedere—per casum—et antecedens est dubitandum; igitur consequens est dubitandum'. Note that this response is not even superficially persuasive unless (16) is read for (15). For otherwise, while perhaps $\sim K \sim s$ cannot be denied (since, one might argue, its antecedent s would have to be denied too, and not doubted), there would be no corresponding reason why $\sim K \sim s$ should not be conceded, as it is on Burley's view. The passage continues: 'Et quando arguitur "Ista minor est vera et impertinens; igitur est concedenda", dico quod primo modo loquendo de impertinenti consequentia non valet. Sed secundo modo loquendo de impertinenti dubitandum est utrum minor sit vera et impertinens' (252–266). For the 'primus modus' and the 'secundus modus', see footnotes 70 and 71.

69 In the passage quoted in footnote 60, Kilvington suggests that order does not count in determining which sentences are to be *conceded*. Since conceding a sentence is equivalent to denying its contradictory, the same passage therefore suggests that order also does not count in determining which sentences are to be denied. It might be thought that, since order does not count in determining the conceded and the denied sentences, it follows that order does not count in determining the doubted sentences either, because sentences that are neither conceded nor denied must be doubted. In that case the passage would imply that order does not count at all, so that Kilvington is committing himself to (4e)-consistency. Furthermore, since (4e)-inconsistency is a trivial corollary of (4d)-inconsistency, as shown in section 2, (4d)-consistency is a corollary of (4e)-consistency. Hence (4d)-consistency would already be implied by the text in footnote 60, and the present discussion would add nothing new. But this is wrong. Since on Burley's theory sentences can be *both* doubted *and* either conceded or denied, fixing the conceded and the denied sentences does not automatically fix the doubted sentences. The text in footnote 60 commits Kilvington only to (4f)-consistency, not to (4e)-or (4d)-consistency. The present discussion does add something new.

There is yet a fifth puzzling passage. Kilvington recognises that if we retain Burley's standard notions of relevance and irrelevance, his remarks may be viewed as an implicit rejection of (3); some true and irrelevant sentences need not be conceded, as for example step 1 of (9) or step 1 of (11a).[70] He does not say what rule would replace (3) in that case. On the other hand, he also suggests that his remarks may be viewed as revising the notions of relevance and irrelevance. This is the direction we shall investigate. Kilvington does not explicitly say that if we make such a revision he will accept (3), and although the suggestion seems implicit in his remarks, it is difficult to reconcile it with the rest of his theory. In any case Kilvington does not make it very clear just how the revision is to go. In the revised sense, he says, an 'irrelevant' sentence is a sentence that is true but that nevertheless, if the positum were so, would not *on that account* be true.[71]

This is not much help as it stands. The restriction to true sentences is probably not a feature of the general theory so much as it is a mere reflection of the fact that, in the context, Kilvington is talking about a sentence that is in reality true, step 1 of (9). Deleting this restriction, we can say that on the revised notion an irrelevant sentence is one that, if the positum were so, would not *on that account* be true. And it is probably not too much to add that, if the positum were so, the sentence in question would not *on that account* be false either. This speculative reconstruction suggests that on Kilvington's revision only the positum has to be taken into account when assessing relevance and irrelevance. And this in turn amounts to replacing (2) above by

(17) X_i contains only the positum,

This revision would have at least one desired effect: the order of proposed sentences in a disputation would in no way affect the correct responses to them. (Hence the subscript could be omitted). Moreover, this revision is of special interest because by itself it yeilds exactly the theory Roger Swyneshed will accept. Nevertheless, Kilvington's view must involve more than this. For otherwise Kilvington would never disagree with Burley about the correct response to the first proposed sentence in a disputation, but only about the sentences proposed later. In fact, however, he does disagree with Burley about the correct responses to step 1 of (9) and step 1 of (11a).[72]

70 Kilvington (footnote 57), 228–232: 'Et quando arguitur "Ista est vera et impertinens; igitur ista est concedenda", ad illud dico quod loquendo de impertinenti ut communiter sumitur—pro propositione non sequenti vel repugnanti posito vel concesso, et ita de aliis—non sequitur "Haec propositio est vera et impertinens; igitur est concedenda"'. In order to violate (3), such a sentence must not only be true but also be known to be true. See footnote 25.

71 Kilvington (footnote 57), 232–239: 'Si tamen accipiatur iste terminus "impertinens" pro propositione quae nunc est vera et quae non foret vera ex hoc quod ita foret ex parte rei sicut significatur per positum, tunc dico quod ista propositio "'Tu es Romae' et 'Tu es episcopus' sunt similia" est impertinens [see footnote 72] huic posito, quod est "Tu es Romae". Quia si tu esses Romae et non esses episcopus, haec foret neganda: "'Tu es Romae' et 'Tu es episcopus' sunt similia"'. Compare the above discussion of (12).

72 At a crucial point some manuscripts of Kilvington (footnote 57), 236, say that step 1 of (9) is 'relevant', while others say it is 'irrelevant' In virtue of the developments below, I suggest that the correct reading is 'relevant'

6. Outline of Kilvington's theory

Kilvington apparently intended a theory of obligationes in which the responses to proposed sentences do not depend on their order in the disputation. Whereas Burley determined the responses to sentences step by step as the disputation unfolded, Kilvington seems to have decided that the responses should be fixed in one fell swoop as soon as the positio is admitted. Since the basic idea behind obligationes is to reason counterfactually about what would happen if the positum were true but everything else were as much as possible the same, Kilvington's decision suggests a simple view in which what is implied by the positum should be conceded, what is incompatible with the positum should be denied, and everything else should stay the same—that is, should be conceded, denied or doubted according to our knowledge of the facts.

On the other hand, we have seen that such a view—represented by (1), (17) and (3)—is not the one Kilvington adopts. And there is good reason for his not adopting it: it is (4c)-inconsistent. Let (10) be posited. It must then be conceded whenever it is proposed. But, on the view under consideration, both $\sim Ks$ and $\sim K\sim s$ are irrelevant and known to be false, and so must likewise be conceded whenever they are proposed. Yet these three concedable sentences form an inconsistent set. Hence, just as on Burley's theory, if $A \,\Box\!\!\rightarrow B$ and $A \,\Box\!\!\rightarrow C$, it does not in general follow that $A \,\Box\!\!\rightarrow B\&C$. If Kilvington had any objection to Burley's theory on these grounds, this was hardly the way to correct the situation.

Whether Kilvington reasoned in this way or not, he seems in any case to have combined his decision to fix all responses in one fell swoop with another consideration. I suggest that he decided there are certain sentences that are 'basic' in the sense that once the response to them is fixed, the responses to all other sentences are fixed as well. While he does not use the principles (1), (17) and (3) for all sentences across the board, he does use them for the 'basic' sentences, recognising that the others will then take care of themselves.

The responses to sentences in general are determined in effect by looking to their truth values in a certain class Y of possible worlds. The correct responses to the 'basic' sentences in particular are determined by looking to their truth values in that same class Y. But the responses to the 'basic' sentences turn out the same if we look to the class Z of all worlds differing from worlds in Y at most with respect to *non*-basic sentences; we are only looking to the truth values of the basic ones. Since the responses to the basic sentences fix the responses to all other sentences, $Y = Z$. In short, not only does fixing the responses to the basic sentences fix the responses to all other sentences, fixing the truth values of the basic sentences fixes the truth values of all other sentences too. If we think of the truth conditions for sentences as being recursively specifiable,[73] then the 'basic' sentences are just those the truth conditions for which are given in the basis clause of the recursion.

Today we should do this by making the basic sentences atomic. But that is not the only way to do it. Mediaeval practice tended to take the truth values of singular

73 Although a theory of recursion was of course not available to mediaeval logicians, the practice of giving something like a recursive account of the truth conditions was by no means unknown to them. See, e.g., Ockham (footnote 12), II.

categorical sentences, including negative ones and so not just atomic sentences, as the basis for generating the truth values of other sentences. But in any event, not *all* categorical sentences or even all atomic sentences can count as 'basic' in the sense required for this interpretation of Kilvington; the class of basic sentences will have to be narrower than that. For *Ks* is atomic and so, if all atomic sentences were basic, would have to be denied as irrelevant and known to be false in any disputation with (10) as positum. But Kilvington says it is to be doubted, not denied, and he argues for this claim on the basis of the fact that *s* itself is to be doubted.[74] Hence, while the latter may be a basic sentence, the former is not.[75]

Once the response to each basic sentence has been determined on the basis of (1), (17) and (3), the responses to all other sentences are fixed automatically. One way of explaining how this works, a way Kilvington would *not* have used, is the following. Let X be a smallest set containing the positum and such that, where A is a basic sentence, (a) if A is to be conceded, then $A \varepsilon X$, (b) if A is to be denied, then $\sim A \varepsilon X$, and (c) if A is to be doubted, then either $A \varepsilon X$ or $\sim A \varepsilon X$ but not both. (Where at least one basic sentence is to be doubted, there will be more than one such set X.) Since the truth values of all other sentences are generated recursively from the truth values of basic sentences, each such set X will determine a class of possible worlds. Any given sentence, whether basic or not, is to be conceded if and only if it is true in all those worlds, denied if and only if it is false in all those worlds, and doubted if and only if it is true in some of those worlds but false in others.

This seems to be in effect Kilvington's view. But when it comes to translating this 'possible worlds' account into the traditional vocabulary of obligationes, difficulties arise. Once the basic sentences are fixed, the respondent's replies to the non-basic ones are fixed as well, so that in replying to them he does not have to ask whether or not he knows they are in fact true or knows they are in fact false. In short, if (3) applies to non-basic sentences, no non-basic sentence is irrelevant. But certainly there are non-basic sentences that must be doubted; *Ks* is such a sentence where (10) is the positum. Hence, if (3) applies to non-basic sentences, there must be a kind of relevance other than sequential relevance and incompatible relevance. For with those kinds of relevance the relevant sentence is not to be doubted. On the other hand, (3) does indeed apply to basic sentences, and there is no need there for a kind of relevance other than sequential relevance and incompatible relevance. It is little wonder, in view of all this, that Kilvington seems unable to explain clearly just how he has revised the notions of relevance and irrelevance, and that he never really says whether, with those revised notions, he accepts (3) or not.

74 See the discussion in section 4, at (15) and (16), and the texts quoted there.

75 If Kilvington really means that the truth conditions of atomic epistemic sentences must be generated recursively from the truth conditions of more basic non-epistemic ones, then he is perhaps demanding the impossible. That appears to be what he does mean, but in any event the difficulty would affect only the implementation of his theory, the actual picking of basic sentences in terms of which the truth conditions of all other sentences are to be specified, not the theory itself of how such a class of basic sentences, once it is specified, functions in the context of obligationes.

An equivalent of Kilvington's view as described above may be summarised in such a way that the classes X may be defined directly, without recourse to (1), (17) or (3), as follows:

(18) Where A is the positum and 'B' ranges over all the basic sentences, let X be a smallest set containing A and such that
  (a) if A implies B, then BX;
  (b) if A implies $\sim B$, then $\sim BX$;
  (c) if A implies neither B nor $\sim B$ and
    (i) B is known to be true, then $B \varepsilon X$;
    (ii) B is known to be false, then $\sim B \varepsilon X$;
    (iii) otherwise either $B \varepsilon X$ or $\sim B \varepsilon X$ but not both.

Then

(19) A sentence C, whether basic or non-basic, is relevant if and only if
  (a) every X implies C (sequential relevance), or
  (b) every X implies $\sim C$ (incompatible relevance).
 C is irrelevant if and only if it is not relevant.

(20) (a) If C is sequentially relevant, it is to be conceded.
  (b) If C is incompatibly relevant, it is to be denied.
  (c) If C is irrelevant, it is to be doubted.

On Kilvington's theory, Burley's (1), (2) and (3) are in effect replaced by (19), (18) and (20), respectively.

This account of Kilvington's theory fits the texts.[76] First, (18)–(20) guarantee that the order of the proposed sentences will in no way affect the responses to them, just as Kilvington wants. The relevance or irrelevance of any proposed sentence in a disputation depends solely on that sentence's logical relations with the positum and the basic sentences, not on whatever other sentences happen to be proposed. Hence in (9), step 1 plays no role in determining the response to B at step 2. If B is not to be conceded 'because of the positum', it is not to be conceded at all. Thus (12).

Second, in Kilvington's actual example, B in (9) is a basic sentence.[77] Thus, since B is not implied by A and is known to be false in the actual world, it will also be false in all the worlds specified by the sets X of (18). Hence step 1 (which is not a basic sentence since its truth value is generated from the truth values of A and B) will likewise be false in all those worlds, so that it ought to be denied in the actual world, as (13) says. This explains (14).

Third, since (10) implies neither the basic sentence s nor its contradictory $\sim s$, and since s is in fact doubtful, it follows that when (10) is posited s is irrelevant and, although it is not in fact proposed in either (11a) or (11b), would have to be doubted if it were inserted in either disputation at any step.

76 See the five puzzling passages discussed in section 5.

77 See footnote 53.

Fourth, as Kilvington suggests, it is because the basic sentence s is to be doubted that the non-basic sentences Ks and $K{\sim}s$, and their negations, must be doubted too in virtue of (16).

Fifth, if we use Burley's notion of relevance, Kilvington rejects (3). And we have seen why Kilvington has so much trouble explaining his revision of that notion.

7. Outline of Roger Swyneshed's theory

Kilvington's view appears very attractive. Provided only that the sets X of (18) are consistent, his theory is (4c)-consistent and therefore (4b)- and (4a)-consistent too. It is also (4d)-, (4e)- and (4f)-consistent. The consequent of a true counterfactual is always to be conceded in all disputations with its antecedent as positum. When a falsehood is posited, Kilvington does not have to concede all other compossible falsehoods whatever. And if $A \,\Box\!\!\rightarrow B$ and $A \,\Box\!\!\rightarrow C$, it follows in every case that $A \,\Box\!\!\rightarrow B \,\&\, C$.

These are powerful recommendations. Unfortunately, they are predicated on the assumption that the sets X of (18) are consistent. And that is not always so. Let A and B compossible basic sentences, both of which are known to be false and neither of which implies the other. Then whenever $A \vee B$ is posited, both A and B will have to be denied on Kilvington's view, and their denials ${\sim}A$ and ${\sim}B$ will have to be conceded. But $A \vee B$, ${\sim}A$ and ${\sim}B$ form an inconsistent subset of each of the sets X described in (18), so that Kilvington's theory is (4c)-inconsistent, and therefore (4b)- and (4a)-inconsistent too. Hence with respect to certain posita, every sentence whatever is sequentially relevant and, since if a sentence is sequentially relevant its contradictory is incompatibly relevant, every sentence is incompatibly relevant as well. In some cases, therefore, a disputation simply cannot be conducted; Kilvington's rules do not allow the respondent a unique reply at each step. In short, the theory breaks down.[78]

Roger Swyneshed discusses such a case. Swyneshed's view simply maintains (1), (17), and (3) across the board. The response to a sentence is determined only by the respondent's knowledge of the facts and by the sentence's logical relation to the positum alone, not by its logical relations to any other proposed sentences or to a privileged class of 'basic' sentences. Order does not matter. On this view, Swyneshed has to concede step 1 of (9) and deny step 2. Again, step 1 of both (11a) and (11b) is to be conceded and step 2 is to be denied. As these cases illustrate, Swyneshed—like Burley—may disagree with Kilvington at any step of a disputation. On the other hand, Swyneshed always agrees with Burley at the first step, although he sometimes disagrees with Burley at later steps.

In his *Obligationes*, Swyneshed presents his view almost entirely without motivation.[79] But in one passage he considers the disjunction 'You are in Rome or

78 It is worth pointing out that, if basic sentences are selected in such a way that the truth value of any one is independent of the values of the others either individually or together, then this inconsistency does not arise where the positum is a basic sentence or a conjunction of basic sentences. As long as Kilvington's theory is restricted to these cases, it may provide a completely consistent and quite admirable account of counterfactual reasoning.

79 Swyneshed (footnote 2). See especially the statement of principles in section 2 of the edition.

you are running'. After explaining his own theory about how to conduct a correct disputation with that sentence as the positum,[80] Swyneshed recognises an objection:[81]

> There is an argument against this view, as follows. No incompatibles are to be conceded in the context of an obligatio. But this view concedes incompatibles in the context of an obligatio. Therefore, it is wrong. Proof of the minor: If the first sentence [i.e., 'You are in Rome or you run'] is posited, then it is to be conceded in the context of the obligatio. And if 'You are not in Rome' is proposed afterwards, it is to be conceded in the context of the obligatio. And if after that 'You do not run' is proposed, it is to be simply conceded, according to this view. These three are clearly incompatible.

In his reply to this objection, Swyneshed says merely, 'The solution: It must be conceded that three incompatibles are to be conceded, and four, and so on'.[82] That is, he explicitly recognises and accepts the (4c)-inconsistency of his theory.

Although Swyneshed nowhere says exactly why his theory should be preferred to the others, it is noteworthy that 'You are in Rome' and 'You are running' both appear to be 'basic' sentences. In effect then what Swyneshed has shown is not only the (4c)-inconsistency of his own view, which accepts (1), (17), and (3) across the board, but also the (4c)-inconsistency of Kilvington's view, which in effect applies (1), (17) and (3) to basic sentences only.

Now whereas the (4c)-inconsistency of Kilvington's theory commits him also to (4b)- and (4a)-inconsistency, the (4c)-inconsistency of Swyneshed's theory does not, and in this sense Swyneshed might well have thought his theory was to be preferred.

80 Swyneshed (footnote 2), par. 98–99. Swyneshed's discussion here is complicated by his allowing a 'composite' positum, one part of which is posited at the outset of the disputation, but the other part of which is introduced only at a later step. We shall ignore this complication, which does not affect the point under consideration.

81 Swyneshed (footnote 2), par. 100:

> Contra illam responsionem arguitur sic: Nulla repugnantia sunt concedenda infra tempus obligationis. Sed illa responsio concedit repugnantia infra tempus obligationis. Igitur, male. Minor probatur: Si ponitur prima, tunc ista est concedenda infra tempus obligationis. Et si postea proponitur 'Tu non es Romae' illa est concedenda infra tempus obligationis. Et si post proponatur 'Tu non curris' ista est concedenda simpliciter secundum illam responsionem. Et ista tria repugnant manifeste.

82 Swyneshed (footnote 2), par. 101: 'Solutio: Concedenda est conclusio quod tria repugnantia sunt concedenda et quattuor et sic deinceps'. Swyneshed goes on to say that indeed two contradictories may sometimes have to be conceded in the same disputation in virtue of a change in the facts. For instance, if 'You are in Rome' is posited and then the sentence 'You are sitting' is proposed while you are in fact sitting, it is to be conceded. But if you then stand up and the sentence 'You are not sitting' is proposed, it is to be conceded too, even though you have earlier conceded its contradictory, because the circumstances have been altered. We shall ignore this complication, in effect thinking of obligational disputations as though they took place at an instant. Otherwise Swynesed's theory will be not only (4c)-inconsistent but (4b)-inconsistent too. It will not, however, be (4a)-inconsistent. From the fact that one must concede both *A* and *B*, it does not follow on Swyneshed's view that one must concede their conjunction *A & B*. See Swyneshed (footnote 2), par. 32: 'Propter concessionem partium copulativae non est copulativa concedenda'.

For since an impossibility never logically follows from a possible positum alone, the respondent will never have to concede an impossibility. Hence Swyneshed's theory is (4a)-consistent. Likewise, if A is to be conceded, it is either because it follows logically from the positum alone (in which case $\sim A$ must be denied as incompatibly relevant), or else neither follows from nor is inconsistent with the positum but is known to be true (in which case $\sim A$ is irrelevant and known to be false). In neither case will $\sim A$ have to be conceded. Hence Swyneshed's theory is also (4b)-consistent. And since the order of the proposed sentences makes no difference on Swyneshed's theory, that theory is (4d)-, (4e)- and (4f)-consistent as well.

These considerations give Swyneshed's theory a decisive advantage over Kilvington's. But it is not so clear that it has the advantage over Burley's. Since order does not count on Swyneshed's theory, any sentence that has to be conceded in a given disputation would also have to be conceded if it were proposed at the first step. Thus, since Swyneshed and Burley never disagree on the first step, every counterfactual true on Swyneshed's theory is true also on Burley's. But the converse does not hold. In virtue of Swyneshed's (4f)-consistency, he is never committed to both $A \,\Box\!\!\rightarrow B$ and $A \,\Box\!\!\rightarrow \sim B$, whereas Burley sometimes is because his theory is (4f)-inconsistent.

For Swyneshed, $A \,\Box\!\!\rightarrow B$ is true if and only if either A logically implies B, or else A does not logically imply $\sim B$ and B is true. For Burley, there is a third alternative: as (9) shows, $A \,\Box\!\!\rightarrow B$ is also true for Burley if A is false and does not logically imply $\sim B$.[83] This means that the two disagree over exactly those cases in which A logically implies neither B nor $\sim B$ and both A and B are false. In such cases, $A \,\Box\!\!\rightarrow B$ is true for Burley but false for Swyneshed. It was Burley's third alternative that committed him sometimes to both $A \,\Box\!\!\rightarrow B$ and $A \,\Box\!\!\rightarrow \sim B$,[84] and so was responsible for his (4f)-inconsistency. We now see why those undesirable features are missing from Swyneshed's theory.

On the other hand, Swyneshed's theory is by no means an attractive account of counterfactuals. Burley's theory was (4f)-inconsistent but had the compensating virtue of being (4c)-consistent. Swyneshed's theory is (4f)-consistent but has the compensating vice of being (4c)-inconsistent. This means that while on Burley's theory, but not on Swyneshed's, $A \,\Box\!\!\rightarrow B$ may be true even though B does not have to be conceded in all disputations with A as positum, which seems odd if obligational disputations are a form of counterfactual reasoning, on Swyneshed's theory but not on Burley's it turns out in some cases that one also has to concede in all those disputations two or more other sentences that are jointly incompatible with B, and that is just as odd. As a result of these facts, both theories have the undesirable feature that if $A \,\Box\!\!\rightarrow B$ and $A \,\Box\!\!\rightarrow C$, it does not in general follow that $A \,\Box\!\!\rightarrow B \& C$. Both theories also have the feature that $A \,\Box\!\!\rightarrow B$ is true whenever A does not imply $\sim B$ and B is true. This is too strong to conform to ordinary usage.

83 There is no fourth alternative for Burley. If all three alternatives fail, then A does not logically imply B, but either A does logically imply $\sim B$ or else A is true and B false. In either case, then, $A \,\Box\!\!\rightarrow B$ is false. In effect, if A is possible, then for Burley $A \,\Box\!\!\rightarrow B$ is true just in case the *material* conditional $A \supset B$ is true and A does not logically imply $\sim B$.

84 See footnote 54.

Swyneshed's theory thus shares some of the difficulties of Burley's theory. Others it does not share but replaces with difficulties just as bad. The only real advantage of Swyneshed's theory over Burley's is that the former is never committed to both $A \Box\!\!\rightarrow B$ and $A \Box\!\!\rightarrow \sim B$, since it does not hold in general that $A \Box\!\!\rightarrow B$ is true if A is false and does not logically imply $\sim B$.

Nevertheless the difficulties with Burley's view can be resolved if we adopt the 'relativised' interpretation described in section 4. This option is not open to us on Swyneshed's theory; since for him order does not count, all disputations beginning with the same positum are equal. Hence in the end it is not clear that Swyneshed has any real advantage over Burley.

8. Summary and conclusion

The theory of obligationes, if I am correct, was a theory of counterfactuals. Burley's theory never required one to concede a contradiction, never required one to concede two contradictories in separate steps, and for that matter never required one to concede each member of an inconsistent set. On the other hand, Burley's theory committed him to the view that $A \Box\!\!\rightarrow B$ is true whenever A is false and does not logically imply $\sim B$, and in some cases committed him to both $A \Box\!\!\rightarrow B$ and $A \Box\!\!\rightarrow \sim B$. These features of Burley's theory arise because for him the order of the proposed sentences affects the responses to them. They and other difficulties can be avoided by adopting an interpretation of Burley's theory that relativises counterfactuals to particular disputations. But while there is a faint suggestion of this interpretation in Burley's text, there is no real evidence that he or anyone else saw or pursued this possibility.

Richard Kilvington, trying to avoid the undesirable consequences of Burley's theory, decided to make the order of the sentences not count by fixing the responses to all sentences at once. This decision suggests the approach that Swyneshed later actually adopted. But Kilvington instead restricted that approach to 'basic' sentences only, sentences covered by the basis clause in a recursive account of truth conditions, and let the responses to them determine the responses to all other sentences. While Kilvington does not say why he does this, it is not implausible to suppose that he recognised that the more sweeping policy Swyneshed would later adopt required one in some cases to concede each member of an inconsistent set, so that such a theory leads to many of the same difficulties Burley's theory had.

Kilvington's theory is subtle, but unfortunately is in the end crippled by inconsistency of the strongest kind. It not only sometimes requires one to concede each member of an inconsistent set, it also requires one to concede outright contradictions all at once. Perhaps in response to this decisive inconsistency, Roger Swyneshed adopted the view Kilvington hesitated to adopt. That view is not committed to the inconsistencies of Kilvington's theory, but neither does it solve many of the problems that prompted that theory.

Kilvington's theory appears to have had no future; no one other than Kilvington himself seems to have held it. Certainly this was in part because the theory is so hard to articulate and explain in the traditional vocabulary of obligationes. But in any case the inherent difficulties of the view would suffice to make it unattractive.

Historically, Burley's theory and Swyneshed's were the main alternatives. And while if we do not take into account the possibility of a 'relativised' interpretation of Burley's view, Swyneshed's theory shows some advantage over Burley's, nevertheless most later authors were content to retain Burley's more traditional theory. It is hard to see whey they did so unless they were at least implicitly using that theory in its relativised form. Further research will have to determine whether there is any positive evidence for this.

Acknowledgments

I would like to thank Romane L. Clark, Daniel H. Cohen, J. Michael Dunn, Norman Kretzmann and Eleonore Stump for their very helpful conversations and comments on a previous draft of this paper.

ADDENDA ET CORRIGENDA

<u>STUDY I - Recent Research</u>

p. 5 line 20: The critical edition of Ockham's works by the Franciscan Institute is now completed.

p. 5 line 31: The authenticity of Boehner (1945) is not in doubt. See S. F. Brown's introduction to the critical edition in William of Ockham, <u>Opera philosophica</u> II, (St. Bonaventure, NY: The Franciscan Institute, 1978), pp. 28*-30*.

p. 5 lines 35-6: Scott (forthcoming) was published in 1977.

p. 6 line 8: Other parts of the <u>Logica magna</u> have been edited and translated by Norman Kretzmann (Part I, fasc. 1: "Tractatus de terminis," 1979) and by Patricia Clarke (Part I, fasc. 7: "Tractatus de scire et dubitare," 1981).

p. 8 line 1: Green's work is still forthcoming.

p. 8 lines 1-2 & line 5: The two papers listed as forthcoming have appeared in <u>Rivista critica di storia della filosofia</u> 33 (1978), pp. 225-42, and in <u>Mediaeval Studies</u> 42 (1980), pp. 41-60.

p. 10 line 17-9: On the doctrine of the modes of personal supposition, see my "The Logic of the Categorical: The Medieval Theory of Descent and Ascent," in Norman Kretzmann, ed., <u>Meaning and Inference in Medieval Philosophy: Studies in Memory of Jan Pinborg</u>, (Dordrecht: D. Reidel, forthcoming).

p. 11 line 27: Ashworth (forthcoming) was published in 1978.

p. 11 line 30: Mohan's volume is still forthcoming.

p. 13 line 3: Published in 1978.

p. 15 line 19: Green's work is still forthcoming.

p. 16 line 40: Mohan's volume is still forthcoming.

p. 18 line 13: Scott (forthcoming) was published in 1977.

p. 18 line 29: Published 33 (1978), pp. 225-42.

p. 18 line 31: Published 42 (1980), pp. 41-60.

STUDY II - The Origins

p. 292 n. 2: My *The Mediaeval Liar* was published in 1975.

p. 293 lines 26-7: There is a passage in Alexander Neckham, from the second half of the 12th century, showing that the problems associated with *insolubilia* were fully realized at least that early. See my "Five Early Theories in the Mediaeval *Insolubilia*-Literature," forthcoming in *Vivarium*.

p. 294 n. 9 lines 9-10: Lambert of Auxerre's treatise has now been published. See Alessio (1971) in the Bibliography to *Study I* above.

p. 300 n. 36: A critical edition of the Latin text may be found in Bernard G. Dod, ed., *De sophisticis elenchis*, ("Aristoteles Latinus," VI, 1-3; Leiden: E. J. Brill, 1975).

STUDY III - Ockham on Self-Reference

p. 298 line 8 & p. 300 n. 2: The chapter from Ockham's *Summa logicae* is numbered III-3, 46, in the critical edition by Gedeon Gál and Stephen F. Brown: William of Ockham, *Opera philosophica* I, (St. Bonaventure, NY: The Franciscan Institute, 1974).

p. 298 lines 8-9 & p. 300 n. 3: Ockham's commentary on the *Sophistici elenchi* has been critically edited by Francesco del Punta: William of Ockham, *Opera philosophica* III, (St. Bonaventure, NY: The Franciscan Institute, 1979). For the passage under discussion, see *ibid*. p. 268 lines 8-19.

p. 299 lines 2-20 & p. 300 n. 6: The chapter from Ockham's *Summa logicae* is numbered III, 3, 39 in the edition by Gál and Brown. For the passage quoted here, see III, 3, 39, lines 20-34.

p. 300 n. 9: The volume was published in 1975.

p. 300 n. 11: The anonymous author of the first text is in fact the late 14th century writer Richard Brinkley. See Gedeon Gál and Rega Wood, "Richard Brinkley and His *Summa logicae*," *Franciscan Studies* 40 (1980), 59-101.

STUDY IV - Bradwardine's Theory

p. 116 n. 6 line 3: The title of the last paper mentioned has been changed to "Five Early Theories in the Mediaeval *Insolubilia-Literature*," forthcoming in *Vivarium*.

p. 119 n. 14: There is a treatise on consequences attributed to Bradwardine. See N. J. Green-Pedersen, "Bradwardine (?) on Ockham's Doctrine of Consequences. An Edition," *Cahiers de l'institut du moyen-âge grec et latin* (Université de Copenhague), fasc. 42 (1982), pp. 85-150. The treatise rejects "as of now" consequences. Green-Pedersen's introduction discusses the question of the treatise's authenticity.

p. 127 n. 42: The *De veritate et falsitate propositionis* attributed to Heytesbury is in fact by Henry Hopton. See L. M. De Rijk, *Some 14th Century Tracts on the Probationes Terminorum: Martin of Alnwick O.F.M., Richard Billingham, Edward Upton and Others*, ("Artistarium," vol. 3; Nijmegen: Ingenium, 1982), p. *39. See also Joel Biard, "La signification d'objets imaginaires dans quelques textes anglais du XIVe siècle (Guillaume Heytesbury, Henry Hopton)," in P. Osmund Lewry, ed., *The Rise of British Logic: Acts of the Sixth European Symposium on Medieval Logic and Semantics, Balliol College, Oxford, 19-24 June 1983*, ("Papers in Mediaeval Studies," vol. 7; Toronto: Pontifical Institute of Mediaeval Studies, 1985), pp. 265-283.

STUDY V - William Heytesbury's Position

p. 114 n. 1 lines 4-5: The translation and study have appeared as *William Heytesbury on "Insoluble" Sentences: Chapter One of His Rules for Solving Sophisms*, Paul Vincent Spade, tr., ("Mediaeval

Sources in Translation," vol. 21; Toronto: Pontifical Institute of Mediaeval Studies, 1979).

p. 115 n. 8: See Study VII in this volume.

p. 115 line 13: Richard Kilmington. The preferred spelling of his surname is 'Kilvington'.

STUDY VI - John Buridan

On the interpretation of Buridan developed in this paper, see the comment in Study IV in this volume, p. 133 n. 51.

STUDY VIII - Swyneshed's Theory

p. 111 n. 9 lines 4-5: See Study IV in this volume.

STUDY IX - Ockham's Rule

p. 65 n. 7 lines 6-12: See the correction in Study XIII in this volume, p. 21 n. 55.

p. 69 line 27 - p. 70 line 1: See the correction in Study XI in this volume, p. 62 n. 23.

STUDY XI - Ockham's Distinctions

p. 56 n. 3: See Study X in this volume.

p. 63 lines 14 ff.: On the claim that there is no synonymy in mental language, see the further discussion in Study XIII in this volume.

p. 71 n. 51: The note is based on a misunderstanding. The Latin refers not to a "verbal adjective" but to an "adjectival verb". On this notion, see Alfonso Maierù, *Terminologia logica della tarda scolastica*, (Rome: Edizioni dell'Ateneo, 1972), p. 202.

STUDY XII - Priority of Analysis

p. 265 lines 16-22, p. 267 n. 14 lines 3ff., & p. 269 line 8 - p. 270 end: I have changed my mind about the claims made in these places. See my "The Logic of the Categorical", cited in the addenda to Study I above.

STUDY XV - Les modalités aléthiques

p. 29 n. 1: The reference is to Venerabilis inceptoris Guillelmi de Ockham Summa logicae, Gedeon Gál & Stephen F. Brown, eds., (Opera philosophica I; St. Bonaventure, NY: The Franciscan Institute, 1974).

p. 34 n. 9 line 1: The reference is to Johannes Buridanus: Sophismata, T. K. Scott, ed., (Stuttgart-Bad Cannstatt: Frommann-Holzboog, 1977).

STUDY XVI - Roger Swyneshed's Obligationes

p. 243 line 15: The treatise attributed to Sherwood is probably not in fact by him. See Paul Vincent Spade and Eleonore Stump, "Walter Burley and the Obligationes Attributed to William of Sherwood," History and Philosophy of Logic 4 (1983), pp. 9-26.

p. 243 n. 3 lines 7-10: These papers have appeared as "Robert Fland's Obligationes: An Edition," Mediaeval Studies 42 (1980), pp. 41-60; and "Richard Lavenham's Obligationes: Edition and Comments," Rivista critica di storia della filosofia 33 (1978), pp. 225-42.

p. 244 n. 3: Green's work is still forthcoming.

p. 245 line 21: The suggestion here is pursued further in Study XVII in this volume.

p. 246 n. 16 line 3: See Study VII in this volume.

p. 247 n. 21 line 1 & p. 266 n. 60 lines 4-6: The treatise published under Peter of Ailly's name is in fact by Marsilius of Inghen.

STUDY XVII - Three Theories

p. 1 n. 1 line 6: Stump's Boethius's In Ciceronis Topica is forthcoming from Cornell University Press. The studies cited in the last sentence of the note will be published in a separate volume, also by Cornell University Press.

p. 2 n. 4 line 3: Green's work is still forthcoming.

p. 2 n. 5 line 2: Perreiah's "What Obligations Really Are" is still forthcoming.

p. 3 n. 6 lines 10-2 & n. 7 lines 2-4: The Cambridge History of Later Medieval Philosophy was published in 1982.

p. 4 n. 9 lines 12-3: The paper has been published. See the addenda to Study XVI above.

p. 19 n. 57: The Kretzmanns' work on Kilvington is still forthcoming.

INDEX

The index is selective. It is intended to be used in conjunction with the Table of Contents. Where it is obvious from a title that an entire article deals with a certain person or topic, I have omitted the reference in the index.